THE IRISH

A TREASURY OF
ART AND LITERATURE

THE IRISH

A TREASURY OF ART AND LITERATURE

Edited by Leslie Conron Carola

Hugh Lauter Levin Associates, Inc.

ACKNOWLEDGMENTS

The following individuals have contributed to this book in many ways, and it is with great pleasure that I offer them my appreciation: The publisher Hugh Lauter Levin who started it all; Kate Stofko, project manager, and Debby Zindell, editor, true collaborators who made what at times looked impossible, possible and fun; Ken Scaglia, designer; Jan Scaglia; Peter Harbison and Letitia Pollard from *Ireland of the Welcomes*; Ralph Keeley from Bord Failte, Dublin; Dr. Patricia Donlon, Director, and especially Elizabeth Kirwan, Prints and Drawings Librarian, the National Library of Ireland; Paula Hicks, the National Gallery of Ireland; Wesley Graham, The National Museum of Ireland; Pat McLean, the Ulster Museum, Belfast; Peter Murray, the Crawford Municipal Gallery, Cork; Ruth Costelloe, Irish Tourist Board, New York; Thomas Horan, Irish-American Historical Society; the staff of the Westport Library. And thank you to Eileen and George Lawton for sharing their collection of Irish memorabilia, books, and magazines, and to Jim Smith for editorial assistance. A special thanks is due to Professor John Conron of Clark University who reviewed the text, offered insightful and useful comments, listened endlessly, and let me win a few arguments. And without the enthusiasm and moral support of Bob, Maria, and Matthew Carola this project would not have happened.

Leslie Conron Carola

In memory of John J. Conron, Jr. who gave each of his children a love for the written word, and for Eunice McCormick Conron who carried on with elan.

CONTENTS

THE IRISH

A TREASURY OF
ART AND LITERATURE

INTRODUCTION

The Irish have a reputation for having "a way with words." This book confirms that well-earned reputation and demonstrates the poetry of Irish art as well. There is no single Irish voice, but rather a rich variety of voices—voices that sing, sigh, mourn, and whisper, or shout, rouse, cajole, and tease. The extraordinary tonal, textural images of text and art complement each other in a passionate expression of the Irish experience.

The past is never very far away for the Irish. In fact, some people have said that the Irish are haunted by the past. One look at the landscape dotted with powerful reminders of history, from the huge stone "tables" of the ancient portal dolmen graves, to the ring forts, and standing stones with their primitive ogham script, to the High Crosses and Round Towers, to the crumbling monastery and castle ruins, confirms the place of history in the Irish consciousness.

The land itself is very much part of Irish history and understanding the sense or spirit of place is essential to understanding the Irish. It seems natural, therefore, that the identification with place occupies so much of the art and literature.

Although the literary tradition in Ireland did not begin until about the eighth century, the sagas then chronicled are actually the myths and legends of pre-literate, pagan Ireland — legends which survived for hundreds of years through a strong oral tradition. It is through these ancient sagas, tales that had flourished through the art of the storyteller, that we learn of Celtic life.

These written accounts were not organized; there is no one definitive book we can turn to to find the sagas because they are contained in several manuscripts including the *Book of the Dun Cow*, the *Yellow Book of Lecan*, and *The Book of Leinster*. The past has remained woven in the literary tradition ever since. Irish history, full of pathos and passion, has always been a wellspring of material for artists and writers.

Early Irish legends describe the brave deeds of mythic heroic figures. Scholars have classified these heroic tales into four categories or cycles: the mythological cycle, mainly about the gods and goddesses (we have included *The Dream of Oenghus*); the Ulster cycle, about the Knights of the Red Branch, the warriors of Ulster; the Fenian cycle, about Finn McCool and his special warrior-poets; and the king's cycle, about the early Irish kings. We first look at two tales from the *Tain bo Cuailnge (The Cattle Raid of Cooley)*, the best known and oldest epic of the Ulster cycle. *The Cattle Raid of Cooley* is to the Irish what the Homerian epics are to the Greeks. *The Tain* has often been compared with *The Iliad*. In the Celtic agrarian society cattle were the chief form of wealth, and cattle raids were the means to add to one's wealth. According to the Irish legend, Queen Maeve's armies invade Ulster to capture and bring home to Connacht the magnificent brown bull of Cooley to satisfy the Queen's need to have more possessions than her husband. Cuchulainn, the Irish Achilles, has eluded the strange affliction that has stricken all the other men of Ulster and is left alone to defend Ulster from the onslaught of the armies of Connacht. Although the story itself is preposterous and improbable, we learn about the rich and powerful warrior life in ancient Ireland. And Cuchulainn, the most dazzling hero of all the epics, remains in the memory of Irishmen the world over.

The Celts were a warrior society; they were fierce fighters with a strong sense of justice. They were also rich in the arts and civilized life. Celtic society was rigidly stratified as the Brehon law tracts indicate, but the poets and storytellers were as revered as the aristocratic warriors. The clearest picture of the cultivation and imagination of the Celts can be seen in the richly ornamented metalwork in the La Tene style.

When the first Christian missionaries came to Ireland is not known, but in the fifth century St. Patrick introduced Latin, writing, and the Christian creed to the Irish. The selection from his *Confession* which we have included here recounts St. Patrick's wish to return to Ireland (he had been taken as a captive several years before and spent six years tending sheep in Antrim) as a Christian missionary after having a dream in which he was given a letter and heard the "voice of the Irish" ask him to "come and walk among us once more." *The Confession*, from his last years, is one of only two written works left by St. Patrick.

Over the next five centuries the Irish developed many monasteries that flourished as centers of learning. These monasteries influenced all of Ireland, and the missionaries sent from them brought classical learning to the European countries. According to some reports, anyone who spoke Greek on the continent in the ninth century was an Irishman, or had been taught by an Irishman. The monasteries that dotted the countryside—places like Glendalough, Clonmacnoise, Kells, Armagh—were not only respected centers of learning, but producers of extraordinary art including illuminated manuscripts and glorious liturgical objects in intricately-designed metalwork. Monasteries became large and important centers of wealth and cultural activity. The period is chiefly marked by the splendor of its religious art, of manuscript illumination (The *Book of Kells* and the *Book of Durrow*) and stone sculpture (South Cross at Clonmacnoise and Muiredach's Cross at Monasterboice), and by the magnificence of its metalworking which captures three-dimensionally the heavily-decorated manuscript pages (Ardagh Chalice, Tara Brooch, many book shrines and reliquaries).

Artistic achievement was given a new purpose by linking it to religious practice. In the monasteries, the very act of writing became a form of prayer. The scribes became the masters of Christian scholarship and their artwork became one of the greatest glories of Irish monasticism. As the monasteries grew, so did the demand for manuscripts. The production of manuscripts became important and large-scale. The earliest Irish manuscript, the *Cathach* of St. Columba, is a fragmentary liturgical book with simple initial decorations. This form found its highest expression in the extraordinary illuminated manuscript of the *Book of Kells*, a masterpiece of the finest calligraphy and painting.

In counterpoint to these busy, flourishing, scholarly centers were the small bands of self-exiled monks who sought the isolation and asceticism of life on a craggy island or mountaintop far from the world and its problems. The monastic village perched atop the lonely rock of Skellig Michael in the Atlantic Ocean off the coast of Kerry is the site of six small beehive stone huts which have survived along with a small oratory where the monks gathered for prayer, and the ruins of a small church and a few tombstones. This was certainly a lonely and difficult way to worship God, but it also freed the monks from worldly interruptions and constraints, not to mention temptation. The lure of those ascetic monks is haunting, as you will see in the illustrations we have included.

The illiterate, pagan Viking raiders who disrupted Irish manuscript production and monastic life in the ninth and tenth centuries were not interested in the literary or artistic achievements, but rather in the valuable, precious metals used for the book shrines and liturgical objects. The Irish response to the attacks was, understandably, terror; the Vikings came to conquer. But these invaders were also sea-faring merchants who established the town of

Dublin, and other coastal towns of Waterford, Wexford, Limerick, and Cork. By the middle of the tenth century these towns were thriving centers of trade with the rest of Europe. The Viking influence on the Irish economy was important; they minted the first coinage in Dublin, and opened Ireland up to the outside world through coastal traffic. With such long-term co-existence, there had to be some cultural exchanges. Viking craftsmen contributed the popular Ringerike style of carving and produced many significant works of art. And the Irish scholars introduced the literature of Greece and Rome to the Norse. Stone churches built with mortar began to replace the wooden ones throughout the country, and stone round towers appeared on the landscape, usually within the monasteries. They were used as storage for the records and treasures of the monastery and as places of refuge for the members of the community.

Although much of the Norse influence was beneficial to the Irish, they *were* invaders. When the Vikings sought to expand their power, the Irish stopped them. The Irish won a decisive victory under Brian Boru (self-described in the *Book of Armagh* as the Emperor of the Irish) at Clontarf in 1014. This battle was particularly significant; it was the last successful Irish stand against a foreign invader.

By the end of the twelfth century the Normans had arrived in Ireland, a country of many small, often warring, kingdoms. In 1170 Dermot MacMurrough, the king of Leinster, sought the help of the English, especially Richard de Clare, the Norman Earl of Pembroke ("Strongbow"), in defeating the Irish king Rory O'Connor who had banished Dermot from his own kingdom. For his assistance Dermot offered not only his fealty to the Normans, but the hand of his daughter in marriage to Strongbow. This drama is illustrated here by a painting of the wedding of Princess Aoife and Strongbow, as well as the poem "Dermot and the Earl." Thus began a period of conquest and colonization, a dispossession that would not end for eight centuries. The Norman lords built castles and towns for themselves. It was a time of transformation and upheaval, but in the end the Normans did not effectively conquer the country. In fact, the Normans were assimilated into the Irish culture, becoming "more Irish than the Irish"; they learned Gaelic, their names were Gaelicized (De Burgos became Burke, Geraldine became Fitzgerald).

Effective English control was now limited to "the Pale," the area including Dublin and about twenty to thirty miles surrounding it. Everything that went on outside these borders was simply "beyond the Pale"—unacceptable, the turf of barbarians with varying degrees of loyalty to the English crown. A portion of a letter written by Captain de Cuellar, one of the few survivors of the 1588 wreck of the Spanish Armada off the coast of Ireland, describes his harrowing escape in this "barbarian" territory beyond the Pale.

Wanting even more control over the Irish, the English government started a long process of "colonizing" Ireland, removing property from the Irish noblemen, forcing the Irish off their land and settling "plantations" of English settlers, not unlike what was done to the native Americans in the United States. The Ulster land of Hugh O'Neill, the leading spirit of the Ulster resistance, was planted with thousands of Scots Presbyterians. The political and religious problems between Ulster and the rest of Ireland may well have started here.

The seventeenth century was one of utter defeat for the Irish. The Battle of Kinsale in 1601, a revolt led by Hugh O'Neill, confirmed the end of the old Irish world and the downfall of the last of the Gaelic lordships. Less than fifty years later, Cromwell's massacre of hundreds of Irish at Drogheda in September 1649 was one of the most savage attacks in history. We see in the selection included from Cromwell's letter to the Speaker of the Parliament of England that he righteously rationalized the attack as being in God's name. But the English government wanted the land of Ireland and that meant they had to eliminate the present landowners—the Catholics. The Catholics were moved to Connacht or Clare; land in the rest of Ireland was confiscated for government use. The Cromwellian settlement aimed to transfer the sources of wealth and power from the Catholics to the Protestants. As the poet Egan O'Rahilly said, "foreign devils have made our land a tomb."

The Irish rally to support the Catholic James II of England, was quelled by the Protestant armies at the Battle of the Boyne in 1690, the third defeat for the Catholic cause in seventeenth century Ireland. On top of this misery was added the incredibly harsh Penal Laws. No Catholic could own land, vote, worship, hold public office, receive an education, own a horse worth more than 5 pounds, and on and on.

The new settlers in Ireland levelled the forests to build their homes. The eighteenth century anonymous poem "Kilcash" chronicles the sorrow of the lost woods, homes, and a longing "that the great come home again." Jonathan Swift, dean of St. Patrick's, attacked the society that could tolerate the terrible conditions of the poor. George Berkeley, Protestant bishop at Cloyne, directed attention to the social and economic evils of the country by asking hundreds of questions in *The Querist*. Maria Edgeworth portrayed the excesses of wasteful landlords in *Castle Rackrent*. William Carleton and Charles Kickham wrote of the "dispossessed," the Irish peasants, while Charles Lever concentrated on the privileged atmosphere of Trinity College in Dublin.

One man, Daniel O'Connell, dominated politics in the first half of the nineteenth century. One of the first Catholics to enter the law, he became a successful barrister and the first Catholic to serve in the Irish parliament. O'Connell won emancipation for the Catholics, earning himself the title "the Liberator." Irish oratory has long been admired and the words of Theobald Wolfe Tone, Daniel O'Connell, and Charles Stewart Parnell justify the admiration, as do the words of the fictional Conor Larkin in the excerpt we have included from Leon Uris' *Trinity*.

The famine of 1847 was one of the lowest points in Irish history. The selections we have included are among the most moving reflections of that time: Justin McCarthy writes of his first assignment as a sixteen-year-old journalist, to describe the devastation of the famine for the Cork *Examiner*; Peter O'Leary, priest and writer, remembers as a young boy witnessing the compassion of neighbors; an eighty-one-year old woman remembers that "The Famine killed everything."

Long after his death in October 1891, Charles Stewart Parnell remained a hero to many Irishmen. Parnell, son of an Anglo-Irish landlord and an American mother, campaigned for revolutionary changes in the Irish land system. Until this point, Irish landlords could raise rents and evict tenants at will. Parnell and Michael Davitt (founder of the Land League) put a stop to that in 1880, earning Parnell the title "the Uncrowned King" from the huge numbers of Irish tenants. Parnell's fall from power in 1890, partly caused by his involvement in the divorce case of Captain William and Katharine O'Shea, halted his campaign for home rule for Ireland. Both William Butler Yeats and James Joyce, two of Ireland's greatest writers, refer to Parnell frequently in their work. We have included a scene from Joyce's *A Portrait of the Artist as A Young Man* in which a passionate discussion about Parnell dominates the Christmas dinner-table conversation.

Although many Irish came to America before 1845, most of the Irish emigrants came to escape the ravages of the famine. From 1846 to 1848, 1,700,000 Irish arrived here. They were poor, uneducated, unskilled, and filled with hope for a life in the new world. What they met here was not always what they had expected, but they were not defeated. Many American roads, bridges, and skyscrapers were built by immigrant Irish; and thousands of Irish immigrants distinguished themselves in the Civil War, sometimes fighting one another on opposing sides. Among the documents we have included are: an article on John Barry, Father of the American Navy; a letter from John Dunlop, the Irish-born printer of the United States Declaration of Independence, encouraging his brother-in-law in Ireland to urge the young men of Ireland "who wish to be free and happy" to come to America; and an article on John Boyle O'Reilly, Irish-American journalist and battler for civil rights in nineteenth century America.

In Ireland at the turn of the century, William Butler Yeats and Lady Augusta Gregory led the Celtic literary revival. Their goal was to rekindle interest in the Irish language and cultural roots. Their efforts resulted in the formation of an Irish national theatre, eventually to become the Abbey Theatre in Dublin. Yeats encouraged J. M. Synge to go to the Aran Islands to "Express a life that has never found expression." *Riders to the Sea*, written after Synge's stay on Inishmore island, was presented at the Abbey Theatre to critical acclaim. (His *Playboy of the Western World* caused an uproar when it was presented.) Sean O'Casey's *The Plough and the Stars* (set in Dublin at the time of the 1916 Easter Rising) was also presented at the Abbey Theatre. Yeats responded to an opening night riot by admonishing the audience: "Is this going to be a recurring celebration of Irish genius: Synge first and then O'Casey?"

One of the most significant events of twentieth century Ireland was the 1916 Easter Rising. Patrick Pearse, one of the leaders, read aloud The Proclamation of the Provincial

Government (included here in its entirety) from the steps of the general post office in Dublin, calling on all Irish men and women to fight for freedom from British rule. After six days of fighting, in which several hundred people were killed, the leaders of the Rising were arrested and then executed a few weeks later at Kilmainhaim Jail, thus securing their places in the Irish memory forever, and recreating the tradition of Cuchulainn and the belief that "better is short life with honor than long life with dishonor." A magnificent bronze statue of the dying mythic Cuchulainn was later erected in the general post office to commemorate the young martyrs.

Many of the twentieth century writers, including among others, Patrick Kavanagh, John Montague, Seamus Heaney, Sean O'Faolain, and Eavan Boland draw from historical images in their work, images of landscapes of the past, of haunting memories. Heaney's wonderful essay "The Sense of Place" proposes the idea that the nourishment which comes from the sense of being part of a place (which has a past) is probably talked about more in Ireland than elsewhere, but is not necessarily exclusive to the Irish. Ita Daly's poignant story "The Lady with the Red Shoes" isolates the long-term effect of the past on her characters — both the observer and the observed.

Some selections were chosen for this book to show history in the making, others to show the response to that history. By no means a comprehensive or academic study of Irish art and literature, this book is a sampling—a treasury—of many voices and images that reflect the Irish experience. We hope you will be enticed to look to the originals and to the works of many writers and artists who are not included here. "If you want to know Ireland body and soul," wrote W. B. Yeats, "you must read its poems and stories."

NOTE: There are many references to translators in the headnotes because much of the material written in Ireland before the nineteenth century was written in Irish. There are many variations in the spelling of names and places. We have not altered the spellings.

COLORPLATE I

Entrance Stone to Passage Grave. Newgrange, County Meath. 2500 B.C. Megalithic tomb. Irish Tourist Board, Dublin. *Ireland's most famous prehistoric monument. The huge stone at the entrance to the burial place of kings is covered with a pattern of carved spirals in the Ultimate La Tene style, frequently seen in early Irish art.*

COLORPLATE 2

Portal Dolmen, County Clare. 2500–2000 B.C. Stone Age tomb. Irish Tourist Board, Dublin. *A prehistoric single-chamber grave marked with a massive capstone weighing about 40 tons resting atop three upright stones (two of equal height, one of lesser height), provides a stark, dramatic silhouette against the sky. The word "dolmen" comes from the Breton "stone table."*

COLORPLATE 3 *(opposite)*

Standing Stone, Glencolumbkille, County Donegal. 2000 B.C. Irish Tourist Board, Dublin.
This solitary stone pillar may have marked a burial site or served some unknown religious purpose.

COLORPLATE 4

Staigue Fort, County Kerry. C. 300 B.C.–A.D. 400. Stone ring-fort. Diameter: 90 ft. (27.4 m). Irish Tourist Board, Dublin. *The dry-stone walls of this fort are 13 ft. (3.9 m) thick and up to 18 ft. (5.5 m) high. Internal staircases lead up to the top of the ramparts. Many stone ring-forts, called cashels, were protective enclosures, but Staigue Fort, strategically placed with mountains behind it and a clear view to the sea in front, was certainly a defensive fort.*

COLORPLATE 5

Dun Aenghus, Inishmore, Aran Islands, County Galway. Prehistoric stone fort. Irish Tourist Board, Dublin.
On the edge of a cliff 300 feet above the Atlantic, Dun Aenghus, one of the most dramatic sights in Ireland,
is the finest example of a cliff or promontory fort. There are three semi-circular rings of stone walls. Outside
of the outer ring an array of pointed stone stakes, a chevaux de frise, *made access to the fort very difficult.*

COLORPLATE 6

Two Gold Armlets. Derrinboy, County Offaly. 1200–1000 B.C. Gold sheet with folded edges, punched and ridged. Height: 2⁷/8 in. (7.2 cm). National Museum of Ireland, Dublin.

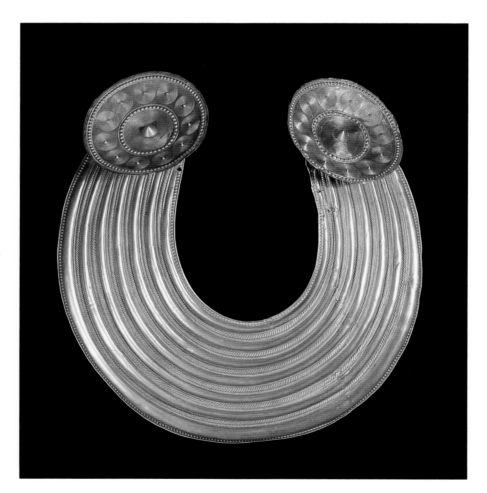

COLORPLATE 7

Gold Collar. Gleninsheen, County Clare. c. 700 B.C. 12³/8 x 4¹/8 in. (31.4 x 10.5 cm). National Museum of Ireland, Dublin. *This gold collar, one of the finest achievements of the Later Bronze Age goldsmiths, was found in 1932 concealed in a rock fissure.*

Gold Disc. Tedavnet, County Monaghan. 2000–1800 B.C. Diameter: 2⁷/₁₆ in. (11.3 cm).
National Museum of Ireland, Dublin. *One of a pair of gold discs, made from sheet gold, found in the roots of an old oak tree and acquired by the museum in 1872.*

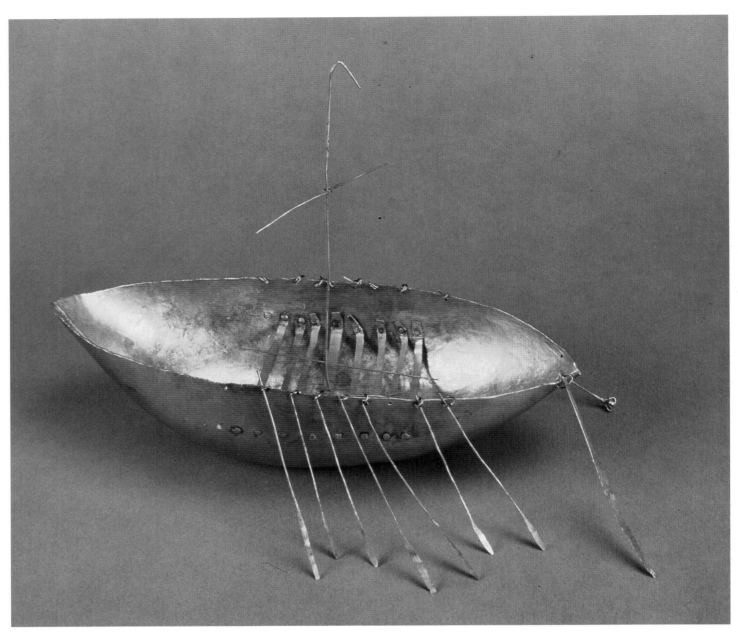

COLORPLATE 9

Gold Boat. Probably 1st century A.D. Found at Broighter, County Londonderry. 7 11/16 x 3 3/16 x 2 in. (19.6 x 8.2 x 5 cm). National Museum of Ireland, Dublin. *This miniature boat, complete with benches, mast, and oars, was part of a hoard of gold jewelry and objects found at Broighter.*

PREHISTORY: ANCIENT MYTHS AND LEGENDS

FROM THE CATTLE RAID OF COOLEY

"The Weakness of the Ulstermen"

This important lead-in to The Cattle Raid of Cooley (The Tain bo Cuailnge) *explains the strange sickness that debilitates the Ulster warriors and leaves the hero Cuchulainn to stand alone against the invading armies of Queen Medb for most of the epic which then follows. Translated by J. J. Campbell.*

———————

Crunnchu was wealthy and prosperous, living in the lonely hills with his wife and four sons. His wife died, and for years he and his sons lived without a woman in the house. One day a young woman, dignified and beautiful, came to the house and sat down by the fire. She said nothing, and Crunnchu watched her, silent also, as she rose again and set about the duties of a housewife, preparing food, milking the cows, directing the servants.

When night came she went to Crunnchu and he spoke to her then:

"Will you be my wife?"

"On condition that you speak my name to no one nor tell aught to anyone about me," she replied. And so it was agreed between them. They lived happily together, and with her his prosperity increased.

One day he told her that he was going to one of the great assemblies of the men of Ulster, where there would be races and games and entertainments and combats. She begged him not to go.

"You may by accident speak of me," she said, "and I am very happy here with you, and would not like to leave. But our union is at an end if you speak of me to anyone."

He would not heed her; but assured her vehemently that he would not endanger their union by one word. And it was a glorious day of entertainment. In all the contests of chariot-racing the horses of the king were victorious, and the mouths of all the people were full of praise for them. And the poets sang the praises of the king and his wife. And they praised the horses, saying:

"No two such horses have ever been seen. Their speed could not be matched anywhere."

But Crunnchu, provoked by all the praise, and forgetting his promise, shouted:

"My wife could run faster than the horses you praise."

The king was enraged and cried out:

"Seize the man who said that."

The attendants seized Crunnchu and brought him to the king.

"Now," said the king, "you will prove that boast or pay for it." And he sent messengers to bring the man's wife at once to the assembly. Meanwhile Crunnchu was kept in bonds until his wife should be brought.

The Hill of Tara. 1980. Photograph. Irish Tourist Board, Dublin.
Tara was the ancient seat and assembly place of the High Kings of Ireland from the 3rd century.

The messengers went to his house, where they were welcomed by the woman. When she inquired why they had come to her they said:

"Your husband has boasted to the king, in the presence of the whole assembly, that you can run more swiftly than the horses of the king. And he will not be released until you come to the assembly."

"My husband," said she, "spoke rashly. I am unwell. I am expecting a child."

"Your husband will pay with his life for his boast," said they, "if you do not come."

She demurred no more, but went with them. The great crowds in the assembly gathered round her and gazed at her. She was humiliated and embarrassed before them all and protested:

"It is not fitting that one such as I should be before all men's gaze. Say quickly what it is you wish of me."

"To race against the horses of the king," they all shouted; and there were cries of mockery and jeering.

She drew back. "But my time is near," she said. "I cannot do this."

"Very well," said the king. "Your husband dies." And he ordered his attendants to draw their swords.

She cried out in great distress: "Will no one help me?" She looked round the mob: "A mother bore each one of you. Have you no pity for me?" She turned to the king and begged him: "Give me but a short respite, until my deliverance is come, and I will do what you ask me."

"You run now, or your husband dies," he replied.

"For this shame you put upon me," she cried, "you and all your people will pay, in years to come."

The king ignored this, but ordered her to tell her name, before the race began.

"My name, and my offspring's name," she said, "will be on this place of assembly to mark the great shame of your deed today. I am Macha. And my descent is from Ocean."

She called for the horses to be brought, and she outran them to the end of the course; and her time came; and her twins were born. So the name Emain Macha.

All who were there felt a strange weakness on them, a weakness like hers in her pain.

And she spoke to them a prophecy:

"The shame you have put upon me will be punished in each man of you. When crisis or danger is nigh to you, this weakness you feel now will come upon you, and upon your children to the ninth generation."

Her word was true. For though the weakness came upon the men it did not affect the women or children of Ulster, nor did it affect any men but those of Ulster, nor did it affect Cuchulainn, who was begotten of Lu. And that is why Cuchulainn stood alone against the warriors of Maeve, because of the weakness put upon the men of Ulster by Macha.

FROM THE CATTLE RAID OF COOLEY
"The Hound of Culann"

In this tale of The Cattle Raid of Cooley, *centerpiece of the eighth century Ulster cycle of heroic tales, the brave young Hound of Culann earns his name. Medieval monks recorded these Celtic tales in their manuscripts after centuries of an oral tradition. Fragments of the texts can be found in the Book of the Dun Cow compiled at the monastery of Clonmacnoise in the 12th century, the Yellow Book of Lecan compiled in the late 14th century, and the Book of Leinster. Translated by J.J. Campbell.*

The following year the smith Culann invited Conor to a banquet, and asked him to bring only a few of his companions, as he had neither the space nor the means for a grand entertainment. Conor accepted, and, before he set out, he went as was his custom to see and say farewell to the boys of the corps.

He watched them at four games. In the first, Setanta kept goal against all the three fifties, and they could not score; yet when they all kept goal together he scored against them as he wished. In the second, Setanta guarded the hole, and though each of the hundred and fifty balls came to the edge of the hole, not one did he let in; yet when they all guarded together he had no difficulty in getting the ball past them into the hole. The third game was the tearing-off of mantles: Setanta tore all the hundred and fifty mantles off in a trice; they could not as much as touch his brooch. In the fourth game they wrestled, and with all the corps against him Setanta stood firm on his feet, yet when he turned to the attack he left not one standing.

Conor said to Fergus, who stood with him:

"If that lad's deeds when he is full-grown are in keeping with his deeds today, we are a lucky land to have him."

"Is there any reason to believe," said Fergus, "that his prowess, alone of all, will not increase with the years?"

But Conor said: "Let him come with us to Culann's feast. He is worthy."

"I cannot go just yet," said Setanta.

The king was surprised that the boy did not at once leave everything for the opportunity of going to a banquet with the select royal party.

"Why so?" he asked.

"Because the boys are not finished playing," said Setanta, "and I cannot leave until the games are finished."

"We cannot wait so long," said Conor.

"You need not wait. I shall follow you."

"You do not know the way."

"I shall follow the tracks of your chariots."

That was agreed. And Conor's party arrived at Culann's house, where they were welcomed to the feast which was ready laid for them. Culann said to Conor when the company were settling to the feast:

"Before we begin, tell me, is this all the company? There is none to follow?"

"None," said Conor: "all are here." He had already forgotten about Setanta.

"The reason I ask," said Culann, "is that I have a magnificent hound, which is my watchdog, and only myself can handle him or exact obedience from him; and none dare approach the neighbourhood when I loose him to guard the house. And I should like to loose him now before we begin."

"You may loose the hound," said Conor. The hound was loosed, and he made a circuit of the place and sat down with his head on his paws, a huge, fearsome guard.

Meanwhile the six-year-old boy had left his fellows of the boy-corps of Emain Macha, and was on his way to the house of Culann, the smith. He had no arms of defence, but passed the time of the journey with his hurling stick and ball. The hound bayed a fearsome challenge as he came to the house, but the boy continued his play until the hound sprang at him. Then he hurled the ball so that with terrific force it went right down the hound's throat, past the great open jaws and teeth, and as the hound reared back with the force of the blow and the pain, he grasped it by the hind legs and smashed its head to pulp on the stones of the yard.

At the sound of the hound's baying Conor had leaped to his feet remembering the boy. They all rushed out, certain Setanta was being torn by the hound, and were overjoyed to see him alive—all except Culann, who was filled with sorrow as he gazed on the hound.

"It was an unlucky day I made a banquet for Conor," he said. He turned to the boy. "You are welcome, boy, for your father's and mother's sake but not for your own. You have slain the only guard and protector of my house and my substance, of my flocks and my herds."

"Do not grieve," said the boy. "I shall see you are none the worse for what has happened."

"How can that be?" asked Culann, looking at the six-year-old boy.

"If there is a whelp of that dog's siring in all Ireland," said Setanta, "I shall rear and train it until it is able to guard and protect you as well as its sire; and until then I myself will guard your house and your property, even as your hound did."

"That is fair," said Conor.

"And you will be Cu Chulainn, the Hound of Culann, in the meantime," said Cathbhad the druid. "And that shall be your name, Cuchulainn."

"Indeed, I prefer my own name, Setanta, son of Sualtam," said the boy.

"But the name Cuchulainn will be on the lips of all the men of Ireland and the world, and their mouths will be full of its praise," said the druid.

"For that I would accept any name," said the boy; and from that time he was known as Cuchulainn.

LEFT:
Bowl Food Vessel.
2000–1300 B.C. Pottery.
Dunamase, County Laois.
3 3/4 x 5 3/8 in.
(9.6 x 13.6 cm).
National Museum of
Ireland, Dublin. *The
bowl food vessels are
closely associated with
the beaker pottery
tradition, and for the most
part have been found in
Bronze Age graves.*

RIGHT:
Bowl Food Vessel.
2000–1300 B.C. Pottery.
Dunamase, County Laios.
4 3/4 x 5 13/16 in.
(12 x 14.7 cm).
National Museum of
Ireland, Dublin.

FROM THE DREAM OF OENGHUS

This story, part of the early Irish mythological cycle about the divine Tuatha de Danann who occupied Ireland before the Celts, presents the Otherworld as an idealized version of the real world; an idyllic place of love and happiness. The elusive Sidhe (fairy) who first appears as a beautiful woman in Oenghus' dream, has the magical power to exist in both worlds, and, through love, to transform Oenghus. Translated by Kenneth Hurlstone Jackson.

Oenghus was asleep one night, when he saw a girl coming towards him as he lay on his bed. She was the loveliest that had ever been in Ireland. Oenghus went to take her hand, to bring her to him in his bed. As he looked, she sprang suddenly away from him; he could not tell where she had gone. He stayed there till morning, and he was sick at heart. He fell ill because of the apparition which he had seen and had not talked with. No food passed his lips. She was there again the next night. He saw a lute in her hand, the sweetest that ever was; she played a tune to him, and he fell asleep at it. He remained there till morning, and that day he was unable to eat.

He passed a whole year while she visited him in this way, so that he fell into a wasting sickness. He spoke of it to no one. So he fell into wasting sickness, and no one knew what was wrong with him. The physicians of Ireland were brought together; they did not know what was wrong with him in the end. They went to Fínghin, Conchobhar's physician, and he came to him. He would tell from a man's face what his illness was, and would tell from the smoke which came from the house how many people were ill in it.

He spoke to him aside. 'Ah, unhappy plight!' said Fínghin, 'you have fallen in love in absence.' 'You have diagnosed my illness,' said Oenghus. 'You have fallen into a wretched state, and have not dared to tell it to anyone,' said Fínghin. 'You are right,' said Oenghus; 'a beautiful girl came to me, of the loveliest figure in Ireland, and of surpassing aspect. She had a lute in her hand, and played it to me every night.' 'No matter,' said Fínghin, 'it is fated for you to make a match with her. Send someone to Boann, your mother, that she should come to speak with you.'

They went to her, and Boann came then. 'I am attending this man,' said Fínghin, 'a serious illness has fallen upon him.' They told his story to Boann. 'Let his mother take care of him,' said Fínghin; 'a serious illness has fallen on him. Have the whole of Ireland scoured to see if you may find a girl of this figure which your son has seen.'

They spent a year at this. Nothing like her was found. Then Fínghin was called to them again. 'No help has been found in this matter,' said Boann. Said Fínghin, 'Send to the Daghdhae, that he should come to speak with his son.' They went to the Daghdhae, and he came back with them. 'Why have I been summoned?' 'To advise your son,' said Boann; 'it is as well for you to help him, for it is sad that he is perishing. He is wasting away. He has fallen in love in absence, and no help is to be found for him.' 'What is the use of talking to me?' said the Daghdhae, 'I know no more than you do.' 'More indeed,' said Fínghin, 'you are the king of the fairy hills of Ireland. Send someone to Bodhbh, king of the fairy hills of Munster; his knowledge is noised throughout all Ireland.'

They went to him. He welcomed them. 'Welcome to you, men of the Daghdhae,' said Bodhbh. 'That is what we have come for.' 'Have you news?' said Bodhbh. 'We have; Oenghus the son of the Daghdhae has been wasting away for two years.' 'What is the matter with him?' said Bodhbh. 'He has seen a girl in his sleep. We do not know where in Ireland is the girl whom he has seen and loved. The Daghdhae bids you seek throughout Ireland for a girl of that figure and aspect.' 'She shall be sought,' said Bodhbh, 'and let me have a year's delay to find out the facts of the case.'

They came back at the end of the year to Bodhbh's house at the Fairy Hill beyond

Feimhen. 'I went round the whole of Ireland until I found the girl at Loch Bél Dragon, at Crotta Cliach,' said Bodhbh. They went to the Daghdhae, and they were made welcome. 'Have you news?' said the Daghdhae. 'Good news; the girl of that figure which you described has been found. Bodhbh bids you let Oenghus come away with us to him, to know whether he recognizes the girl when he sees her.'

Oenghus was taken in a chariot to the Fairy Hill beyond Feimhen. The king had a great feast ready for them, and he was made welcome. They were three days and three nights at the feast. 'Come away now,' said Bodhbh, 'to know whether you recognize the girl when you see her. Even if you do recognize her, I have no power to give her, and you may only see her.'

They came then to the lake. They saw three times fifty grown girls, and the girl herself among them. The girls did not reach above her shoulder. There was a chain of silver between each couple; and a necklet of silver round her own throat, and a chain of refined gold. Then Bodhbh said, 'Do you recognize that girl?' 'I do indeed,' said Oenghus. 'I can do no more for you,' said Bodhbh. 'That is no matter, then,' said Oenghus, 'since it is she that I saw; I cannot take her this time. Who is this girl, Bodhbh?' said Oenghus. 'I know, truly,' said Bodhbh, 'she is Caer Ibhormheith, daughter of Ethal Anbhuail from the fairy hill of Uamhan in the land of Connaught.'

Then Oenghus and his people set off for their own country. Bodhbh went with him, and talked with the Daghdhae and Boann at Bruigh Maic ind Óaig. They told them their news, and told how she seemed, in figure and aspect, just as they had seen; and they told her name and the name of her father and grandfather. 'We feel it to be discourteous that we cannot content you,' said the Daghdhae. 'What you should do, Daghdhae,' said Bodhbh, 'is to go to Ailill and Medhbh, for they have the girl in their province.'

The Daghdhae went till he reached the lands of Connaught, with three score chariots in his company. The king and queen made them welcome. They spent a full week banqueting round the ale after that. 'What has brought you?' said the king. 'You have a girl in your country,' said the Daghdhae, 'and my son has fallen in love with her, and has become sick. I have come to you to find out whether you may give her to the lad.' 'Who?' said Ailill. 'The daughter of Ethal Anbhuail.' 'We have no power over her,' said Ailill and Medhbh, 'if we had she should be given him.' 'This would be good—let the king of the fairy hill be summoned to you,' said the Daghdae.

Ailill's steward went to him. 'You have been ordered by Ailill and Medhbh to go to speak with them.' 'I will not go,' said he, 'I will not give my daughter to the son of the Daghdhae.' That is told to Ailill; 'He cannot be made to come, but he knows why he is summoned.' 'No matter,' said Ailill, 'he shall come, and the heads of his warriors shall be brought with him.' At that, Ailill's household troops and the men of the Daghdhae rose up against the fairy hill, and overran the whole hill. They brought out three score heads, and the king, so that he was in captivity at Cruachu.

Then Ailill said to Ethal Anbhuail, 'Give your daughter to the son of the Daghdhae.' 'I cannot,' said he, 'her magic power is greater than mine.' 'What is this great magic power she has?' said Ailill. 'Easily told; she is in the shape of a bird every other year, and in human shape the other years.' 'What year is she in the shape of a bird?' said Ailill. 'It is not for me to betray her,' said her father. 'Off with your head, unless you tell us!' said Ailill. 'I will not hold out any longer,' said he; 'I will tell you,' said he, 'since you are so persistent about her. Next All Hallows she will be at Loch Bél Dragon in the shape of a bird, and wonderful birds will be seen with her there, there will be three times fifty swans around her; and I have made preparations for them.' 'I do not care, then,' said the Daghdhae; 'since you know her nature, do you bring her.'

Then a treaty was made between them, between Ailill and Ethal and the Daghdhae, and Ethal was let go. The Daghdhae bade them farewell and came to his house and told his news to his son. 'Go next All Hallows to Loch Bél Dragon, and call her to you from the lake.' The Mac Óag went to Loch Bél Dragon. He saw three times fifty white birds on the lake with their silver chains, and curls of gold about their heads. Oenghus was in human shape on the brink of the lake. He called the girl to him. 'Come to speak to me, Caer!' 'Who calls me?' said Caer. 'Oenghus calls you.' 'I will go, if you will undertake on your honour that I may come back to the lake again.' 'I pledge your protection,' said he.

She went to him. He cast his arms about her. They fell asleep in the form of two swans, and went round the lake three times, so that his promise might not be broken. They went away in the form of two white birds till they came to Bruigh Maic ind Óaig, and sang a choral song so that it put the people to sleep for three days and three nights. The girl stayed with him after that.

FROM THE VOYAGE OF MAEL DÚIN

A Bridge of Glass

The extraordinary adventures of Mael Dúin and his companions are told as a folk-tale, in a straightforward style without any distinction between natural and supernatural events. Translator Kenneth Hurlstone Jackson suggests that these tales should be accepted in the same spirit as Cinderella's pumpkin.

A little while after that they saw an island with a fortress in it, and a bridge of glass at its door. As often as they tried to go up on the bridge they would fall down back again. They saw a woman come out of the fortress with a bucket in her hand. She lifted up a plank of glass from the floor of the bridge and filled her bucket from the well which was beneath the plank. Then she went into the fortress. 'Let the steward come to receive Mael Dúin,' said Germán. 'Mael Dúin, indeed!' said the woman, as she shut the door behind her; and she made the brazen pillars and the brazen net which was on them shake at that, and the noise these made was soft sweet-stringed music, and it put them to sleep until the next morning. When they woke up in the morning, they saw the same woman come out of the fortress with her bucket in her hand, and she filled it from the same well which was beneath the plank. 'But let the steward come to receive Mael Dúin,' said Germán. 'Much I care for Mael Dúin!' said she, as she closed the door. The same music prostrated them and put them to sleep again until the next day. For three days and three nights they continued like this. Then on the fourth day the woman came to them, and in a lovely guise she came. A white cloak round her, and a circlet of gold round her hair. Her hair was golden. Two silver shoes on her pink and white feet. A silver brooch with golden filigree in her cloak, and a filmy robe of silk next to her white body. 'Welcome, Mael Dúin,' she said, and she called every man in turn by his own proper name. 'For a long time your coming here has been known and accepted,' she said. Then she took them with her into a great house which was close to the sea, and had their boat pulled up on land. They saw then in the house ready for them a bed for Mael Dúin and a bed for every three of his followers. She brought them food in a hamper, like cheese or sour buttermilk, and she gave out helpings for three at a time. Each man found in it whatever taste he desired. Then she served Mael Dúin by himself. She filled a bucket beneath the same plank, and poured drink for them. She made a trip for every three men in turn. She saw when they had had enough, and ceased pouring for them. 'A woman fit for Mael Dúin is this woman,' said every man of his followers. After that she left them, with her hamper and her bucket. His men said to Mael Dúin, 'Shall we speak to her to ask whether she would sleep with you?' 'What harm would it do you,' said he, 'if you speak to her?' She came the next day at the same time to serve them, as she did before. They said to the girl, 'Will you make a match with Mael Dúin, and sleep with him? Why not stay here tonight?' She said that she had not learned and did not know what sin was. Then she went away to her house, and came the next day at the same time with her service for them. When they were surfeited and drunk, they said the same words to her. 'Tomorrow then,' said she, 'you shall be given an answer about this.' She went after that to her house, and they fell asleep on the beds. When they awoke, they were in their boat on a rock, and they did not see the island nor the fortress nor the woman nor the place where they were before.

Myles Dillon

FROM THE CYCLE OF THE KINGS

Cormac MacArt, Greatest of the Ancient Irish Kings

Grandson of Conn of the Hundred Battles, Cormac MacArt reigned in the 3rd century at Tara in County Meath, seat of the pagan high kings. In addition to his many intellectual and cultural contributions, Cormac is reputed to have been responsible for the magnificent rebuilding of the great banqueting hall at Tara.

Etain was then pregnant and resolved to go to the house of Lugna Fer Tri so that her child should be born there. When she reached his country the birth-pains seized her, and she got down from her chariot and was delivered of a son on a bed of fern. A peal of thunder greeted his birth, and Lugna, hearing this, knew that it was for the birth of Cormac, son of the true prince Art, and he set out in search of him.

Etain slept after her delivery, and entrusted the boy to her maid till they should continue their journey. The maid fell asleep, and a she-wolf came and carried off the child to her lair in the place now known as Cormac's Cave. Lugna came to where she lay, and she told him all that had happened. He brought her to his house, and proclaimed that whosoever should find tidings of the child should obtain in reward whatever he asked.

Grec MacArod was abroad one day, and coming upon the cave, he saw the whelps playing before it and the child creeping among them. He brought the news to Lugna, and was granted the territory where the Grecraige now dwell. The child and the whelps were brought home from the cave, and the child was named Cormac, for that was the name his father had given him. He was the delight of many for his beauty and grace and dignity and strength and judgment.

One day, as he was playing with Lugna's sons, he struck one of them. The lad exclaimed that it was too much to suffer a blow from one whose race and kindred were unknown, save that he was a fatherless child. Cormac complained to Lugna, and Lugna told him that he was the son of the true prince Art, son of Conn of the Hundred Battles, and that it was prophesied that he should steer his father's rudder, for there would be no prosperity in Tara until he should reign there. "Let us go," said Cormac, "to seek recognition in my father's house in Tara." "Let us go then," said Lugna.

They went to Tara, and MacCon welcomed them and took Cormac into fosterage. There was a woman hospitaller in Tara at that time named Bennaid. Her sheep grazed the queen's woad. MacCon awarded the sheep to the queen in compensation for the grazing of the woad.

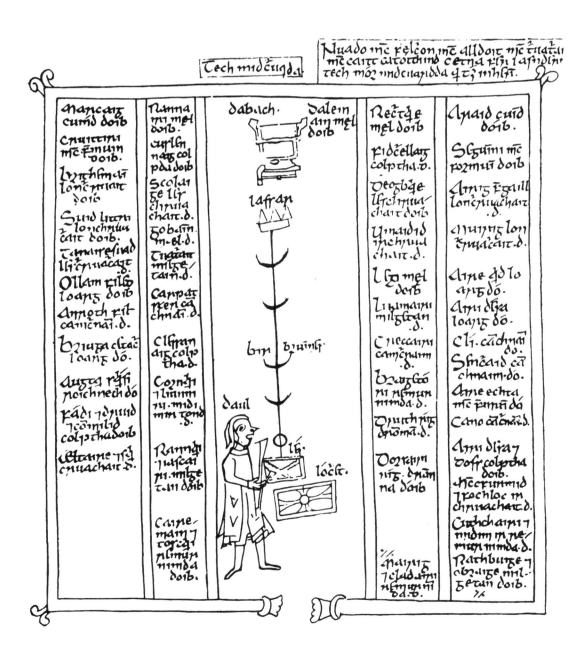

Imaginary Ground Plan of Great Banqueting Hall of Legendary High Kings at Tara. Book of Leinster. 12th century. Manuscript. Courtesy The Board of Trinity College Dublin.

"No," said Cormac. "The shearing of the sheep is enough in compensation for the grazing of the woad, for both will grow again." "It is a true judgment!" said all. "It is the son of a true prince who has given judgment!" The side of the house on which the false judgment had been given fell down the slope. It will stay thus for ever. That is the Crooked Mound of Tara.

The men of Ireland expelled MacCon and gave the kingship to Cormac. Everything prospered while he lived. His wolves remained with him, and the reason for the great honor he received was that he had been reared by wolves.

Tara was restored by Cormac so that it was grander than ever before, houses, fences, and buildings. Well was it with Ireland in his time. The rivers teemed with fish, the woods with mast, the plains with honey, on account of the justice of his rule. Deer were so plentiful that there was no need to hunt them. Cormac built the noblest building that ever was raised in Tara. Though he was opposed by the Ulstermen, he was never deprived of the kingship till his death. He died in the *raith* of the hospitaller in Cletech when a salmon bone stuck in his throat.

Cormac ordered that he should not be buried in Bruig na Boinne, for he did not adore the same god as those who were buried there. He ordered his burial in Ros na Rig with his face due east towards the rising sun.

Cormac MacArt

FROM SELECTIONS FROM ANCIENT IRISH POETRY

"Instructions of a King"

This text, sometimes ascribed to Cormac who died in A.D. 267, is more likely the product of a much later period. Cormac engages his son Cairbre in a dialogue which outlines the duties of a king, and offers a picture of a remarkably wise leader with a superlative code of ethics. This selection is from Kuno Meyer's version.

"O grandson of Conn, O Cormac," said Cairbre, "what is best for a king?"

"Not hard to tell," said Cormac. "Best for him—firmness without anger, patience without strife, affability without haughtiness, guarding of ancient lore, giving justice, truth, peace, giving many alms, honoring poets, worshipping the great God.

". . . Let him attend to the sick, benefit the strong, possess truth, chide falsehood, love righteousness, curb fear, crush criminals, judge truly, foster science, improve his soul, utter every truth. For it is through the truth of a ruler that God gives all.

"Let him restrain the great, slay evil-doers, exalt the good, consolidate peace, check unlawfulness, protect the just, confine the unjust.

"He should question the wise, follow ancient lore, fulfil the law, be honest with friends, be manly with foes, learn every art, know every language, hearken to elders, be deaf to the rabble.

"Let him be gentle, let him be hard, let him be loving, let him be merciful, let him be righteous, let him be patient, let him be persevering, let him hate falsehood, let him love truth, let him be forgetful of wrong, let him be mindful of good, let him be attended by a host in gatherings, and by few in secret councils, let his covenants be firm, let his levies be lenient, let his

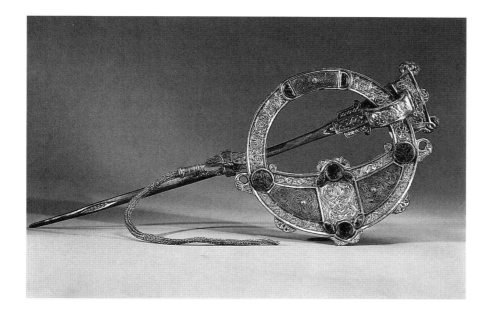

Tara Brooch. 8th century. Silver-gilt with gold filligree, amber and polychrome glass ornaments. Diameter of ring: 3⁷/₁₆ in. (8.7 cm); length of pin: 12⁹/₁₆ in. (32 cm). National Museum of Ireland, Dublin.

judgments and decisions be sharp and light. . . . For it is by these qualities, kings and lords are judged."

"O grand-son of Conn, O Cormac," said Cairbre. "What were your habits when you were a lad?"

"Not hard to tell," said Cormac.

> "I was a listener in woods,
> I was a gazer at stars,
> I was unseeing among secrets,
> I was silent in a wilderness,
> I was conversational among many,
> I was mild in the mead-hall,
> I was fierce in the battlefield,
> I was gentle in friendship,
> I was a nurse to the sick,
> I was weak toward the strengthless,
> I was strong toward the powerful,
>   *   *   *
> I was not arrogant though I was wise,
> I was not a promiser though I was rich,
> I was not boastful though I was skilled,
> I would not speak ill of the absent,
> I would not reproach, but I would praise,
> I would not ask, but I would give—

For it is through these habits that the young become old and kingly warriors."

"O grandson of Conn, O Cormac," said Cairbre, "what is good for me?"

"Not hard to tell," said Cormac, "if you listen to my teaching—

> "Do not deride the old, though you are young;
> Nor the poor, though you are wealthy;
> Nor the lame, though you are swift;
> Nor the blind, though you are given sight;
> Nor the sick, though you are strong;
> Nor the dull, though you are clever;
> Nor the foolish, though you are wise.
>   *   *   *

Be not too wise, be not too foolish;
Be not too conceited, be not too diffident;
Be not too haughty, be not too humble;
Be not too talkative, be not too silent;
Be not too harsh, be not too feeble.

If you be too wise, they will expect (too much) of you;
If you be too foolish, you will be deceived;
If you be too conceited, you will be thought vexatious;
If you be too humble, you will be without honor;
If you be too talkative, you will not be heeded;
If you be too silent, you will not be regarded;
If you be too harsh, you will be broken,
If you be too feeble, you will be crushed."

Membership in the Fianna

Under the leadership of Finn McCool, the Fianna were a roving band of specially-trained professional warriors whose mission was to uphold justice on behalf of the kings and lords of Ireland. Translator Standish H. O'Grady details the rigid criteria required for membership in this select group.

This is the enumeration and description of Finn's people: their strength was seven score and ten officers, each man of these having thrice nine warriors, every one bound (as was the way with Cuchullin in the time when he was there) to certain conditions of service, which were: that in satisfaction of their guarantee violated they must not accept material compensation; in the matter of valuables or of meat must not deny any; no single individual of them to fly before nine warriors.

Of such not a man was taken into the Fianna; nor admitted whether to the great Gathering of Usnach, to the Convention of Taillte, or to Tara's Feast; until both his paternal and his maternal correlatives, his peoples and kindreds, had given securities for them to the effect that,

The Giant's Causeway. Unique rock formation. County Antrim, Northern Ireland. National Library, Dublin. *History says that these strange tubular basalt structures are the result of volcanic action, but legend tells us that Finn McCool, leader of the Fianna, built the causeway as a pathway across to Scotland.*

though at the present instant they were slain, yet should no claim be urged in lieu of them: and this in order that to none other but to themselves alone they should look to avenge them. On the other hand: in case it were they that inflicted great mischiefs upon others, reprisals not to be made upon their several people.

Of all these again not a man was taken until he were a prime poet versed in the twelve books of poesy. No man was taken till in the ground a large hole had been made (such as to reach the fold of his belt) and he put into it with his shield and a forearm's length of a hazel stick. Then must nine warriors, having nine spears, with a ten furrows' width betwixt them and him, assail him and in concert let fly at him. If past that guard of his he were hurt then, he was not received into Fianship.

Not a man of them was taken till his hair had been interwoven into braids on him and he started at a run through Ireland's woods; while they, seeking to wound him, followed in his wake, there having been between him and them but one forest bough by way of interval at first. Should he be overtaken, he was wounded and not received into the Fianna after. If his weapons had quivered in his hand, he was not taken. Should a branch in the wood have disturbed anything of his hair out of its braiding, neither was he taken. If he had cracked a dry stick under his foot as he ran he was not accepted. Unless that at his full speed he had both jumped a stick level with his brow, and stooped to pass under one even with his knee, he was not taken. Also, unless without slackening his pace he could with his nail extract a thorn from his foot, he was not taken into Fianship: but if he performed all this he was of Finn's people.

CHRISTIANITY AND THE GOLDEN AGE

Saint Patrick

FROM THE CONFESSION

A Humble Meditation

St. Patrick first came to Ireland as a captive and spent six years tending sheep in the mountains before escaping home to Britain. At his own request Patrick returned to Ireland as a missionary several years later. This 5th century text preserved in the Book of Armagh, translated here from the Latin by Ludwig Bieler, demonstrates how the saint's humility and sincerity were grounded in the message of the Gospels.

---

§1. I am Patrick, a sinner, most unlearned, the least of all the faithful, and utterly despised by many. My father was Calpornius, a deacon, son of Potitus, a priest, of the village Bannavem Taburniae; he had a country seat nearby, and there I was taken captive.

I was then about sixteen years of age. I did not know the true God. I was taken into captivity to Ireland with many thousands of people—and deservedly so, because we turned away from God, and did not keep His commandments, and did not obey our priests, who used to remind us of our salvation. And the Lord *brought over us the wrath of His anger and scattered us among many nations*, even *unto the utmost part of the earth*, where now my littleness is placed among strangers.

§2. And there *the Lord opened the sense of my unbelief* that I might at last remember my sins and *be converted with all my heart to the Lord my God*, who *had regard for my objection*, and mercy on my youth and ignorance, and watched over me before I knew Him, and before I was able to distinguish between good and evil, and guarded me, and comforted me as would a father his son. . . .

§23. And again after a few years I was in Britain with my people, who received me as their son, and sincerely besought me that now at last, having suffered so many hardships, I should not leave them and go elsewhere.

And there I saw in the night the vision of a man, whose name was Victoricus, coming as it were from Ireland, with countless letters. And he gave me one of them, and I read the opening words of the letter, which were, 'The voice of the Irish'; and as I read the beginning of the letter I thought that at the same moment I heard their voice—they were those beside the Wood of Voclut, which is near the Western Sea—and thus did they cry out *as with one mouth*: 'We ask thee, boy, come and walk among us once more.'

And I was quite broken in heart, and could read no further, and so I woke up. Thanks be to God, after many years the Lord gave to them according to their cry. . . .

§41. Hence, how did it come to pass in Ireland that those who never had a knowledge of God, but until now always worshipped idols and things impure, have now been made a people of the Lord, and are called sons of God, that the sons and daughters of the kings of the Irish are seen to be monks and virgins of Christ?

§42. Among others, a blessed Irishwoman of noble birth, beautiful, full-grown, whom I had baptised, came to us after some days for a particular reason: she told us that she had received a message from a messenger of God, and he admonished her to be a virgin of Christ and draw near to God. Thanks be to God, on the sixth day after this she most laudably and eagerly chose what all virgins of Christ do. Not that their fathers agree with them; no—they often even suffer persecution and undeserved reproaches from their parents; and yet their number is ever increasing. How many have been reborn there so as to be of our kind, I do not know—not to mention widows and those who practice continence.

But greatest is the suffering of those women who live in slavery. All the time they have to endure terror and threats. But the Lord gave His grace to many of His maidens; for, though they are forbidden to do so, they follow Him bravely.

§43. Wherefore, then, even if I wished to leave them and go to Britain—and how I would have loved to go to my country and my parents, and also to Gaul in order to visit the brethren and to see the face of the saints of my Lord! God knows it that I much desired it; but I am bound by the Spirit, who gives evidence against me if I do this, telling me that I shall be guilty; and I am afraid of losing the labour which I have begun—nay, not I, but Christ the Lord who bade me come here and stay with them for the rest of my life, if the Lord will, and will guard me from every evil way that I may not sin before Him. . . .

§48. You know, and so does God, how I have lived among you from my youth in the true faith and in sincerity of heart. Likewise, as regards the heathen among whom I live, I have been faithful to them, and so I shall be. God knows it, I have over-reached none of them, nor would I think of doing so, for the sake of God and His Church, for fear of raising persecution against them and all of us, and for fear that through me the name of the Lord be blasphemed; for it is written: *Woe to the man through whom the name of the Lord is blasphemed.* . . .

§59. And if ever I have done any good for my God whom I love, I beg Him to grant me that I may shed my blood with those exiles and captives for His name, even though I should be denied a grave, or my body be woefully torn to pieces limb by limb by hounds or wild beasts, or the fowls of the air devour it. I am firmly convinced that if this should happen to me, I would have gained my soul together with my body, because on that day without doubt we shall rise in the brightness of the sun, that is, in the glory of Christ Jesus our Redeemer, as sons of the living God and *joint heirs with Christ, to be made comfortable to His image;* for *of Him,*

St. Patrick's Bell and Shrine. Bell: 6th to 8th century; Shrine: A.D. 1100 Bell: Bronze-coated iron; Shrine: Bronze with gilt silver frames surrounding gold filligree panels arranged in the form of a ringed cross; late Medieval cabochon of rock crystal in a gilt-silver filligree frame in the center. Bell: 7 9/16 x 5 3/16 in. (19.3 x 13.2 cm); Shrine: 10 1/2 x 6 1/8 in. (26.7 x 15.5 cm). National Museum of Ireland, Dublin.

and by Him, and in Him we shall reign.

§60. For this sun which we see rises daily for us because He commands so, but it will never reign, nor will its splendour last; what is more, those wretches who adore it will be miserably punished. Not so we, who believe in, and worship, the true sun—Christ—who will never perish, nor will he *who doeth His will*; but he *will abide for ever as Christ abideth for ever*, who reigns with God the Father Almighty and the Holy Spirit before time, and now, and in all eternity. Amen.

Cogitosus

FROM THE LIFE OF SAINT BRIGIT

The Miracle of The Garment Thrown Over a Sunbeam

This is the earliest "Life" of St. Brigit to survive. Not much is known about the author except that he was most likely a member of the community at the famous monastery of Kildare. Cogitosus is apparently a Latinized version of an Irish name.

———————

Here, I think I ought to slip in for your Reverences this other miracle in which the pure mind of the virgin and God's cooperating hand clearly appear to combine. As she was grazing her sheep in the course of her work as a shepherdess on a level grassy plain, she was drenched by a very heavy downpour of rain and returned to the house with her clothes wet. There was a ray of sunshine coming into the house through an opening and, as a result, her eyes were dazzled and she took the sunbeam for a slanting tree growing there. So, she put her rainsoaked clothes on it and the clothes hung on the filmy sunbeam as if it were a big solid tree. And the occupants of the house and the neighbours, dumbfounded by this extraordinary miracle, began to extol this incomparable lady with fitting praise.

Vinnian

FROM THE PENITENTIAL OF VINNIAN

Rules of Penance

Irish Penitentials are guides for the confessor (the "soul-friend"). Penances vary in length and severity according to the nature of the sin and the state of the sinner. Penances consist mainly of prayer, fasting, and alms-giving. The Penitential of Vinnian, *the earliest known Penitential of any length, served as a model for that of St. Columbanus.*

In the name of the Father and of the Son and of the Holy Ghost.

1. If anyone has sinned by thought in his heart and immediately repents, he shall beat his breast and seek pardon from God and make satisfaction, and (so) be whole.

2. But if he frequently entertains (evil) thoughts and hesitates to act on them, whether he has mastered them or been mastered by them, he shall seek help from God by prayer and fasting day and night until the evil thought departs and he is whole.

3. If, however, he has thought evil and intended to do it and has not been able to do it, since opportunity has failed him, it is the same sin but not the same penance; for example, if he intended fornication or murder, he has, by his intention, already committed the sin in his heart which he did not complete by a deed; but if he quickly does penance, he can be helped. His penance is this: half a year he shall do penance on an allowance of bread and water, and he shall abstain from wine and meat for a whole year.

4. If anyone has sinned in word by inadvertence and immediately repented, and has not said any such thing of set purpose, he ought to submit to penance, but he shall keep (only) one special fast; but thereafter let him be on his guard throughout his life, lest he commit further sin.

5. If one of the clerics or ministers of God makes strife, he shall do penance for a period of seven days with bread and water and salt, and seek pardon from God and his neighbour, with full confession and humility; and thus can he be reconciled to God and his neighbour.

6. If anyone has decided on a scandalous deed and plotted in his heart to strike or kill his neighbour, if (the offender) is a cleric, he shall do penance for half a year with an allowance of bread and water and for a whole year abstain from wine and meat, and thus he will be reconciled to the altar; 7. but if he is a layman, he shall do penance for a period of seven days; since he is a man of this world, his guilt is lighter in this world and his reward less in the world to come.

COLORPLATE 10

Canon Table. From the *Book of Kells.* Folio 5r. 8th century. Vellum. 13 x 9⅞ in. (33 x 25 cm).
340 folios. Courtesy The Board of Trinity College Dublin. *The* Book of Kells *is the finest illuminated
manuscript from the "golden age" of Ireland, and the finest surviving example of manuscripts in the
majuscule script saved for luxurious books to be used on the altar for important occasions. It contains
a Latin text of the four gospels, with prefaces, summaries of the narrative, and canon tables or
concordances of gospel passages.*

COLORPLATE 11

Chi-Rho. Opening Page of St. Matthew's Gospel. From the *Book of Kells.* Folio 34r. 8th century. Vellum.
13 x 9⁷/₈ in. (33 x 25 cm). Courtesy The Board of Trinity College Dublin. *The script is embellished with*
zoomorphic ornament and elaborate initials and opening words of the gospels. This ornate page,
dominated by the abbreviated Greek form of the name of Christ (Chi and Rho), is often referred to as the
highpoint of the manuscript and the culmination of the style.

COLORPLATE 12

Portrait of Christ. Opening page of Gospel. From the *Book of Kells.* Folio 32v. 8th century. Vellum.
13 x 9⅞ in. (33 x 25 cm). Courtesy The Board of Trinity College Dublin. *The Latin text is from the eventually "authorized" Vulgate translation done by St. Jerome in the 4th century at the request of Pope Damasus.*

COLORPLATE 13

Symbols of the Evangelists. From the *Book of Kells*. Folio 27v. 8th century. Vellum. 13 x 9⁷/₈ in. (33 x 25 cm). Courtesy The Board of Trinity College Dublin. *The symbols for the evangelists (from the Vulgate)—the man for Matthew, the lion for Mark, the calf for Luke, and the eagle for John—recur throughout the manuscript. Clearly, more than one scribe and artist worked on this magnificent manuscript.*

COLORPLATE 14

Eagle Symbol of Apostle Mark. From the *Book of Durrow*. Folio 84v. 7th century. Vellum. 9 5/8 x 29 5/16 in. (24.5 x 74.5 cm). 248 folios. Courtesy The Board of Trinity College Dublin. *The* Book of Durrow *contains the four gospels, canon tables, etc. decorated with framed evangelical symbols, carpet pages, and illuminated opening words of the gospels. The evangelical symbols used here follow a pre-Vulgate order in which Mark is represented by the eagle. An early 9th century inscription at the end of the manuscript ascribes its production to St. Columba (Columcille) at Durrow.*

COLORPLATE 15

Eagle Symbol for St. John. From the *Book of Dimma*. Folio 104v. Late 8th century. Vellum. 6 7/8 x 5 9/16 in. (17.5 x 14.2 cm). 74 folios. Courtesy The Board of Trinity College Dublin. *Written in miniscule script by Dimma, a scribe in the monastery of Roscrea, County Tipperary, this small, easily transportable "pocket" Gospel book, made for private devotion, contains the four gospels in the old Latin translation of the Vulgate.*

COLORPLATE 16

Domnach Airgid Shrine. Late 8th–early 9th century; mid-14th century. Wood; Silver plates. 9 x 6 9/16 in.
(23 x 16.7 cm). National Museum of Ireland, Dublin. *The name* Domnach Airgid (*Silver church or shrine*)
*comes from a shrine of the same name given by St. Patrick to St. Mac Cairthainn. The reliquary is a yew
box with a lid to which decorated silver plates were subsequently added (in the 14th century). In the center,
a worn figure of the crucified Christ is flanked by Mary and St. John.*

COLORPLATE 17

Shrine of the Stowe Missal.
Mid-11th and late 14th centuries.
Body: Wood box covered with bronze
plates. Lid: Lengths of bronze covered
with silver; semi-precious stones.
7 3/8 x 6 1/4 in. (18.7 x 15.8 cm). National
Museum of Ireland, Dublin. *A lengthy
inscription in Irish around the edge calls
for a blessing on the King of Cashel and
a prayer for Donnchadh Mac Briain, the
king of Ireland and the son of Brian
Boru, who died in 1064. The four-lobed
silver mounted stone was added in the
14th century.*

COLORPLATE 18

Soiscel Molaise Shrine. 11th century. Bronze and silver. 5^{13}/$_{16}$ x 4^{5}/$_{8}$ in. (14.75 x 11.70 cm). National Museum of Ireland, Dublin. *The earliest surviving Irish book shrine, the* Soiscel Molaise— *the Gospels of St. Molaise—is named for a 6th century Irish saint who founded an island monastery at Devenish, County Fermanagh. The four panels on the front contain representations of the four evangelists with the name of each and his symbol inscribed in Latin beside each panel.*

COLORPLATE 19

Crucifixion Plaque. Probably 8th century A.D. Openwork, hammered gilt-bronze with engraved ornament. 8⁵/₁₆ x 5¹/₂ in. (21.1 x 13.9 cm). National Museum of Ireland, Dublin. *This plaque, perhaps the decoration for a book shrine or altar, is one of the earliest surviving representations of the crucifixion in Irish art. The Ultimate La Tene style of concentric circles dominates.*

8. But if he is a cleric and strikes his brother or his neighbour or sheds blood, it is the same as if he had killed him, but the penance is not the same: he shall do penance with bread and water and salt and be deprived of his clerical office for an entire year, and he must pray with weeping and tears, that he may obtain mercy of God, since Scripture says: Whosoever hateth his brother is a murderer; how much more he who strikes him. 9. But if he is a layman, he shall do penance forty days and give some money to him whom he has struck, according as some priest or arbiter determines. A cleric, however, ought not to give money to either man or woman.

10. But if one who is a cleric falls miserably through fornication and loses his crown, if it happens once (only) and it is concealed from men but known before God, he shall do penance for an entire year with an allowance of bread and water and for two years abstain from wine and meat, but he shall not lose his clerical office. For, we say, sins can be absolved in secret by penance and by very diligent devotion of heart and body. 11. If, however, they have long been in the habit of sin and it has not come to the notice of men, he shall do penance for three years with bread and water and lose his clerical office, and for three years more he shall abstain from wine and meat, since it is not a smaller thing to sin before God than before men.

Rock of Cashel.
12th–13th century.
County Tipperary. Irish
Tourist Board, Dublin.
Royal site of the kings of
Munster until the 12th
century, then the location
of the Cathedral of
Cashel.

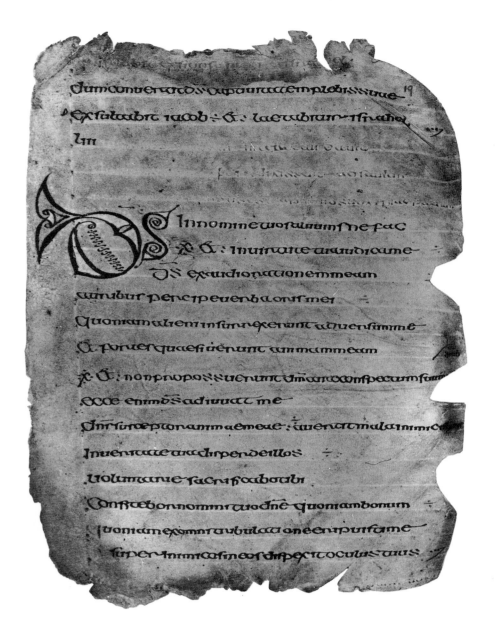

The Cathach. Psalm 53: "Deus in nomine tuo saluum," folio 19. 6th century. Manuscript. Royal Irish Academy, Dublin. *This is the oldest Irish manuscript, attributed to St. Columba. This may be the illegal copy of a psalter for which Columba was in litigation.*

FROM THE RULES OF SAINT COLUMBANUS

The Monk's Perfection

Columbanus (A.D. 543–615) headed the monastic school at Bangor. He travelled as a pilgrim and missioner to France, eventually settled in Italy, and formed the monastery at Bobbio that was to become one of the most renowned in Europe. The Rules and Penitentials of St. Columbanus demand that the monk regularly confess every sinful thought *as well as sinful deed.*

Let the monk live in a community under the discipline of one father and in company with many, so that from one he may learn lowliness, from another patience. For one may teach him silence and another meekness. Let him not do as he wishes, let him eat what he is bidden, keep as much as he has received, complete the tale of his work, be subject to whom he does not like.

Let him come weary to his bed and sleep walking, and let him be forced to rise while his sleep is not yet finished. Let him keep silence when he has suffered wrong, let him fear the superior of his community as a lord, love him as a father, believe that whatever he commands is healthful for himself, and let him not pass judgement on the opinion of an elder, to whose duty it belongs to obey and fulfil what he is bidden, as Moses says, Hear, O Israel, and the rest.

Poems of Devotion

Columcille the Scribe

The beloved Irish saint, Columcille (A.D. 521–597), "Dove of The Church," founded many monasteries—Derry, Durrow, and Kells among them—before he was exiled as the result of what may have been the first copyright battle. One of his masters claimed that a copy of a Book of Psalms, scribed and carried away by Columcille, was stolen property. The judgment was made against Columcille—with the colorful phrase "to every cow her calf."

My hand is weary with writing,
My sharp quill is not steady.
My slender beaked pen pours forth
A black draught of shining dark-blue ink.

A stream of the wisdom of blessed God
Springs from my fair brown shapely hand:
On the page it squirts its draught
Of ink of the green skinned holly.

My little dripping pen travels
Across the plain of shining books,
Without ceasing for the wealth of the great—
Whence my hand is weary with writing.

The Hermit's Song

The fervor and dedication to religious life of medieval monks in the land of saints and scholars is legendary. This anonymous 9th–century poem evokes images of both the hermit in his cell and the monk in the monastic community. Translated by Kuno Meyer (1859–1919).

I wish, O Son of the living God,
O ancient, eternal King,
For a hidden little hut in the wilderness
That it may be my dwelling.

An all-grey lithe little lark
To be by its side,
A clear pool to wash away sins
Through the grace of the Holy Spirit.

Quite near, a beautiful wood,
Around it on every side,
To nurse many-voiced birds,
Hiding it with its shelter.

And facing the south for warmth;
A little brook across its floor,
A choice land with many gracious gifts
Such as be good for every plant.

A few men of sense—
We will tell their number—
Humble and obedient,
To pray to the King:—

Four times three, three times four,
Fit for every need,
Twice six in the church,
Both north and south:—

Six pairs
Besides myself,
Praying forever to the King
Who makes the sun shine.

A pleasant church and with the linen altar-cloth,
A dwelling for God from Heaven;
Then, shining candles
Above the pure white Scriptures.

One house for all to go to
For the care of the body,
Without ribaldry, without boasting,
Without thought of evil.

This is the husbandry I would take,
I would choose, and will not hide it:
Fragrant leek,
Hens, salmon, trout, bees.

Raiment and food enough for me
From the King of fair fame,
And I to be sitting for a while
Praying God in every place.

Geoffrey Keating

FROM HISTORY OF IRELAND

The Tale of The Three Treasures

Geoffrey Keating, born in County Tipperary around 1580, studied in France at the
University of Bordeaux. He was supposedly killed by Cromwellian soldiers in 1650. The

asceticism and mystery of this little tale is characteristic of early Irish Christianity.

Mo Chua and Colmcille were contemporaries, and when Mo Chua, or Mac Duach, was alone in the wilderness, the only worldly wealth he had was a cock and a mouse and a fly. The cock's function used to be to wake him for midnight matins. As for the mouse, he only used to let him have five hours sleep, night or day, and whenever he used to wish for more sleep, because he was tired from all the cross vigils and prostrations, the mouse used to lick his ear and wake him like that. The fly also: its function was to walk along each line as he read his psalter, and when he rested from chanting his psalms it used to stay on the line he left until he came again to read his psalms. It happened soon after that those three treasures died, and Mo Chua wrote to Colmcille, who was in Iona in Scotland, complaining about the death of that little flock. Colmcille wrote to him and he said: 'My brother you should not be surprised at the death of the flock that has departed from you because misfortune only strikes where there is wealth.'

FROM THE VOYAGE OF SAINT BRENDAN

Journey to the Land of Promise

This popular story of Brendan's quest for the "Land of Promise and of the Saints," translated here by Lady Augusta Gregory, has been translated into many languages. Supposedly Brendan found the Americas long before Columbus's famous voyage in 1492. A few years ago, several young adventurers set out from Ireland to retrace Brendan's route in a similar handmade boat. The new voyagers made it to Greenland.

His Vision of the Land of Promise
It is a monk going through hardship Blessed Brendan was, that was born in Ciarraige Luachra

Croagh Patrick and Clew Bay, County Mayo. Photograph. Irish Tourist Board, Dublin. *St. Patrick's mountain.*

of a good father and mother. It was on Slieve Daidche beside the sea he was one time, and he saw in a vision a beautiful island with angels serving upon it. And an angel of God came to him in his sleep and said, "I will be with you from this out through the length of your lifetime, and it is I will teach you to find that island you have seen and have a mind to come to." When Brendan heard those words from the angel he cried with the dint of joy, and gave great thanks to God, and he went back to the thousand brothers that were his people.

The News of the Hidden Country
It happened now there was a young man by name Mernoke that was a brother in another house, and that went out in a ship looking for some lonely place where he might serve God at will. And he came to an island that is convenient to the Mountain of Stones, and he liked it well and stopped there a good while, himself and his people. But after that he put out his ship again and sailed on eastward through the length of three days. And it seemed to him on a sudden that a cloud came around them, the way they were in darkness the whole of the day, till by the will of our dear Lord the cloud passed away and they saw before them a shining lovely island. There was enough of joy and of rejoicing in that island, and every herb was full of blossom and every tree was full of fruit; and as for the ground it was shining with precious stones on every side, and heaven itself could hardly be better. There came to them then a very comely young man, that called every one of them by name and gave them a pleasant welcome; and he said to them, "It would be right for you to give good thanks to Jesus Christ that is showing you this hidden place, for this is the country he will give to his darlings upon earth at the world's end, and it is to this place He himself will come. And there is another island besides this one," he said; "but you have not leave to go on to it or to have sight of it at all. And you have been here through the length of half a year," he said "without meat or drink or closing your eyes in sleep." They thought now they had not been the length of half an hour in that place, they had been so happy and so content. And he told them that was the first dwelling place of Adam and Eve, and there never came darkness there, and the name of it was the Earthly Paradise. Then he brought them back to their ship again and when they were come to it he vanished out of their sight, and they did not know where was it he went.

Then they set out over the sea again, and where they came to land was the place where Brendan was and his brothers, and they questioned Mernoke's people as to where they had been. "We have been," they said, "before the gates of Paradise, in the Land of Promise, and we had every sort of joy there and of feasting, and there is always day in it and no night at all." And their clothes had the sweetness of that place about them yet and the brothers said, "We are certain indeed you have been in that place, by the happy smile of you." And when Brendan heard all these tidings he stood still for a while thinking with himself; and after that he went about among the brothers and chose out twelve of them that he thought more of than of all the rest; and he consulted them and asked an advice of them. "Dear Father," they said, "we have left our own will and our friends and all our goods, and have come as children to you; and whatever you think well to do," they said, "we will do it."

The Beginning of Brendan's Search
So with that Brendan made his mind up to search out that place by the help of God; and he fasted forty days and did hard penance. And he made a very large ship having strong hides nailed over it, and pitch over the hides, that the water would not come in. And he took his own twelve with him and took his leave of the brothers and bade them good-bye. And those he left after him were sorry every one, and two among them came when he was in the ship and begged hard to go with him. And Brendan said, "You have leave to sail with me; but one of you will be sorry that he asked to come." But for all that they would go with him. Then they rowed out into the great sea of the ocean in the name of our Lord and were no way daunted at all. And the sea and the wind drove the ship at will, so that on the morning of the morrow they were out of sight of land. And so they went on through forty days and the wind driving them eastward.

Skellig Michael
(foreground) *with Little*
Skellig (background).
Photograph. Irish Tourist
Board, Dublin. *Medieval*
monastic settlement off
the coast of County Kerry.

The Very Comely Hound

And at the last they saw to the north a very large island having hard rocks on every side, and they sailed around it for three days before they could come near any place of landing; but at the last they found a little harbour, and landed every one. Then there came of a sudden a very comely hound and it fell down at Brendan's feet and bade him welcome in its own way. "Good brothers," said Brendan, "there is nothing for us to be in dread of, for I know this is a Messenger to lead us into a right place." Then the hound brought them into a great hall where there was a table having a cloth upon it, and bread and fish; and there was not one of them but was glad of that, and they sat down and eat and drank; and after their supper they found beds ready for them and they took their fill of sleep. . . .

The Paradise of Birds

They went on then to the westward through the length of three days, and very downhearted they were seeing no land. But not long after by the will of God they saw a beautiful island full of flowers and herbs and trees, and they were glad enough to see it and they went on land and gave thanks to God. And they went a long way through that lovely country, till they came to a very good well and a tree beside it full of branches and on every branch were beautiful white birds, so many of them there were that not a leaf hardly could be seen. And it was well for them to be looking at such a tree, and the happy singing of the birds was like the noise of Heaven. And Brendan cried for joy and he kneeled down and bade the Lord to tell him the meaning of the birds and their case. Then a little bird of the birds flew towards him from the tree and with the flickering of his wings he made a very merry noise like a fiddle, and it seemed to Brendan never to have heard such joyful music. Then the little bird looked at him and Brendan said, "If you are a Messenger tell me out your estate and why you sing to happily." And it is what the bird said: "One time we were every one of us angels, but when our master Lucifer fell from heaven for his high pride we fell along with him, some higher and some lower. And because our offence was but a little one," he said, "our Lord has put us here without pain in great joy and merriment to serve what way we can upon that tree. And on the Sunday that is a day of rest," he said, "we are made as white as any snow that we may praise him the better. And it is twelve months," he said, "since you left your own place, and at the end of seven years there will be an end to your desire. And through these seven years," he said, "it is here you will be keeping your Easter until you will come into the Land of Promise." Then the bird took his leave of them and went back to his fellows upon the tree. It was upon an Easter Day now all this happened. Then all the birds began to sing the Vespers, and there could be no merrier music if God himself was among them. And after supper Blessed Brendan and his comrades went to bed; and they rose up on the morning of the morrow and the birds sang the matins and said the verses of the psalms, and sang all the Hours as is the habit with Christian men. And Brendan and his people stopped there for eight weeks till after the Pentecost; and they sailed back again to the Island of the Sheep, and there they got good provision and took their leave of the old man their Helper, and went back into their ship. . . .

The Bird's Foretelling

And when they had kept their Easter with great honour they went on to the island having the tree of birds. And the little bird gave them a good welcome and it is lively was the sound of his song. So they stopped there from Easter to Candlemas the same as the year before, very happy and content, listening to the merry service that was sung upon the tree. Then the bird told Blessed Brendan he should go back again for Christmas to the Island of the Abbey, and at Easter he should come hither again and the rest of the year he should be labouring in the great sea in trouble and in danger. "And so it will be with you from year to year to the end of forty years," he said, "and then you will reach to the Land of Promise; and then through forty days you will have your fill of joy. And after that you will return to your own country," he said, "quite easily and without any annoy, and there you will end your life." Then the Angel that was their helper brought all sorts of provision and loaded the ship and made all ready. So they thanked our Lord for his great goodness that he had showed them so often in their great need, and they sailed out into the sea among great storms.

The Dangers of the Sea

And soon there came after them a horrible great fish that was following their ship and that was casting up such great spouts of water out of his mouth that they had like to be drowned, and he was coming so fast that he had all but reached to them. Then they cried on Jesus Christ to help them in that great danger. And with that there came another fish bigger than the first out of the west, and made an attack on him and beat him and at the last made three halves of him and went away again as he came, and they were very glad and gave thanks to Jesus Christ. And after that again they were very downhearted through hunger, for all their food was spent. And there came to them then a little bird having with him a great branch of red grapes, and they lived by them through fourteen days and had their fill. And when that failed them they came to a little island that was full of beautiful trees, and fruit on every bough of them. And Brendan landed out of the ship and gathered as much of that fruit would last them through forty days, and they went sailing and ever sailing through storm and through wind. And of a sudden there came sailing towards them a great monster and it made an attack upon them and on their ship and had like to have destroyed them, and at that they cried pitifully and thought themselves as good as dead. And then the little bird that had spoken with them from the tree at Easter time came at the monster and struck out one of his eyes with the first attack and the other eye with the second and made an end of him that he fell into the sea; and it is well pleased Brendan was when he saw that bird coming. Then they gave thanks to God, and they went on sailing until Saint Peter's Day, and they sang the service in honour of the Feast. And in that place the water was so clear that they could see to the bottom, and it was all as if covered with a great heap of fishes. And the brothers were in dread at the sight of all the fishes and they advised Brendan to speak softly and not to waken the fishes for fear they might break the ship. And Brendan said, "Why would you that have these two years kept the Feast of the Resurrection upon the great fish's back be in dread of these little fishes?" And with that he made ready for the Mass and sang louder than before. And the fishes awoke and started up and came all around the ship in a heap, that they could hardly see the water for fishes. But when the Mass was ended each one of them turned himself and swam away, and they saw them no more.

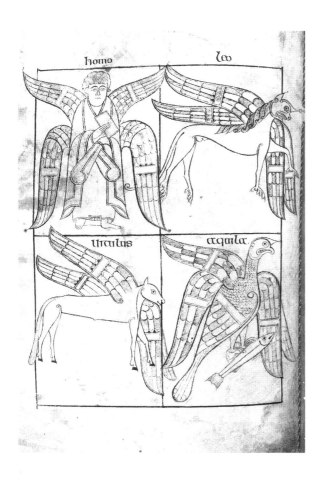

A Border of Hell

For seven days now they were going on through that clear water, and there came a south wind that drove them on and they did not know were they were going. And at the end of eight days they saw far away in the north a dark country full of stench and of smoke; and as the ship drew near it they heard great blowing and blasting of bellows, and a noise of blows and a noise like thunder, the way they were all afeared and blessed themselves. And soon after there came one starting out all burning, and he turned away again and gave out a cry that could be heard a long way off. . . .

A Most Wretched Ghost

Then the wind turned and drove the ship southward through seven days, and they came to a great rock in the sea, and the sea breaking over it. And on the rock was sitting a wretched ghost, naked and in great misery and pain, for the waves of the sea had so beaten his body that all the flesh was gone from it and nothing was left but sinews and bare bones. And there was a cloth tied to his chin and two tongues of oxen with it, and when the wind blew, the cloth beat against his body, and the waves of the sea beat him before and behind, the way no one could find in any place a more wretched ghost. And Brendan bade him tell who was he in the name of God, and what he had done against God and why he was sitting there. "I am a doleful shadow," he said, "that wretched Judas that sold our Lord for pence and I am sitting here most wretchedly; and this is not my right place," he said, "for my right place is in burning hell, but by our Lord's Grace I am brought here at certain times of the year, for I am here every Sunday and from the evening of Saturday, and from Christmas to Little Christmas and from Easter to the Feast of Pentecost and on every feast day of Our Lady; for he is full of mercy. But at other times I am lying in burning fire with Pilate, Herod, Annas and Caiaphas; and I am cursing and ever cursing the time when I was born. And I bid you for the love of God," he said, "to keep me from the devils that will be coming after me." And Brendan said, "With the help of God we will protect you through the night. And tell me what is that cloth that is hanging from your head," he said. "It is a cloth I gave to a leper when I was on earth, and because it was given for the love of God, it is hanging before me. But because it was not with my own pence I bought it but with what belonged to our Lord and his brothers," he said, "it is more harmful to me than helpful, beating very hard in my eyes. And those tongues that you see hanging," he said, "I gave to the priests upon earth and so they are here and are some ease to me, because the fishes of the sea gnaw upon them and spare me. And this stone that I am sitting upon," he said, "I found it lying in a desolate place where there was no use for it, and I took it and laid it in a boggy path where it was a great comfort to those that passed that way; and because of that it comforts me now, and there are but few good deeds I have to tell of," he said. On the evening now of the Sunday there came a great troop of devils blasting and roaring and they said to Brendan, "Go from this, God's man, you have nothing to do here, and let us have our comrade and bring him back to hell for we dare not face our master and he not with us." "I will not give you leave to do your master's orders," said Brendan, "but I charge you by the name of our Lord Jesus Christ to leave him here this night until tomorrow." "Would you dare," said the devils, "to help him that betrayed his master and sold him to death and to great shame?" But Brendan laid orders on them not to annoy him that night, and they cried horribly and went away, and with that Judas thanked Blessed Brendan so mournfully that it was a pity to hear him. And on the morning of the morrow the devils came again and cried out and scolded at Brendan. "Away with you," they said, "for our master the great devil tormented us heavily through the night because we had not brought him with us; and we will avenge it on him," they

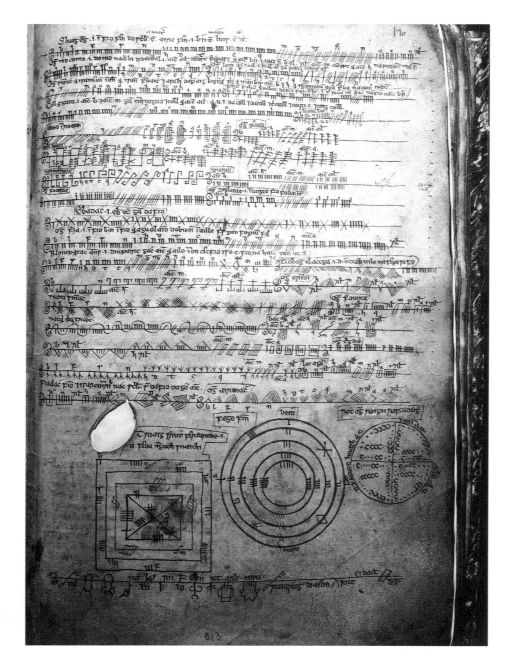

Tract on Ogham Script. From *The Book of Ballymote.* 14th century. Vellum. Ms. 23, p. 12, folio 170r. Royal Irish Academy, Dublin. *Compiled in 1390 at the home of a Gaelic lord, this manuscript contains many early genealogies, histories, legends, classic tales, poems, and legal treatises.*

said, "and he will get double pains for the six days to come." And then they turned and took away with them that wretched one, quailing and trembling as he went. . . .

A Lucky Journey

Then they went back to the ship and they were driven towards the south by a great wind through the forty days of Lent. And on Easter Eve they reached to their good Helper and he gave them good treatment as he had done before. And then he led them to the great fish and it was upon his back they said their Matins and their Mass. . . .

The Land of Promise

And after that they took their ship and sailed through forty days eastward. And at the end of the forty days there came a great shower of hail and then a dark mist came about them, and they were in it for a long time. Then their Helper came to them and said, "Let you be glad now and hearten yourselves for you are come to the Land of Promise." Then they came out of the dark mist and they saw to the east the loveliest country that any one could see. Clear it was and lightsome, and there was enough in it of joy, and the trees were full of fruit on every bough, and the apples were as ripe as at harvest time. And they were going about that country through forty days and could see no end to it, and it was always day there and never night, and the air neither hot nor cold but always in the one way, and the delight that they found there could never be told. Then they came to a river that they could not cross but they could see beyond it the country that had no bounds to its beauty. Then there came to them a young man the comeliest that could be, and he gave them all a welcome, and to Brendan he showed great honour and took him by the hand and said to him, "Here is the country you have been in search of, but it is our Lord's will you should go back again and make no delay, and he will show you more of his hidden things when you will come again into the great sea. And charge your ship with the fruit of this country," he said, "and you will soon be out of the world for your life is near its end. And this river you see here is the mering," he said, "that divides the worlds, for no man may come to the other side of it while he is in life; and when our Lord will have drawn every man to him, and when every man will know him and be under his law, it is then there will be leave to see this country, towards the world's end." Then Brendan and his comrades did not fast from the fruit, but brought away what they could of it and of precious stones, and put them in their ship and went away homewards, and sorry enough they were to go.

Brendan's Home-coming

And they sailed home in their ship to Ireland and it is glad the brothers they had left after them were to see them come home out of such great dangers. And as to Brendan he was from that time as if he did not belong to this world at all, but his mind and his joy were in the delight of heaven. And it is in Ireland he died and was buried; and that God may bring us to the same joy his blessed soul returned to!

FROM CRITH GABLACH
A Catalogue of Property

The ancient Irish laws are popularly referred to as the "Brehon Laws" after the Irish term for the official lawgiver—the very learned legal expert. Although only a fraction of this ancient law literature, written down around A.D. 700, survives today, it occupies five large volumes. Crith Gablach, *one volume, defines the rights and privileges of the various ranks of society. All freemen were landowners. The brehon catalogued elaborate subdivisions of each class according to property qualifications. Here is a detailed inventory of the contents of the home of a bóaire, or higher grade of freemen. The furnishings in the home of an aristocrat would be similar although more luxurious.*

All the furniture of his house is in its proper place—
    a cauldron with its spit and handles,
    a vat in which a measure of ale may be brewed,
    a cauldron for everyday use,
    small vessels: iron pots and kneading trough and wooden mugs, so that he has
        no need to borrow them;
    a washing trough and a bath,
    tubs, candlesticks, knives for cutting rushes;
    rope, an adze, an auger, a pair of wooden shears, an axe;
    the work-tools for every season—every one unborrowed;
    a whetstone, a bill-hook, a hatchet, spears for slaughtering livestock;
    a fire always alive, a candle on the candlestick without fail;
    a full ploughing outfit with all its equipment . . .
There are two vessels in his house always:
    a vessel of milk and a vessel of ale.
He is a man of three snouts:
    the snout of a rooting boar that cleaves dishonour in every season,
    the snout of a flitch of bacon on the hook,
    the snout of a plough under the ground;
    so that he is capable of receiving a king or a bishop or a scholar or a brehon
      from the road, prepared for the arrival of any guest-company.
He owns seven houses:
    a kiln, a barn, a mill (a share in it so that it grinds for him),
    a house of twenty-seven feet,
    an outhouse of seventeen feet,
    a pig-stye, a pen for calves, a sheep-pen.
He has twenty cows, two bulls, six oxen, twenty pigs, twenty sheep, four domestic
    boars, two sows, a saddle-horse, an enamelled bridle, sixteen bushels of seed
    in the ground.
He has a bronze cauldron in which there is room for a boar.
He possesses a green in which there are always sheep without having to change
    pasture.
He and his wife have four suits of clothes.

Donatus of Fiesole

"Ireland's Golden Age"

These lines written in Latin in the mid-9th century by Donatus of Fiesole, an Irish bishop living in Italy, are translated here by Liam de Paor. The poet describes Ireland in her golden age, a period which culminated in the extraordinary illuminated masterpiece of the Book of Kells.

The noblest share of earth is the far western world
Whose name is written Scotia in the ancient books;
Rich in goods, in silver, jewels, cloth and gold,
Benign to the body in air and mellow soil.
With honey and with milk flow Ireland's lovely plains,
With silk and arms, abundant fruit, with art and men.

Worthy are the Irish to dwell in this their land
A race of men renowned in war, in peace, in faith.

FROM THE VIKINGS TO 1700

"The Viking Terror"

This anonymous little poem, found in the margin of an 8th or 9th century manuscript, was written by an Irish monk of the time, grateful to hear the sounds of the storm outside as he worked on his manuscript, knowing that the monastery (usually the invader's first target) would be safe from Norse plunderers this night. Translated by F.N. Robinson.

—————————

Fierce is the wind tonight,
It ploughs up the white hair of the sea
I have no fear that the Viking hosts
Will come over the water to me.

Viking Ship. 8th century. Carving/drawing on bark. National Museum of Ireland, Dublin.

Seamus MacManus

FROM THE STORY OF THE IRISH RACE

Viking Influence

The arrival of the Vikings in Ireland was terrifying. But there is much evidence of a positive Norse influence on Irish life. A predominantly rural lifestyle shifted to the coastal towns, and the Irish learned to look out at the expanding world in a new way.

The Viking age was by no means a starless night in Ireland, nor was society so horribly disorganised as is generally believed. It was a period marked by the lives of Irish chiefs of outstanding ability, of some of the greatest figures in Nordic history, and of women of unusual personality. Even in those days of terror and danger from foreign invasion, when an enemy fleet stood in every port and soldiers were encamped in many parts of the country, Ireland was still in the full current of European life. Though internecine feuds and battles with the Danes took up much of the chieftains' time, other things besides spears and swords were exchanged between the Irish and the invader. In no other land in which these two peoples of such different culture came together did each learn so much from the other as in Ireland. In matters of agriculture and cattle raising the Irish were the teachers of the Norsemen, but in other purely material pursuits the civilisation of the Norse was superior to that of the Irish. Though by the middle of the seventh century, in the pre-Viking period, Ireland had made considerable progress in the art of ship construction, it was above all from the hardy sailors of the north that they learned to build and sail great ships and to organise fleets, to use iron armour, to fight on horseback and no longer from chariots or on foot, to build stone forts and bridges, and to live in fortified cities surrounded by walls. By the middle of the tenth century, Dublin, Limerick, Cork, Waterford, all Viking establishments, were strong walled places.

Nor were the Vikings mere sea robbers; they were merchants as well. Since they controlled the seas, for a long time all trade and shipping between Limerick and other Irish ports and the west of France and Spain was in their hands. They exported Ireland's products and imported all that Ireland wanted, as wheat, wine, costly silks, and fine leather, and they helped to introduce foreign fashions into Ireland. The first Irish coins that were struck in Ireland were minted by Norse kings who held court in Dublin; they have been found in Norway and elsewhere, and point to the trade carried on between the two countries. The Irish probably also adopted the northern system of weights and measures.

How much Irish society and domestic life were influenced by Norse occupation is seen in the Irish language itself, in which there is scarcely a word meaning a large ship or its parts or markets or trade that is not borrowed from the Norse, if it is not from the Latin. Even the name by which, in English, we call Erin, is from the Old Norse Iraland, and the English names of three of the present-day provinces, Munster, Leinster and Ulster, have a Norse termination, *stadr*, "place," added to the Gaelic stem. Donegal (Dun na Gall), "the Fort of the Foreigners," got its name from a fort built by the Vikings. But these are the exceptions. There are scarcely more than a dozen Norse place names on the whole map of Ireland and these are mostly on or near the sea coast, while there are over a thousand in middle and northern England. This is one of the surest signs that there was no real conquest or occupation of the country. The Norse and the Irish had to understand each other to some appreciable extent, and it was the language of the invader that gave way to that of the invaded. . . .

Though the Viking invasions checked the normal development of Irish civilisation, undid what the efforts of successive centuries had realised, and gave Ireland such a shock that learning scarcely ever fully recovered from it, a brilliant intellectual life prevailed during that period

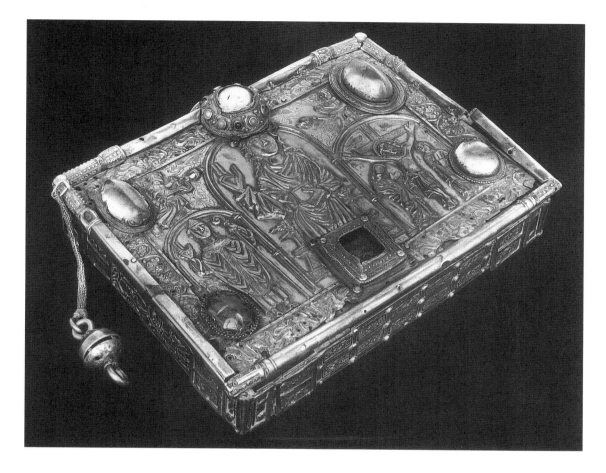

Book Shrine for the Cathach. 11th century. Cast metal. National Museum of Ireland, Dublin. *Made between 1072 and 1098, almost certainly at Kells, by a craftsman of Viking origin named Sitric who used the popular Ringerike style of ornamentation.*

and, in all the things that pertained to the mind, the Irish were far superior to their invaders and Irish genius made itself felt upon them. The names of Norse students are found among those who attended Ireland's most celebrated university, Clonmacnois, in the first half of the eleventh century. Streams of professors, students and missionaries continued to flow to the continent, some of them no doubt fleeing from the Vikings.

Irish sculpture, building, metal work, art, and ornament, flourished and influenced the art of the Scandinavians. The most important and most beautifully illuminated manuscripts, both in Latin and Irish, date from that period, and some of the greatest poets in Irish literature . . . flourished in it. It was Irish scholars who introduced the literature of Greece and Rome to the men of the north.

FROM THE ANNALS OF CLONMACNOISE
"Brian Boru and the Battle of Clontarf"

Brian Boru, most civilized Irish king, self-described in the Book of Armagh *as "Emperor of the Irish," won the famous battle of Clontarf in 1014, but lost his life in the conflict. This translation by Conall MacGeoghegan from 1627 chronicles this pivotal struggle for dominance between the great provincial leaders, and is particularly valuable since the original Irish text has been lost.*

Bryan Borowa tooke the kingdome and government thereof out of the handes of king Moyleseachlin in such manner as I doe not Intend to Relate in this place. Hee was very well worthy of the place and government, and raigned 12 years, the most famous king for his time that ever was before or after him of the Irish nation for manhood, fortune, manners, laws, liberties, religion, and many other good partes, hee neuer had his peere amongst them all, though some chroniclers of the kingdome made comparisons between him and Conn Cedcahagh, Conairey more, and king Neale of the nine hostages. Yett hee in regard of the state of the kingdome when hee came to the government thereof was judged to beare the bell away from them all. At his first entry into the kingdom the whole realme was overrun and overspread by the Danes every where, the churches, abbyes, and other religious howses were by them quite Razed, and Debased, or otherwise turned to vile, base, servile, and abominable uses. Most of all, yea almost all the noblemen, gentlemen and those that were of any account were turned out of theire landes and liveings without any hopes of recovery or future redress; Yea some of the best sort were compelled to servitude and bounden slavery; both human lawe and Godes feare were set aside. In summe, it was strange how men of any fashion could use men as the Danes did use the Irish men at that time. King Bryan Borowa was a meet salve to cure such festred sores, all the phisick in the world could not cure it else, where in a small time he bannished the Danes, made up the churches and religious houses, restored the nobilityes to their auntient patrimonies and possessions, and in fine brought all to a notable reformation. At lenth in the yeare of our Lord God 1007 the 22nd of march being good ffryday hee assembled together all his forces to give battle to the Danes at Clontarffe, and on the other side Brwader Earle of the Island of the Orcades called together and assembled all the Danes of Denmark out of all parts and kingdoms that owed them any service to that place as Generall and captain of the Danes, where there was a bloody battle between them fought at Clontarffe aforesaid. Brwader himself with his thousand men in shirtes of maile were slaine, the rest of his army were both slaine and drowned in the sea. Mulmurray McMurrogh M^cffinn king of Leinster and McBrogaroann prince of Affaile that partaked with the Danes with many Leinstermen about them were slaine alsoe in this battle, and of the other side king Bryan Borowa sonn of Kennedy McLorckan then greatest monarch in these partes of Europe, then of the age of 88 years, his nephew Conyng

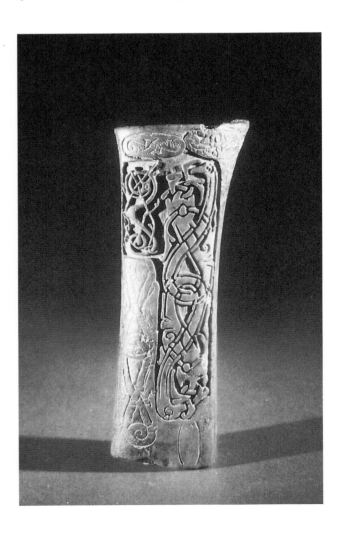

Bone Trial Piece. 11th–12th century. Bone. 4¹/₂ x 1¹¹/₁₆ in. (11.4 x 4.2 cm). National Museum of Ireland, Dublin. *Metalworkers made preliminary sketches of designs and metalworking apprentices made practice sketches on bone rather than precious metal. Bone had no grain and provided an ideal cutting surface for "trial pieces" such as this one.*

COLORPLATE 20

Pseudo-penannular Brooch. Roscrea, County Tipperary. 9th century. Cast silver with gold filligree and amber ornaments with engraved motifs. Diameter of ring: 3³/₈ in. (8.62 cm). Length of pin: 7¹/₁₆ in. (17.9 cm). National Museum of Ireland, Dublin.

COLORPLATE 21

Ardagh Chalice. 8th century. Polished silver and cast gilt bronze panels with gold filligree kerbschnitt and glass ornaments. 7 x 8¹/₈ in. (17.8 x 23.1 cm). National Museum of Ireland, Dublin.

COLORPLATE 22

Ardagh Chalice. View of underside. Irish-made liturgical vessels are rare. The Ardagh Chalice *is the finest expression of 8th century Irish metalworking we have. The chalice was used for dispensing eucharistic wine to the faithful during liturgical rituals. Found with other objects in 1868 by a boy digging potatoes within a ring-fort near Ardagh, County Limerick, the chalice and other treasures are thought to have been hidden during a Viking raid in the 10th century.*

COLORPLATE 23

Lismore Crozier. c. A.D. 1100. Lismore, County
Waterford. Sheet bronze wrapped around a wood staff;
hollow crook with a small box-shaped reliquary; gold
foil; blue and white *millefiori* glass. 45¹¹/₁₆ in.
(116 cm). National Museum of Ireland, Dublin. *An
inscription around the crook reads: "A prayer for Nial
Mac Meic Aeducain who caused this crozier to be
made. A prayer for Neachtain the craftsman who
made the work." Nial Mac Meic Aeducain was bishop
of Lismore in 1090, and died in A.D. 1113.*

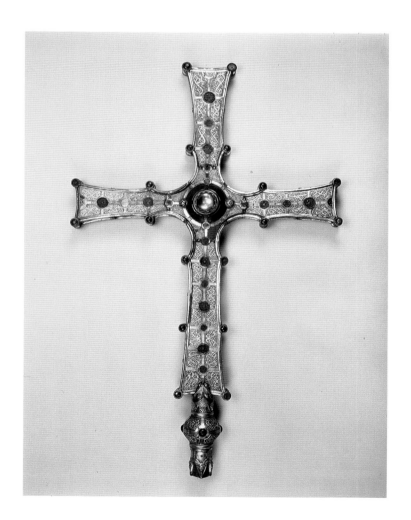

COLORPLATE 24

Cross of Cong. Early 12th century. Processional cross
of oak cased in copper and silver with decorations in
gold and gilt bronze. 30¹/₈ in. (76.5 cm). National
Museum of Ireland, Dublin. *A circular rock crystal set
in a silver mount housed a fragment of the true cross.
Inscriptions date the cross to about 1125.*

COLORPLATE 25

Muiredach's Cross at Monasterboice. County Louth. Detail:
The Arrest of Christ. c. 923. Carved white sandstone flecked
with black mica. 18 ft. (54 m). Irish Tourist Board, Dublin.
*This High Cross, one of the sculptural masterpieces of Ireland,
is decorated on all sides with intricate, sharply-cut scenes
from the Bible. The name of Muiredach, probably the abbot of
Monasterboice, is carved in the base of the cross.*

COLORPLATE 26

Muiredach's Cross at Monasterboice.
County Louth. Detail: *Doubting Thomas.*
c. 923. Carved white sandstone flecked
with black mica. 18 ft. (54 m). Irish Tourist
Board, Dublin. *Scenes from the New
Testament dominate the west face of the
massive High Cross.*

COLORPLATE 27 *(opposite)*

South Cross, Clonmacnoise. County Offaly. 9th century. Stone Celtic Cross. Irish Tourist Board, Dublin.
*Earliest of the Early Christian High Crosses at Clonmacnoise Monastery, most of the surface is adorned
with carved, abstract ornamental designs. Very much part of the monastic scenery (more than 100 examples
have survived), the exact purpose of these High Crosses is not certain. They were not grave markers, but
perhaps gathering places outside the small churches, or sacred totems to ward off evil spirits.*

COLORPLATE 28

Monastic ruins, Skellig Michael. 6th or 7th century. Early Christian monastic settlement off the coast of County Kerry. Irish Tourist Board. *Ruins of six small stone beehive cells which were the monks' ascetic living quarters (each measuring 9–16 ft. [2.74–4.8 m] high with barely enough room for a man to lie down inside), a medieval chapel and two dry-stone oratories where the monks prayed and worshipped are perched on a rocky island rising more than 700 feet above the sea. Dedicated to St. Michael, patron saint of high places, the ruins are reached by the stairway of the monks— 600 uneven steps crudely cut in the rock face.*

COLORPLATE 29

Gallerus Oratory. County Kerry. A.D. 800–1200. Small stone chapel of dry-stone wall. 10 x 15 ft. (3 x 4.5 m). Irish Tourist Board, Dublin. *Such oratories, of which this is the best-preserved example, were common to early-Christian monastic settlements. Shaped like an upturned boat, with a high-ridged roof and dry-stone construction, the oratory has remained waterproof for more than a thousand years.*

COLORPLATE 30

Clonfert Cathedral. County Galway. c. 1160. Red sandstone. Irish Tourist Board, Dublin.
The famous monastery founded on this site by Brendan the Navigator in A.D. *563 (and the place of his burial in 584), was destroyed in the 12th century. Much of the cathedral built then has survived. The elaborately-carved, great west doorway shown here is considered by many to be the ultimate example of Irish Romanesque art.*

COLORPLATE 31

Ardmore Round Tower. County Waterford. 12th century. Mortared stone tower. Height: 90 ft. (27.43 m).
Photograph. Irish Tourist Board, Dublin. *Round towers, of which this is one of the best preserved examples
in Ireland, were built in response to Viking attacks on monasteries. In addition to serving as belfries from
which handbells were rung summoning the monks to prayer, they also functioned as watch towers, as
strongholds of monastic records and treasures, and as hiding places for the members of the community
in the face of danger. The single doorway was normally 10–15 feet above the ground reached only by a
ladder which was lowered and then retrieved back into the tower.*

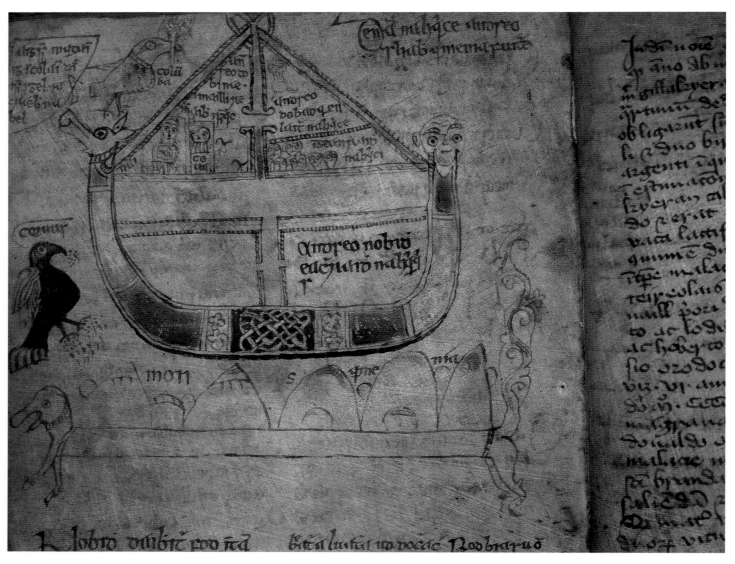

COLORPLATE 32

Noah's Ark. Mid-14th century. Vellum. National Library of Ireland, Dublin. *This miniature from an illuminated manuscript by Gaelic scribe Adam O'Ceanan (d. 1373), shows compartments in the ark for Noah and his family, the animals, and birds.*

COLORPLATE 33

The Brian Boru Harp. 15th or 16th century. Wood harp. Height: 33 7/8 in. (86 cm). Courtesy The Board of Trinity College Dublin. *The oldest surviving harp in Ireland. Although once associated with Brian Boru, high king of Ireland who died in 1014, this association is no longer tenable. A silver badge depicting the arms of the O'Neill family, dating from the 16th or 17th century was found attached to the instrument. The harp has become an important Irish artistic motif and a national symbol.*

COLORPLATE 34

Portrait of King John. 1399. From *The Royal Charters of Waterford City.*
With permission from the Waterford Corporation.

COLORPLATE 35

Portrait of Edward III. 1399. From *The Royal Charters of Waterford City.*
With permission from the Waterford Corporation.

COLORPLATE 36

DANIEL MACLISE. *The Marriage of the Princess Aoife of Leinster with Richard de Clare, Earl of Pembroke (Strongbow).* 1854. Oil on canvas. 121 11/16 x 198 13/16 in. (309 x 505 cm). National Gallery of Ireland, Dublin. *This very large painting commemorates a politically significant union in Irish history—the merging of the old Gaelic order with the Norman settlers. The event, however, was socially and culturally destructive to the native way of life. Notice the responses of some of the crowd in the painting, and the burning city in the background.*

COLORPLATE 37

JAN WYCK. *The Battle of the Boyne.* 1693. Oil on canvas. 86¹/₄ x 118⁷/₈ in. (219 x 302 cm).
National Gallery of Ireland, Dublin. *On July 1, 1690, in the war of the two kings, William of Orange
(Protestant husband of James's daughter) defeated the Catholic James II at the Boyne. The battle
was a struggle between Catholics and Protestants, the older inhabitants and the newer settlers.*

COLORPLATE 38

ENGLISH SCHOOL. *The Fair Geraldine (Elizabeth, Daughter of Garret Og Fitzgerald)*. 16th century. Oil on panel. 18¹/₈ x 13³/₈ in. (46 x 34 cm). National Gallery of Ireland, Dublin.

McDon Cwan, prince Murrogh his son then of the age of 63 yeares, were killed, Terence the kings grand-child, then about the age of 15 yeares was found drowned neare the fishing wier of Clontarffe with both his hands fast bounde in the haire of a Danes head, whome he pursued to the sea at the time of the flight of the Danes, . . . [and] all [these] noblemen with many others were slaine in that battle, to the great greefe of the whole Realme. . . .

Moyleseachlin, after king Bryan was thus slaine, succeeded againe king of Ireland and reigned 8 years, dureing which time hee fought 25 battles both great and small against his enemies, wherein he for the most part had the victory.

Giraldus Cambrensis (Gerald of Wales)
FROM THE HISTORY AND TOPOGRAPHY OF IRELAND, c. 1187
A Visitor Observes the Irish

Giraldus Cambrensis (1146–1223), also called Gerald of Wales, was a member of a Norman Welsh family involved in the Norman invasion of Ireland in the late 12th century. His basically unflattering portrait of the Irish as uncivilized barbarians, reserving his only positive comments for their musical skill, caused great offense to the Irish, but because there are so few sources about medieval Ireland available, his books are still consulted today.

I have thought it not superfluous to say a few things about the nature of this people both in mind and body, that is to say, of their mental and physical characteristics.

To begin with: when they are born, they are not carefully nursed as is usual. For apart from the nourishment with which they are sustained by their hard parents from dying altogether, they are for the most part abandoned to nature. They are not put in cradles, or swathed; nor are their tender limbs helped by frequent baths or formed by any useful art. The midwives do not use hot water to raise the nose, or press down the face, or lengthen the legs. Unaided nature according to her own judgement arranges and disposes without the help of any art the limbs that she has produced.

As if to prove what she can do by herself she continually shapes and moulds, until she finally forms and finishes them in their full strength with beautiful upright bodies and handsome and well-complexioned faces.

But although they are fully endowed with natural gifts, their external characteristics of beard and dress, and internal cultivation of the mind, are so barbarous that they cannot be said to have any culture.

They use very little wool in their dress and that itself nearly always black—because the sheep of that country are black—and made up in a barbarous fashion. For they wear little hoods, close-fitting and stretched across the shoulders and down to a length of about eighteen to twenty-two inches, and generally sewn together from cloths of various kinds. Under these they wear mantles instead of cloaks. They also use woollen trousers that are at the same time boots, or boots that are at the same time trousers, and these are for the most part dyed.

When they are riding, they do not use saddles or leggings or spurs. They drive on, and guide their horses by means of a stick with a crook at its upper end, which they hold in their hand. They use reins to serve the purpose both of a bridle and a bit. These do not keep the horses, accustomed to feeding on the grass, from their food.

Moreover, they go naked and unarmed into battle. They regard weapons as a burden, and they think it brave and honourable to fight unarmed. They use, however, three types of weapons—short spears, two darts . . . and big axes well and carefully forged, which they have taken over from the Norwegians and the Ostmen. . . .

They are quicker and more expert than any other people in throwing, when everything else fails, stones as missiles, and such stones do great damage to the enemy in an engagement.

They are a wild and inhospitable people. They live on beasts only, and live like beasts. They have not progressed at all from the primitive habits of pastoral living.

While man usually progresses from the woods to the fields, and from the fields to settlements and communities of citizens, this people despises work on the land, has little use for the money-making of towns, contemns the rights and privileges of citizenship, and desires neither to abandon, nor lose respect for, the life which it has been accustomed to lead in the woods and countryside.

They use the fields generally as pasture, but pasture in poor condition. Little is cultivated, and even less sown. The fields cultivated are so few because of the neglect of those who should cultivate them. But many of them are naturally very fertile and productive. The wealth of the soil is lost, not through the fault of the soil, but because there are no farmers to cultivate even the best land: 'the fields demand, but there are no hands.' How few kinds of fruit-bearing trees are grown here! The nature of the soil is not to be blamed, but rather the want of industry on the part of the cultivator. He is too lazy to plant the foreign types of trees that would grow very well here.

The different types of minerals too, with which the hidden veins of the earth are full, are not mined or put to any use, precisely because of the same laziness. Even gold, of which they are very desirous—just like the Spaniards—and which they would like to have in abundance, is brought here by traders that search the ocean for gain.

They do not devote their lives to the processing of flax or wool, or to any kind of merchandise or mechanical art. For given only to leisure, and devoted only to laziness, they think that the greatest pleasure is not to work, and the greatest wealth is to enjoy liberty.

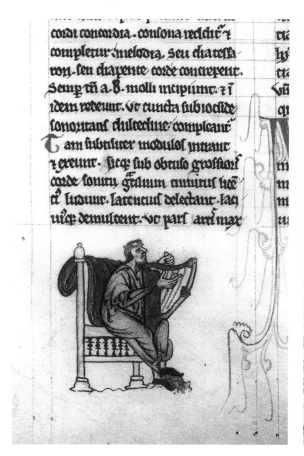

This people is, then, a barbarous people, literally barbarous. Judged according to modern ideas, they are uncultivated, not only in the external appearance of their dress, but also in their flowing hair and beards. All their habits are the habits of barbarians. Since conventions are formed from living together in society, and since they are so removed in these distant parts from the ordinary world of men, as if they were in another world altogether and consequently cut off from well-behaved and law-abiding people, they know only of the barbarous habits in which they were born and brought up, and embrace them as another nature. Their natural qualities are excellent. But almost everything acquired is deplorable. . . .

It is only in the case of musical instruments that I find any commendable diligence in the people. They seem to me to be incomparably more skilled in these than any other people that I have seen.

The movement is not, as in the British instrument to which we are accustomed, slow and easy, but rather quick and lively, while at the same time the melody is sweet and pleasant. It is remarkable how, in spite of the great speed of the fingers, the music proportion is maintained. The melody is kept perfect and full with unimpaired art through everything—through quivering measures and the involved use of several instruments—with a rapidity that charms, a rhythmic pattern that is varied, and a concord achieved through elements discordant. They harmonize at intervals of the octave and the fifth, but they always begin with B flat and with B flat end, so that everything may be rounded with the sweetness of charming sonority. They glide so subtly from one mode to another, and the grace notes so freely sport with such abandon and bewitching charm around the steady tone of the heavier sound, that the perfection of their art seems to lie in their concealing it, as if 'it were the better for being hidden. An art revealed brings shame.'

Hence it happens that the very things that afford unspeakable delight to the minds of those who have a fine perception and can penetrate carefully to the secrets of the art, bore, rather than delight, those who have no such perception—who look without seeing, and hear without being able to understand. When the audience is unsympathetic they succeed only in causing boredom with what appears to be but confused and disordered noise.

One should note that both Scotland and Wales, the former because of her affinity and intercourse, the latter as it were by grafting, try to imitate Ireland in music and strive in emulation. Ireland uses and delights in two instruments only, the harp namely, and the timpanum. Scotland uses three: the harp, timpanum, and the crowd. Wales uses the harp, the pipes, and the crowd. They also use strings made of bronze, and not from leather. In my opinion, however, of many, Scotland has by now not only caught up on Ireland, her instructor, but already far outdistances and excels her in musical skill. Therefore people now look to that country to the fountain of the art.

"The Song of Dermot and the Earl"

Dermot MacMurrough, king of Dublin and Leinster, was banished from his kingdom by the high king Rory O'Connor for various misdemeanors. Dermot sought help to restore his kingship from England, especially from Strongbow (Richard de Clare), the "Earl" of the poem, for which favor Dermot promises his daughter in marriage to Strongbow.

When Dermot, the valiant king, before King Henry had come at this time, before the English king, very courteously he saluted him fairly and finely before his men: 'May God who dwells on high guard and save you, King Henry, and give you also heart and courage and will to avenge my shame and my misfortune that my own people have brought upon me! Hear, noble King Henry, whence I was born, of what country. Of Ireland I was born a lord, in Ireland a

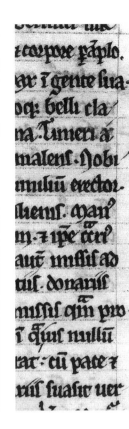

king; but wrongfully my own people have cast me out of my kingdom. To you I come to make my plaint, good sire, in the presence of the barons of your empire. Your liege man I shall become henceforth all the days of my life, on condition that you be my helper so that I do not lose at all: you I shall acknowledge as sire and lord, in the presence of your barons and lords.' Then the king promised him, the powerful king of England, that wilfully would he help him as soon as he should be able.

The earl at this time was a bachelor. He had neither spouse nor wife. When he hears from King Dermot that he was willing to give him his daughter on condition that he would come with him and subdue his land for him, the earl replies before his men: 'Rich king, hearken unto me. Here I assure you loyally that I shall assuredly come to you. But I should wish in these matters to crave licence of the English king, for he is the lord of my landed estate; wherefore I cannot go from his territory without obtaining licence in this way.' The king assured the earl that he would give him his daughter when he should come to his aid to Ireland with his barons. When they had concluded this accord, the king turned straight towards Wales, and never ceased journeying there until he came to St. David's.

Angus O'Gillan

"The Dead At Clonmacnoise"

Translated by T.W. Rolleston (1857–1920) from the Irish of 14th century poet Angus O'Gillan. Ogham-inscribed stones mark the graves of the dead High Kings buried in the quiet hillside of the celebrated Clonmacnoise monastery founded in the 6th century by St. Kieran.

In a quiet water'd land, a land of roses,
    Stands Saint Kieran's city fair:
And the warriors of Erin in their famous generations
    Slumber there.

There beneath the dewy hillside sleep the noblest
    Of the clan of Conn,
Each below his stone with name in branching Ogham
    And the sacred knot thereon.

There they laid to rest the seven Kings of Tara,
    There the sons of Cairbré sleep—
Battle-banners of the Gael, that in Kieran's plain of crosses
    Now their final hosting keep.

And in Clonmacnoise they laid the men of Teffia,
    And right many a lord of Breagh;
Deep the sod above Clan Creidé and Clan Conaill,
    Kind in hall and fierce in fray.
Many and many a son of Conn, the Hundred-Fighter,
    In the red earth lies at rest;
Many a blue eye of Clan Colman the turf covers,
    Many a swan-white breast.

Egan O'Rahilly
"A Time Of Change"

Egan O'Rahilly (c. 1700) a well-educated scribe and poet, was forced to leave his native county Kerry and live in poor conditions some twenty miles west. This poem reflects the agony of his disposession by the oppressors. Translated by Eavan Boland.

Without flocks or cattle or the curved horns
Of cattle, in drenching night without sleep
My five wits on the famous uproar
Of the wave toss like ships
And I cry for boyhood, long before
Winkle and dogfish had defiled my lips.

O if he lived, the prince who sheltered me
And his company who gave me entry
On the river of the Laune,
Whose royalty stood sentry
Over intricate harbours, I and my own
Would not be desolate in Dermot's country.

Fierce McCarthy Mor whose friends were welcome,
McCarthy of the Lee a slave of late,
McCarthy of Kenturk whose blood
Has dried underfoot:
Of all my princes not a single word—
Irrevocable silence ails my heart.

My heart shrinks in me, my heart ails
That every hawk and royal hawk is lost;
From Cashel to the far sea
Their birthright is dispersed
Far and near, night and day, by robbery
And ransack, every town oppressed.

Take warning, wave, take warning, crown of the sea
I, O'Rahilly—witless from your discords—
Were Spanish sails again afloat
And rescue on our tides,
Would force this outcry down your wild throat,
Would make you swallow these Atlantic words.

Francisco de Cuellar, Captain of the Spanish Armada

FROM A LETTER TO KING PHILLIP OF SPAIN, OCTOBER 4, 1589

Adventures After a Shipwreck

In this letter to King Phillip II of Spain, Captain Francisco de Cuellar recounts the shipwreck off the west coast of Ireland in 1588 that claimed more than twenty Spanish ships and their crews. His story is one of survival in most inhospitable surroundings.

When the Englishman saw that I had a gold chain and money, he wanted to keep me prisoner, thinking that he would be offered a ransom for me. I told him that I had nothing to give, as I was only a poor soldier, and that I had got that gold aboard ship. The girl was very sorry to see the ill usage they did me, and entreated them to give me back my clothes and do me no more harm. They all went back to the savage's cabin, and I was left under the trees, bleeding fast from the cut that the Englishman had given me. I put on my doublet and coat. They had even taken away my shirt and some precious relics which I wore in a little jacket of the brotherhood of the Holy Trinity, and which had been given to me at Lisbon. The girl took these and put them around her neck, making signs to me that she wished to keep them, and telling me that she was a Christian, and so she was—like Mahomet. They sent a boy to me from the hut bearing a poultice made of herbs to put on my wound, also milk, butter, and a piece of oaten bread for me to eat. I poulticed myself and ate. Then the boy went with me along the road, pointing out the direction in which I ought to go, and keeping me away from a village which was in sight of the road, where many Spaniards had been killed, and not a single man on whom the inhabitants could lay hands had escaped. The Frenchman was the cause of doing me this good turn, for he had been a soldier at Terceira, and he was very sorry to see me so maltreated. When the boy turned to go back, he bade me keep straight on to some mountains that seemed to be some six leagues from us, behind which lay a friendly country that belonged to a great lord who was a good friend to the King of Spain, and who harboured all the Spaniards that came to him, and was very kind to them, and had taken in more than eighty of the men from our ships who had gone to him naked. At this news I plucked up courage somewhat, and stick in hand started to walk as best I could, striking north for the mountains that the boy had pointed out. That night I came to some huts where they did me no harm because there was a young man there who knew Latin, and God was pleased that owing to the necessity of the occasion we should understand one another in that language. I told him my misfortunes. The Latin scholar took me into his hut for the night, and gave me medicine and some supper and a place on the straw to sleep. In the middle of the night his father and brothers came home laden with the spoils of our things, but the old man did not mind that they had taken me into his house and had treated me well. In the morning they gave me a boy and a horse to take me over a mile of road which was so bad that the mud was up to the horse's pasterns. After we had gone past it by a bow-shot we heard a great noise, and the boy said to me, making signs, "Save yourself, Spain," for that is what they call us. "Many Saxons are coming on horseback, and they will kill you unless you hide. Come here quick!" They call the English Saxons. We hid in the cleft of some rocks, where we lay safe without being seen. There were more than one hundred and fifty of them on horseback, and they were going all along the coast to rob and kill all the Spaniards that they could find. God delivered me from them, but as we went on our way we met more than forty savages on foot who wanted to murder me, for they were all Protestants, but they did not do it because the boy who was with me told them that his master had captured

Cross of the Order of Santiago. 16th century. Gold and red enamel. 1³/₄ in. (4.4 cm). Ulster Museum, Belfast, Northern Ireland. *This cross is one of many pieces of jewelry found after the wreck of the Spanish Armada galleon* Gerona *off the coast of County Antrim in 1588.*

me and I was his prisoner, and that he was sending me on horseback so that I might get well. All this did not suffice to secure my going on in peace, for two of those robbers seized me and gave me half a dozen blows, bruising my back and arms, and stripped me of everything I had on, and left me naked as when I was born. By the Holy Baptism that I received, this is true. Then, seeing myself in this plight, I gave thanks to God, supplicating His Divine Majesty to fulfil His will upon me, for that was my will also. The savage's boy then turned to go home with his horse, weeping to see me so naked, beaten, and cold. I besought God very earnestly to take me where I might confess myself and then die in His grace. Then I plucked up courage, being in the worst extreme of misfortune that ever a man was, and covered myself with some fern leaves and a bit of an old mat, and protected myself from the cold the best I could. I journeyed on, little by little, in a direction they had pointed out, in search of the lands of that chieftain with whom the other Spaniards had taken refuge, and I came to that peak which they had pointed out as a mark. There I found a lake around which there were some thirty huts, all completely empty, and I looked about for a place to spend the night. Having nowhere to go, I went up to the biggest cabin, as that seemed the best place to take shelter in for the night, for all of them were deserted and empty. As I was going in the door I saw there many bundles of oats, which are made into the bread that those savages usually eat, and I thanked God that on them I had a good place to sleep, when of a sudden I saw three naked men get up at one side, and come forward and stare at me. It gave me a start, for I thought without doubt they were devils, and they knew no better what I could be, wrapped up in my mat and leaves. They were so frightened that they did not speak to me, nor I to them, and I could not see them distinctly, for the hut was rather dark; and being much confounded I exclaimed, "Oh, Mother of God, be with me and deliver me from all evil." When they heard me speak Spanish and call on the Mother of God, they also exclaimed, "Holy Virgin, be with us." Then I was reassured, and went up to them and asked if they were Spaniards. They answered, "Yes, we are, for our sins. Eleven of us together were robbed of everything on the beach, and naked as we were we went to look for some place where Christians dwelt, and on the way we met a troop of the enemy, who killed eight of us. The three of us here escaped into a wood which was so thick that they could not find us, and that night God led us thither to these huts, and here we stayed to recover from our fatigue, although there were no people and nothing to eat." I told them always to commit themselves to God and to be of good cheer, for we were in the neighbourhood of friends and Christians, for I had information of a village that was about three or four leagues away from us, which belonged to my Lord Ruerque (O'Rourke), where many of the wrecked Spaniards had taken refuge, and that although I was very badly used up and wounded we should start on our journey thither the next day. The poor fellows were delighted, and asked me who I was. I told them that I was Captain Cuellar. They could hardly believe it, for they thought I was drowned, and rushed up to me and hugged me almost to death. One of them was a sergeant and the other two common soldiers. And as this tale is ludicrous, and true as I am a Christian, I have written it all out for your Majesty's diversion. I buried myself deep in the straw, taking care not to disturb it or disarrange it from the way it was; and, having agreed to get up early in the morning for our journey, we went to sleep without supper, and without having had anything to eat except mulberries and water-cress. While it was still daytime I was already wide awake with a great pain in my legs, and I heard noises and talking, and just then a savage came to the door with a battle-axe in his hand, and looked around at the oats, muttering to himself. I and my companions, who had also waked up, lay still without drawing a breath, peering attentively through the straw at the savage to see what he would do. God willed that he went out and betook himself, with a number of others who had come with him, to work at reaping near the huts, in such a place that it was impossible for us to go out without their seeing us. We lay still, buried alive, talking over what we had better do, and agreed not to get out of the straw or to move from that place as long as those savages and heretics were there; for they belonged to that neighbourhood where the people treated the poor Spaniards whom they caught so dreadfully, and they would have done the like to us if they had found us there, where there was no one to help us but God. All day passed in this way, and when night came those wretches betook themselves to their huts. We waited for the moon to rise, and then, wrapped up in straw and hay, because it was bitter cold, we left that dangerous place without waiting for daylight.

Hugh O'Neill, Earl of Tyrone. 16th century. Engraving.
National Library of Ireland, Dublin.

Hugh O'Neill, Earl of Tyrone

A Letter of Resolve

Hugh O'Neill, Earl of Tyrone, last of the great Gaelic chieftains, was the motivating spirit behind the Ulster lords' struggle against English rule which culminated in the Battle of Kinsale and the death of the old Gaelic order. This little letter expresses defiance with a characteristically Irish blend of humor and satire.

Our greetings to you, McCoughleyn. We have received your letter, and what we make out from it is that you offer nothing but sweet words and procrastination. For our part in the matter, whatever man would not be on our side and would not spend his efforts for the right, we take it that that man is a man against us. For this reason, whatever you yourself are doing well, hurt us as much as you are able, and we shall hurt you to the best of our ability, with God's will.

O'NEILL

At Knocduffmaine, 6th Feb. 1600.

Oliver Cromwell

FROM A LETTER ON THE ATTACK AT DROGHEDA

Cromwell's ruthless attack on the medieval walled town of Drogheda in September 1649 was swift and efficient; no one escaped. The Protestant Ascendancy and the systematic transplantation of the Irish landowners out of all the arable land in Ireland had begun harshly. With self-righteousness, Cromwell tells the Honorable William Lenthall, Speaker of the Parliament of England, that "that which caused your men to storm so courageously, it was the Spirit of God."

Dublin, 17th September 1649.

SIR,

Upon Tuesday the 10th of this instant, about five o'clock in the evening, we began the Storm: and after some hot dispute we entered, about seven or eight hundred men; the Enemy disputing it very stiffly with us. And indeed, through the advantages of the place, and the courage God was pleased to give the defenders, our men were forced to retreat quite out of the breach, not without some considerable loss; Colonel Castle being there shot in the head, whereof he presently died; and divers officers and soldiers doing their duty killed and wounded. There was a Tenalia to flanker the south Wall of the Town, between Duleek Gate and the corner Tower before mentioned;—which our men entered, wherein they found some forty or fifty of the Enemy, which they put to the sword. And this 'Tenalia' they held: but it being without the Wall, and the sally-port through the Wall into that Tenalia being choked up with some of the Enemy which were killed in it, it proved of no use for an entrance into the Town that way.

Although our men that stormed the breaches were forced to recoil, as is before expressed; yet, being encouraged to recover their loss, they made a second attempt: wherein God was pleased so to animate them that they got ground of the Enemy, and by the Goodness of God, forced him to quit his entrenchments. And after a very hot dispute, the Enemy having both horse and foot, and we only foot, within the Wall—they gave ground, and our men became masters both of their retrenchments and 'of' the Church; which indeed, although they made our entrance the more difficult, yet they proved of excellent use to us; so that the Enemy could not 'now' annoy us with their horse, but thereby we had advantage to make good the ground, that so we might let in our own horse; which accordingly was done, though with much difficulty.

Divers of the Enemy retreated into the Mill-Mount: a place very strong and of difficult access; being exceedingly high, having a good graft, and strongly palisadoed. The Governor, Sir Arthur Ashton, and divers considerable Officers being there, our men getting up to them, were ordered by me to put them all to the sword. And indeed, being in the heat of action, I forbade them to spare any that were in arms in the Town: and, I think, that night they put to the sword about 2,000 men;—divers of the officers and soldiers being fled over the Bridge into the other part of the Town, where about 100 of them possessed St. Peter's Church-steeple, some the west Gate, and others a strong Round Tower next the Gate called St. Sunday's. These being summoned to yield to mercy, refused. Whereupon I ordered the steeple of St. Peter's Church to be fired, when one of them was heard to say in the midst of the flames: "God damn me, God confound me; I burn, I burn."

The next day, the other two Towers were summoned; in one of which was about six or seven score; but they refused to yield themselves: and we knowing that hunger must compel them, set only good guards to secure them from running away until their stomachs were come

Cromwell's Bridge, Glencarriff. 17th century. Engraving by A. Grey. National Library of Ireland, Dublin.

down. From one of the said Towers, notwithstanding their condition, they killed and wounded some of our men. When they submitted, their officers were knocked on the head; and every tenth man of the soldiers killed; and the rest shipped for the Barbadoes. The soldiers in the other Tower were all spared, as to their lives only; and shipped likewise for the Barbadoes. . . .

I sent a party of horse and dragoons to a House within five miles of Trim, there being then in Trim some Scots Companies, which the Lord of Ardes brought to assist the Lord of Ormond. But upon the news of Tredah, they ran away; leaving their great guns behind them, which also we have possessed.

And now give me leave to say how it comes to pass that this work is wrought. It was set upon some of our hearts, That a great thing should be done, not by power or might, but by the Spirit of God. And is it not so, clearly? . . .

It is remarkable that these people, at the first, set up the Mass in some places of the Town that had been monasteries; but afterwards grew so insolent that, the last Lord's day before the storm, the Protestants were thrust out of the great Church called St. Peter's, and they had public Mass there: and in this very place near 1,000 of them were put to the sword, fleeing thither for safety. I believe all their friars were knocked on the head promiscuously but two; the one of which was Father Peter Taaff, brother to the Lord Taaff, whom the soldiers took, the next day, and made an end of. The other was taken in the Round Tower, under the repute of a Lieutenant, and when he understood that the officers in that Tower had no quarter, he confessed he was a Friar; but that did not save him. . . .

I most humbly pray the Parliament may be pleased 'that' this Army may be maintained; and that a consideration may be had of them, and of the carrying on affairs here, 'such' as may give a speedy issue to this work. To which there seems to be a marvellous fair opportunity offered by God. And although it may seem very chargeable to the State of England to maintain so great a force; yet surely to stretch a little for the present, in following God's providence, in hope the charge will not be long—I trust it will not be thought by any (that have not irreconcilable or malicious principles) unfit for me to move, For a constant supply; which, in human probability as to outward things, is most likely to hasten and perfect this work. And indeed if God please to finish it here as He hath done in England, the War is like to pay itself.

We keep the field much; our tents sheltering us from the wet and cold. But yet the Country-sickness overtakes many: and therefore we desire recruits, and some fresh regiments of foot, may be sent us. . . . Craving pardon for this great trouble, I rest,

Your most obedient servant,

OLIVER CROMWELL.

from THE JACOBITE WAR

For the Irish, the war of the two kings—Ri Seamus and Ri Liam—was a struggle between Catholic and Protestant, the older inhabitants and the newer settlers, both sides fighting with foreign assistance. The first of these anonymous poems is about Patrick Sarsfield (d. 1693), a Jacobite and one of the most beloved Irish heroes, and was translated by Frank O'Connor. The second selection praises both the heroism of the opposing side, the Williamites, and English Protestantism.

JACOBITE

PATRICK SARSFIELD

> Farewell, Patrick Sarsfield, wherever you may roam,
> You crossed the seas to France and left empty camps at home,
> To plead our cause before many a foreign throne
> Though you left ourselves and poor Ireland overthrown.
>
> Farewell, Patrick Sarsfield, you were sent to us by God,
> And holy forever is the earth that you trod;
> May the sun and the white moon light your way,
> For you trounced King Billy and won the day.
>
> With you, Patrick Sarsfield, goes the prayer of everyone,
> My own prayer too and the prayer of Mary's Son;
> As you passed through Birr the Narrow Ford you won,
> You beat them off at Cullen and took Limerick town.
>
> I'll climb the mountain, a lonely man,
> And I'll go east again if I can,
> 'Twas there I saw the Irish ready for the fight,
> The lousy crowd that wouldn't unite.
>
> Who's that I see now yonder on Howth Head?
> "One of Jamie's soldiers, sir, now the King has fled;
> Last year with gun and knapsack I marched with joyous tread,
> But this year, sir, I'm begging my bread."
>
> And God, when I think of how Diarmuid was attacked,
> His limbs wrenched asunder, his standard cracked,
> And Christ himself couldn't fight a way through
> As they chopped off his head and held it in our view.
>
> The ears tumbled fast as the scythes went on,
> The first we lost were the twelve Kilkennymen,
> My two brothers followed—my very breath—
> But the death that broke me was Diarmuid's death.
>
> At the Boyne Bridge we took our first beating,
> From the bridge at Slane there was great retreating,
> And then we were beaten at Aughrim too—
> Ah, fragrant Ireland, that was goodbye to you!

The fumes were choking at the house went alight,
And Black Billy's bastards were warming to the fight,
And every shell that came, wherever it lit,
Colonel Mitchell asked was Lord Lucan hit.

Farewell to you, Limerick, and your houses so fair,
And all the good company that was quartered with us there;
We played cards at night by the watchfires' glare,
And often the priests called us in to prayer.

But on you, Londonderry, may misfortune come
Like the smoke that lit with every bursting gun,
For all the fine soldiers you gathered together
By your walls without shelter from wind or weather.

Many and many a soldier, all proud and gay,
Seven weeks ago they passed this way,
With guns and swords and pikes on show,
And now in Aughrim they're lying low.

Kelly's Aughrim has manure that's neither lime nor sand
But sturdy young soldiers stretched over the land,
The lads were left behind on the battlefield that day,
Torn like horsemeat by the dogs where they lay.

Oversea they all are, Ireland's best,
The Dukes and the Burkes, Prince Charlie and the rest,
And Captain Talbot their ranks adorning,
And Patrick Sarsfield, Ireland's darling.

WILLIAMITE

THE BOYNE WATER

July the First, of a morning clear one thousand six hundred and ninety,
King William did his men prepare—of thousands he had thirty—
To fight King James and all his foes, encamped near the Boyne Water
He little feared, though two to one, their multitudes to scatter.

Battle of the Boyne.
17th century. Engraving.
National Library of
Ireland, Dublin.

Prospect of Carrickfergus. Being the Place where King William Landed in Ireland. 17th century. Watercolor sketch. National Library of Ireland, Dublin.

King William called his officers, saying: "Gentlemen, mind your station,
And let your valour here be shown before this Irish nation;
My brazen walls let no man break, and your subtle foes you'll scatter,
Be sure you show them good English play as you go over the water."

* * *

Within four yards of our fore-front, before a shot was fired,
A sudden snuff they got that day, which little they desired;
For horse and man fell to the ground, and some hung in their saddle:
Others turned up their forked ends, which we call *coup de ladle.*

Prince Eugene's regiment was the next, on our right hand advanced,
Into a field of standing wheat, where Irish horses pranced—
But the brandy ran so in their heads, their senses all did scatter,
They little thought to leave their bones that day at the Boyne Water.

* * *

Now, praise God, all true Protestants, and heaven's and earth's Creator,
For the deliverance that He sent our enemies to scatter . . .
The Church's foes will pine away, like churlish-hearted Nabal.
For our deliverer came this day like the great Zorobabel.

So praise God, all true Protestants, and I will say no further,
But had the Papists gained the day, there would have been open murder,
Although King James and many more were ne'er that way inclined,
It was not in their power to stop what the rabble they designed.

John Langley

An Irish Will

A Cromwellian settler makes an Irish last will and testament.

I, John Langley, born at Wincanton, in Somersetshire, and settled in Ireland in the year 1651, now in my right mind and wits, do make my will in my own handwriting. I do leave all my house, goods, and farm at Black Kettle of 253 acres to my son, commonly called 'Stubborn

Jack,' to him and his heirs forever, provided he marries a Protestant, but not Alice Kenrick, who called me 'Oliver's whelp.' My new buckskin breeches and my silver tobacco stopper with 'J.L.' on the top I give to Richard Richards, my comrade, who helped me off at the storming of Clonmel when I was shot through the leg. My said son John shall keep my body above ground six days and six nights after I am dead; and Grace Kenrick shall lay me out, who shall have for so doing five shillings. My body shall be put upon the oak table in the brown room, and fifty Irishmen shall be invited to my wake and every one shall have two quarts of the best aqua vitae, and each one one skein, dish and knife before him, and when the liquor is out nail up the coffin, and commit me to the earth whence I came. This is my will; witness my hand this 3rd day of March, 1674.

Seamus MacManus

FROM THE STORY OF THE IRISH RACE
Penal Laws

After the siege of Limerick, Catholics were subjected to new restrictive laws that fortified the age of Protestant Ascendancy in Ireland.

The Penal Laws enacted or re-enacted in the new era succeeding the siege of Limerick, when under the pledged faith and honour of the English crown, the Irish Catholics were to be "protected in the free and unfettered exercise of their religion," provided amongst other things that:

Penal Cross (front and back). Late 17th–early 18th century. Wood. The National Museum of Ireland, Dublin. *This small, roughly-carved wooden cross, one that could be easily concealed, is typical of those belonging to Catholics who suffered religious persecution under Cromwell's harsh Penal Laws.*

The Irish Catholic was forbidden the exercise of his religion.

He was forbidden to receive education.

He was forbidden to enter a profession.

He was forbidden to hold public office.

He was forbidden to engage in trade or commerce.

He was forbidden to live in a corporate town or within five miles thereof.

He was forbidden to own a horse of greater value than five pounds.

He was forbidden to purchase land.

He was forbidden to lease land.

He was forbidden to accept a mortgage on land in security for a loan.

He was forbidden to vote.

He was forbidden to keep any arms for his protection.

He was forbidden to hold a life annuity.

He was forbidden to buy land from a Protestant.

He was forbidden to receive a gift of land from a Protestant.

He was forbidden to inherit land from a Protestant.

He was forbidden to inherit anything from a Protestant.

He was forbidden to rent any land that was worth more than thirty shillings a year.

He was forbidden to reap from his land any profit exceeding a third of the rent.

He could not be guardian to a child.

He could not, when dying, leave his infant children under Catholic guardianship.

He could not attend Catholic worship.

He was compelled by the law to attend Protestant worship.

He could not himself educate his child.

He could not send his child to a Catholic teacher.

He could not employ a Catholic teacher to come to his child.

He could not send his child abroad to receive education.

THE EIGHTEENTH CENTURY

"Kilcash"

Translated by Frank O'Connor. Kilcash was the home of one branch of the Butler family. Although it is doubtful that Yeats, who had Butler blood in him, knew this, it was one of his favorite poems, and there is a good deal of his work in it.

———————

What shall we do for timber?
   The last of the woods is down.
Kilcash and the house of its glory
   And the bell of the house are gone,
The spot where that lady waited

COLORPLATE 39

NATHANIEL HONE THE ELDER. *The Piping Boy (Camillus, Son of the Artist).* 1769. Oil on canvas.
14 3/16 x 12 3/16 in. (36 x 31 cm). National Gallery of Ireland, Dublin.

COLORPLATE 40

GEORGE BARRET. *View of Powerscourt, County Wicklow*. c. 1760–62. Oil on canvas. 28⅞ x 38¼ in.
(73.4 x 97.2 cm). Yale Center for British Art, Paul Mellon Collection. *Great Palladian house designed by German architect Richard Castle. The house was destroyed by fire in 1974, but the gardens are intact.*

COLORPLATE 41

NATHANIEL HONE THE ELDER. *Horace Hone Sketching*. 18th century. Oil on canvas. 50³/8 x 41¹⁵/16 in.
(128 x 105 cm). National Gallery of Ireland, Dublin.

COLORPLATE 42

FRANCIS WHEATLEY. *The Dublin Volunteers in College Green, 4th November 1779.* Oil on canvas.
68 7/8 x 127 3/16 in. (175 x 323 cm). National Gallery of Ireland, Dublin. *The outbreak of the American Revolutionary War provided the impetus for Ireland's patriots to form troops of mostly Protestant Volunteers to defend Irish shores. The corps were splendidly uniformed and had frequent colorful parades and reviews.*

BLARNEY Castle 3ᴹ from Cork County of Cork.

COLORPLATE 45

WILLIAM ASHFORD. *A View of Dublin Bay*. 1794. Oil on canvas. 27 3/16 x 49 5/8 in. (69 x 126 cm). National Gallery of Ireland, Dublin.

COLORPLATE 43 *(opposite, above)*

GABRIEL BERANGER. *Blarney Castle*. 18th century. Watercolor on paper. 11 3/4 x 9 1/2 in. (30 x 24.13 cm). Royal Irish Academy, Dublin.

COLORPLATE 44 *(opposite, below)*

JAMES MALTON. *The Custom House, Dublin*. 1793. Watercolor over ink on paper. 21 1/8 x 30 5/16 in. (53.6 x 77 cm). National Gallery of Ireland, Dublin.

COLORPLATE 46

JOHN MULVANEY. *A View of Killmalock*. Late 18th–early 19th century. Oil on canvas. 26³/₄ x 31¹/₂ in. (68 x 80 cm). National Gallery of Ireland, Dublin.

Kilcash Castle, Roscommon. Pencil on paper. National Library of Ireland, Dublin.

Who shamed all women for grace
When earls came sailing to greet her
    And Mass was said in the place.

My grief and my affliction
    Your gates are taken away,
Your avenue needs attention,
    Goats in the garden stray.
The courtyard's filled with water
    And the great earls where are they?
The earls, the lady, the people
    Beaten into the clay.

No sound of duck or geese there,
    Hawk's cry or eagle's call,
No humming of the bees there
    That brought honey and wax for all,
Nor even the song of the birds there
    When the sun goes down in the west,
No cuckoo on top of the boughs there,
    Singing the world to rest.

There's mist there tumbling from branches,
    Unstirred by night and by day,
And darkness falling from heaven,
    For our fortune has ebbed away,
There's no holly nor hazel nor ash there,
    The pasture's rock and stone,
The crown of the forest has withered,
    And the last of its game is gone.

I beseech of Mary and Jesus
    That the great come home again
With long dances danced in the garden,
    Fiddle music and mirth among men,
That Kilcash the home of our fathers
    Be lifted on high again,
And from that to the deluge of waters
    In bounty and peace remain.

Jonathan Swift

FROM DRAPIER'S LETTER IV

Jonathan Swift (1667–1745), born in Dublin of English parents, was educated at Trinity College, Dublin. Ordained into the Church of Ireland in 1695, he was eventually appointed dean of St. Patrick's Cathedral in Dublin, Ireland's largest church, where he is buried beneath the epitaph he composed himself. In the 1720s Ireland needed new coinage, and the English proposed to have it supplied by their own William Wood. In this excerpt from "Drapier's Letter IV" Swift inspires the Irish to oppose the government's plan to mint inferior coinage.

Let me place this offer in as clear a light as I can, to show the unsupportable villainy and impudence of that incorrigible wretch. First (says he) 'I will send two hundred thousand pounds of my coin into your country; the copper I compute to be in real value eighty thousand pounds, and I charge you with an hundred and twenty thousand pounds for the coinage; so that you see, I lend you an hundred and twenty thousand pounds for thirty years, for which you shall pay me three *per cent*. That is to say three thousand six hundred pounds *per ann.* which in thirty years will amount to an hundred and eight thousand pounds. And when these thirty years are expired, return me my copper and I will give you good money for it.'

This is the proposal made to us by *Wood* in that pamphlet written by one of his *commissioners*; and the author is supposed to be the same infamous Coleby one of his *underswearers* at the *committee of council*, who was tried for *robbing the treasury here*, where he was an under-clerk.

By this proposal he will first receive two hundred thousand pounds, in goods or sterling, for as much copper as he values at eighty thousand pounds, but in reality not worth thirty thousand pounds. Secondly, he will receive for interest an hundred and eight thousand pounds. And when our children come thirty years hence to return his halfpence upon his executors (for before that time he will be probably gone *to his own place*) those executors will very reasonably reject them as raps and counterfeits, which probably they will be, and millions of them of his own coinage.

Methinks I am fond of such a *dealer* as this who mends every day upon our hands, like a Dutch reckoning, where if you dispute the unreasonableness and exorbitance of the bill, the landlord shall bring it up every time with new additions.

Although these and the like pamphlets published by *Wood* in London be altogether unknown here, where nobody could read them without as much *indignation* as *contempt* would allow, yet I thought it proper to give you a specimen how the *man* employs his time, where he rides alone without one creature to contradict him; while OUR FEW FRIENDS there wonder at our silence, and the English in general, if they think of this matter at all, impute our refusal to *wilfulness* or *disaffection* just as *Wood* and his *hirelings* are pleased to represent.

But although our arguments are not suffered to be printed in England, yet the consequence will be of little moment. Let *Wood* endeavour to *persuade* the people *there* that we ought to *receive* his coin, and let me *convince* our people *here* that they ought to *reject* it under pain of our utter undoing. And then let him do his *best* and his *worst*.

Before I conclude, I must beg leave in all humility to tell Mr. *Wood*, that he is guilty of great *indiscretion*, by causing so honourable a name as that of Mr. W[alpole] to be mentioned so often, and in such a manner, upon his occasion. A short paper printed at Bristol and reprinted here reports Mr. *Wood* to say, that he 'wonders at the impudence and insolence of the Irish in refusing his coin, and what he will do when Mr. W[alpole] comes to town.' Where, by the way, he is mistaken, for it is the *true English people* of Ireland who refuse it, although we take it for granted that the Irish will do so too whenever they are asked. He orders it to be printed in another paper, that 'Mr. W[alpole] will cram this brass down our throats.' Sometimes it is given out that we must 'either take these halfpence or eat our brogues.' And, in another newsletter but of yesterday we read that the same great man 'hath sworn to make us swallow his coin in fire-balls.'

This brings to my mind the known story of a Scotchman, who receiving sentence of death, with all the circumstances of *hanging, beheading, quartering, embowelling* and the like, cried out, 'What need all this COOKERY?' And I think we have reason to ask the same question; for if we believe *Wood*, here is a *dinner* getting ready for us, and you see the *bill of fare*, and I am sorry the drink was forgot, which might easily be supplied with *melted lead* and *flaming pitch*.

What vile words are these to put into the mouth of a great councillor, in high trust with His Majesty, and looked upon as a prime minister. If Mr. *Wood* hath no better a manner of representing his patrons, when I come to be a *great man* he shall never be suffered to attend at my *levee*. This is not the style of a great minister, it savours too much of the *kettle* and the *furnace*, and came entirely out of Mr. *Wood's forge*.

As for the threat of making us *eat our brogues*, we need not be in pain; for if his coin should pass, that *unpolite covering for the feet* would no longer be a *national reproach*; because then we should have neither *shoe* nor *brogue* left in the kingdom. But here the falsehood of Mr. *Wood* is fairly detected; for I am confident Mr. W[alpole] never heard of a *brogue* in his whole life.

As to 'swallowing these halfpence in fire-balls,' it is a story equally improbable. For to execute this *operation* the whole stock of Mr. *Wood's* coin and metal must be melted down and moulded into hollow *balls* with *wild-fire*, no bigger than a *reasonable* throat can be able to swallow. Now the metal he hath prepared, and already coined, will amount to at least fifty millions of halfpence to be *swallowed* by a million and a half of people; so that allowing two halfpence to each *ball*, there will be about seventeen *balls* of *wild-fire* a-piece to be swallowed by every person in this kingdom. And to administer this dose there cannot be conveniently fewer than fifty thousand *operators*, allowing one *operator* to every thirty, which, considering the *squeamishness* of some stomachs and the *peevishness* of *young children*, is but reasonable. Now, under correction of better judgments, I think the trouble and charge of such an experiment would exceed the profit; and therefore I take this *report* to be *spurious*, or at least only a new *scheme* of Mr. *Wood* himself, which to make it pass the better in Ireland he would father upon a *minister of state*. . . .

I am,
My dear countrymen,
Your loving fellow-subject,
fellow-sufferer, and humble servant.
M.B.

Oct. 13, 1724

The Unfortunate Wolfe Tone. 18th century.
Engraving. National Library of Ireland, Dublin.

Theobald Wolfe Tone

FROM SPEECHES FROM THE DOCK
A Protestant Defends Catholic Public Virtue

Wolfe Tone was one of the founders of the Society of the United Irishmen in Belfast in 1791, originally a legal and constitutional reform group intending to remove the injustices suffered by the Catholics of Ireland, but which was eventually reorganized as a secret, illegal society. The Protestant Tone, arrested and tried as a traitor, here speaks from the dock, where he expresses an outburst of gratitude towards the Catholics of Ireland, a sentiment that was suppressed at his trial.

I have labored to create a people in Ireland by raising three millions of my countrymen to the rank of citizens. I have labored to abolish the infernal spirit of religious persecution, by uniting the Catholics and Dissenters. To the former I owe more than ever can be repaid. The services I was so fortunate as to render them they rewarded munificently; but they did more: when the public cry was raised against me—when the friends of my youth swarmed off and left me alone—the Catholics did not desert me; they had the virtue even to sacrifice their own interests to a rigid principle of honor; they refused, though strongly urged, to disgrace a man who, whatever his conduct towards the government might have been, had faithfully and conscientiously discharged his duty towards them; and in so doing, though it was in my own case, I will say they showed an instance of public virtue of which I know not whether there exists another example.

Mary Delany

FROM A LETTER DESCRIBING DUBLIN SOCIAL LIFE, 1731

This is one of the many letters Mary Delany (1700–1788) wrote home to her sister and other friends in England which provide a vivid account of social life in Dublin in the 1730s. While in Dublin she met Patrick Delany who would become her second husband, and his friend, Jonathan Swift who became a friend and correspondent.

I must tell you all that has passed since my writing to you last, which was on Thursday. . . . Sunday to church we went—staid at home all the afternoon, Mrs. Percival and Mrs. Usher of the company. Monday being St. Cecilia's Day it was celebrated with great pomp at St. Patrick's Cathedral. We were there in the greatest crowd I ever saw; we went at 10 and staid till 4; there is a very fine organ, which was accompanied by a great many instruments, Dubourg at the head of them; they began with the 1st concerto of Corelli; we had Purcell's Te Deum and Jubilate; then the 5th concerto of Corelli; after that an anthem of Dr. Blow's, and they conclud-

ed with the 8th concerto of Corelli. Perhaps you think this was entertainment enough for one day; pardon me, we are not here so easily satisfied as to let one diversion serve for the whole day and we *double and treble* them. Lord Mountjoy made a fine ball for the Duke and Duchess of Dorset and their retinue, our house was among the invited people, and Monday was the day fixed on.

After our music we returned home, eat our dinner as expeditiously as we could, and by seven (the hour named) we were all equipped for the ball; Mrs. Graham, Miss Granville, and Miss Usher called on us, and we all went away together, nobody was admitted but by tickets. There was four-and-twenty couple, 12 danced at a time, and when they had danced 2 dances, the other 12 took their turn. No lookers on but the Duchess and Mrs. Clayton, who thought it beneath the dignity of a Bishop's wife to dance. The Duke danced with Lady Allen (the Duchess had the headache) Lord Mountjoy with Lady Caroline, Mr. Coot with Lady Lambert, Capt. Pierce with Mrs. Donellan, and Mr. Usher with me; the rest were people you don't know at all. . . . Before the dancing began, the company were all served with tea and coffee; at 9, every lad took out his lass. At 11, those who were not dancing followed the Duke and Duchess up stairs to a room where was prepared all sorts of cold meats, fruits, sweetmeats, and wines, placed after the same manner as the masquerades. We eat and drank as much as we liked, and then descended to make way for the rest of the company. Mrs. Clayton went away at 12, the Duchess soon after that, and Phil and I staid till 1, and then with much difficulty made our escapes, the rest staid till 4 in the morning. On the whole, the entertainment was more handsome than agreeable, there being too much company.

The next morning we rose at 9 o'clock, put on our genteel dishabille, and went to the Parliament House, at 11, to hear an election determined: the parties were Brigadier Parker the sitting member, and Mr. Ponsonby the petitioner, Mr. Southwell's interest was the first, and the last was Sir R^d Mead's. I believe we were the most impartial hearers among all the ladies that were there, though rather inclined to Mr. Southwell's side, but the cause was determined in favour of Sir R. M.'s. I was very well entertained there. Our cousins were also there. About 3 o'clock Mrs. Clayton went home to dinner with her Bishop; we were stout, and staid. Mr. Hamilton, a gentleman I have mentioned to you, brought us up chickens, and ham, and tongue, and everything we could desire. At 4 o'clock the speaker adjourned the House 'till 5. We then were conveyed, by some gentlemen of our acquaintance into the Usher of the Black Rod's room, where we had a good fire, &c., and meat, tea, and bread and butter. Were we not well taken care of?

When the House was assembled, we re-assumed our seats and staid till 8; loth was I to go away then, but I thought that my kind companions were tired, and staid out of a compliment to me, so home we came, not a little fatigued with what we had undergone for two days together. Yesterday our assembly, today we shall spend peaceably by our own fireside, and talk over the passed hurries. Miss Forth's two sisters come to town, who are to be introduced to me today, 'tis one of them that paints *so finely*. I believe I did not write you word that Mrs. Foster is parted from her husband. Dean Berkeley and his family are returned to England; they are not at Greenwich. They talk of coming to Dublin early in the spring; I wish they may for I want to be acquainted with him. Mrs. Barber is still in England, she has not yet published her works; I wish she may not spend more money in pursuing this affair than the subscription will answer.

Adieu, my dear sister,—how I long for the packets! 'Tis terribly cold, but I wish for an easterly wind, though I would make me ten times colder; I know then I should have my heart warmed by some expressions of yours, without which I could hardly live, or live miserably, like the poor creatures in Greenland, when they lose their sun.

Yours for ever,
ASPASIA

George Berkeley

FROM THE QUERIST

On the Causes of Ireland's Problems

George Berkeley (1685–1753), Ireland's most famous philosopher, travelled widely throughout Europe and lived for almost three years in Middletown, Rhode Island. Upon his return to Ireland he became the bishop of Cloyne in 1734. This selection from "The Querist" (a collection of more than 200 political and economic queries, published in Dublin 1735–1737) indicates his keen awareness of Ireland's social and political problems.

89. Whether our hankering after our woollen trade be not the true and only reason which hath created a jealousy in England towards Ireland? And whether anything can hurt us more than such jealousy?

90. Whether it be not the true interest of both nations to become one people? And whether either be sufficiently apprised of this?

91. Whether the upper part of this people are not truly English, by blood, language, religion, manners, inclination, and interest?

92. Whether we are not as much Englishmen as the children of old Romans, born in Britain, were still Romans?

93. Whether it be not our true interest not to interfere with them; and, in every other case, whether it be not their true interest to befriend us?

94. Whether a mint in Ireland might not be of great convenience to the kingdom; and whether it could be attended with any possible inconvenience to Great Britain? And whether there were not mints in Naples and Sicily, when those kingdoms were provinces to Spain or the house of Austria?

95. Whether anything can be more ridiculous than for the north of Ireland to be jealous of

a linen manufacturer in the south?

96. Whether the county of Tipperary be not much better land than the county of Armagh; and yet whether the latter is not much better improved and inhabited than the former?

97. Whether every landlord in the kingdom doth not know the cause of this? And yet how few are the better for such their knowledge? . . .

99. Whether, as our exports are lessened, we ought not to lessen our imports? And whether these will not be lessened as our demands, and these as our wants, and these as our customs or fashions? Of how great consequence therefore are fashions to the public?

100. Whether it would not be more reasonable to mend our state than to complain of it; and how far this may be in our own power?

101. What the nation gains by those who live in Ireland upon the produce of foreign countries? . . .

105. Whether, as our trade is limited, we ought not to limit our expenses; and whether this be not the natural and obvious remedy?

106. Whether the dirt, and famine, and nakedness of the bulk of our people might not be remedied, even although we had no foreign trade? And whether this should not be our first care; and whether, if this were once provided for, the conveniences of the rich would not soon follow? . . .

115. Whether, if the arts of sculpture and painting were encouraged among us, we might not furnish our houses in a much nobler manner with our own manufactures?

116. Whether we have not, or may not have, all the necessary materials for building at home?

117. Whether tiles and plaster may not supply the place of Norway fir for flooring and wainscot?

118. Whether plaster be not warmer, as well as more secure, than deal? And whether a modern fashionable house, lined with fir, daubed over with oil and paint, be not like a fire-ship, ready to be lighted up by all accidents? . . .

123. Whether one may not be allowed to conceive and suppose a society or nation of

JOHN SMIBERT. *George Berkeley, Philosopher, (1685–1733) with his Wife and Friends.* Oil on canvas. 24 x 27 9/16 in. (61 x 70 cm). National Gallery of Ireland, Dublin.

human creatures, clad in woollen cloths and stuffs, eating good bread, beef and mutton, poultry and fish, in great plenty, drinking ale, mead, and cider, inhabiting decent houses built of brick and marble, taking their pleasure in fair parks and gardens, depending on no foreign imports either for food or raiment? And whether such people ought much to be pitied?

124. Whether Ireland be not as well qualified for such a state as any nation under the sun?

125. Whether in such a state the inhabitants may not contrive to pass the twenty-four hours with tolerable ease and cheerfulness? And whether any people upon earth can do more? . . .

132. Whether there be upon earth any Christian or civilized people so beggarly, wretched, and destitute as the common Irish?

133. Whether, nevertheless, there is any other people whose wants may be more easily supplied from home? . . .

142. Whether it be not certain that from the single town of Cork were exported, in one year, no less than one hundred and seven thousand one hundred and sixty-one barrels of beef; seven thousand three hundred and seventy-nine barrels of pork; thirteen thousand four hundred and sixty-one casks, and eighty-five thousand seven hundred and twenty-seven firkins of butter? And what hands were employed in this manufacture?

143. Whether a foreigner could imagine that one half of the people were starving, in a country which sent out such plenty of provisions? . . .

176. Whether a nation might not be considered as a family?

Oliver Goldsmith

FROM A LETTER FROM AN ENGLISH GENTLEMAN

A Surprisingly Pleasant Stay

Oliver Goldsmith (1728–1774), physician turned prolific writer, editor, and poet is most probably the author of this letter which first appeared in the Weekly Magazine, *December 29, 1759. Assuming the voice of an almost foreigner to view the native Irish character, he characteristically combines a gentle nostalgia with a moral commitment to accurately inform his readers.*

But in order to give you a more minute description of the inhabitants, I shall present you with one month's adventures in the country, where I was invited from Dublin by a Gentleman who had a handsome country seat upon the western shore. I set out on horseback attended only with one servant, and he an English man, being resolved to observe the manners of the inhabitants more minutely than they had been examined before.

When I had got about forty miles from the capital, I found the country begin to wear a different appearance from what it before appeared to me in. The neat inclosures, the warm and well built houses, the fine cultivated grounds, were no more to be seen, the prospect now changed into, here and there a gentleman's seat, grounds ill cultivated, though seemingly capable of cultivation, little irregular fences made of turf, and topped with brush wood, cut from some neighbouring shrub, and the peasants houses wearing all the appearance of indigence and misery. You will not be surprised, sir, as you know me, that I had curiosity enough to enter one of those mansions, which seemed by its appearance to be the habitation of despair: ordering

Images of Ireland.
18th century. Hand-colored pastel drawing used for engraving in Mr. and Mrs. S.C. Hall's *Ireland (1841–43).* National Library of Ireland, Dublin.

my servant therefore to walk his horses to a neighbouring inn, I alighted and walked into the peasant's hovel. The first sight that struck me was a cow, tied by the horns at one end of the cottage, and a fire of turf without any chimney in the midst. By this sat the mistress of the house, and her daughter knitting stockings, the first seemed about fifty, her eyes bleared with smoak, the daughter about fifteen, and beautiful as an angel. To say the truth, I was surprized to the last degree to see so much beauty where I expected nothing but objects of compassion. For only conceive an hut the walls of which were about four feet high, and made of clay, thatched only with rushes, dirt, and straw, with a door which I was obliged to stoop to enter, conceive this I say, and how could it be expected to find the goddess of beauty lodged so meanly.

In every thing however I was greatly disappointed, for though nothing seemed more wretched than their situation, both seemed alert and lively, and quite insensible of their uncomfortable way of living. They both desired I might be seated upon a straw truss placed by the fire side, probably designed for the husband against his return. The daughter who could speak a little English was excessively chearful and no way surprized at the appearance of a stranger, for by her mother's directions she invited me to supper.

Though I could not imagine where they could procure any thing fit to be eaten, yet in order to see life I complied with their request; for had I refused, it would have been looked upon by the Irish as the highest affront, and the most unpardonable piece of ill breeding. The daughter and I therefore, immediately entered into conversation till the husband's return, who was by trade a labourer, by which occupation he earned four pence a day without meat and drink, but then as he had two sons and they put their profits into one stock, the daughter assured me they all contrived to live pretty comfortably.

The father and his two sons soon returned, and all instead of surprize testified the sincerest satisfaction at the arrival of their new guest, informing me at the same time that nothing was more common than for great folks to lodge a night in their house, when the neighbouring inn could hold no more. The pot was therefore put down with potatoes, and the whole family were busily employed in providing supper; all but the father who it seems is ever exempted from domestic occupations. Supper was soon upon the table, which consisted of nothing more than potatoes and milk, for the rest of the family, but for the father and me, we were honoured each with a wooden knife, and a print of butter.

We accordingly fell to, and as I had a good appetite, I assure you I never made a more comfortable meal. In order however to do things genteely I offered my landlord half a crown when supper was over for my entertainment, but this he refused with the utmost indignation, telling me at the same time that he scorned to keep an inn, and was resolved never to be such a disgrace to his family. It was with the utmost entreaties therefore, that I was permitted to send to the neighbouring alehouse for a shilling's worth of beer, which the daughter ran and fetched in a moment. The circulation of the beer soon threw us all into tip top spirits, I could not behold without the utmost satisfaction the faces of my fellow creatures which were but a little before wrinkled with fatigue and labour, expanding gradually into smiles, and forgetting those miseries which I had before foolishly deemed insupportable. My landlord offered to tell me the story of Kaul Kroodareg, but continues he it will be nothing in English, but in Irish it is finer than fine itself. I declined his offer, pretending to have heard it before, for I had a greater inclination to have some conversation (such Jack is the fraility of us mortals) with the daughter. I therefore attempted to prelude my discourse by a kiss, but guess my surprize, when a favour which the English girls think nothing of bestowing, was denied me. I was therefore obliged in spite of me to let the conversation take a general turn, and answer the news of the day, which was asked me by every one of the family. To these questions I answered to the best of my power, but I found they looked upon my answers as no way satisfactory, they wanted something *strange*, and I had only *news*, to tell them. 'Lord my dear Soul,' says my landlord. 'Taking Quebec, burning the French fleet, ruining what d'ye call him, Tierconneldrago, what signifies all that, where is the wonder there, we have been told here that the king of Prussia, took the whole French army, and fifty pieces of cannon prisoners of war, there is something in such news as that; between ourselves my dear soul, I hate the doubled hearted French, for they have always deceived the Irish, but for all that my dear I love king James in my heart, and God knows I have a good right for my father lost a very good estate by him.' With such discourse it began to grow late, and I thought it time to go to my inn; to this my host objected, for says he, 'we shall have some clean straw, and you may lie by the fire side, as for us here, we all lie together, my wife, my daughter, and I, at the head of the bed, and Laughlin, and Thady, and our dog at the feet.' I thanked him for his offer, and went to my inn where the servant had secured me the best and perhaps the only feather-bed in the house.

Before I left that part of the country, I went to see a wake or funeral, which is entirely peculiar to these people. As soon as a person dies he is immediately carried out into the best appartment, and the bed on which he died is burned at the door. The body is wrapped in linnen all but the face, and thus laid upon the door of the house, which on this occasion is taken off the hinges, and claped under their large square table. Beer, pipes, and tobacco are immediately procured, and all the neighbours are invited to sit up the ensuing night, with the corpse, which they call waking it.

Upon this occasion all the old men and women who are generally fond of beer and tobacco, and all the young ones of both sexes, who are equally fond of diversion assemble at the house of the deceased, in order to howl, to romp, and to tell stories. If the deceased was of any substance there is always employed on this occasion a man whose only employment is story telling, and a woman whose only business is to bear a chorus in every howl. At night fall the plays begin, the young folks no way terrified at the scene of death before them, toy and play tricks and have twenty pastimes suited to the occasion, the old ones smoak, guzzle, and upon the appearance of every stranger, howl in the most dismal manner, to a particular tune which you may have seen set to music. This custom of rejoicing instead of sorrow upon the death of a relation, is still preserved among the Tartars, and I fancy from them it is that the native Irish have taken it. When they have thus watched one night for they never keep the body two, it is next day carried upon men's shoulders to the churchyard, and the women continue howling all the way.

. . . In short I spent a month in a part of the kingdom where I expected to meet nothing but savages in as good company, with as good cheer, and as hearty a reception as I ever remember to have seen. . . .

I am, &c.

Oliver Goldsmith

FROM THE HISTORY OF CAROLAN, THE LAST IRISH BARD

The Harpist Remembered and Revered

In this essay on Turlogh Carolan (1670–1738), the "earliest mention of Carolan in literature," Oliver Goldsmith offers a real sense of Carolan's revered status as "the last and the greatest" of the Irish bards.

───────────

Of all the bards this country ever produced, the last and the greatest was Carolan the blind. He was at once a poet, a musician, a composer, and sung his own verses to his harp. The original natives never mention his name without rapture; both his poetry and music they have by heart; and even some of the English themselves who have been transplanted there, find his music extremely pleasing. A song beginning *O'Rourke's noble fare will ne'er be forgot*, translated by Dean Swift, is of his composition; which though perhaps by this means the best known of his pieces, is yet by no means the most deserving. His songs, in general, may be compared to those of Pindar, as they have frequently the same flights of imagination, and are composed (I don't say written, for he could not write) merely to flatter some man of fortune upon some excellence of the same kind. In these one man is praised for the excellence of his stable, as in

FRANCIS BINDON. *Carolan the Harper.* 18th century. Oil on copper. 7 3/8 x 6 11/16 in. (20 x 17 cm). National Gallery of Ireland, Dublin.

116

Pindar, another for his hospitality, a third for the beauty of his wife and children, and a fourth for the antiquity of his family. Whenever any of the original natives of distinction were assembled at feasting or revelling, Carolan was generally there, where he was always ready with his harp, to celebrate their praises. He seemed by nature formed for his profession; for as he was born blind, so also he was possessed of a most astonishing memory, and a facetious turn of thinking, which gave his entertainers infinite satisfaction. Being once at the house of an Irish nobleman, where there was a musician present, who was eminent in the profession, Carolan immediately challenged him to a trial of skill. To carry the jest forward, his lordship persuaded the musician to accept the challenge, and he accordingly played over on his fiddle the fifth concerto of Vivaldi. Carolan, immediately taking his harp, played over the whole piece after him, without missing a note, though he had never heard it before: which produced some surprise; but their astonishment increased, when he assured them he could make a concerto in the same taste himself, which he instantly composed, and that with such spirit and elegance, that it may compare (for we have it still) with the finest compositions of Italy.

His death was not more remarkable than his life. Homer was never more fond of a glass than he; he would drink whole pints of Usquebaugh, and, as he used to think, without any ill consequence. His intemperance, however, in this respect, at length brought on an incurable disorder, and when just at the point of death, he called for a cup of his beloved liquor. Those who were standing round him, surprised at the demand, endeavoured to persuade him to the contrary; but he persisted, and when the bowl was brought him, attempted to drink but could not; wherefore, giving away the bowl, he observed with a smile, that it would be hard if two such friends as he and the cup should part at least without kissing; and then expired.

Eileen O'Leary

FROM THE LAMENT FOR ART O'LEARY

Eileen O'Leary was the aunt of Daniel O'Connell who would eventually bring about the emancipation of Catholics. This poem laments her husband who was killed for refusing to sell his horse to a Protestant for 5 pounds. (Catholics, under the penal laws, were not permitted to own a horse of greater value than this.) Translated by Frank O'Connor.

Could my calls but wake my kindred
In Derrynane beyond the mountains,
Or Capling of the yellow apples,
Many a proud and stately rider,
Many a girl with spotless kerchief,
Would be here before tomorrow,
Shedding tears about your body,
Art O'Leary, once so merry.

My love and my secret,
Your corn is stacked,
Your cows are milking;
On me is the grief
There's no cure for in Munster.
Till Art O'Leary rise
This grief will never yield
That's bruising all my heart

GEORGE PETRIE.
*Gougane Barra Lake
with the Hermitage of
St. Finbarr, Co. Cork.*
c. 1831. Watercolor on
paper. 12 3/16 x 15 5/8 in.
(30.9 x 39.7 cm).
National Gallery of
Ireland, Dublin.

Yet shut up fast in it,
As 'twere in a locked trunk
With the key gone astray,
And rust grown on the wards.

My love and my calf,
Noble Art O'Leary,
Son of Conor, son of Cady,
Son of Lewis O'Leary,
West of the Valley
And east of Greenane
Where berries grow thickly
And nuts crowd on branches
And apples in heaps fall
In their own season;

What wonder to any
If Iveleary lighted
And Ballingeary
And Gougane of the saints
For the smooth-palmed rider,
The unwearying huntsman
That I would see spurring
From Grenagh without halting
When quick hounds had faltered?
My rider of the bright eyes,
What happened you yesterday?
I thought you in my heart,
When I bought you your fine clothes,
A man the world could not slay.

Maria Edgeworth

FROM CASTLE RACKRENT

A New Mistress Arrives

Maria Edgeworth (1768–1849) is one of the few women literary figures of the late 18th and early 19th centuries. In this selection long-standing servant Thady Quirk, ironic-toned narrator of Castle Rackrent, *immediately senses the advent of change at the castle upon the arrival of the master Sir Kit Murtagh and his new wife.*

Then, in a private postscript, he condescended to tell us that all would be speedily settled to his satisfaction, and we should turn over a new leaf, for he was going to be married in a fortnight to the grandest heiress in England, and had only immediate occasion at present for £200, as he would not choose to touch his lady's fortune for travelling expenses home to Castle Rackrent, where he intended to be, wind and weather permitting, early in the next month; and desired fires, and the house to be painted, and the new building to go on as fast as possible, for the reception of him and his lady before that time; with several words besides in the letter, which we could not make out, because, God bless him! he wrote in such a flurry. My heart warmed to my new lady when I read this: I was almost afraid it was too good news to be true; but the girls fell to scouring, and it was well they did, for we soon saw his marriage in the paper, to a lady with I don't know how many tens of thousand pounds to her fortune; then I watched the post office for his landing; and the news came to my son of his and the bride being in Dublin, and on their way home to Castle Rackrent. We had bonfires all over the country, expecting him down the next day, and we had his coming of age still to celebrate, which he had not time to do properly before he left the country; therefore, a great ball was expected, and great doings upon his coming, as it were, fresh to take possession of his ancestors' estate. I never shall forget the day he came home; we had waited and waited all day long till eleven o'clock at night, and I was thinking of sending the boy to lock the gates, and giving them up for that night, when there came the carriages thundering up to the great hall door. I got the first sight of the bride; for when the carriage door opened, just as she had her foot on the steps, I held the flame full in her face to light her, at which she shut her eyes, but I had a full view of the rest of her, and greatly shocked I was, for by that light she was little better than a blackamoor, and seemed crippled; but that was only sitting so long in the chariot.

'You're kindly welcome to Castle Rackrent, my lady,' says I (recollecting who she was). 'Did your honour hear of the bonfires?'

His honour spoke never a word, nor so much as handed her up the steps—he looked to me no more like himself than nothing at all; I know I took him for the skeleton of his honour. I was not sure what to say to one or t' other, but seeing she was a stranger in a foreign country, I thought it but right to speak cheerful to her; so I went back again to the bonfires.

'My lady,' say I, as she crossed the hall, 'there would have been fifty times as many; but for fear of the horses, and frightening your ladyship, Jason and I forbid them, please your honour.'

With that she looked at me a little bewildered.

'Will I have a fire lighted in the stateroom tonight?' was the next question I put to her, but never a word she answered; so I concluded she could not speak a word of English, and was from foreign parts. The short and the long of it was, I couldn't tell what to make of her; so I left her to herself, and went straight down to the servants' hall to learn something for certain about her. Sir Kit's own man was tired, but the groom set him a-talking at last, and we had it all out before ever I closed my eyes that night. The bride might well be a great fortune—she

was a *Jewish* by all accounts, who are famous for their great riches. I had never seen any of that tribe or nation before, and could only gather that she spoke a strange kind of English of her own, that she could not abide pork or sausages, and went neither to church or mass. Mercy upon his honour's poor soul, thought I; what will become of him and his, and all of us, with his heretic blackamoor at the head of the Castle Rackrent estate? I never slept a wink all night for thinking of it; but before the servants I put my pipe in my mouth, and kept my mind to myself, for I had a great regard for the family; and after this, when strange gentlemen's servants came to the house, and would begin to talk about the bride, I took care to put the best foot foremost, and passed her for a nabob in the kitchen, which accounted for her dark complexion and everything.

The very morning after they came home, however, I saw plain enough how things were between Sir Kit and my lady, though they were walking together arm in arm after breakfast, looking at the new building and the improvements.

'Old Thady,' said my master, just as he used to do, 'how do you do?'

'Very well, I thank your honour's honour,' said I; but I saw he was not well pleased, and my heart was in my mouth as I walked along after him.

'Is the large room damp, Thady?' said his honour.

'Oh, damp, your honour! How should it be but as dry as a bone,' says I, 'after all the fires we have kept in it day and night? It's the barrack room your honour's talking on.'

'And what is a barrack room, pray, my dear?' were the first words I ever heard out of my lady's lips.

'No matter, my dear,' said he, and went on talking to me, ashamed-like I should witness her ignorance. To be sure, to hear her talk one might have taken her for an innocent, for it was, 'What's this, Sir Kit?' and 'What's that, Sir Kit?' all the way we went. To be sure, Sir Kit had enough to do to answer her.

'And what do you call that, Sir Kit?' said she; 'that—that looks like a pile of black bricks, pray, Sir Kit?'

'My turfstack, my dear,' said my master, and bit his lip.

Where have you lived, my lady, all your life, not to know a turfstack when you see it? thought I; but I said nothing. Then, by-and-by, she takes out her glass, and begins spying over the country.

'And what's all that black swamp out yonder, Sir Kit?' says she.

'My bog, my dear,' says he, and went on whistling.

'It's a very ugly prospect, my dear,' says she.

COLORPLATE 47

JAMES MALTON. *Trinity College Through the Portico of the Houses of Parliament, College Green.* 1790.
Ink and watercolor on paper. 19$^{1}/_{4}$ x 25$^{3}/_{16}$ in. (49 x 64 cm). National Gallery of Ireland, Dublin.

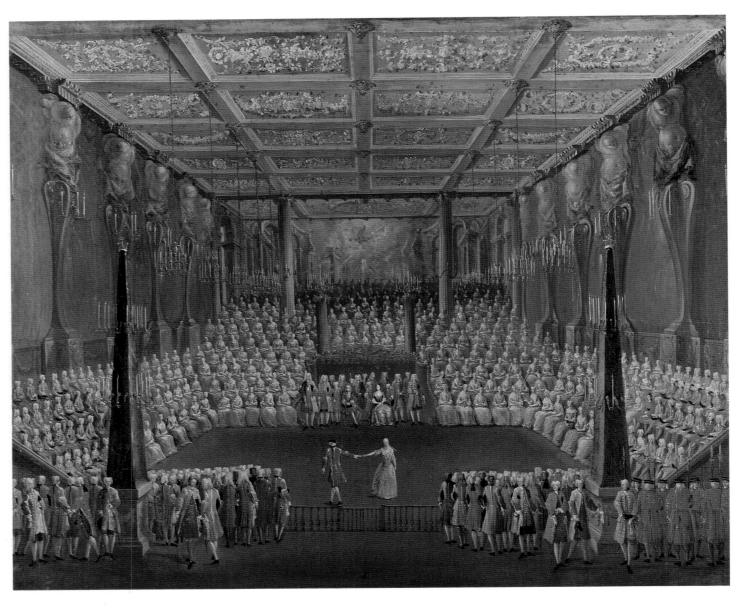

COLORPLATE 48

WILLIAM VAN DER HAGEN. *State Ball in Dublin Castle*. 1731. Oil on canvas. Private collection.
Photo: ET Archive, London.

COLORPLATE 49

JAMES MALTON. *Long Room, Trinity College Library*. Late 18th century. Watercolor over ink on paper. 213 ft. (65 m). Courtesy The Board of Trinity College Dublin. *The main chamber of the Old Library, the Long Room houses about 200,000 of the Library's oldest books. Trinity College Library holds the largest collection of manuscripts and printed books in Ireland.*

COLORPLATE 52

NATHANIEL GROGAN. *View of Cork*. Late 18th century. Oil on canvas. 29³/4 x 47¹/4 in. (75.5 x 120 cm).
Crawford Municipal Art Gallery, Cork.

COLORPLATE 50 *(opposite, above)*

Attributed to NATHANIEL GROGAN. *A View of Cork Harbor*. Late 18th century. Oil on canvas.
60 ¹/4 x 35¹³/16 in. (153 x 91 cm). National Gallery of Ireland, Dublin.

COLORPLATE 51 *(opposite, below)*

WILLIAM SADLER. *The French in Killala Bay (1798)*. 18th century. Oil on panel. 4³/4 x 7 ¹/2 in.
(12 x 19 cm). National Gallery of Ireland, Dublin.

COLORPLATE 53

GEORGE BARRET. *A View of Powerscourt Waterfall*. 18th century. Oil on canvas. 39³/8 x 50 in.
(100 x 127 cm). National Gallery of Ireland, Dublin. *Approximately four miles from the now-destroyed house, the spectacular waterfall is about 400 feet high and one of the great scenic sights in Ireland.*

COLORPLATE 54

JONATHAN FISHER. *A View of the Eagle's Nest, Killarney*. 18th century. Oil on canvas. 46¹/₁₆ x 46¹/₁₆ in. (117 x 117 cm). National Gallery of Ireland, Dublin.

COLORPLATE 55

JAMES BARRY. *Ulysses and Polyphemus*. 18th century. Oil on canvas. 50 x 40⅛ in. (127 x 102 cm).
Crawford Municipal Art Gallery, Cork.

'You don't see it, my dear,' says he; 'for we've planted it out; when the trees grow up in summertime——' says he.

'Where are the trees,' said she, 'my dear,' still looking through her glass.

'You are blind, my dear,' says he: 'what are these under your eyes?'

'These shrubs?' said she.

'Trees,' said he.

'Maybe they are what you call trees in Ireland, my dear,' said she, 'but they are not a yard high, are they?'

'They were planted out but last year, my lady,' says I, to soften matters between them, for I saw she was going the way to make his honour mad with her: 'they are very well grown for their age, and you'll not see the bog of Allyballycarricko'shaughlin at-all-at-all through the skreen, when once the leaves come out. But, my lady, you must not quarrel with any part or parcel of Allyballycarricko'shaughlin, for you don't know how many hundred years that same bit of bog has been in the family; we would not part with the bog of Allyballycarricko'shaughlin upon no account at all; it cost the late Sir Murtagh two hundred good pounds to defend his title to it and boundaries against the O'Learys, who cut a road through it.'

Now one would have thought this would have been hint enough for my lady, but she fell to laughing like one out of their right mind, and made me say the name of the bog over, for her to get it by heart, a dozen times; then she must ask me how to spell it, and what was the meaning of it in English—Sir Kit standing by whistling all the while. I verily believed she laid the cornerstone of all her future misfortunes at that very instant; but I said no more, only looked at Sir Kit.

THE NINETEENTH CENTURY

Charles Kickham

FROM KNOCKNAGOW; OR, THE HOMES OF TIPPERARY

Father Hannigan's Sermon

Charles Kickham (1825–1882), from County Tipperary, was one of the leaders of the Fenian movement in Ireland. Eventually arrested as a traitor and sentenced to fourteen years' penal servitude, he was released due to poor health after serving four years. This warm, humorous sermon revels in the common humanity of the small farming and shopkeeping parishioners.

But though Father Hannigan had delivered his regular discourse after the first gospel, it was his habit to address a few homely words to the people at the conclusion of the Mass, upon what we may call local and individual topics. He now turned round and began, in his deep *big* voice, with:

"Now, what's this I was going to say to ye?"

He pressed the fore-finger of his left hand against his temple, as if trying to recall something that had escaped his memory. Mr. Lowe thought he was about giving up the attempt in despair, when he suddenly jerked up his head, exclaiming—

"Ay! ay! ay! D'ye give up stealing the turf in the name o' God?"

"Every one," he continued after a pause, "must steal turf such weather as this that hasn't it of their own. But sure if ye didn't know it was wrong, ye wouldn't be telling it to the priest. And ye think it would be more disgraceful to beg than to steal it. That's a great mistake. No dacent man would refuse a neighbour a hamper of turf such weather as this. And a poor man is not a beggar for asking a hamper of turf such weather as this when he can't get a day's work, and the Easter water bottles bursting. Ye may laugh; but Judy Manogue stopped me on the road yesterday to know what she ought to do. Her bottle of Easter water that she had under her bed was in a lump of ice, and the bottle—a big, black bottle that often gave some of ye a headache—an' maybe twasn't without giving more of you a heartache—before Judy took my advice and gave up that branch of her business: well, the big, black bottle was split in two with the fair dint of the frost—under the poor woman's bed. And the Lord knows no Christian could stand without a spark of fire to keep the life in him—let alone looking at a houseful of children shivering and shaking, and he able and willing to work, and not a stroke of work to be got. But ye all know that stealing is bad; and ye ought fitter make your cases known to the priest, and maybe something might be done for ye. *Pride* is a good thing—dacent, manly pride—and 'twill often keep a man from doing a mane act even when he's sorely tempted. *Sperit* is a good thing. But, take my word for it, there's nothing like HONESTY. And poverty, so long as it is not brought on by any fault of his own, need never bring a blush to any man's cheek. So, in the name o' God, d' ye give up stealing the turf."

Here he paused, and Phil Lahy, supposing the discourse ended, advanced with a bowl of holy water with a kind of brush laid across it, for the purpose of sprinkling the congregation before they dispersed. But Father Hannigan motioned him back and proceeded.

"Father O'Neill is against the beagles. He says 'tis a shame to hear the horn sounding, and see ye scampering over ditches and hedges on the Lord's Day. Well, I don't know what to say to that. 'Tis the only day ye have for diversion of any sort. And as long as ye are sure not to lose Mass, I won't say anything against the beagles. The farmers tell me they don't mind the loss to them to let their sons keep a dog or two. And if ye meet after Mass—mind, I say, *after* divine service—I don't see much harm in it. I'm told, too, the gentlemen of the neighbourhood—that is, such of them as *are* gentlemen—don't object to it, as ye are honourable sportsmen and spare the hares. But then there's the hurling. There's a deal of bad blood when ye hurl the two sides of the river. If there's any more of the work that was carried on at the last match, ye'll be the disgrace of the country, instead of being, as ye are, the pride of the barony. 'Tis given up to the Knocknagow boys to be as spirited and well-conducted as any in the county. Didn't I point ye out to the Liberator himself the day of the Meeting, and he said a finer body of men he never laid his eyes on. Such men, said he, are the bone and sinew of the country. Some of the best boys ye had are gone since that time, short as it is——"

Here there was a murmur amongst the women; and a low, suppressed wail from two or three whose sons had but lately emigrated, made him pause for a moment.

"Well," he continued, shaking his head as the low wail died away; "thank God the crowbar brigade didn't pay ye a visit like other places; and I hope there is no danger of it, as the landlords here are not exterminators like some I could mention. I was in Cloonbeg the other day at a funeral—I was curate there six years ago—'twas the first parish I was sent to after being ordained, and it broke my heart to see the change. I could hardly believe 'twas the same place. The people swept away out of a whole side of a country, just as if 'twas a flood that was after passing over it. I married some of 'em myself and christened their children, and left 'em happy and comfortable. 'Tis little I thought I'd ever pass the same road and not find a human face to welcome me. Well, please God, there's no danger of ye that way, at any rate. And yet, sure, 'tis little security ye have—but I won't say anything that might discourage ye."

Father Hannigan turned toward the altar, and Phil Lahy was again advancing with the holy water; but after taking a pinch of snuff he resumed his address:—

"I want ye to keep up the good name ye have. And talking of funerals reminds me of your conduct at the berrin' of that poor man ye brought to Kilree the week before last. 'Twas a charitable thing to carry him thirteen long miles through the teeming rain, and I know ye had pains in your shoulders next morning after him. 'Twas a charitable thing to lay his poor old bones alongside of his wife and children, as it was his last wish—though he hadn't a chick or child living belonging to him. I say that was a charitable, Christian, Irish act—and may God reward ye for it. But that was no excuse for the way ye behaved. The parish priest of Kilree said such a set never came into his parish. And ould Peg Naughton, that keeps the shebeen house at the church, declared to myself that, though she is there goin' on fifty-two years, 'twas the drunkenest little funeral she ever laid her eyes on. Isn't that a nice cha-*rac*-ter ye're airning for yourselves? But I hope now ye'll remember my words. And now I have one request to ask of you. I want ye to promise me that ye'll dig the Widow Keating's stubbles for her. She hasn't a sowl to do a hand's turn for her since her boy lost his health. Will he promise me now that as soon as the weather is fitting ye'll dig the Widow Keating's stubbles? 'Tis short 'twill take ye if ye all joint together."

William Carleton

FROM PARTY FIGHT AND FUNERAL

"The Curse"

William Carleton (1798–1869), the youngest of fourteen children of a farmer in County Tyrone, grew up surrounded by Gaelic tales and songs. He was educated by hedge school-masters since formal education was denied the Catholic peasant. In this simple tale a griev-ing widow's vengeful curse is softened by the recipient's honest, human response.

When he had been *keened* in the street, there being no hearse, the coffin was placed upon two handspikes which were fixed across, but parallel to each other, under it. These were borne by four men, one at the end of each, with the point of it touching his body a little below his stom-ach; in other parts of Ireland the coffin is borne on the shoulders, but this is more convenient and less distressing.

When we got out upon the road the funeral was of great extent—for Kelly had been highly respected. On arriving at the *merin* which bounded the land he had owned, the coffin was laid down, and a loud and wailing *keena* took place over it. It was again raised, and the funeral proceeded in a direction which I was surprised to see it take, and it was not until an acquain-tance of my brother's had explained the matter that I understood the cause of it. In Ireland, when a murder is perpetrated, it is usual, as the funeral proceeds to the graveyard, to bring the corpse to the house of him who committed the crime, and lay it down at his door, while the relations of the deceased kneel down, and, with an appalling solemnity, utter the deepest imprecations, and invoke the justice of Heaven on the head of the murderer. This, however, is usually omitted if the residence of the criminal be completely out of the line of the funeral, but if it be possible, by any circuit, to approach it, this dark ceremony is never omitted. In cases where the crime is doubtful, or unjustly imputed, those who are thus visited come out, and lay-ing their right hand upon the coffin, protest their innocence of the blood of the deceased, call-ing God to witness the truth of their asseverations; but in cases where the crime is clearly proved against the murderer, the door is either closed, the ceremony repelled by violence, or the house abandoned by the inmates until the funeral passes.

The death of Kelly, however, could not be actually, or, at least, directly, considered a mur-der, for it was probable that Grimes did not inflict the stroke with an intention of taking away his life, and besides, Kelly survived it four months. Grimes' house was not more than fifteen perches from the road; and when the corpse was opposite the little bridle-way that led up to it, they laid it down for a moment, and the relations of Kelly surrounded it, offering up a short prayer, with uncovered heads. It was then borne towards the house, whilst the *keening* com-menced in a loud wailing cry, accompanied with clapping of hands, and every other symptom of external sorrow. But, independent of their compliance with this ceremony as an old usage, there is little doubt that the appearance of anything connected with the man who certainly occasioned Kelly's death awoke a keener and more intense sorrow for his loss. The wailing was thus continued until the coffin was laid opposite Grimes' door; nor did it cease then, but, on the contrary, was renewed with louder and more bitter lamentations.

CHARLES GREY. *William Carleton, Author, with his Dog.* 19th century. Ink on paper. 10 x 6⁹/₁₆ in. (25.3 x 16.7 cm). National Gallery of Ireland, Dublin.

As the multitude stood compassionating the affliction of the widow and orphans, it was the most impressive and solemn spectacle that could be witnessed. The very house seemed to have a condemned look; and, as a single wintry breeze waved a tuft of long grass that grew on a seat of turf at the side of the door, it brought the vanity of human enmity before my mind with melancholy force. When the *keening* ceased, Kelly's wife, with her children, knelt, their faces towards the house of their enemy, and invoked, in the strong language of excited passion, the justice of Heaven upon the head of the man who had left her a widow, and her children fatherless. I was anxious to know if Grimes would appear to disclaim the intention of murder; but I understood that he was at market—for it happened to be market day.

'Come out!' said the widow—'come out and look at the sight that's here before you! Come and view *your own work!* Lay but your hand upon the coffin, and the blood of him that you murdhered will spout, before God and these Christhen people, in your guilty face! But, oh! may the Almighty God bring *this home to you!*—May you never lave this life, John Grimes, till worse nor has overtaken me and mine falls upon you and yours! May our curse light upon you this day;—the curse, I say, of the widow and the orphans, and that your bloody hand has made us, may it blast you! May you and all belonging to you wither off the 'arth! Night and day, sleeping and waking,—like snow off the ditch may you melt, until your name and your place will be disremimbered, except to be cursed by them that will hear of you and your hand of murdher! Amin, we pray God this day!—and the widow and orphan's prayer will not fall to the ground while your guilty head is above. Childher, did you all say it?'

At this moment a deep, terrific murmur, or rather ejaculation, corroborative of assent to this dreadful imprecation, pervaded the crowd in a fearful manner; their countenances dark-

SAMUEL BROCAS. *Trinity College and College Green, Dublin.* 1818. Ink and watercolor on paper. 9⅝ x 15¹³/₁₆ in. (24.4 x 40.2 cm). National Gallery of Ireland, Dublin.

ened, their eyes gleamed, and their scowling visages stiffened into an expression of determined vengeance.

When these awful words were uttered, Grimes' wife and daughters approached the window in tears, sobbing, at the same time, loudly and bitterly.

'You're wrong,' said the wife—'you're wrong, Widow Kelly, in saying that my husband *murdhered* him! he did *not* murdher him; for, when you and yours were far from him, I heard John Grimes declare, before the God who's to judge him, that he had no thought or intention of taking his life; he struck him in anger, and the blow did him an injury that was not intended. Don't curse him, Honor Kelly,' said she—'don't curse him so fearfully; but, above all, don't curse me and my innocent childher, for *we* never harmed you, nor wished you ill! *But it was this party work did it!* Oh! my God!' she exclaimed, wringing her hands, in utter bitterness of spirit, 'when will it be ended between friends and neighbours, that ought to live in love and kindness together, instead of fighting in this bloodthirsty manner!'

Shen then wept more violently, as did her daughters.

'May God give me mercy in the last day, Mrs. Kelly, as I pity from my heart and soul you and your orphans,' she continued; 'but don't curse us, for the love of God—for you know we should forgive our enemies, as we ourselves, that are the enemies of God, hope to be forgiven.'

'May God forgive me, then, if I have wronged you or your husband,' said the widow, softened by their distress; 'but you know that, whether he intended his life or not, the stroke he gave him has left my childher without a father, and myself dissolate. Oh, heavens above me!' she exclaimed, in a scream of distraction and despair, 'is it possible—is it thrue—that my manly husband, the best father that ever breathed the breath of life, my own Denis, is lying dead—murdhered before my eyes! Put your hands on my head, some of you—put your hands on my head, or it will go to pieces. Where are you, Denis, where are you, the strong of hand, and the tender of heart? Come to me, darling, I want you in my distress. I want comfort, Denis; and I'll take it from none but yourself, for kind was your word to me in all my afflictions!'

All present were affected; and, indeed, it was difficult to say whether Kelly's wife or Grimes' was more to be pitied at the moment. The affliction of the latter and of her daughters was really pitiable: their sobs were loud, and the tears streamed down their cheeks like rain. When the widow's exclamations had ceased, or rather were lost in the loud cry of sorrow which was uttered by the *keeners* and friends of the deceased, they, too, standing somewhat apart from the rest, joined in it bitterly; and the solitary wail of Mrs. Grimes, differing in character from that of those who had been trained to modulate the most profound grief into strains of a melancholy nature, was particularly wild and impressive. At all events, her Christian demeanor, joined to the sincerity of her grief, appeased the enmity of many; so true is it that a soft answer turneth away wrath. I could perceive, however, that the resentment of Kelly's male relations did not at all appear to be in any degree moderated.

Charles Lever

FROM TRINITY COLLEGE

Roommates

Charles Lever (1806–1872), son of a Dublin architect, was a student at Trinity College and with a friend—the original model for Frank Webber, the irrepressibly-dashing roommate in this selection—lived the high-spirited, privileged life described here. In truth, however, it was Lever himself who wrote ballads and sung them as he wandered the streets in disguise.

MY FIRST DAY IN TRINITY

No sooner had I arrived in Dublin than my first care was to present myself to Dr. Mooney, by whom I was received in the most cordial manner. In fact, in my utter ignorance of such persons, I had imagined a college fellow to be a character necessarily severe and unbending; and, as the only two very great people I had ever seen in my life were the Archbishop of Tuam, and the Chief Baron, when on circuit, I pictured to myself that a university fellow was, in all probability, a cross between the two, and feared him accordingly.

The doctor read over my uncle's letter attentively, invited me to partake of his breakfast, and then entered upon something like an account of the life before me, for which Sir Harry Boyle had, however, in some degree prepared me.

'Your uncle, I find, wishes you to live in college; perhaps it is better too; so that I must look out for chambers for you. Let me see; it will be rather difficult, just now, to find them.' Here he fell for some moments into a musing fit, and merely muttered a few broken sentences, as, 'To be sure, if other chambers could be had,—but—then—and, after all, perhaps as he is young—besides, Frank will certainly be expelled before long, and then he will have them all to himself. I say, O'Malley, I believe I must quarter you for the present with a rather wild companion; but as your uncle says you're a prudent fellow'—here he smiled very much, as if my uncle had not said any such thing—'why, you must only take the better care of yourself, until we can make some better arrangement. My pupil, Frank Webber, is at this moment in want of a "chum," as the phrase is, his last three having only been domesticated with him for as many weeks; so that, until we find you a more quiet resting-place, you may take up your abode with him.'

During breakfast the doctor proceeded to inform me that my destined companion was a young man of excellent family and good fortune, who, with very considerable talents and acquirements, preferred a life of rackety and careless dissipation to prospects of great success in public life, which his connection and family might have secured for him; that he had been originally entered at Oxford, which he was obliged to leave; then tried Cambridge, from which he escaped expulsion by being rusticated—that is, having incurred a sentence of temporary banishment; and lastly, was endeavouring, with what he himself believed to be a total reformation, to stumble on to a degree in the 'Silent Sister.'

'This is his third year,' said the doctor, 'and he is only a freshman, having lost every examination, with abilities enough to sweep the university of its prizes. But come over now, and I'll present you to him.'

I followed down stairs, across the court, to an angle of the old square, where, up the first floor left, to use the college direction, stood the name of Mr Webber, a large No. 2 being conspicuously painted in the middle of the door, and not over it, as is usually the custom. As we reached the spot, the observations of my companion were lost to me in the tremendous noise and uproar that resounded from within. It seemed as if a number of people were fighting, pretty much as banditti in a melodrama do, with considerable more of confusion than requisite; a fiddle and a French horn also lent their assistance to shouts and cries, which, to say the best, were not exactly the aids to study I expected in such a place.

Three times was the bell pulled, with a vigour that threatened its downfall, when, at last, as the jingle of it rose above all other noises, suddenly all became hushed and still; a momentary pause succeeded, and the door was opened by a very respectable-looking servant, who, recognizing the doctor, at once introduced us into the apartment where Mr Webber was sitting.

In a large and very handsomely furnished room, where Brussels carpeting and softly-cushioned sofas contrasted strangely with the meager and comfortless chambers of the doctor, sat a young man at a small breakfast-table, beside the fire. He was attired in a silk dressing-gown and black velvet slippers, and supported his forehead upon a hand of most lady-like whiteness, whose fingers were absolutely covered with rings of great beauty and price. His long silky brown hair fell in rich profusion upon the back of his neck and over his arm, and the whole air and attitude was one which a painter might have copied. So intent was he upon the volume before him, that he never raised his head at our approach, but continued to read aloud, totally unaware of our presence.

'Dr Mooney, sir,' said the servant.

'*Ton dapamey bominos, prosephe, crione Agamemnon,*' repeated the student, in an ecstasy, and not paying the slightest attention to the announcement.

'Dr Mooney, sir,' repeated the servant, in a louder tone, while the doctor looked round on every side for an explanation of the late uproar, with a face of the most puzzled astonishment.

'*Be dakiown para thina dolekoskion enkos,*' said Mr Webber, finishing a cup of coffee at a draught.

'Well, Webber, hard at work I see,' said the doctor.

'Ah, doctor, I beg pardon! Have you been long here?' said the most soft and insinuating voice, while the speaker passed his taper fingers across his brow, as if to dissipate the traces of deep thought of study.

While the doctor presented me to my future companion, I could perceive, in the restless and searching look he threw around, that the fracas he had so lately heard was still an unexplained and *vexata questio* in his mind.

'May I offer you a cup of coffee, Mr O'Malley?' said the youth, with the air of almost timid bashfulness. 'The doctor, I know, breakfasts at a very early hour.'

'I say, Webber,' said the doctor, who could no longer restrain his curiosity, 'what an awful row I heard here as I came up to the door. I thought Bedlam was broke loose. What could it have been?'

'Ah, you heard it, too, sir?' said Mr Webber, smiling most benignly.

'Hear it!—to be sure I did. O'Malley and I could not hear ourselves talking with the uproar.'

'Yes, indeed; it is very provoking; but, then, what's to be done? One can't complain, under the circumstances.'

'Why, what do you mean?' said Mooney, anxiously.

'Nothing, sir, nothing. I'd much rather you'd not ask me; for, after all, I'll change my chambers.'

'But why? Explain this at once. I insist upon it.'

'Can I depend upon the discretion of your young friend?' said Mr Webber, gravely.

'Perfectly,' said the doctor, now wound up to the greatest anxiety to learn a secret.

'And you'll promise not to mention the thing except among your friends?'

'I do,' said the doctor.

'Well, then,' said he, in a low and confident whisper, 'it's the dean!'

'The dean!' said Mooney, with a start. 'The dean! Why, how can it be the dean?'

'Too true,' said Mr Webber, making a sign of drinking; 'too true, doctor. And then, the moment he is so, he begins smashing the furniture. Never was anything heard like it. As for me, as I am now become a reading man, I must go elsewhere.'

Now, it so chanced that the worthy dean, who albeit a man of most abstemious habits, possessed a nose which, in colour and development, was a most unfortunate witness to call to character; and as Mooney heard Webber narrate circumstantially the frightful excesses of the great functionary, I saw that something like conviction was stealing over him.

'You'll, of course, never speak of this except to your most intimate friends?' said Webber.

'Of course not,' said the doctor, as he shook his hand warmly, and prepared to leave the room. 'O'Malley, I leave you here,' said he; 'Webber and you can talk over your arrangements.'

Webber followed the doctor to the door, whispered something in his ear, to which the other replied, 'Very well, I will write; but if your father sends the money, I must insist—' The rest was lost in protestations and professions of the most fervent kind, amidst which the door was shut, and Mr Webber returned to the room.

Short as was the interspace from the door without to the room within, it was still ample enough to effect a very thorough and remarkable change in the whole external appearance of Mr Frank Webber; for scarcely had the oaken panel shut out the doctor, when he appeared no longer the shy, timid, and silvery-toned gentleman of five minutes before, but, dashing boldly forward, he seized a key-bugle that lay hid beneath a soft-cushion and blew a tremendous blast.

'Come forth, ye demons of the lower world,' said he, drawing a cloth from a large table, and discovering the figures of three young men coiled up beneath. 'Come forth, and fear not, most timorous freshmen that ye are,' said he, unlocking a pantry, and liberating two others. 'Gentlemen, let me introduce to your acquaintance Mr O'Malley. . . .'

FRANK WEBBER

Among the many peculiar tastes which distinguished Mr Francis Webber was an extraordinary fancy for street-begging; he had, over and over, won large sums upon his success in that difficult walk; and so perfect were his disguises, both of dress, voice, and manner, that he actually, at one time, succeeded in obtaining charity from his very opponent in the wager. He wrote ballads with the greatest facility, and sang them with infinite pathos and humour; and the old woman at the corner of College-green was certain of an audience when the severity of the night would leave all other minstrelsy deserted. As these feats of *jonglerie* usually terminated in a row, it was a most amusing part of the transaction to see the singer's part taken by the mob against the college men, who, growing impatient to carry him off to supper somewhere, would invariably be obliged to have a fight for the booty.

Now, it chanced that, a few evenings before, Mr Webber was returning with a pocket well lined with copper from a musical *réunion* he had held at the corner of York Street, when the idea struck him to stop at the end of Grafton Street, where a huge stone grating at that time exhibited—perhaps it exhibits still—the descent to one of the great main sewers of the city.

The light was shining brightly from a pastry-cook's shop, and showed the large bars of stone between which the muddy water was rushing rapidly down, and plashing in the torrent that ran boisterously several feet beneath.

To stop in the street in any crowded city is, under any circumstances, an invitation to others to do likewise, which is rarely unaccepted; but when, in addition to this, you stand fixedly in one spot, and regard with stern intensity any object near you, the chances are ten to one that you have several companions in your curiosity before a minute expires.

Now, Webber, who had at first stood still, without any peculiar thought in view, no sooner perceived that he was joined by others, than the idea of making something out of it immediately occurred to him.

'What is it, agra?' inquired an old woman, very much in his own style of dress, pulling at the hood of his cloak.

'And can't you see for yourself, darlin?' replied he, sharply, as he knelt down, and looked most intensely at the sewer.

'Are ye long there, avick?' inquired he of an imaginary individual below, and then, waiting as if for a reply, said, 'Two hours! Blessed Vargin! he's two hours in the drain!'

By this time the crowd had reached entirely across the street, and the crushing and squeezing to get near the important spot was awful.

'Where did he come from?' 'who is he?' 'how did he get there?' were questions on every side, and various surmises were afloat, till Webber, rising from his knees, said, in a mysterious whisper, to those nearest him, 'He's made his escape tonight out o' Newgate by the big drain, and lost his way; he was looking for the Liffey, and took the wrong turn.'

To an Irish mob, what appeal could equal this? A culprit, any time, has his claim upon their sympathy! but let him be caught in the very act of cheating the authorities and evading the law, and his popularity knows no bounds. Webber knew this well; and, as the mob thickened around him, sustained an imaginary conversation that Savage Landor might have envied, imparting now and then such hints concerning the runaway as raised their interest to the highest pitch, and fifty different versions were related on all sides—of the crime he was guilty of—the sentence that was passed on him—and the day he was to suffer.

'Do you see the light, dear?' said Webber, as some ingeniously benevolent individual had lowered down a candle with a string—'do ye see the light? Oh, he's fainted? the creature.' A cry of horror from the crowd burst forth at these words, followed by a universal shout of 'Break open the street!'

Pickaxes, shovels, spades, and crowbars seemed absolutely the walking accompaniments of the crowd, so suddenly did they appear upon the field of action, and the work of exhumation was begun with a vigour that speedily covered nearly half of the street with mud and paving-stones. Parties relieved each other at the task, and, ere half an hour, a hole capable of containing a mail-coach was yawning in one of the most frequented thoroughfares in Dublin. Meanwhile, as no appearance of the culprit could be had, dreadful conjectures as to his fate began to gain ground. By this time the authorities had received intimation of what was going forward, and attempted to disperse the crowd; but Webber, who still continued to conduct the prosecution, called on them to resist the police, and save the poor creature. And now began a most terrific fray; the stones, forming a ready weapon, were hurled at the unprepared constables, who, on their side, fought manfully, but against superior numbers; so that at last it was only by the aid of a military force the mob could be dispersed, and a riot, which had assumed a very serious character, got under. Meanwhile, Webber had reached his chambers, changed his costume, and was relating over a supper-table the narrative of his philanthropy to a very admiring circle of his friends.

Such was my chum, Frank Webber; and as this was the first anecdote I had heard of him, I relate it here that my readers may be in possession of the grounds upon which my opinion of that celebrated character was founded, while yet our acquaintance was in its infancy.

William Carleton

FROM TRAITS AND STORIES OF THE IRISH PEASANTRY
The Hedge School

When the Penal Laws forbade the children of Catholics to attend school, the Irish peasants found their own way to educate their children, usually by a scholar who gathered his group together anywhere—even in the shelter of the hedges of the remote countryside. It was not unheard of for students to memorize their Greek and Latin lessons as they took turns looking out for the British soldiers.

There never was a more unfounded calumny than that which would impute to the Irish peasantry an indifference to education. I may, on the contrary, fearlessly assert that the lower orders of no country ever manifested such a positive inclination for literary acquirements, and that, too, under circumstances strongly calculated to produce carelessness and apathy on this particular subject. Nay, I do maintain that he who is intimately acquainted with the character of our countrymen, must acknowledge that their zeal for book learning not only is strong and ardent, when opportunities of scholastic education occur, but that it increases in proportion as these opportunities are rare and unattainable. The very name and nature of hedge schools are proof of this: for what stronger point could be made out, in illustration of my position, than the fact that, despite of obstacles whose very idea would crush ordinary enterprise—when not even a shed could be obtained in which to assemble the children of an Irish village, the worthy pedagogue selected the first green spot on the sunny side of a quickset-hedge which he conceived adapted for his purpose, and there, under the scorching rays of a summer sun, and in defiance of spies and statutes, carried on the work of instruction. From this circumstance the name of hedge school originated; and, however it may be associated with the ludicrous, I maintain that it is highly creditable to the character of the people, and an encouragement to those who wish to see them receive pure and correct educational knowledge. A hedge school, however, in its original sense, was but a temporary establishment, being only adopted until such a schoolhouse could be erected as was in those days deemed sufficient to hold such a number of children as were expected, at all hazards, to attend it.

The opinion, I know, which has been long entertained of hedge schoolmasters was, and still is, unfavourable; but the character of these worthy and eccentric persons has been misunderstood, for the stigma attached to their want of knowledge should have rather been applied to their want of morals, because, on this latter point only, were they indefensible. The fact is that

J. HAVERTY. *The Monster Meeting in the Irish Highlands, Clifden.* O'Connell Addressing the Crowd. 1843. Lithograph from on-the-spot drawing. National Library of Ireland, Dublin.

hedge schoolmasters were a class of men from whom morality was not expected by the peasantry; for, strange to say, one of their strongest recommendations to the good opinion of the people, as far as their literary talents and qualifications were concerned, was an inordinate love of whisky, and if to this could be added a slight touch of derangement, the character was complete.

On once asking an Irish peasant why he sent his children to a schoolmaster who was notoriously addicted to spirituous liquors, rather than to a man of sober habits who taught in the same neighbourhood—

"Why do I sind them to Mat Meegan, is it?" he replied; "and do you think, sir," said he, "that I'd sind them to that dry-headed dunce, Mr. Frazher, with his black coat upon him, and his caroline hat, and him wouldn't taste a glass of poteen wanst in seven years? Mat, sir, likes it, and teaches the boys ten times betther whin he's dhrunk nor when he's sober; and you'll never find a good tacher, sir, but's fond of it. As for Mat, when he's *half gone*, I'd turn him agin the country for deepness in larning; for it's then he rhymes it out of him, that it would do one good to hear him."

"So," said I, "you think that a love of drinking poteen is a sign of talent in a schoolmaster."

"Ay, or in any man else, sir," he replied. "Look at tradesmen, and 'tis always the cleverest that you'll find fond of the dhrink! If you had hard Mat and Frazher the other evening at it—what a hare Mat made of him; but he was just in proper tune for it, being, at the time, purty well, I thank you, and did not lave him a leg to stand upon. He took him in Euclid's Ailments and Logicals, and proved in Frazher's teeth that the candlestick before them was the church-steeple, and Frazher himself the parson; and so sign was on it, the other couldn't disprove it, but had to give in."

"Mat, then," I observed, "is the most learned man on this walk."

"Why, thin, I doubt the same, sir," replied he, "for all he's so great in the books; for, you see, while they were ding dust at it, who comes in but mad Delany, and he attacked Mat, and in less than no time rubbed the consate out of *him*, as clane as *he* did out of Frazher."

"Who is Delany?" I inquired.

"He was the makings of a priest, sir, and was in Maynooth a couple of years, but he took in the knowledge so fast that, bedad, he got *cracked wid larnin'*—for a *dunce*, you see, never cracks wid it, in regard of the thickness of the skull: no doubt but he's too many for Mat, and can go far beyand him in the books; but then, like that, he's still brightest whin he has a sup in his head."

These are prejudices which the Irish peasantry have long entertained concerning the character of hedge schoolmasters; but granting them to be unfounded, as they generally are, yet it is an indisputable fact that hedge schoolmasters were as superior in literary knowledge and acquirements to the class of men who are now engaged in the general education of the people as they were beneath them in moral and religious character.

Daniel O'Connell

FROM A SPEECH ON THE FLOOR OF THE COMMONS, 1837

On the Renewal of Irish Pride

Daniel O'Connell (1775–1847)—the Liberator—dominated Irish politics during the first half of the 19th century. One of the first Catholics to enter the legal profession (1798), he became one of the most successful barristers and then the most prominent politician/hero in Ireland, winning emancipation for the Catholics thereby giving dignity and self-respect back to the Irish people after centuries of repression. His campaign to repeal the union between Ireland and England failed, but stimulated the founding of the Young Ireland movement.

If we were seven millions of mere, dull, uneducated, degraded serfs, a mere mass of helotism, to our seven millions little regard should be paid. Once, indeed, we were sunk by the Penal Code. But a marvellous change has taken place. Men often talk of the great improvement which has taken place in Ireland, and in doing so they refer merely to its external aspect. Its moral one has undergone a still greater alteration. Not only has the plough climbed to the top of the mountain and cultivation pierced the morass, but the mind of Ireland has been reclaimed.

You educate our people, and with the education of our people, the continuance of unnatural and unjust institutions is incompatible. But if education has done much, agitation has done more. Public opinion, which before did not exist, has been created in Ireland. The minds of men of all classes have been inlaid with the great principles on which the rights of the majority depended. This salutary influence has ascended to the higher classes, spread among the middle, and descended among the lower. The humblest peasant has been nobly affected by it.

Even in the most abject destitution he has begun to acquire a sentiment of self-respect. "He venerates himself a man." I remember the time when, if you struck an Irish peasant, he cowered beneath the blow. Strike him now, and the spirit of offended manhood starts up in a breast covered with rags. . . .

No, sir, we are not what we were. We have caught the intonations of your rhymes. Englishmen, we are too like you to give you leave to keep us down. Nay, in some points we have surpassed you.

We are an undecaying and imperishable people.

Justin McCarthy

FROM AN IRISHMAN'S STORY

On the Causes of the Famine

Justin McCarthy (1830–1912), journalist and politician, was a member of the Irish Parliamentary Party, of which Parnell was elected leader in 1880. And it was Justin McCarthy who led forty-five members of the party out of Committee Room 15 at Westminster on December 1, 1890 in protest to Parnell's manifesto. The resulting split in the party lead to Parnell's fall. In this article about his first assignment as a journalist at the age of sixteen, McCarthy writes movingly about the misery of the famine, of the thousands of people starving on the shore as rotting supplies of wheat and flour were dumped into the harbor.

My work as a journalist began under depressing and inauspicious conditions. I had not long been engaged as a reporter on the "Cork Examiner" when the earliest evidences of the great coming famine cast their gloom over the land. The first work of any importance I had to undertake was to act as one of the reporters who were sent into different parts of the country as "special correspondents" to describe the devastating effects of the failure of the potato crop. It is hardly necessary to say that in those days the great majority of the working population of Ireland were living almost exclusively on the potato, and the sudden failure of the crop paralyzed all the efforts of the Irish government and the local authorities to resist the encroachments of the famine. It is no part of my intention to attempt a history of those famine months, which have found ample and abiding record in many carefully compiled volumes. I saw enough for myself to cast a gloom over my memory, which even at the present moment cannot be recalled without a thrill of pain. It was a common sight to see men and women, during that ghastly winter, lie down in the streets of the country towns, and die of actual starvation. The parochial and charitable institutions proved wholly inadequate to grapple with this invasion of hunger, and the burial-grounds themselves in some places were unable to find space for the coffins of the newly dead. In some parts of the south and west of Ireland, the coffins had to do double and treble duty. A coffin was made with one of its sides so adjusted as to be capable of

THE FAMINE IN IRELAND.—FUNERAL AT SKIBBEREEN.—FROM A SKETCH BY MR. H. SMITH, CORK.—(SEE NEXT PAGE.)

[COUNTRY EDITION.]

The Famine in Ireland. Funeral at Skibbereen. 1847. Lithograph from a sketch by H. Smith. National Library of Ireland, Dublin.

easy removal. The dead body thus coffined was lowered into the grave, the coffin was then lifted up so that the corpse fell from its wooden shroud into the cold, soft bosom of Mother Earth, and the coffin was removed altogether and made to do duty for successive inanimate occupants.

The weather during that winter proved remarkably cold for Ireland, and in many parts of the south and west of the island the snow lay deep on the ground for days and days together. Some of the villages presented, under these conditions, the most ghastly sights that human imagination can picture. The unhappy creatures, men, women, and children, who were already sinking from hunger, had their dying agonies increased by the intensity of the cold, and by the drifts of snow which made their way into every miserable hovel whenever the door was open, or even through the chinks and fissures of the rotten and broken old doors when no wider opening was made for the admission of the snowy gusts. It must be owned that this was a trying time for a boy of sixteen to begin his work of descriptive reporting. I grew terribly familiar, in those days, with the frequent sight of death in some of its most heart-rending shapes. Again and again have I seen the corpse of some man, woman, or child, the victim of hunger and cold, with a face of greenish pallor, lying across the threshold of a cabin or on the pathway of some village street. The workhouses were crowded out of all proportion to their capacity for the reception of inmates, and the utmost effects of active beneficence proved utterly unable to make head against the ever increasing spread of the famine.

It is only right to say that nothing was wanting which public and private beneficence could do to check the ravages of that terrible season. I can well remember the mingled sensations created by the sounding of joy bells from many steeples in the city of Cork, when the news went abroad that an American war frigate had come into the harbour heavily laden with food supplies wherewithal to resist the work of the famine. The mere thought that public rejoicing should have come to be associated with the arrival from across the Atlantic of donations of food for the starving poor whom the local authorities were not able to save from starvation, was of itself enough to fill the heart with a new and a keener sense of the misery surrounding us on all sides. Other countries followed the generous example of America. As a writer in one of the national newspapers said at the time, "Even the heart of the Turk at the far Dardanelles was touched, and he sent us in pity the alms of a beggar."

Owing to an extraordinary idea of political economy prevailing at the time among the governing authorities in Ireland, great supplies of wheat and flour were kept stored in some public buildings used as temporary granaries, lest if the whole supplies were poured out too lavishly, the result might be an undue interference with the possible profits of the private trader. In more than one instance it happened—it may have happened in many instances for aught I know, but I am only speaking of those which came within the range of my observation—that the food thus stored was badly packed, so that it actually rotted and had to be poured into the sea, while numbers were starving on the near shores who might have been kept alive if the grain and flour had been devoted in good time to their relief. To quote again from one of the national newspapers, it may truly be said that all through the south and west of Ireland there seemed to be "but one silent, vast dissolution." The people of the island underwent during these terrible months a sudden and immense reduction, from which it has never since recovered. With the famine, and after it, there set in that flood of emigration to the United States and Canada, but more especially to the United States, which has gone on increasing in volume from that time to our own days . . . .

When the famine had done its worst, and there was time to think about something else than deaths from starvation, it soon became evident that among the majority of the Irish people the peaceful and constitutional policy of Daniel O'Connell had sunk into utter discredit. The famine in Ireland was the immediate cause of the triumphs secured by the advocates of free trade, but it was the immediate cause also of the Irish rebellion in 1848. The younger race of Irish nationalists had already broken away from O'Connell's leadership when he endeavoured to pledge them to a strictly peaceful and constitutional policy, and the mood of mind produced throughout the country by the ravages of the famine was naturally favourable to any incitement against the system of rule which was believed to be the main cause of the whole calamity. The Young Ireland party, the followers that is to say of the new group of national leaders, came into something like genuine power, and it would not have required a very far-seeing judgment to fill an observer just then with the conviction that an attempt at armed rebellion would be the next event in the national history.

Peter O'Leary

FROM MY OWN STORY

A Bitter Memory

Peter O'Leary (1839–1920), Catholic priest and prolific writer in Irish, was a founding member of the Gaelic League, an organization dedicated to reviving the Gaelic language. This selection from his famous autobiography Mo Sgeal Fein (My Own Story) *recounts with compassion the horrifying stories of the 1840s' famine in County Cork.*

As soon as understanding comes to a child, it is usual for people to be asking him what would his vocation in life be, when he would be big. I well recall that question being put to me very often. I don't recall having any other answer to give to it but the one, solitary answer: that I would be a priest. From the beginning that much was settled in my mind and I don't recall that there was ever anything other than that. Neither do I recall when my mind first settled on my becoming a priest when I would be grown up.

I know well that people used to be making fun of the story, for it was clear to everyone that my father had nowhere near the necessary capital to set about such an undertaking. As soon as I got any sense, I also knew that he hadn't got the capital, but that did not prevent me from being steadfast in my mind about becoming a priest, whatever way this would come about. If it were not for the blight coming on the potatoes and the bad times that came afterwards, I don't say that he would not have been able to give me the necessary amount of schooling. But the bad times turned everything upside down.

A strange thing—it was the big, strong farmers who were the first to fall! The man who had only a small farm, the grass of six or seven cows, kept his hold; the man with the big, broad, spacious farm was soon broken when the changed times came. He, who had only a little, lost only a little. Before this, there was no big rent or big demands on him. He was accustomed to living without much extravagance. It wasn't too difficult for him to tighten his belt a little bit more, and to answer the small demands on him without too much hardship. But he, who had a big farm, was accustomed to the expensive way of life. He was independent as long as his farm responded. When the change came, the returns from the farm came to a sudden stop. The loss, the extravagance, the demands were too great. It was impossible to meet them and they swept him off his feet. I well recall how I would hear the latest news and how it caused amazement: 'Oh! Did you hear? Such a person is burst! His land is up for sale. He's gone. He slipped away. His land is up!'

You would often hear 'His land is up!'—but you wouldn't hear at all that time 'His land has been taken by another person.' Nobody had any wish to take land. Things used to be very bad for those who had lost their land. They'd have neither food nor credit and there was nothing they could do but go looking for alms. They would not be long begging when they used to go into a decline and they'd die. As they were not accustomed to hunger or hardship, they couldn't stand it long when the hunger and hardship would come on them. Often, when the hunger was very severe, they'd have to rise and move out and head for the house of some neighbour (who, perhaps, would be as needy as themselves, or close to it) to see if they could

COLORPLATE 56

W. F. WAKEMAN. *Trim Castle, County Meath.* 1843. Watercolor on paper. National Library of Ireland, Dublin. *Trim Castle, on the banks of the Boyne River, is an impressive Norman fortress. It was built in 1172 by Hugh de Lacey, destroyed by Rory O'Connor, and rebuilt around 1190. The main gatehouse was used both residentially and defensively.*

COLORPLATE 57

On the Road at Full Pace. Car Travelling in the South of Ireland. 1836. Print, after a drawing by M. A. Hayes. National Library of Ireland, Dublin. *Charles Bianconi's Establishment set up a transport system of these long cars drawn by four horses which lasted through much of the 19th century.*

COLORPLATE 58

JAMES HENRY BROCAS. *Old Baal's Bridge, Limerick.* c. 1810. Watercolor over ink on paper. 9 3/16 x 15 9/16 in. (23.3 x 39.5 cm). National Gallery of Ireland, Dublin. *The medieval Old Baal's Bridge which links the separate communities of Irishtown and Englishtown across the Abby river was demolished and rebuilt in 1831 as Ball's Bridge.*

COLORPLATE 59

MICHAEL ANGELO HAYES. *Sackville Street, Dublin.* c. 1853. Watercolor over pencil, with gum arabic and white highlights on paper. 21⁷/₁₆ x 30⁹/₁₆ in. (54.5 x 77.6 cm). National Gallery of Ireland, Dublin. *Sackville Street, renamed O'Connell Street in 1930, has long been the central thoroughfare in Dublin. On the left is the portico of the General Post Office across the street from what is now Clery's Department Store.*

COLORPLATE 60

DANIEL MCDONALD. *Bowling Match*. 19th century. Oil on canvas. 40³/16 x 51³/16 in. (102 x 130 cm). Crawford Municipal Art Gallery, Cork.

COLORPLATE 61

WILLIAM TURNER DE LOND. *The Market Place and Court House at Ennis.* c. 1820. Oil on canvas.
Frost and Reed Gallery, London. *This is the site of Parnell's famous speech at Ennis on September 20, 1880
where he defined the technique of non-violent intimidation soon to be known as boycotting.*

COLORPLATE 62

EDWIN HAYES. *An Emigrant Ship, Dublin Bay, Sunset.* 1853. Oil on canvas. 22 3/16 x 33 7/8 in.
(58 x 86 cm). National Gallery of Ireland, Dublin.

COLORPLATE 63

WILLIAM BURTON. *The Meeting on the Turret Stairs.* 1864. Watercolor on paper. 37⁹/₁₆ x 23¹⁵/₁₆ in. (95.5 x 60.8 cm). National Gallery of Ireland, Dublin.

get a mouthful of something to eat, which might take the frenzy of hunger off them. . . .

I remember one evening during the period, when the people were running in and out and they talking away. In the winter, it was. The night was after falling. I heard someone saying, 'It was down by Carriginanassey I heard the shout!' 'There it is again!' said another, and they all ran out. A while afterwards, they came back in with a poor, old fellow between them. They put him standing on the floor—he was hardly able to stand. I was facing him and I had a view of his features. His mouth was wide open and his lips, upper and lower both, were drawn back, so that his teeth—the amount he had of them—were exposed. I saw the two, big, long, yellow eye-teeth in his mouth, the terror in his eyes and the confusion in his face. I can see them now as well as I could see them then. He was a neighbour. It is how the hunger drove him out to see if he could find anything to eat and the poor man went astray in the bog that was below Carriginanassey. When he found himself going astray, he became afraid that he would fall into a hole and be drowned. He stopped then and began to shout. That was a custom—there was a certain shout for the purpose—for anyone going astray. Each one knew how to send up that *liúgh*, so that, when they heard it, everybody would know the meaning of it, and the people would gather and seek the person who was going astray.

Maire ni Grianna

FROM MEMORIES OF THE FAMINE

Maire ni Grianna, from Rannafast, County Donegal, recorded with poignant clarity these memories of the 1847 Famine on May 5, 1945 when she was eighty-one years old. Although Donegal, in the north west of Ireland, was not as severely affected as were regions in the south, the natives believed that throughout the country the years of the hunger destroyed the strength and spirit that were once an integral part of Irish rural life. Translated by Emer Deane.

The years of the Famine, of the bad life and of the hunger, arrived and broke the spirit and strength of the community. People simply wanted to survive. Their spirit of comradeship was lost. It didn't matter what ties or relations you had; you considered that person to be your friend who gave you food to put in your mouth. Recreation and leisure ceased. Poetry, music and dancing died. These things were lost and completely forgotten. When life improved in other ways, these pursuits never returned as they had been. The Famine killed everything.

The old people said that in the summer of 1846 the potato blight struck for the first time. People went to sleep at night with the potato fields looking green and healthy; when they got up the next day, every stem in the fields was ruined by the disease. It was too early in the season for the potatoes to be ready and when the blight came they developed no further. Nothing could be done with the potatoes. In one night they were scorched and the people could do nothing but stand and watch them. No matter how hard they worked after that, the potatoes didn't grow. It is said that the blight had never struck before then, but every year after that for the next six or seven years, it happened again but never so disastrously as in that first year. Even now the same thing is happening; it's liable to break out now and then. Hardly anyone planted potatoes in 1847. Because of the ruin of the year before, they didn't have one potato to sow in the ground in the spring of '47. That's when the hunger struck and it was from that point on that the deaths began.

Not many people died from hunger here. There were good years for oats here, and during the Famine anyone who saved the oats made meal from it. Those people were alright. But those who were dependent on the potatoes were lost. Their families died. The poor creatures, they thought they would be able to live on seafood, but they weren't. They needed a little of the produce of the soil to stay alive. They used to stay inside in their cabins, not able to walk, so weak were they with hunger. They would go out in the fields on all fours and eat their fill of grass and weeds and then they'd be able to walk home. Mothers lay in their beds with the children beside them and they were so weak they were not able to get up. They used to lie there until one after another they died of hunger. The hunger killed the old and the children for the most part. Stronger people were able to survive the hardship.

THE GRUEL CAULDRON

When the people began to die of hunger, a big cauldron was set up in Rannafast to make broth or gruel to keep people alive. No-one knew where it came from or who had sent it. Bones were boiled to make the broth and there's no record of where those bones came from. Anyone who had anything at all to eat or any way of getting it would get no broth at all. But there weren't many here who could do that. Every one got one serving of broth per day. Crowds would be milling around as they gave out the broth and they'd be pushing and shoving, nearly killing one another to get up to the cauldron. Everyone was trying to get in before others, so great was the hunger. No one had mercy for anyone else. At any rate, between broth and whatever the soil produced and seafood or weeds, they were kept alive, but barely so. That cauldron was in Rannafast until a few years ago. . . .

THE FEVER

Far more died of fever than of hunger. The people were so wasted and weak with hunger and starvation that, when the fever came, they could not withstand the disease and therefore hundreds of them died. There were no hospital or doctor in this area either. . . .

Conor Cruise O'Brien

On Charles Stewart Parnell,

Uncrowned King of Ireland

Conor Cruise O'Brien, noted academic, political commentator and author on a wide range of subjects, served in the Irish diplomatic service for many years. In this article on Charles Stewart Parnell he offers his own dispassionate report on the man called The Uncrowned King of Ireland.

————————

Charles Stewart Parnell (1846–1891) was the son of an Anglo-Irish landlord, John Henry Parnell, and of an American heiress, Delia Tudor Stewart. John Henry's political views do not seem to have varied significantly from those of other members of his class, although he was more liberal than most of them.

Delia, on the other hand, was greatly given to anti-British utterances, and sympathetic to Irish nationalism. She was a daughter of Commodore Stewart—'Old Ironsides'—a hero of the War of 1812. . . .

Charles Stewart Parnell's later career ran counter to all the assumptions and allegiances of his father's class. Some of these indeed had favoured Home Rule—a separate parliament for Ireland—but they had assumed that this would be an aristocratic body, dominated by their class. The achievement of Charles Stewart Parnell, on the other hand, was to put the Home Rule cause on a populist base, linking it with an attack on landlord privileges. This made him an extraordinarily unorthodox member of the Anglo-Irish landlord class. The most obvious source of unorthodoxy in the Parnell household at Avondale is that American mother. Two of Parnell's siblings—his sisters, Anna and Fanny—were also populist nationalists, and more extreme in that direction than Charles Stewart was. Delia's influence over Anna and Fanny is not disputed, and I don't think it can possibly have been without effect on her son, Charles Stewart Parnell. . . .

Parnell was elected to the Parliament of the United Kingdom as Member for Meath in 1875. He sat as a member of the Home Rule Party, then led by Isaac Butt (1813–1879). Under Butt's leadership the Home Rulers had attempted a moderate posture based on a moral suasion and had got nowhere. By 1877, however, Parnell was becoming the leader of a small group of Home Rule members engaged in a determined effort to obstruct all other business of Parliament as long as Home Rule was denied. These activities attracted widespread attention both in Ireland itself, and among politically-minded Irish-Americans. By 1879, Parnell was already beginning to be seen as the emerging leader of a broadly based agrarian-nationalist movement. The movement became known as the New Departure.

The New Departure linked obstructive agitation at Westminster with agrarian agitation in Ireland itself. The Land League was founded by Michael Davitt (1846–1906), a Fenian who had served a long sentence in Dartmoor for revolutionary activities. After his release from prison, Davitt sought out Parnell and persuaded him, in 1879, to put himself at the head of the new movement. Within three years the New Departure had brought about revolutionary changes in the Irish land system.

Up to this time, Irish landlords had had unrestricted authority over their lands. They could raise their rents as they chose, and evict tenants at will. Parnell and Davitt set about changing that. They concentrated on making evictions difficult, by singling out particularly painful cases, organising mass-demonstrations, followed by the ostracism of obnoxious parties: evicting landlords and land-agents and 'grabbers'—tenants who leased lands from which the previous tenants had been evicted.

The Land League's most spectacular victory, in 1880, was to give a new word to the languages of the world: the word 'boycott.' Captain Boycott was an unpopular land agent and small landlord in Co. Mayo. Through the activities of the Land League he had become entirely isolated, and could get no workers to bring in his harvest. The British Government brought in Protestant labourers, from distant Eastern Ulster, under military escort, to gather Captain Boycott's harvest. The episode aroused widespread international ridicule and provided the New Departure with a superb advertisement. Throughout Ireland, evictions were falling steeply as landlords became increasingly afraid to evict. In consequence Parnell became hugely popular among the tenantry of rural Ireland, and was soon to be called 'the Uncrowned King.'

Under these pressures, the then Prime Minister, William Ewart Gladstone, decided to concede virtually the whole Land League programme. Gladstone's Land Act of 181 revolutionised the Irish land system, by curbing the landlord's freedom to evict, and by providing for judicially-fixed rents.

On the agrarian front, Parnell's victory was complete by the end of 1881. He now decided to concentrate on the political front; the use of the ballot-box and party organisation to win Home Rule for Ireland. Parnell had become leader of the Home Rule Party in Parliament in April 1880. From 1881 his authority was such—in every constituency in Ireland outside the Protestant North-East—that his nominees won in every by-election from 1881 to 1885 and won 86 seats (the representation of all Catholic Ireland) in the elections of 1885. With those 86 seats, Parnell held the balance of power in the new Parliament. As Prime Minister, Gladstone, dependent on Parnell for power, would introduce a Home Rule Bill.

But before that, Parnell had an ugly personal and political crisis to overcome. William Henry O'Shea was a Home Rule Member of Parliament, who had voted for Parnell in the leadership contest of April, 1880. O'Shea's wife Katharine—later vulgarly known as 'Kitty O'Shea'—had become Parnell's mistress about the same time, and the two remained lovers for the rest of Parnell's life. The liaison was well known in political circles by 1885, although it did not become known to the general public until five years later. Parnell now—in February 1886—put his personal authority behind the candidature of Captain O'Shea in a by-election in Galway City. There can be little doubt that Parnell was blackmailed into taking this step. It produced a revolt by two of his lieutenants, but Parnell's authority was still sufficient to have O'Shea elected.

Gladstone, supported by Parnell, introduced his Home Rule Bill in April 1886. It was defeated as a result of the defection of some of Gladstone's followers, led by Joseph Chamberlain. Still, Parnell's 'conversion' of Gladstone and the Liberal Party to Home Rule was regarded as a great success, and Home Rule was confidently expected to follow the next return of the Liberals to power, with Parnell's support.

Parnell's immense popularity in Ireland—and also his reputation in England—was enhanced in February 1889, when charges made against him by *The Times* in connection with the Phoenix Park murders (1882) were proved to rest on forgeries. The alliance between Parnell and Gladstone seemed solidified and the triumph of their political partnerships secure.

By the end of that same year, irreparable disaster struck. On Christmas Eve, 1889, Captain O'Shea filed a divorce petition, citing Parnell as co-respondent. Parnell's supporters at first tried to treat this move as 'another *Times* forgery.' But when the case came—on 15–17 November 1890—the suit was undefended, and the verdict therefore went against Mrs. O'Shea and Parnell. Even after that, Parnell's support held, for about a week. A public meeting in Dublin, on the day after the verdict, reaffirmed the Party's confidence in Parnell, and he was re-elected Chairman of the Party on 25 November. Even the Catholic Hierarchy—later blamed for excess of zeal against Parnell—seems to have been prepared at this point to acquiesce silently, if reluctantly, in Parnell's continued leadership, and this is a measure of the astonishing authority Parnell's achievements had won for him in Ireland.

The revolt against Parnell began, not in Ireland but in England. Gladstone's lieutenants reported to him that non-conformist indignation against a continued alliance with 'a convicted adulterer' was such that the Liberals could not win a General Election while allied with Parnell. Gladstone so informed the Irish Parliamentary Party which now realised that it could not win Home Rule with Parnell as its leader. The Party consequently split, after a bitter debate. Forty-five members seceded from Parnell's leadership, and Parnell was left with only 28 followers in Parliament.

After the Party had split on a political issue, the Catholic Church came publicly down against Parnell over 'the moral issue.' Every altar in the land thundered against 'the convicted adulterer.' In those conditions, Parnell fought and lost three ghastly by-elections in 1891. Exhausted, he succumbed to rheumatic fever.

After the divorce, Parnell had married Katharine O'Shea, in June 1891. Five months later, on 6 October 1891, he died in Brighton, in his wife's arms.

To many who were young in Ireland, at the time of the Parnell Split, Parnell remained a hero. He left his imprint on the imagination of the country. Both W. B. Yeats and James Joyce turn to him repeatedly in their work: Yeats wrote:

> And here's a final reason
> He was of such a kind
> Every man that sings a song
> Keeps Parnell in his mind.

Charles Stewart Parnell
FROM SPEECH AT ENNIS
"Boycotting" Defined

Charles Stewart Parnell (1846–1891), was born to an American mother and an Anglo-Irish landlord father. His life-long efforts for Irish home rule were not successful, due in part to his fall from power because of his scandalous involvement in a divorce case. Parnell is favorably remembered for his superb leadership that prepared the way for the final stages in the struggle for independence. This selection, from his famous speech at Ennis on September 19, 1880, defines a technique of non-violent intimidation—boycotting.

Now [he said to the excited crowd] what are you to do with a tenant who bids for a farm from which his neighbour has been evicted [Various shouts, among which 'Kill him' and 'Shoot him']. Now I think I heard somebody say, 'Shoot him' ['Shoot him']. But I wish to point out to you a very much better way, a more Christian and more charitable way which will give the lost sinner an opportunity of repenting. When a man takes a farm from which another has been evicted, you must show him on the roadside when you meet him, you must show him in the streets of the town, you must show him at the shop-counter, you must show him in the fair and at the marketplace, and even in the house of worship, by leaving him severely alone, by putting him into a sort of moral Coventry, by isolating him from the rest of his kind as if he were a leper of old, you must show him your detestation of the crime he has committed, and you may depend upon it if the population of a county in Ireland carry out this doctrine, that there will be no man so full of avarice, so lost to shame, as to dare the public opinion of all right-thinking men within the county and to transgress your unwritten code of laws.

Eviction Scene (Battering Ram). 1888. Photograph. National Library of Ireland, Dublin. The Lawrence Photographic Collection.

Thomas Flanagan

FROM THE TENANTS OF TIME

The Fenian Rebellion Begins

Thomas Flanagan (b. 1923) has written a sweeping epic about the 1867 Fenian rising. The story revolves around three young men—Hugh MacMahon, Bob Delaney, and Ned Nolan— whose lives, while inextricably bound in the Fenian cause, subsequently take very different paths. In this excerpt, Patrick Prentiss, a young historian attempting to put the Rising into perspective forty years later, speaks with John Devoy, a Fenian leader who had been involved with the rising and is now a New York journalist.

It had begun, what historians (if he should ever finish his history) would someday call the Fenian rebellion, long before 'sixty-seven or even 'sixty-five—a decade earlier, in 1856. It had begun when James Stephens—veteran of the 1848 rising—returned to Ireland to take the country's temperature. For months he tramped the roads of the four provinces, disguised as beggarman, casual labourer, commercial traveller, talking to the young and the disaffected. His three-thousand-mile walk, he called it later; by that time he was the legendary "Number One" of the Fenian conspiracy. In 1865, holding the strings of insurrection in those hands which everyone remembered as small and ladylike, he was the hero of the famous escape from Richmond Prison; in 'sixty-seven, he was a leader discredited, sentenced to more than thirty years of garrulous recollection, long-bearded by then, a shabby sage living penniless in a sub-urban lodging.

But in 1856, in the year of his ramble, James Stephens had been a will-o'-the-wisp, never forgotten, dimly remembered. *An seabhac*, he was called in the Gaelic-speaking districts, "the Hawk," and that passed over into police reports as "Shook," "Mr. Shook." "It is reported," wrote the sergeant in Castletown Bearhaven, harbor town in a spur of West Cork, "that Shook, who was last month reported in Waterford by the *Gazette*, has been this week in Castletown, and met with a score of men in the shop of a farrier named Grady. What he said to them is not known, but they were men of a lowly condition, except for Grady himself, who is known for his intemperate habits." It was a decade after the famine, the great hunger, and Mr. Shook visited the districts more sorely damaged, Skull and Crosshaven and Skibbereen, where he talked to a young hothead named Jeremiah O'Donovan, who claimed that lineage entitled him to call himself "O'Donovan Rossa."

With difficulty, Prentiss sought an image of that early Stephens, unsmeared by gossip, failure. He saw him at nightfall, cresting a hill, before him a village imperfectly cradled against sea winds, huts straggling towards dull water, a darkening strand. In beggar's disguise, long greatcoat, boots patched and dusty, canvas pack strapped to his back, he pauses. Here, in the village before him, ten years earlier, the dead lay untended in their cabins, and beyond them, in the fields, the crop of potatoes rotted black and putrescent. Their stench clings to the air, invincible against seaborne freshening winds. He remembers, perhaps, the Tipperary peasants of 1848, polite and apathetic, puzzled, as Smith O'Brien preached resistance to them, mild-voiced patrician strayed into rebellion, counting out for them on delicate fingers their numberless wrongs. In the front of the small crowd, a cottier hawked, spat precisely between his boots, nudged his neighbour. A fairday treat, these gentlemen from Dublin, frock-coated, preaching a genteel rebellion, constables to be halted on the road, disarmed without injury to their person. Young Stephens stood among them, not of them, loaded carbine resting on forearm. Beside him O'Mahony, chieftain of the Comeraghs, a Tipperary man known to them, bred of fighting stock; a tall, handsome man, his coat open and two pistols shoved into his waistband. O'Mahony could have led them, or Stephens himself, but not these gentlemen from Dublin. It was over in a few hours, that rising in 'forty-eight: an attack upon a barracks, a rattle of rifle fire, and two men dead in a field. Never again, O'Mahony and Stephens vowed in Paris exile, exhilarated by talk of Blanquist barricades, dark-eyed *carbonari* in ill-lit cafés off the Boul' Mich.' "Use the faction fighters," Stephens said, "take hostages, tear up the rails." And pushed the bottle of wine towards O'Mahony, who, temperate in those Paris years, smiled, and shook his head. But later, from New York, O'Mahony wrote to him of hundreds of thousands of famine Irish, washed up on the shores of Boston and New York, bewildered, wrathful, peasants unused to brick and asphalt and clanging horse trams, saloon bullies, their minds clinging to sun-shadowed hills, bog cotton, a twist of road, the voices and heat of winter taverns. "A second Ireland here," he wrote. "Unbroken. They can send money, men. England drove them from their homes, and well they know it." They must have a sign, he wrote; they must know that the country is not dead.

And so Stephens set out upon his ramble, his trail left behind him in scattered, puzzled police reports, in memories of old men swollen and magnified by time, by pride in their own vanished youth. . . .

But Hugh MacMahon was, characteristically, more acerb. "There was not one man of the Kilpeder circle whose oath ran back to the time of James Stephens's ramble. Bob and Vincent and myself were the first, and we brought back the oath from Cork. He was never in Kilpeder, that I have heard, although 'tis said that he was in Macroom. At the time of his ramble, we were all of us schoolboys at work on our spelling and our sums. Long after, I met men who claimed to have met him, to be sure, and some who claimed to have been given the oath by Mr. Shook himself. But by 'sixty-five, Stephens was Number One, COIR was his title, Chief Organiser of the Irish Republic, and he was everywhere at once, in New York, in Paris, in London, in disguise in Dublin itself. But I remember the escape from Richmond Prison in 'sixty-five. It was the talk of all Ireland, and London as well, I have no doubt. Man, it was prodigious. There they had him caught at last, on the very eve of the Rising, as we then believed, the Hawk netted. The government made great play of it, and the lackey newspapers, as we called them. They had drawings of it, to drive home the point: James Stephens with shirt collar unfastened, manacled wrist and ankle, being led through the entranceway of sombre

JOHN B. YEATS. *John O'Leary, Fenian.* 1904. Oil on canvas. 44 x 34¼ in. (112 x 87 cm). National Gallery of Ireland, Dublin.

stone. Dame Street was thronged for his arraignment, and all the gentlemen and ladies were down from the viceregal lodge to get a look at him. 'I deliberately repudiate the existence of British law in Ireland,' he said, 'and I defy any punishment it can inflict on me. I have spoken.'" MacMahon's laugh ended in a dry cough. "'I have spoken.' Brave words, by God, but they put us in a panic. Bob and Kevin Mangan, who was in command in Macroom, rode down to Cork, but of course they knew no more than we did, and Bob rode home in a fury. 'Never fear,' Jackie Keegan had said to him. 'They have not yet built a cage strong enough to hold the Hawk.' Then he put his hand on Bob's shoulder. 'They all talk like penny dreadfuls,' Bob said to me, but we put on a brave front for the men, and if I remember aright, Bob borrowed Jackie Keegan's words with a clear conscience. And by the living God, wasn't Keegan right? They arraigned Stephens, but they never tried him. Two weeks later, he was free as a bird. It was a great sensation, and the effect upon the movement was prodigious."

It was indeed, and for this Prentiss had needed only to consult the yellowing files of newspapers. But in fact, the escape had been described to him in New York by John Devoy himself, who led the band of men waiting outside the prison walls. Straight and inflexible as a poker, like Ned Nolan one of the unforgiving men, wedded to the oath, gaolbird, conspirator, looking not Irish but like a Yankee colonel, retired. "It was simple enough," he said, "and why not? An inside job, as they say over here. The two warders on his block were sworn Fenians, Breslin and Byrne. They moved him through the inner wall and across the courtyard, and Kelly and myself and a dozen lads were waiting beyond with rope. I mind that when we reached the North Circular, a fellow named Ryan said to me, 'John, we have tonight witnessed the greatest event in history.' So much for the Crucifixion."

"And what did Stephens say?" Prentiss said.

Devoy smiled grimly and relit his cigar, moving the match carefully, from side to side, twisting the cigar. "Stephens? He had little enough to say that night, although I think he inclined towards Ryan's view of the matter. He was a vain man; it was his besetting sin, and it proved fatal a year later. But what the devil, it was *felix culpa*, without vanity could he have managed what he did ten years before? A man on his own, walking the roads of Ireland, scattering the seeds of revolution. It was spitting rain that night, the dark rain of late November. The one thing we hadn't remembered was an overcoat for Stephens, and so I put my own around his shoulders. You cannot have the Chief Organiser of the Irish Republic shivering along the Royal Canal. But first I transferred my revolver, and until we reached the safe house in the North Circular, I was worried lest the rain damp the cartridges."

"You would have used it," Prentiss said.

Devoy exhaled fragrant Havana smoke. "If a peeler had so much as asked us our destination, I would have blown him out of his boots. I'm sorry it didn't happen. No blood had yet been shed, you know, and that might have tripped the wire. By God, the night that James Stephens flew Richmond, we could have raised half Dublin. Or from then through the Christmas season and into the spring of 'sixty-six. After that came the arrests, and the organisation fell apart. Nor would there have been a rising in 'sixty-seven, had not Stephens been deposed. It was simply done. McCafferty put a cocked revolver to his head, and said, 'Mr. Stephens, you are deposed.' McCafferty had a wonderful simplicity of manner—one of the American officers, a Confederate guerrilla with Mosby. But of all that, I have heard talk only. By February of 'sixty-six, I was myself in Mountjoy Gaol."

"Then in 'sixty-seven," Prentiss said, "when the Rising came, it was McCafferty gave the word? By then McCafferty was Number One?"

Devoy smiled again. "There was never but the one held that title. James Stephens. Mr. Shook. But it would not have been McCafferty. McCafferty was organising the raid on Chester Arsenal. Kelly gave the word, a solid man. I mind the day of the Rising, you could feel it among the warders, and one of them, a decent skin named Clanahan, told me that there were a thousand men in the Dublin hills up above Rathfarnham, and the troops had gone to face them down. Later, we heard about the risings in Cork."

"The Kilpeder rising?"

"The Kilpeder rising, yes, Ned Nolan's rising, but the other ones as well—Ballyknockane and the others. A bloody waste. In the back room in Grantham Street, in January of 'sixty-six, I told James Stephens that it was then or never. I have heard it said in later years that when McCafferty had the hammer cocked he should have finished off the job and squeezed the trigger. But I would never have had part in that, nor would Burke or Kelly. We owed everything to Stephens. He botched it, and he was thrust rightly aside, but we owed him everything. Sorry decades he had of it after that, poor devil, but the funeral was a great occasion, I am told." Devoy drew again on his cigar, and grinned at Prentiss. "Fenians specialise in grand funerals, Mr. Prentiss. We dug up poor Terence MacManus, and shipped him across the world from San Francisco to Glasnevin."

Hawk in a rainy night, Prentiss thought, in borrowed overcoat, the leafless trees dripping, led by armed young men through streets of brown and red brick, along the banks of the dark canal, rainpattered. He died then, not sorry decades later, brought down by history's fowling piece, far behind him his long ramble through Munster and Connaught, the years of scheming and contriving, cadging funds from New York immigrants, riding the cars to address Irishmen encamped with the Federal troops in Tennessee, Virginia valleys. Ahead of him lay only his own months of indecisiveness—terror, perhaps, at the prospect of what he had himself summoned into being, and then moss trooper McCafferty's wide-mouthed revolver pressed against his skull.

"My own specialty," Devoy said, "was the recruiting of Irish soldiers among the British regiments, and a brisk traffic it was. I gave the oath to hundreds of them. But the British aren't fools. By the spring of 'sixty-six, the regiments had all been replaced by true-blues from England, and myself and my recruiters were behind bars. Stephens had given me a title, Chief Organiser of the British army. He was a great man for inventing titles. When they arrested me, I was at the task, with two sergeants in the back room of a public house. I was shopped by an informer."

They had had dinner in a restaurant in the West Twenties, around the corner from Devoy's

James Stephens
Addressing American
Fenian Meeting. 1864.
Engraving.

Fenian newspaper. Coffee sat cold before them, and empty wineglasses.

"They gave you a life sentence, as I recall," Prentiss said.

Devoy shook his head. "Fifteen years' hard. I had never had a chance to fire that revolver I spoke of. That is why I was eligible for the amnesty in 'seventy-one, myself and Rossa. Lads like your man Nolan had to linger on a few years. When Nolan came over, we were here to welcome him."

"Had you know him before," Prentiss said, "in Ireland or in prison?"

"Not at all," Devoy said. "Ned was sent over late in 'sixty-six, or early 'sixty-seven, on the eve of the Rising. And afterwards, I was in Millbank and he in Portland. He had the worse of it. Millbank was accounted a model prison, but Portland was bad. Men went mad in Portland. Not Ned, though. It hammered Ned into hardness. That is the way of it. Prison turned poor Rossa into a fanatic, and Ned into—well, what he became. You know what he became."

But Prentiss did not. They all moved in courses beyond his experience or understanding. Russian nihilists, perhaps, or anarchists, meeting in their Whitechapel clubs and coffeehouses, dark-faced, gesticulating, wide declamatory Slavic sweeps of arm. Not Devoy, close-buttoned, spare, a distant, polite courtesy, devoid of affability. "These days?" Devoy had said to him when they commenced their meal. "These days I am a most respectable old party. My paper tried to keep alive an interest in Irish affairs; we have a Dublin correspondent; there are many fraternal organisations, here and in Jersey. Clambakes, commemorations. Ireland is very quiet now, you know, very constitutional. She has entrusted her future to Mr. Redmond and Mr. O'Brien and Mr. Healy."

Prentiss knew better. Even now there was a shadowy Fenian organization, and Devoy was close to its centre.

"Mr. Healy," Devoy said mildly, "the man who betrayed Parnell. And little Johnny Redmond. There are no Ned Nolans now. All that died in 1891, in the hills of West Cork."

Rudyard Kipling

FROM NAMGAY DOOLA

Unlikely Patriots

Rudyard Kipling (1865–1936), a leading English novelist, poet, and writer of short stories, won the Nobel prize for literature in 1907. In this comic story, he recounts an unusual and unexpected reception in a Tibetan hut.

The door was thrown open and I entered the smoky interior of a Thibetan hut crammed with children. And every child had flaming red hair. A raw cow's-tail lay on the floor, and by its side two pieces of black velvet—my black velvet—rudely hacked into the semblance of masks.

"And what is this shame, Namgay Doola?" said I.

He grinned more willingly than ever. "There is no shame," said he. "I did but cut off the tail of that man's cow. He betrayed me. I was minded to shoot him, Sahib. But not to death. Indeed not to death. Only in the legs."

"And why at all, since it is the custom to pay revenue to the King? Why at all?"

"By the God of my father I cannot tell," said Namgay Doola.

"And who was thy father?"

"The same that had this gun." He showed me his weapon—a Tower musket bearing date 1832 and the stamp of the Honourable East India Company.

"And thy father's name?" said I.

"Timlay Doola," said he. "At the first, I being then a little child, it is in my mind that he wore a red coat."

"Of that I have no doubt. But repeat the name of thy father thrice or four times."

He obeyed, and I understood whence the puzzling accent in his speech came. "Thimlay Dhula," said he excitedly. "To this hour I worship his God."

"May I see that God?"

"In a little while—at twilight time."

"Rememberest thou aught of thy father's speech?"

"It is long ago. But there is one word which he said often. Thus 'Shun.' Then I and my brethren stood upon our feet, our hands at our sides. Thus."

"Even so. And what was thy mother?"

"A woman of the hills. We be Lepchas of Darjeeling, but me they call an outlander because my hair is as thou seest."

The Thibetan woman, his wife, touched him on the arm gently. The long parley outside the fort had lasted far into the day. It was now close upon twilight—the hour of the Angelus. Very solemnly, the red-headed brats rose from the floor and formed a semi-circle. Namgay Doola laid his gun against the wall, lighted a little oil lamp, and set it before a recess in the wall. Pulling aside a curtain of dirty cloth, he revealed a worn brass crucifix leaning against the helmet-badge of a long-forgotten East India regiment. "Thus did my father," he said, crossing himself clumsily. The wife and children followed suit. Then all together they struck up the wailing chant that I had heard on the hillside—

> *Dir hane mard-i-yemen dir*
> *To weeree ala gee*

I was puzzled no longer. Again and again they crooned, as if their hearts would break, their version of the chorus of *The Wearing of the Green*—

> *They're hanging men and women too*
> *For the wearing of the green.*

Maurice Healy

FROM THE OLD MUNSTER CIRCUIT

Legal "Tenders"

Maurice Healy, Irish attorney, introduces some of his favorite, singular characters who appeared at the local circuit courts around the turn of the century.

———————

Once I was opposed to him [Johnnie Moriarity, a colorful local attorney] in an action in the course of which he was completely overwhelmed by a single answer of a witness. Everyone who visited Cork in the first quarter of the present century will remember Flurry O'Donoghue, the porter at the Imperial Hotel. He practically owned the hotel, but accepted your tip with gratitude. He put his savings into the purchase of another hotel at Killarney, which was managed by his wife, who had the misfortune to have an accident when out driving one day. Out of the accident an action arose. In the course of her story Mrs. O'Donoghue happened to describe

HENRY MACMANUS. *Reading "The Nation."* 19th century. Oil on canvas. 12 x 14 in. (30.5 x 35.5 cm). National Gallery of Ireland, Dublin.

her little hotel with some satisfaction and pardonable complacency. Johnnie unwound himself with a sinister smile. "So you live in this earthly paradise?" he asked. "A regular Garden of Eden—tell me, have you any serpent there?" "No, Serjeant, but we'd always be happy to see you!" replied the lady, bringing the cross-examination to an immediate and ignominious conclusion.

* * *

The accused was alleged to have entered the house of an eccentric old lady by night, made his way to her bedroom, and helped himself to some money and articles of value. Dick outlined the story, and called his principal witness into the witness-box, where she was sworn with some difficulty.

"What is your name?" began Dick.

"Bridget Murphy," replied the old lady.

"And how old are you?" asked Dick.

"I won't tell you," replied the witness.

"Oh!" cried Dick, "I assure you I have no matrimonial intentions!" The Judge then interfered, and suggested that perhaps the question was irrelevant to the point at issue, which indeed it seems to have been. Dick, therefore, proceeded to get from the old woman an account of how she had gone to bed, fallen asleep, and been awakened by the sound of footsteps ascending the stairs. "And what did you do?" asked Dick.

"I reached for the holy water, and blessed myself," said the witness.

"Very right and proper," said Dick; "but what else did you do?"

"I commended myself to the protection of Saint Patrick and Saint Bridget," replied Mrs. Murphy.

"Admirable, no doubt," said Dick; "but what practical steps did you take?"

"I got out of bed and took up the poker," said the witness.

"Ah!" said Dick; "and, armed with the poker and the holy water, and under the protection of Saint Patrick and Saint Bridget, what did you do then?"

But here the Judge felt it necessary to check the laughter that had arisen in Court, and to suggest that the religious beliefs of humble people ought not to be made the subject of jest.

* * *

I have never forgotten a trial in Cork, probably in March, 1905, when a little barefoot post-boy was charged with having got a girl of less than statutory age into trouble. Such cases were rare in Ireland; this one was indeed a case of true love gone too impetuously forward. I cannot remember whether there was an actual trial or whether the accused pleaded guilty; but I do know that Stephen Ronan, the Crown Prosecutor, thought it necessary to read a number of letters which the lover had written to his lady; and one phrase burned itself into my brain, and survives to this day, although the rest which I have forgotten were all in tune with it. Barefooted, with no education beyond what a National School could give, this bucolic Petrarch addressed to his Laura the following lovely words: "Far away from where I am now there is a little gap in the hills, and beyond it the sea; and 'tis there I do be looking the whole day long, for it's the nearest thing to yourself that I can see."

I watched the Judge; there was a tear trickling down his nose. "Mr. Ronan," he said, "these young people seem to be very fond of one another. Why couldn't they get married?"

Stephen Ronan sniggered; there was not much romance in his nature, and he had a trick of speech which made every sentence seem to begin with a sneering smile. "Heh!" he said. "Marriage is easy enough where there is money to provide for it, heh!" "I don't suppose it would cost a lot," said Billy. "Heh! More than these young people could afford!" cried Ronan. "Will the Post Office take him back if I bind him over?" asked the Judge. There proved to be little difficulty about that. "Come up here, my girl," said Billy kindly. The little girl, heavy with child, came into the witness-box. "Do you love the boy?" "I do, me Lord." "Will you marry him?" "I will if he'll ax me, me Lord." "Now, prisoner, do you hear that? Will you marry her?" "There's nothing I'm more wishful for, me Lord." "There, now; that's all settled; are the girl's people there?" A little procession went into the Judge's room, where the bride was promptly endowed out of his own pocket; and I hope they all lived happily ever afterwards.

Some Favorite Irish Folk Songs

THE WEARING OF THE GREEN

A street ballad from about 1800, which appeared in several versions, the best-known written by the playwright Dion Boucicault for his play Arrah-na-Pogue. *The color green represented the revolution in Ireland.*

O Paddy dear, and did you hear the news that's going round?
The shamrock is forbid by law to grow on Irish ground;
St. Patrick's day no more we'll keep, his colours can't be seen,
For there's a bloody law again the wearing of the green.
I met with Napper Tandy, and he took me by the hand,
And he said, "How's poor old Ireland, and how does she stand?"
She's the most distressful country that ever yet was seen,
They are hanging men and women for the wearing of the green.

Then since the colour we must wear is England's cruel red,
Sure Ireland's sons will ne'er forget the blood that they have shed.
You may take the shamrock from your hat and cast it on the sod,
But 'twill take root and flourish there, though under foot 'tis trod.
When law can stop the blades of grass from growing as they grow,
And when the leaves in summer-time their verdure dare not show,
Then I will change the colour that I wear in my caubeen,
But 'till that day, please God, I'll stick to wearing of the green.

But if at last our colour should be torn from Ireland's heart,
Her sons with shame and sorrow from the dear old isle will part;
I've heard a whisper of a country that lies beyond the sea,
Where rich and poor stand equal in the light of freedom's day.
O Erin, must we leave you, driven by a tyrant's hand?
Must we ask a mother's blessing from a strange and distant land?
Where the cruel cross of England shall nevermore be seen,
And where, please God, we'll live and die still wearing of the green

I KNOW WHERE I'M GOING

An anonymous Anglo-Irish ballad.

I know where I'm going, she said,
  And I know who's going with me;
I know who I Love—
  But the dear knows who I'll marry.

Feather beds are soft,
  And painted rooms are bonny,
But I'll forsake them all
  To go with my love Johny;

Leave my dresses of silk,
  My shoes of bright green leather,
Combs to buckle my hair,
  And rings for every finger.

O some say he's black,
  But I say he's bonny—
The fairest of them all,
  My winsome handsome Johny.

I know where I'm going, she said,
  And I know who's going with me;
I know who I love—
  But the dear knows who I'll marry.

GREEN GROW THE LILACS

An old Irish song. One engaging story claims that the Mexican word "Gringo" meaning "cowboy" originated when the Mexicans misunderstood the words of this song as it was sung by the Irish soldiers who fought on the American side in the Mexican War.

———————————

Green grow the lilacs, all sparkling with dew,
I'm lonely, my darling, since parting with you.
But by our next meeting I'll hope to prove true,
And change the green lilacs to the Red, White, and Blue.

I used to have a sweetheart, but now I have none,
Since she's gone and left me, I care not for one.
Since she's gone and left me, contented I'll be,
For she loves another one better than me.

I passed my love's window, both early and late,
The look that she gave me, it made my heart ache.
Oh, the look that she gave me was painful to see,
For she loves another one better than me.

I wrote my love letters in rosy red lines,
She sent me an answer all twisted in twines,
Saying, "Keep your love letters and I will keep mine,
Just you write to your love and I'll write to mine."

Green grow the lilacs, all sparkling with dew,
I'm lonely, my darling, since parting with you,
But by our next meeting I'll hope to prove true,
And change the green lilacs to Red, White, and Blue.

COCKLES AND MUSSELS

A traditional Irish folk song.

In Dublin's fair city, where girls are so pretty,
I first set my eyes on sweet Molly Malone,
As she wheel'd her wheelbarrow through streets broad and narrow
Crying, Cockles and Mussels! alive, alive oh!

She was a fish monger, but sure 'twas no wonder,
For so were her father and mother before;
And they each wheel'd their barrow through streets broad and narrow,
Crying, Cockles and Mussels! alive, alive oh!

She died of a fever, and no one could save her,
And that was the end of sweet Molly Malone;
Her ghost wheels her barrow through streets broad and narrow,
Crying, Cockles and Mussels! alive, alive oh!

Alive, alive oh! Alive, alive oh!
Crying, Cockles and Mussels, alive, alive oh!

YOU BRAVE IRISH HEROES

*A traditional ballad infused with mythic power first sung by young Irish men and women
after the famine of the 1840s during the mass emigration to America.*

You brave Irish heroes wherever you be,
I pray stand a moment and listen to me,
Your sons and fair daughters are now going away,
And thousands are sailing to Americay.

So good luck to those people and safe may they land,
They are leaving their country for a far distant strand,
They are leaving old Ireland, no longer can stay,
And thousands are sailing to Americay.

The night before leaving they are bidding goodbye,
And it's early next morning their heart gives a sigh,
They do kiss their mothers and then they will say
'Farewell, dear old father, we must now go away.'

Their friends and relations and neighbours also,
When the trunks are all packed up, all ready to go,
O the tears from their eyes they fall down like the rain,
And the horses are prancing, going off for the train.

COLORPLATE 64

THOMAS ALFRED JONES. *Molly Macree*. 1860s. Watercolor and gouache with gum arabic on paper.
16¹/₈ x 13¹/₁₆ in. (41 x 33.2 cm). National Gallery of Ireland, Dublin.

COLORPLATE 65

WALTER OSBORNE. *The Fish Market, Patrick Street, Dublin.* Late 19th century. Oil on canvas. 23⁵/8 x 31 ¹/2 in. (60 x 80 cm). Hugh Lane Municipal Gallery of Modern Art, Dublin.

COLORPLATE 66

SEAN KEATING. *Aran Fisherman and His Wife*. Early 20th century. Oil on canvas. 49 x 39 in.
(124.5 x 99 cm). Hugh Lane Municipal Gallery of Modern Art, Dublin.

COLORPLATE 67

AUGUSTUS BURKE. *A Connemara Girl*. 1865. Oil on canvas. 14⁹/₁₆ x 29¹/₈ in. (37 x 74 cm).
National Gallery of Ireland, Dublin.

COLORPLATE 68

TREVOR FOWLER. *Children Dancing at a Crossroads*. 19th century. Oil on canvas. $27^{15}/_{16}$ x $36^{1}/_{4}$ in. (71 x 92 cm). National Gallery of Ireland, Dublin.

COLORPLATE 69

JOSEPH HAVERTY. *The First Confession.* 19th century. Oil on canvas. 14³/₁₆ x 11¹³/₁₆ in. (36 x 30 cm). National Gallery of Ireland, Dublin.

COLORPLATE 70

WALTER OSBORNE. *A Scene in the Phoenix Park*. 19th century. Oil on canvas. 27¹⁵/₁₆ x 35¹³/₁₆ in. (71 x 91 cm). National Gallery of Ireland, Dublin.

COLORPLATE 71

MATTHEW LAWLESS. *The Sick Call*. 1863. Oil on canvas. 24¹³/₁₆ x 40⁹/₁₆ in. (63 x 103 cm).
National Gallery of Ireland, Dublin.

COLORPLATE 72

NATHANIEL HONE THE YOUNGER. *Summer Pastures*. Late 19th–early 20th century. Oil on board.
7 1/16 x 9 7/8 in. (18 x 25 cm). National Gallery of Ireland, Dublin.

COLORPLATE 73

NATHANIEL HONE THE YOUNGER. *A View of the Coast (of Clare?).* Late 19th–early 20th century.
Oil on canvas. 24 x 36¹/₄ in. (61 x 92 cm). National Gallery of Ireland, Dublin.

COLORPLATE 74

NATHANIEL HONE THE YOUNGER. *Sheep and A Shepherd by the Sea.* Late 19th–early 20th century.
18 1/8 x 27 3/16 in. (46 x 69 cm). National Gallery of Ireland, Dublin.

COLORPLATE 75

WALTER OSBORNE. *St. Patrick's Close, Dublin.* Late 19th century. Oil on canvas. 27³/₁₆ x 20¹/₁₆ in.
(69 x 51 cm). National Gallery of Ireland, Dublin.

COLORPLATE 76

Rose Barton. *Going to the Levee.* 1897. Watercolor on paper. 14 x 10¹/₂ in. (35.6 x 26.6 cm).
National Gallery of Ireland, Dublin. *In 1892 Rose Barton and her sister were presented at Dublin Castle.*
In this watercolor done five years later she depicts the arrival of the carriages at Dublin Castle.

COLORPLATE 77

JOSEPH HAVERTY. *O'Connell and His Contemporaries; the Clare Election, 1828.* 19th century.
Oil on canvas. 43⁵/₁₆ x 72 in. (110 x 183 cm). National Gallery of Ireland, Dublin.

COLORPLATE 78

JOHN LAVERY. *The Ratification of the Irish Treaty in the English House of Lords, 1921.* 1921.
Oil on board. 14³/₁₆ x 10¹/₄ in (36 x 26 cm). National Gallery of Ireland, Dublin. *Inscribed on reverse:*
"Painted in the House of Lords on the afternoon of 16 December 1921."

COLORPLATE 79

JOHN LAVERY. *Blessing of the Colours; "A Revolutionary Soldier Kneeling to be Blessed."* 20th century.
Oil on canvas. 96 1/16 x 72 in. (244 x 183 cm). Hugh Lane Municipal Gallery of Modern Art, Dublin.

So good luck to those people and safe may they land,
They are leaving their country for a far distant strand,
They are leaving old Ireland, no longer can stay,
And thousands are sailing to Americay.

When they reach the station, you will hear their last cry,
With handkerchiefs waving and bidding goodbye,
Their hearts will be breaking on leaving the shore,
'Farewell, dear old Ireland, will we ne'er see you more?'

O I pity the mother that rears up the child,
And likewise the father who labours and toils,
To try to support them he will work night and day,
And when they are older they will go away.

So good luck to those people and safe may they land,
They are leaving their country for a far distant strand,
They are leaving old Ireland, no longer can stay,
And thousands are sailing to Americay.

THE IRISH IN AMERICA

William D. Griffin

"This Distant Land"

William D. Griffin, professor of history at St. John's University, is the author of A Portrait of the Irish in America *and* The Book of Irish Americans. *The contribution of the Irish immigrant to the development of our nation is everpresent. But the ultimate Irish legacy to the United States is the presence of forty-three million Americans who claim at least partial Irish ancestry.*

It was in the eighteenth century . . . that the Irish began to come to America in large numbers. Many of them were Presbyterians from Ulster, driven by hard times at home, who settled on the rocky farmlands of New Hampshire and the mountain slopes of Virginia and the Carolinas. Irish 'Palatines' of German descent came from the Limerick area to establish the first Methodist Church in New York. Adventurers like William Johnson and George Croghan made their fortunes as Indian agents, while merchants, lawyers and physicians formed Irish fraternal and charitable organisations everywhere from Boston to Baltimore. Immigrants of the bolder sort left the security of the coastal colonies to press inland, into what would later be Kentucky and Tennessee. Most of these settlers were Protestants, for there was little incentive for Catholics to experience in British America the same discriminatory laws that they endured at home. Yet some there clearly were, particularly in Pennsylvania and Maryland.

* * *

During the American Revolution, the Irish in the thirteen British colonies were divided along essentially the same lines as the general population, about one-third supporting Crown or rebels respectively, while the remaining third stood neutral. Irishmen of all religious and regional backgrounds fought both for and against King George or waited for the outcome. Thus, the healing process that was necessary in the newly-independent United States was reflected among Americans of Irish origin. The friendly Sons of St. Patrick, founded in New York City in 1784, for example, made no political or sectarian distinction in its membership, and welcomed arriving Irish immigrants as 'fellow countrymen.' During the next few decades, however, this harmony among the Irish in America, and the general accepting attitude of Anglo-Americans, began to change. The political radicalism attributed to refugees from the failed United Irish rebellion of 1798, combined with suspicion of the growing proportion of Catholics among new arrivals, led to the seemingly contrary objections that the Irish were both Jacobins and supporters of a 'Universal Papal Monarchy.'

With the end of the French Revolutionary and Napoleonic Wars in 1815, the real influx of Irish began. Between 1820 and 1840, some 300,000 Irish immigrants, mostly Catholic, arrived in the United States, in search of economic opportunity. They found a demand for their labor in the work of building roads, canals, and the first stage of the railroad network, as well as in urban construction and mill-work. But their numbers and cultural distinctiveness created growing concern in a country of barely thirteen million people, almost entirely of British stock. The 'second wave' of Ulster Protestants who came to America during this period understood the new negative implications of being identified as mere 'Irish,' and the distinguishing label of 'Scots-Irish' began to be used.

All this was but a prelude to the flood of Irish immigration and the crises that it created during the decades surrounding the Great Famine. From 1840 to 1860 approximately 1,700,000 men, women, and children from Ireland entered the United States. While not all of these were literally fleeing starvation and disease, most of them were poor, uneducated, unskilled, and ill-equipped to deal with the challenges of an expanding frontier. Irish slums and shantytowns, already in being in most Eastern cities, became swollen ghettos. The new-comers experienced social ostracism that often flared into mob violence and became the object of nativist rantings. Excluded from all but menial occupations, they were frequently driven to crime and vice, and then condemned for traits of drunkenness and brutality that justified their exclusion. Nevertheless, it was during this period that the American Irish formed or expanded many of their basic community institutions, ranging from Catholic schools and infirmaries to militia companies and political clubs. Those who abandoned the reassuring companionship of

Priest Blessing Emigrants as they Leave Home. 19th century. Engraving. From *London Illustrated Weekly.*

Arriving in New York.
1893. Watercolor on
paper. Courtesy Kenny's
Bookshop, Galway and
Ireland of the Welcomes,
Dublin.

their kind in Boston, New York, New Orleans and the other port cities for the freer and more
open society of the Mid-West were, on the other hand, already taking advantage of a fluid
social setting to pursue the 'American dream' with some hope of success. In cities like
Chicago and St. Louis there was a better chance for an Irishman to win his share of fame and
fortune.

The Civil War, in so many respects a watershed in American history, also saw the beginning of new and better times for the Irish in America. Tens of thousands of them, from pri-
vates to generals, fought for their adopted country between 1861 and 1865. Irish regiments,
and even brigades, distinguished themselves for bravery and dedication on a hundred
battlefields, and General Philip Sheridan was merely one of many Irish-American officers who
seemed to lend a special panache to the long-bitter struggle. Even the far smaller proportion of
Irish who had settled in the South fought for the Confederacy with a zeal that earned the
respect of their foes. After the War the Irish found a much greater acceptance as comrades-in-
arms who had demonstrated their identification with their new homeland. Moreover, although
they continued to arrive in the United States in significant numbers down to the end of the century, their coming was overshadowed by the steadily increasing hordes of southern and eastern
European immigrants. Compared to these latter, the Irish who came over in the 1880s and
1890s, better educated, often possessing specialised skills, and speaking English, appeared relatively attractive. Joining their American-born kinsfolk, they constituted a familiar and toler-
ated element in the population.

* * *

By 1900 it seemed as if the Irish Americans were everywhere. They were building the
skyscrapers, the bridges and the subway tunnels; they had laid the tracks for the trans-conti-
nental railroad, started the mining boom in the West and followed the trail to Alaska; they had
provided cowboys, cavalrymen, and outlaws from Mississippi to San Francisco's Golden Gate;
they had virtually created the Catholic Church in the United States, giving it both a material
infrastructure and a magisterial hierarchy that has endured to the present day. Nor were all of
these Irish Americans merely unknown and unsung components of a massive community.
They included the greatest American architect of the day, Louis Sullivan (son of an immigrant), the outstanding American sculptor, Augustus St. Gaudens (son of an Irish mother), the
founder of the American automobile industry, Henry Ford (son of an immigrant), and two
brothers who were among the country's leading literary and academic figures, Henry and
William James (grandsons of an immigrant).

On the Quarantine Ground, New York Harbor: Health Officials Coming Aboard. 1893. Watercolor on paper. Courtesy Kenny's Bookshop, Galway and *Ireland of the Welcomes*, Dublin.

The Irish in America were distinguished by more than their sheer volume of immigration and the breadth of their settlement and occupational activity. What set them apart from almost all other ethnic groups was their continuing commitment to their native land. Irish-American support for the national cause in Ireland remained consistent from the era of Daniel O'Connell and the Young Ireland movement through Fenianism and the Home Rule struggle. Money and manpower were always forthcoming for the furtherance of 'Ireland's destiny.' The climax of this commitment was reached during the critical years 1916–1922, and was recognised throughout by Irish nationalist leaders as a vital component of their enterprise.

The establishment of the Irish Free State, coinciding with changed immigration laws, brought an end to this vital interaction between the Irish on both sides of the Atlantic. As the number of Americans born in Ireland steadily declined from 1930 onward, Irish Americans became increasingly preoccupied with social and economic advancement in a purely American context. For every Eugene O'Neill, obsessed by his Irish ancestry, there was a Scott Fitzgerald or a John O'Hara, striving to repudiate it. Dramatists, film-makers, and artists sought a wider audience. Businessmen and politicians devoted themselves to climbing the corporate ladder or campaigning for senate seats or governorships by transcending rather than emphasising their roots in the Irish community. The changing ethnic structure of Catholic parishes and parochial schools, combined with the increased opportunities for higher education after World War II, impelled many young men and women of Irish extraction into an environment where Irishness seemed irrelevant.

With the election of John F. Kennedy as president of the United States of America in 1960, the assimilation of the Irish into the American mainstream seemed complete. Commentators spoke of the 'vanishing Irish,' who had been totally accepted as Americans. Symbolic of the severing of ties was the virtual cessation of immigration from Ireland: during the 1960s the Irish accounted for only one per cent of the total immigration to the United States, as contrasted with the forty-two per cent they had provided a century earlier.

Irish-American consciousness would be reawakened in the 1970s, however, by two developments. One was the general upsurge in ethnic awareness and the quest for roots that was stimulated by the African-American civil rights and cultural movements. The other was the revival of Irish nationalism in its most militant form, growing out of communal strife in Northern Ireland. A renewal of Irish identity, particularly among the younger generations, brought a new interest in Ireland and an increased sensitivity to its contemporary problems. By the early 1990s, a significant number of Irish Americans had abandoned the naive sentimentality or pragmatic indifference of earlier decades for serious commitment, whether on the cultural or the political level.

By the early 1990s, too, the flow of Irish immigrants to America had revived. Though statistics are imprecise, due to the undocumented status of many of these new arrivals, it has been estimated that as many as 100,000 young Irish men and women have entered the United States since the late 1970s. Settling for the most part in areas such as New York and Boston that have retained a nucleus of Irish community life, they have interacted with newly-self-conscious Irish Americans to produce a revivified Irish presence in America. The economic problems of contemporary Ireland are likely to impel further waves of emigration, with many of these new 'exiles of Erin' following the traditional route to the United States, despite its own economic downturn.

The story of Irish emigration to America spans more than 300 years, and includes the steady growth of an Irish presence in the New World during the eighteenth century, a massive flood of men and women seeking opportunity (or mere survival) in the nineteenth century, and a diminishing flow in the twentieth century. In this story, the recent increase of economic exiles is essentially an epilogue rather than a new chapter. The story may now have ended, but the legacy of Irish migration to the United States is a population of some forty-three million who claim at least partial Irish ancestry, the second-largest immigrant group in the country. This great array of Americans and their ancestors have experienced every aspect of American life, from the heights of power and influence to the depths of degradation and poverty. The Irish experience, on one side or the other of the Atlantic, includes invasion, confiscation, bondage, religious discrimination, racial prejudice, economic exploitation, and social exclusion. And yet they survived, and triumphed.

Thomas D'Arcy McGee

FROM A HISTORY OF THE IRISH SETTLERS IN NORTH AMERICA

John Barry, Father of the American Navy

Thomas D'Arcy McGee (1825–1868) was a journalist on both sides of the Atlantic and a leading figure in the Young Ireland movement. A History of the Irish Settlers in North America, *the source for this essay, was published in Boston in 1855. John Barry (1745–1803) was born in County Wexford and while a young teenager followed his love for the sea across the Atlantic to Philadelphia. His formidable skills as a seaman eventually earned him the official title Commodore of the United States Navy, and due to his success in the training of young officers he was popularly called the Father of the American Navy.*

The organization of the infant Navy of the United States was one of the heaviest anxieties of the first Congress. Among a people bred to the use of arms, and annually involved in Indian warfare, it was a much easier matter to raise an army, than, out of the limited shipping of the young seaports, to find vessels and officers to whom the national flag could be intrusted on the other element.

Fortune had thrown in the way of Washington, a man most useful for this department of the public service. This was John Barry, a native of the parish of Tacumshane, Wexford county, Ireland. Barry was born in the year 1745, the son of "a snug farmer," and had but to step out of his own door, to stand beside the sea. He conceived so strong a love for a sailor's life, that, at fourteen or fifteen years of age, he crossed the Atlantic, and began to sail to and from Philadelphia. He rose from one trust to another, teaching himself as he rose, till, at twenty-five years of age, he was captain of "the Black Prince," one of the finest London and Philadelphia packets, afterwards a vessel of war. Mr. Rese Meredith was the owner of this ship, and Washington's host when in Philadelphia. It was in his house the illustrious Virginian met, and marked, the future commodore.

In the latter part of 1775, Congress had purchased a few merchant ships, and hastily fitted them up as vessels of war. Captain Barry was given the command of the principal, the *Lexington*; and in another, "the Alfred," Paul Jones entered as first lieutenant. These vessels both lay in the Delaware, and, when the flag of the Union was agreed on, they were the first to hoist it, afloat.

* * *

From 1783 till his death, Barry was constantly engaged in superintending the progress of the navy. He induced the government to adopt the model for ships of war, which has been found so well suited to its uses. He was particularly fond of aiding the younger officers in the service. . . . He was an exceedingly affable and hospitable man, and, what is unfortunately not usual in his profession, practically religious. He died in September, 1803, and his chief legacy was to the Catholic Orphan Asylum. He has been called, by naval writers, "The Father of the American Navy." He is buried in St. Philadelphia.

The personal character of Commodore Barry was made of noble stuff. When Lord Howe tempted him with a vast bribe, and the offer of a British ship of the line, he replied, "He had devoted himself to the cause of his country, and not the value or command of the whole British fleet could seduce him from it." He never was ashamed of his native land, and, after the peace of Paris, paid a visit to the place of his birth, which fact is still remembered with gratitude in his native parish. When hailed by the British frigates, in the West Indies, and asked the usual questions as to the ship and captain, he answered, "The United States ship *Alliance*, saucy Jack Barry, half Irishman, half Yankee,—who are you?"

Parry Miller

The Captain at Sea

Here, from an article in The Irish Digest, *is a sparkling account of Captain Barry's spirited exploits on the Atlantic as he adroitly outwits his enemies while in the service of his adopted country.*

———————

Early in 1781, [Captain John Barry was] given the thirty-two-gun frigate *Alliance*, which had just got back after a remarkable cruise round the British coast as one of John Paul Jones's squadron. His job was to carry safely to France Colonel Laurens, the new representative of the

President George Washington Presenting Captain John Barry with his Commission. 1797. Engraving. New York Historical Society.

States at the Court at Versailles.

On the way back he met fresh adventures. To start with, he and the captain of a French ship captured a couple of English privateers. Then, while his craft lay becalmed off the coast of Newfoundland one May morning, she was spotted and smartly attacked by two English brigs—the sixteen-gun *Atlanta* and the fourteen-gun *Trepassy*.

For an hour the Englishmen kept up their fire with impunity. Barry himself had a shoulder badly shattered by grape-shot and had to go to his cabin for attention at the hands of the ship's surgeon. Scarce had he got there than a lucky hit from one of the brigs carried away the American flag from the masthead of the *Alliance*.

Barry heard an English hail from across the water, to know if the disappearance of the flag meant the frigate had struck. But at that moment, with everything apparently lost, Barry felt his ship suddenly lurch—lightly enough, but unmistakably. Seaman as he was, he knew well enough what it meant. That lurch meant a breeze. And sure enough, within a little while the *Alliance* had gained steerage way.

Barry knew just what to do now to turn the tables on the Englishmen. Bringing his ship smartly about, he ran her straight between the two brigs with all guns thundering. Then, his men sweating and straining and reloading, he about ship and did it again and again. The play of those powerful broadsides turned the trick. Both the brigs were compelled to strike their flags. Barry went on ranging the seas and striking shrewd blows for his adopted country.

John Dunlop

A LETTER TO HIS BROTHER-IN-LAW, 1785

In this letter written from Philadelphia to his brother-in-law at home in Strabane, County Tyrone, John Dunlop, the Irish-born printer of the American Declaration of Independence, urges his relative to encourage "the young men of Ireland who wish to be free and happy" to embark as quickly as possible for America.

Philadelphia
May 12th, 1785

Dear Brother,

My brother James left this for Kentucky a few weeks ago. I expect him back in the summer. Then perhaps he may take a trip to Ireland. The account he gives of the soil is pleasing but the difficulty of going to it is great from this indeed as the distance is not less [than] thousand miles. And I was there last year and must confess that altho the journey is a difficult one, I did not begrudge the time and labour it cost me. We are told the Parliament of Ireland means to lay restrictions on those who want to come from that country to this. Time will tell whether or no this will answer the purpose they intend. People with a family advanced in life find great difficulties in emigration but the young men of Ireland who wish to be free and happy should leave it and come here as quick as possible. There is no place in the world where a man meets so rich a reward for good conduct and industry as in America. By Mr. Orr who will deliver you this I write your son Billy in answer to a letter he wrote me. Should you think of sending him to this country I will observe your directions in having him taught any business you may point out or if you will leave that to me I will judge the most valuable for him. If you intend he should come, the sooner the better. I wish you would give me some little account of the situation of the house in Strabane, whose hands it is in, where the deeds are and what its value may be.

I am, Dear Sir, your affectionate brother,
John Dunlop

For Mr. Robert Rutherford in Strabane, Ireland

John Doyle

FROM AN IRISH IMMIGRANT'S LETTER TO HIS WIFE, 1818

An Irish immigrant in New York City paints an encouraging picture of life in the new world, assuring his wife that "it's a fine country and a much better place for a poor man than Ireland."

Oh, how long the days, how cheerless and fatiguing the nights since I parted with my Fanny and my little angel. Sea sickness, nor the toils of the ocean, nor the starvation which I suffered, nor the constant apprehension of our crazy old vessel going to the bottom, for ten tedious weeks, could ever wear me to the pitch it has if my mind was easy about you. But when the recollection of you and of my little Ned rushes on my mind with a force irresistible, I am amazed and confounded to think of the coolness with which I used to calculate on parting with my little family even for a day, to come to this *strange* country, which is the grave of the reputations, the morals, and of the lives of so many of our countrymen and countrywomen. . . .

Letter from John Dunlop to Robert Rutherford in Strabane. May 12, 1785. Document T. 1336/1/20. Public Record Office of Northern Ireland, Belfast. Courtesy Trevor Parkhill, Canon Delap and the Deputy Keeper of the Records. *Irish immigrant John Dunlop, the printer of the United States' Declaration of Independence, writes to his brother-in-law back in Ireland, encouraging emigration to the United States.*

We were safely landed in Philadelphia on the 7th of October and I had not so much as would pay my passage in a boat to take me ashore. . . . I, however, contrived to get over, and . . . it was not long until I made out my father, whom I instantly knew, and no one could describe our feelings when I made myself known to him, and received his embraces, after an absence of seventeen years. [The father was a United Irish refugee of 1798]. . . . The morning after landing I went to work to the printing. . . . I think a journeyman printer's wages might be averaged at 7 dollars a week all the year round. . . . I worked in Philadelphia five and one-half weeks and saved 6 pounds, that is counting four dollars to the pound; in the currency of the United States the dollar is worth five shillings Irish. . . . I found the printing and bookbinding overpowered with hands in New York. I remained idle for twelve days in consequence; when finding there was many out of employment like myself I determined to turn myself to something else, seeing that there was nothing to be got by idleness. . . . I was engaged by a bookseller to hawk maps for him at 7 dollars a week. . . . I now had about 60 dollars of my own saved . . . these I laid out in the purchase of pictures on New Year's Day, which I sell ever since. I am doing astonishingly well, thanks be to God, and was able on the 16th of this month to make a deposit of 100 dollars in the bank of the United States.

As yet it's only natural I should feel lonesome in this country, ninety-nine out of every hundred who come to it are at first disappointed. . . . Still, it's a fine country and a much better place for a poor man than Ireland . . . and much as they grumble at first, after a while they never think of leaving it. . . . One thing I think is certain, that if emigrants knew beforehand what they have to suffer for about the first six months after leaving home in every respect, they would never come here. However, an enterprising man, desirous of advancing himself in the world, will despise everything for coming to this free country, where a man is allowed to thrive and flourish without having a penny taken out of his pocket by government; no visits from tax gatherers, constables or soldiers, every one at liberty to act and speak as he likes provided he does not hurt another . . .

Walt Whitman

"Old Ireland"

Walt Whitman (1819–1892), American poet and journalist, grew up in Brooklyn, New York and worked as a printer before gaining recognition as a writer. His most famous collection of poems Leaves of Grass *was published for the first time in 1855, and has been constantly revised and reprinted.*

———————

Far hence amid an isle of wondrous beauty,
Crouching over a grave an ancient sorrowful mother,
Once a queen, now lean and tatter'd seated on the ground,
Her old white hair drooping dishevel'd round her shoulders,
At her feet fallen an unused royal harp,
Long silent, she too long silent, mourning her shrouded hope and heir,
Of all the earth her heart most full of sorrow because most full of love.
Yet a word ancient mother,
You need crouch there no longer on the cold ground with forehead
    between your knees,
O you need not sit there veil'd in your old white hair so dishevel'd,
For know you the one you mourn is not in that grave,
It was an illusion, the son you love was not really dead,
The Lord is not dead, he is risen again young and strong in another country,
Even while you wept there by your fallen harp by the grave,
What you wept for was translated, pass'd from the grave,
The winds favor'd and the sea sail'd it,
And now with rosy and new blood,
Moves to-day in a new country.

Richard Roche

FROM JOHN BOYLE O'REILLY

An Irish-American Hero

John Boyle O'Reilly (1844–1890), journalist, poet, athlete, lecturer, and true Irishman, fresh from a hair-raising escape from an Australian penal colony, battled for civil rights in the United States in the 19th century. "He is one whom children would choose for their friend, women for their lover, and men for their hero," wrote a columnist in The Boston Post, *and he was called "easily the most distinguished Irishman in America" at his death. Richard Roche is a writer in Ireland today.*

A hero he certainly was—to his family, relatives and neighbours at Dowth, near where he was born in 1844; to his Fenian comrades who saw him enlist in the 10th Hussars at Dundalk with the express purpose of recruiting the 100 men in his regiment into his secret revolutionary organisation, only to be arrested, court-martialled and sentenced to death; to his fellow-felons who rejoiced in the commutation of that sentence to 20 years' in a penal colony; to the convicts of that Western Australian Settlement who helped in his escape on a whaler in 1869, and to the many Irish in the United States who welcomed him to that country as a free man and who watched in admiration as he became one of the most famed journalists in Boston, editor and owner of the Boston 'Pilot' and 'the foremost spokesman of his generation' (as he has been described by William Shannon in *The American Irish*).

John Boyle O'Reilly used his agile pen not only in the cause of fellow Irish-Americans but also in defence of the rights of Negroes, Jews and American Indians. 'He seemed to scan the world to search out those who were downtrodden and oppressed,' wrote W. F. P. Stockley. When continual mistreatment of the Indians resulted in the debacle at Little Big Horn in 1876, O'Reilly initiated a campaign for Indian rights in the pages of 'The Pilot.' Almost alone among journalists of the day, he considered Custer not as a martyr but as an ineffective general who had been outsmarted by the Indians. O'Reilly won few friends in that campaign.

He incurred further censure in his defence of Negro rights, yet when he died in 1890 all

A.B. Houghton. *Between Decks in an Emigrant Ship.* Graphic America-Steerage Passengers. 1870. Print. The Metropolitan Museum of Art, Harris Brisbane Dick Fund, 1928.

John Boyle O'Reilly. 19th century. Photograph. Royal Irish Academy, Dublin.

America mourned his passing. His obituary in 'Harper's Weekly,' a journal which had harshly criticised him when alive, said: 'Boyle O'Reilly . . . was easily the most distinguished Irishman in America. He was one of the country's foremost poets, one of its most influential journalists, an orator of unusual power, and he was endowed with such a gift of friendship as few men are blessed with . . . '

Some years before his untimely death, Boyle O'Reilly had written a letter to a friend in Ireland, Rev. James Anderson, an Augustinian who was stationed in Drogheda and later in Dublin:

'I may never go to Drogheda' (the letter said), 'but I send my love to the very fields and trees along the Boyne from Drogheda to Slane. Some time for my sake, go out to Dowth alone, and go up on the moat, and look across the Boyne, over to Rosnaree to the Hill of Tara and Newgrange, and Knowth, and Slane and Mellifont, and Oldbridge, and you will see there the pictures that I carry forever in my brain and heart—vivid as the last day I looked on them. If you go into the old graveyard at Dowth, you will find my initials cut on a stone on the wall of the old church . . . this is from the side of the church nearest the Boyne. I remember cutting 'J. B. O'R.' on a stone with a nail, thirty years ago. I should like to be buried just under that spot, and please God, perhaps I may be . . . '

Boyle O'Reilly never saw those scenes again, nor did he have his wish to be buried at Dowth. He was buried in Holyhood Cemetery, Brookline, where today a massive boulder and plaque mark the grave. The Anderson letter, however, did serve ultimately to mark the exact site on which was erected in 1903 a Celtic cross with an inscription in Irish. In translation it reads: 'John Boyle O'Reilly, hero, poet, orator, true Irishman, lovable, famous. He endured great torment at the hands of the big crow on behalf of Ireland. He had always hoped in his heart to be buried in this spot among the hills and plains where he was born and which he loved so dearly. God grant eternal rest to the soul of one who enhanced the reputation of his country. Amen.'

William D. Griffin

FROM THE BOOK OF IRISH AMERICANS
"The Irishness of Billy the Kid"

Henry McCarty (1859–1881) was born in New York City, and grew up to become Billy the Kid, famed outlaw of the American West. Billy claimed to have killed over twenty people before he was shot down at the age of twenty-one by Sheriff Pat Garrett. In this essay, William D. Griffin's story of Billy the Kid becomes a saga with Irish overtones.

Billy the Kid is the ultimate American outlaw. With the possible exception of Jesse James, no other desperado of the Old West is so widely known. He has been the subject of countless books, magazine articles, stage reproductions, and no fewer than forty motion pictures. He has been portrayed as everything from a pathological killer to a misunderstood young rebel.

What is rarely noted about this famous frontier figure is his Irishness. The facts of his biography bristle with Irish names and contacts. At an uncertain date and place, he was born to a "jolly Irishwoman" named Catherine McCarty. Many reference works assert that he was the product of the Irish slums of New York's Lower East Side. Nothing is known for certain about his father, whose name may have been McCarty, since Catherine is usually referred to as Mrs. McCarty. At any event, her child, known as Henry McCarty and presumably born around 1860, was raised in various Midwestern towns. After the marriage of his mother to William Antrim (presumably also of Irish origin), the boy was sometimes known as Billy Antrim, Jr.

The legends surrounding the early boyhood of Billy the Kid, as he came to be known, suggest everything from a bright, amiable lad to an incipient juvenile delinquent. Whatever the truth of the matter, he was scarcely into his teens before trouble started. After killing a man named Frank Cahill, he stole a horse from a neighbor named Murphy and fled into the mountains. Following many adventures with bandits and Indians, he ended up in Lincoln County, New Mexico. There his associates were men like O'Keefe, O'Folliard, and McCloskey. By this time he was using the name William Bonney.

Billy found himself in the midst of a power struggle between rival landowning and business factions, a struggle that came to be known as the Lincoln County War. He and his friends attached themselves to one Tunstall, a rancher who had befriended the young fugitive and become a father figure to him. Tunstall was the archenemy of an "Irish mafia" headed by Laurence Murphy, a native of Wexford, and the Galway-born James Dolan. These men, who had come west as soldiers during the Civil War, controlled the sheriff, William Brady, and a gang of deputized thugs—Riley, Boyle, etc.

The quarrel between these parties led to the assassination of Tunstall by a posse, and the reprisal killing of Sheriff Brady by Billy. The conflict raged on between 1878 and 1880, finally requiring the intervention of the army. Billy and his comrades gradually passed from revenge-taking into banditry, although regarded by many as being in the Robin Hood tradition of resisting oppression. Finally, in 1881, Billy was trapped and killed by the new sheriff, Patrick Garrett.

Beyond all of these Hibernian surnames, there is something very Irish about the whole epic

A Few Good Men are Wanted. Civil War recruiting poster. New York Historical Society.

of Billy the Kid. The story of the warrior youth who comes out of the wilderness to take part in a struggle between battling clans is reminiscent of ancient Irish tales. So too is his implacable quest for revenge against those who killed his "father," including the slaying of the slayer. The band of comrades, with a price on their heads, defying all odds and enjoying the support of the countryfolk, raises echoes of the Irish experience. And, at the end, there is the martyrdom of the young hero, who goes to his death unarmed (Billy was not carrying a gun) as if welcoming his doom. Whatever the prosaic reality of Henry McCarty's life and death, the story of Billy the Kid, romanticized over the generations, has attained a sagalike quality that gives it a peculiarly Irish aura.

Mary Ann Larkin

"Immigrant Daughter's Song"

Mary Ann Larkin, born in 1945 in Pittsburgh, Pennsylvania to Irish-American parents, is a poet and teacher living in Washington, D.C. A book of her poems, The Coil of Her Skin, *was published in 1982.*

All gone,
the silver-green silk of time
winding down centuries
of custom and kinship
the pouring of the sea
the stars, bright pictures
on the slate of night,
the moon stamping forever
the spire of the church
on the sand,
bird-song, wind-song, mother-song
Even time itself changed
to a ticking, a dot on a line

Customs of grace and gentleness gone
name-saying
and knowing
who begat who
and when and where
and who could work
and who could sing
and who would pray
and who would not
and where the fish ran
and the wild plums hid
and how the old mothers
fit their babies' fingers
to the five-flowered hollows
of blue ladyfingers
And whose father fought whose
with golden swords
a thousand years ago
at Ballyferriter
on the strand below the church

All gone
changed from a silken spool unwinding
to rooms of relics and loss
behind whose locked doors
I dream
not daring to wake

Pete Hamill

FROM THE GIFT

Pete Hamill, born in Brooklyn in 1935, is a columnnist for the New York Post. *In* The Gift, *published in 1972, Hamill remembers the voice of his father "singing about some long-gone green island and his own sweet youth" more than twenty years earlier. He longs to feel his connection to this man and his heritage. Hamill, now a young man home from the service on Christmas leave, finds that connection with his father.*

I looked into the window of Diamond's Bar and Grill on Ninth Street; my father seldom went there any more, but I thought it might be one of those late Fridays when he was traveling. There were a few old men at the far end of the dark bar, but my father wasn't there. Fitzgerald's, on the corner of Tenth Street, was a bright, high-ceilinged place, all polished wood and tile floors. It was a whiskey drinkers' bar, a place for cops and firemen and iron-workers, and before I went away I had started going there. My father didn't go there much. His bar was Rattigan's on Eleventh Street, and it was a place where I had not gone since I was twelve, when I had been stashed in a booth in the back to drink ginger ale with a maraschino cherry and consume most of a bowl of pretzels. Rattigan's was their club: the club of the older men, my father's people, the guys who had come back from World War II, the hard drinkers, the brawlers, the guys who had been, as they said, in the country for a visit. It was across the street from where we lived, and on summer evenings, the bar sounds would roar through the nights: shouting over baseball, angry arguments over politics (they were almost all Democrats there), the boisterous entrance of wives in search of husbands, fierce resistance to outsiders, and through the nights, my father's voice.

That voice, rough-edged, sometimes harsh, drifted up to me through all those summer nights while I tried to sleep in the small room with the bunk beds that I shared with my brother Tommy. The songs were always about Ireland, about Galway Bay, and the strangers who came and tried to teach us their ways; about Patty McGinty's Goat and My Old Scalara Hat and the Night That Rafferty's Pig Ran Away; about Kevin Barry and the Bold Fenian Men, about Innisfree and Tipperary, about Irish men fighting British guns with pikes; songs of laughter, songs of the Green Glens of Antrim, where he had been born, songs of young men who had crossed oceans and chosen exile. Sometimes, in the summer, with the whole house asleep, I would crawl out onto the fire escape, and lie there—eight, ten, twelve, fourteen years old— looking down and across the avenue, looking at the Rattigan's sign hanging out over the tavern, the door open to the night, and hear my father's voice singing there, for strangers and friends, as year faded into year, all years the same, singing about some long-gone green island and his own sweet youth. Across all those summers, just once, I wanted him to sing them to me.

And so on this night, back on the avenue and heading for home, I wanted somehow to see him. I wanted him to see me in my uniform, wanted to have him hug me and buy me a drink, wanted to hear the songs.

* * *

"What was the old country like?"

He looked at me, his eyes wary, and shook his head. "To hell with the old country," he said.

He drained the glass quickly.

"Hit me again, George," he said, sliding the glass a few inches. He looked at me and made an odd little disparaging movement with his hand.

"Ireland . . ."

"I'm serious, Dad. What was it like, when you were, you know, my age?"

"It was a bloody mess."

"Did you kill anyone?"

"What do you mean, kill anybody?"

He looked behind him when he said it, to see where Joe Whitmore was standing. Joe was playing shuffleboard.

"I mean, you were in the IRA."

"I was."

"Well, I thought maybe, well, you might have—"

COLORPLATE 80

Style of NATHANIEL GROGAN. *Emigrants at Cork.* c. 1820. Oil on canvas. 24 x 35⁷/₁₆ in. (61 x 90 cm). Department of Irish Folklore, University College, Dublin. *These Irish citizens emigrating before the famine are obviously not in desperate straits.*

COLORPLATE 81

St. Patrick's Day Parade in America: Union Square, New York. 1870s. Lithograph. Museum of the City of New York. The J. Clarence Davies Collection. *The sheer size of this parade gives some indication of the number of Irish immigrants in New York in the late 19th century.*

COLORPLATE 82

JAMES SHANNON. *Jungle Tales*. 1895. Oil on canvas. 33¼ x 44¾ in. (87 x 113.7 cm).
The Metropolitan Museum of Art. Arthur Hoppock Hearn Fund.

COLORPLATE 83

SAMUEL WAUGH. *The Battery, the Bay and Harbor of New York.* c. 1855. Oil on canvas. 99¹/₈ x 198 in.
(251.7 x 503 cm). Museum of the City of New York. Gift of Mrs. Robert M. Littlejohn.

COLORPLATE 84

Rockwell Kent. *Shipwreck*. 20th century. Oil on canvas. Courtesy of the Rockwell Kent Legacies and the Rockwell Kent Gallery, PSUC Plattsburgh, New York.

COLORPLATE 85

JAMES FITZGERALD. *Connemara Ponies*. 20th century. Oil on canvas. Courtesy Anne and Edgar Hubert.

COLORPLATE 86

St. Patrick's Day Parade, Fifth Avenue, New York. 1987. Photograph. AP/Wide World Photo.

"Nobody got killed who didn't deserve it."

"You mean the British?"

"Those bastards deserved it."

"What about the priests?"

"Worse," he said.

And then Joe Mullins was there, and Whitmore was back from the shuffleboard machine, and the music was louder as the bar grew more crowded. The snow was still falling thinly, driven by the wind. They started to talk about guys they knew, someone who had run off, leaving his wife and four kids behind, a beer racket that was going on at Diamond's on New Year's Eve. That son of a bitch O'Malley. The ballplayers oughtta quit. Who the hell does he think he is? They oughtta lock that bastard up. They moved around my father, between me and him, and some of them talked to me, the same questions about the food and the training and where was I going. My father moved among them, laughing, drinking, moving with the flow of the bar. After a while he came back, and had another one with me. The beer was getting to him. He reached over and squeezed my left leg.

"Christ," he said, "I wish I had your legs."

And I loved him in that moment; wanted to put my arm around him, hold him, tell him that the leg didn't matter, and being poor didn't matter, none of it mattered. He was there, still there, he wasn't on relief, he wasn't begging in subways, he had resisted, he hadn't give up. I touched him, and then Red Cioffi yelled from down the bar.

"Hey, Billy, give us a song!"

My father pointed at the clock. "It's too early, Red."

"Too early, my ass. It's Christmas Eve. Hey, George, turn that goddamn radio off."

"Maybe Billy don't wanna sing," George said.

"Don't wanna sing, my ass."

George turned the radio off, and my father started to sing.

> *"Now Mister Patrick McGinty*
> *An Irishman of note.*
> *He fell into a fortune.*
> *And he bought himself a goat."*

"That's the way, Bill," Red yelled. "Go get 'em."

> *"'A goat's milk,' said Patty.*
> *'I think I'll have me fill.'*
> *But when he got the nanny home—*
> *He found it was a bill."*

The song brought him out of himself and into himself at the same time, the face shining and young and careless, alone on the stage. And then song followed song, full of the things I had wanted him to tell me, all the answers there in the texture of the songs, in the lonely somber tone, filled up with exile and anger and longing, all the things he had carried with him across the sea. All the things that came together that Sunday on a winter field in Brooklyn.

> *"Castles are sacked in war*
> *Chieftains are scattered far*
> *Truth is a fixed star!*
> *Eileen, aroon."*

I cheered with the others and hugged him and bought some beers, and he stood there pleased, standing in the gabardine raincoat, and began to sing, "Come Back, Patty Reilly."

> *"The boy is a man now,*
> *He's toil-worn, he's tough,*
> *Whispers come over the sea . . ."*

Singing the words, he tipped his glass to me and winked. I joined him at the end.

> *"Oh, come back, Patty Reilly.*
> *To Bally James Duff,*
> *Oh, come back, Patty Reilly, to me."*

Patrick Fenton

FROM THE NEW YORK TIMES, DECEMBER 3, 1983

"What Flaherty Was"

A remembrance of Irish writers who came from the Park Slope section of Brooklyn, of "a special time and place in New York when immigrants worked in docks and factories and their children dreamed of ways to escape the neighborhood."

SCHELL and HOGAN. *The Construction of the Brooklyn Bridge* (The Brooklyn Ascent to the Bridge Tower). Drawing for *Harper's Weekly,* March 1877. Museum of the City of New York.

In the late 1940s, when I was growing up in the tenements of Seventeenth Street in the Park Slope section of Brooklyn, the death of Joe Flaherty's father was always spoken about in whispers. It would be winter, and on the kitchen table there would be jelly jars filled with rye whiskey. I would hear my father talk about how they found the body of Joe Flaherty's father, who was a union president on the Red Hook docks, floating in the Gowanus Canal. When I was older and started to hitch rides on the back of fruit trucks to the public swimming pool down in Red Hook, I always thought about the story as the trucks went by the canal.

When Joe Flaherty died six weeks ago, the obituaries praised him as a writer. That he was, but his death also summoned in me memories of a special time and place in New York when immigrants worked the docks and factories and their children dreamed of ways to escape the neighborhood.

Joe Flaherty dropped out of high school when he was sixteen, and eventually joined Local 1266 of the Grain Handlers Association, his father's old union. He took the toughest job on the docks, humping bags of grain out of the holds of ships. He grew up just a few blocks from me, down near the Park Circle section of Brooklyn. My mother, who was born in Ireland, used to take long walks with his mother through Park Slope. If life wasn't full of turns and twists, this story would have ended there. As it turned out, we both became writers.

The odds of growing up in that section of Brooklyn then and becoming a writer were very slim. The Park Slope of that time had no resemblance to the Park Slope of today. Seventeenth Street was once the hub of one of the greatest Irish working-class neighborhoods in Brooklyn. It was filled with large immigrant families, some with as many as thirteen kids. The fathers drove trolley cars for a living, worked behind the stick of Irish bars and labored in the factories of Industry City, a line of gray factory buildings that went on for miles on the Brooklyn waterfront.

If it weren't for a weekly newspaper, *The Park Slope News*, Joe Flaherty might have simply made his peace with the old neighborhood and settled down to a life of cold mornings on the docks or midnight shifts down in Quaker Maid, one of the factories of Industry City. The paper was unique in that it encouraged some of the talent buried in that lower-class Irish neighborhood. Although I too quit high school, I spent three years writing for *The Park Slope News* about bar fights and Saturday nights in the tenements of Seventeenth Street.

Joe Flaherty wrote for *The Park Slope News* before I came there, and eventually had a piece published in the *Village Voice*. *The News* was one of those great places that you hated to leave, but once you got published outside the paper it was time to go. After a few years, I managed to get published in *New York Magazine*, and like Flaherty I moved on.

I knew who Joe Flaherty was when I was growing up in Park Slope, but I didn't meet him until I was about thirty. He was living up in Greenwich Village at the time and he invited me to his apartment to talk. He showed me a scrapbook with all the stuff he had published. On the front of it was an old picture of him when he worked down on the docks. "If you really want to find out about this city," he told me, "go out in the streets and talk to some of the guys who cut meat for a living. Talk to a guy who makes a living behind the stick. Go talk to a guy who drives a cab. They'll tell you what's really wrong with this city. They know more about it than any politician."

A few years after that, I talked to someone about doing a radio show on some of the Irish writers who came from that working-class section of Park Slope. (Pete Hamill grew up in the same area.) I wondered what it would be like to get myself, Joe Flaherty, Pete Hamill, and even Jack Deacy (who came from Bay Ridge, but who also wrote for *The Park Slope News*) to talk about writers with talent being encouraged to write even though they have no formal education. Was that chance being offered to writers from the South Bronx or to writers from whatever neighborhood is left down in Red Hook? I didn't think so.

The radio people liked the idea and asked me to put it on paper. After reading the obituaries of Joe Flaherty, I was sorry I never did that. He was probably one of the last writers to come out of the world of tenements and factories and to make it in this computer age as a newspaperman. He came from "the guys who cut meat for a living," "the guys who work behind the stick." Like Walt Whitman, he was one of "the roughs." Had he lived a little longer, he would have written a novel about our old neighborhood that would have stood up against the works of James T. Farrell.

Harry Golden

FROM ONLY IN AMERICA

"How Tammany Hall Did It"

Harry Golden, publisher, editor, and writer, was born and raised on New York's Lower East Side, home to most of the immigrants—Irish, Jewish, and Italian—at the turn of the century. His distinctive publication, The Carolina Israelite, *has been called the most quoted newspaper of personal journalism. Here Golden turns his thoughts to Irish-American politics and Big Tim Sullivan.*

———————

> *Tammany, Tammany,*
> *Big Chief sits in his tepee,*
> *Cheering braves to victory.*
> *Tammany, Tammany,*
> *Swamp 'em, swamp 'em,*
> *Get the wampum,*
> *Taaammmaaannieeee.*

Big Tim Sullivan was the Tammany Hall power on the Bowery of New York. He was a tremendous man, physically, and a tremendous man, politically. He made a fortune out of his

Departure from Home.
Wood engraving from
Harper's Weekly, June
26, 1859. Museum of the
City of New York.

position as a Tammany district leader—principally from "concessions" to gambling houses—
and "Raines Law" hotels.

What was a "Raines Law" hotel? John Raines, a member of the New York State
Legislature, was a strict Prohibitionist who unwittingly established hundreds of brothels in
New York.

Raines tried and tried, in the State Legislature, to restrict the use of Demon Rum. Finally
he succeeded in putting across a bill prohibiting the sale of intoxicating liquors on Sunday
throughout the State, *except in hotels.* So what happened? Every saloon became a "hotel."
The saloonkeeper knocked out a few walls upstairs and advertised rooms for rent. And what
decent family would occupy rooms above a saloon? So pretty soon the rooms were rented out
to prostitutes and the money just rolled in for everybody concerned (according to the Lexow
and the Mazet investigations).

The police got their share, the politician his cut; the saloonkeeper was able to buy a five-
thousand-dollar pew in his church, and good old Mr. Raines had his "Prohibition" on Sunday.

Well, what I started out to tell you was about Big Tim Sullivan, as colorful a character as
ever wielded political power in this republic. During one of the periodic investigations which

revealed some of his vast wealth, Big Tim made a speech to his constituents: "The trouble with reformers is that they don't know our traditions down here.

"That's why the reformers think just because I have a little money, there must be something wrong. I say 'to hell with reform.'" The crowd cheered. "And," continued Sullivan, "if I have done wrong, I have always thought I have done right, and I was always good to the poor." The women in the crowd wept openly and most of the men were dabbing their wet cheeks with handkerchiefs.

Big Tim gave us kids on the East Side a trip up the Hudson River every year. A trip to Bear Mountain; and the name "Big Tim" was blessed in thousands of households.

In his report to the Tammany Hall chieftain, Richard Croker, at the end of one election day, Big Tim Sullivan wrote: "Boss, Grover Cleveland, 938—Benjamin Harrison, 3. This is one vote more than I expected Harrison to get, but I'll find the guy who did it if it's the last thing I do."

Big Tim's greatest contribution to Tammany power was his organization of "repeaters." He had hundreds of Bowery bums organized in one or two places on election day, and he waited for the reports—"The Fifth District needs two hundred," etc.—and, as each "requirement" came in, Big Tim dispatched a truckload of the required number of bums to the polling place where a henchman went down the line and gave each the name under which he was to vote. The names were usually of those voters who had died between registration day and the election, or of those voters who had not yet voted an hour before the closing of the polls.

Big Tim also had about fifty student barbers working for him on every election day. These barbers performed a great service for Tammany. Here is how it worked. Along about August Big Tim sent word around the Bowery flophouses for the bums to let their beards grow. By election day, Big Tim had at his disposal several hundred Bowery bums, each with a full-grown beard. First, each bum would vote with a full beard under one name. He would then rush to one of the stand-by barbers who immediately clipped off the chin fuzz. So then the bum voted under another name with sideburns, like the Emperor Francis Joseph of the Austro-Hungarian Empire. Then he would rush back to the barber who shaved off the sideburns, and now the bum would vote for the third time with just a moustache; and finally that came off and he would go forth to vote for a fourth time—plain-faced, as Tammany called it.

For this day's work the bum got one dollar, three meals, a pint of whiskey, and, of course, a lesson in civics and good government.

Big Tim and the other Tammany district leaders were careful to keep in the good graces of the foreign-born. The Tammany sachems had henchmen roaming the districts looking for bar mitzvahs, weddings, fiestas, and funerals, but mostly funerals. The presence of the district leader at one of these functions made the voters very proud and they talked about it for years to come. "Just think, Patrick Divver, the leader, *himself*, was at the funeral of my father, God rest his soul."

Sometimes there was lots of trouble at these functions when two Tammany factions were fighting each other, as often happened. Big Tim Sullivan, Tom Foley, and Patrick Divver attended all the funerals and christenings they could find. Each leader had a man stationed at the marriage-license bureau to telephone whenever an Italian couple from the district came to get married. They had a whole system of espionage to find out what kind of present each camp was buying the couple. If the word went down that Foley is giving earrings to the bride, then Divver would give earrings *and* a set of cups and saucers.

Tammany leaders rarely made speeches. The henchmen went down the line getting out the vote and the "repeaters," and that was all that was necessary. Once, however, the Bowery Congressman, Tim Campbell, did make a speech. His opponent in the race was an Italian named Rinaldo. Tim's only political speech was: "There is two bills before the country—one is the Mills bill and the other is the McKinley bill. The Mills bill is for free trade with everything free; the McKinley bill is for protection with nothing free. Do you want everything free, or do you want to pay for everything?

"Having thus disposed of the national issue, I will now devote myself to the local issue, which is the Dago, Rinaldo. He is from Italy. I am from Ireland. Are you in favor of Italy or Ireland?"

James Carroll

FROM MORTAL FRIENDS

Boston Irish Politics

James Carroll lives in Boston, the setting for this scene from his sprawling novel about Colman Brady, Irish farmer immigrant to the United States. At this point in the story, Brady is right hand man to James Michael Curley in his race for mayor of Boston. The feisty Irish Catholic Curley speaks to his supporters at a political rally in the Brahmin aristocratic Louisburg Square.

Election Day was the second Tuesday in September.

The rally for Curley at Louisburg Square was set for Sunday afternoon.

Brady had made arrangements that satisfied him. Hoping to avoid any incident, he had secured permission from Chief McGrath to close the streets adjoining Louisburg Square. A small platform was set up at the intersection of Willow and Mt. Vernon. Part of the crowd could thus be kept on the closed-off public street, and Curley himself would address them from city property. With any luck, Brady told himself when it was all arranged, by Sunday afternoon it would be raining.

But Indian summer came that day. The gold warm air descended upon the city and blew softly through its streets, waking up the bright, crisp leaves that kicked over, stretched, made ready to fall. A gaily colored crowd swarmed across Boston Common from the subways at Park Street and Arlington. There were women merrily pushing baby buggies and men, walking in clumps, dressed for the occasion in dark suits and ties and soft tweed hats. Some men had their pockets turned inside out. As they came down from Joy or came up Mt. Vernon from Charles, moving evenly, like balls in their slots into the Beacon Hill reserve, they gave off a certain tangible trepidation, mingled with pride and eagerness. Boston policemen funneled the crowd into the Willow Street intersection as far as the platform. The people cheerfully greeted the police, who returned their salutations merrily. There seemed to be no inclination to invade the precincts of the square itself.

Brady was standing on Mt. Vernon Street up the hill several dozen yards, nearly in front of the Otis mansion, with Chief McGrath.

"So far so good, Chief, eh?"

"This takes the biscuit, Brady, if you ask me. Of course nobody asks me, damn fool thing to do."

"Well, with luck we'll keep them where they are and it'll be a grand picnic of a finale for the mayor."

"A finale for me if we *don't* keep them there."

"Aw, Chief, what's the harm?" Brady had resigned himself. He had the capacity to draw his feelings smartly up behind his self-interest. He was drawing easily on a long thin cigar. He was wearing his white linen suit. The ends of his tie made a perfect equation halfway down his shirt.

"The harm is they'll get bashed, and *then* watch."

"Restraint, Chief. We must all exercise great restraint."

"I got to work this precinct, don't forget. I'm not worth a plugged nickel up here if these people think I won't protect them."

"I don't see any signs of them. Where the hell are they? They must have all gone to Gloucester for the weekend."

"Wouldn't you? But don't kid yourself. They're watching every move, right now."

Brady scanned the windows of the houses opposite. There were no signs of life in them. He turned toward the square. A third-floor curtain fluttered and caught his eye. He saw a hand withdraw and disappear.

The nineteenth-century houses were stony and mute, but they seemed to be staring down their bay windows—like noses—on the gathering throng indifferently.

"Just hope to high heavens," the officer said, "they keep their Pinkertons out."

"That's your job."

"No, it ain't, Brady. They've the right. Unless I get a warrant, they can have *me* thrown off that square. Just hope James Michael keeps his hat on, that's all."

Curley seemed oblivious to the fact that the rally was not occurring quite on the exact turf of Louisburg Square. He was buoyed by the tremendous cheer the crowd gave him when he arrived, and he walked happily through their midst, squeezing hundreds of hands as he went. The people roared at the sight of him. He cut a grand figure in his velvet-collared Chesterfield coat and striped pants. He mounted the platform and, with his back to the empty Louisburg Square, he raised his megaphone to the crowd who were pressed together along the entire length of Willow Street and up and down Mt. Vernon. He began speaking through the cone, but dropped it and went on with his rich, sonorous voice at its loudest. The people were attentive, even rapt.

"Here we are gathered in the very center of the power and the glory that was in the beginning, is now and—after Tuesday—never shall be again!"

The crowd roared.

"This is the center of the descendancy of those citizens who came over on the Mayflower to *de*-flower the New World! Well, their bloom has faded and we have come to pluck them! I am the vinedresser and *they* are the vine, and I say it's time to cut them down!"

Jets of approval and laughter followed one another out of the convulsed crowd.

"The Massachusetts of the Puritan is dead! Dead as Caesar! Dead as ancient Rome! But there is no need to mourn the fact, because their successors are here! Their successors are the Irish!"

"Hurray for Curley!" someone called, *"Erin go bragh!"*

"And the Irish," he hollered, "are not cowed by the phony finery of Blue-blood Hill! The Irish had letters and learning and culture and high civilization when the ancestors of the Puritans were savages running half-naked through the forests of Britain and relieving themselves squatting over lice-infested logs!"

The assembly interrupted him again, bellowing and clapping.

"It has taken the Irish to make Massachusetts a fit place to live in and it will take the Irish to make Boston a decent and honorable city at last. For never forget—as history will never forget—that the wealth and comfort surrounding us here was stolen by scoundrels who got rich selling opium to the Chinese and rum to the Indians and guns to the Kaiser and slaves to the plutocrats down south!"

At that Curley turned half away from the crowd and raised his fist to the upper stories of the great Bulfinch mansion of the Otis family, and he hollered, "You're nothing but a pack of second-story workers, milkbottle robbers, and doormat thieves! I'll be elected mayor of Boston and you don't like it! Well, here I am! Does any one of you bums want to step down here and make anything of it?"

As the gathering egged him on with its cheering, Curley slowly turned in a semicircle as if looking for a taker to his challenge. That was how his gaze came to fall on Louisburg Square.

"And look at that!" He pointed to the enclosed park. "Their little game reserve!" He leaned forward and with great show read the nearby sign in a voice booming with contempt. "'Private Property, Public access at the discretion of the residents!' Well, the hell with that! Come on!"

Curley leapt down off the platform and led a swarm across Mt. Vernon Street. The high iron spikes deterred the first arrivals from entering the park itself, but when several boys scampered up and over the fence and down onto the lawn, there was a momentary gasp as if a sacred space had been violated. But quickly they were followed by dozens of others, who were over the hurdle and into the forbidden precinct. A squad of large men carefully raised Curley himself to the level of the fence top and handed him over so that he too had gone in. The crowd was delirious.

Curley raised his hands for quiet.

With great drama, his chin thrust high, his chest out, his fist raised, he announced, "We claim this land for the people of the city of Boston!" He paused. The crowd was absolutely still. He glared up at the grand houses and cried, "What are you going to do about it?"

The question hung in the silence.

Not a curtain stirred in the windows. There was not a sign that anyone had noticed that Louisburg Square had been violated. The great residences stood mute and detached. Soon the silence itself began to dissipate the effect of Curley's challenge.

He knew it, and rather than let the impact of the silence grow, he hollered again, "Well? What are you going to do about it?"

Nothing.

Only the leaves of the huge elms moved. The crowd was transfixed as if suddenly witness to a great spectacle. But it was the opposite of spectacle.

Curley had thrust his hand into the bowels of the sleeping beast, but the beast did not wince. As far as anyone could tell, all of the residents of Louisburg Square were still snug in their late Sunday naps.

"Perfect," Brady muttered to himself; "perfect." He stifled an admiring smile and chastised himself again for disloyalty. But they were so much better at it. They responded to Curley's demagoguery with nothing, with nothingness itself. Perfect. Curley would be elected easily Tuesday, and he would be approaching the peak of his power. But he had just been defeated again. Drastically defeated. Brady wondered if he knew it.

A bell began to toll, a church bell, and almost simultaneously, the door to the large mansion at the end of the square opened and six full-habited nuns walked out in single file, each clasping a prayer book. They walked single file down the hill past the rally as if no one were there. The people were Catholics nearly to a person, and they stared slack-jawed at the line of nuns. The nearest Catholic church was St. Joseph's in the West End. What were nuns doing on Beacon Hill?

Brady leaned into Chief McGrath and said in a low voice, "What the hell are they doing up here among the Freemasons?"

"That's their convent right there," McGrath said, pointing to the mansion. "St. Margaret's."

Sure enough, there was a yard-high cross engraved over the lintel. Why hadn't Brady noticed it before? "Convent?" Brady was shocked. Nothing he knew of Boston made sense if there was a convent of nuns on Louisburg Square. "A convent of Catholic nuns?"

McGrath laughed. He enjoyed the joke of it before Brady understood. "They're Protestants," the chief said. "They're going down to the Advent Church for evensong."

Brady was stunned. Whoever heard of Protestant nuns? The Advent—the Church of England?

Its bell still tolled.

Then Brady got it. Curley's crowd was silent, mystified, totally confused. The nuns ignored them absolutely, as if no one were there.

"Perfect," Brady said again. This time he smiled.

William V. Shannon

FROM THE AMERICAN IRISH

"President John F. Kennedy"

William Shannon was a member of the editorial board of The New York Times *and Ambassador to Ireland. In this article he analyzes the election of John F. Kennedy as President in terms of what it meant to Irish Americans, and examines the impact of his assassination, when Kennedy "joined the company of lost leaders—Michael Collins, Charles Stewart Parnell, Wolfe Tone, Patrick Sarsfield, and all the others, reaching back in an unbroken line through the mists of defeat and old pain."*

John Kennedy's election was charged with a special significance for the American Irish. The winning of the Presidency culminated and consolidated more than a century of Irish political activity. It wiped away the bitterness and disappointment of Al Smith's defeat in 1928; it removed any lingering sense of social inferiority and insecurity. To a people for whom politics had long been one of their chosen professions, the election of Kennedy was a deeply satisfying accomplishment in which every Irishman could take vicarious pleasure.

The shift in values implicit in the change from Dwight Eisenhower, conservative and relying upon the business community, to John Kennedy, liberal and dependent on the political and intellectual professions, signified another kind of Irish success. The new President and his administration bodied forth in full and accurate form the three main themes of the history of the Irish in this country: the poetry, the power, and the liberalism. Kennedy was a man of words, an inveterate reader, an orator of considerable power, a companion and admirer of men of the highest intellectual attainments, a man of good taste, sensibility, and imagination. . . .

The search for power has been the main motif of Irish history in the country. Kennedy was a man of power, who openly pursued the authority of the Presidency, and relished its exercise. Beginning with the first of those who came out of the immigrant ships, the Irish have had an instinct for power and an understanding that political power exists to be used. They made the vocation of politician an honorable one, and used their political machines as one means to lift themselves out of exploitation and poverty. . . .

John Kennedy was an aristocrat and the representative of an American dynasty with all the advantages in life that such an inheritance confers. Although four years younger than Richard Nixon, his Republican opponent for the Presidency, he was, in a sense, twenty years ahead of Nixon from the day he was born because he entered the race of life with that serenity, security from abrasive money worries, and self-confident style that inherited wealth and family prestige can provide.

By the time he was born in May, 1917, his grandfather had been twice mayor of Boston, and his father, a rising young businessman, was already well on the way toward his first million. Young John was brought up to believe that, as a matter of course, all men of his family were successful and that any barrier would come tumbling down if enough energy, brains, and determination were applied to the assault. If an East Boston politician's son could become Ambassador to the Court of St. James's, might not the ambassador's son become President of the United States?

Joseph Kennedy was a classic dynasty-founder, empire-builder type. He had ravenous ambition, cupidity, energy, audacity, and charm. The astonishing thing was that such a man did not break or cow the spirit of his sons. Instead, they inherited his energy and brains, and he successfully instilled in them his exceptional competitive drive. John was the second of four sons. His older brother, Joseph, Jr., who was killed in World War II, and his younger brothers, Robert and Edward, more nearly resembled their father in their outgoing temperament. John, by contrast, was a loner, a self-contained person. It may be that in the intensely competitive family situation he withdrew somewhat into himself, learned to keep his own counsel, and put a layer of insulation between himself and other people. Members of his family cannot remember any instance when he cried or had a tantrum as a child. Likewise, as an adult, he was even-tempered and coolly self-disciplined. He was not cold, and he could be a most charming and companionable man, but there was a part of himself always reserved, kept aloof, not completely dissolved in the chemistry of the situation. That is why long before he became President he was always a dignified figure, though his hair was rumpled and everybody called him "Jack." That is why people sometimes described him as cold, though he had extraordinary emotional intensity and verve.

Kennedy had an excellent mind, and received a quality education at Choate and Harvard. Like many boys from a privileged background, he was not strongly motivated toward winning academic honors. His academic record, therefore, was spotty. In his first years at Harvard, he was probably more concerned with making the swimming team than the dean's list, but he finished strong and graduated in the top half of his class. More important, somewhere along the way he acquired the habit of reading. He was one of the top politicians of his time who regularly read serious books as a form of relaxation. Kennedy had an exceptionally absorptive mind: he soaked up information and remembered it. He was quick and keen at understanding complicated problems, respected learning and expertise, and was at ease with scholars.

It was a happy circumstance for the Irish that Kennedy was a mediocre athlete and became a bookish man. The Irish have contributed more than their share to the national cult of football and to the impoverishing ideal of man as simply a sweaty, locker-room figure. Since too many Irish boys have grown up with the idea that the most important goal in four years of college is not in attaining intellectual excellence but in making the team, it is just as well that Kennedy was a skinny, often sickly 150-pounder, not heavy enough or fast enough to make any varsity team, despite his earnest ambitions. The sports that became popularly associated with Kennedy in the White House—swimming, sailing, and "touch" football—are those in which even women can participate. Physical stamina and physical courage were basic elements in Kennedy's makeup, as his gallant wartime heroism demonstrated, but important as they were, they did not comprise the whole man. Instead of just reading Westerns or detective stories, Kennedy wrote two books and was a regular reader of history, biography, political analysis, and serious novels. Americans are so fact-conscious and so technique-oriented that Kennedy's course in rapid reading and ability to read 1,200 words a minute received more attention than the excellent quality of what it was he read. Nevertheless, his intellectual interests became well-known and provided a useful example. Although the Irish have produced men of letters and learning since the Dark Ages, and innumerable good teachers, neither the American Irish in their picture of themselves nor the popular folklore about the Irish gives much place to them as people who are important for what they do with their minds. Kennedy's intellectual distinction helped change that picture.

Fate intervened three times in Kennedy's early life. His older brother had political ambitions and, if he had not been killed, he would have sought the congressional seat that Kennedy won. Second, Kennedy had a miraculous escape from death as a PT boat skipper in the Pacific. Fate intervened a third time in 1954–1955 when he was critically ill from a war-time back injury. If a delicate operation involving the fusion of two spinal discs had failed, he might have died or been crippled. Instead, he made a complete recovery. Any man can look back at his life and see critical turning points, but Kennedy, as the second son of a family with the highest ambitions and an almost royal sense of destiny and as a man twice near death, had a more than ordinary awareness of fortune's role. This awareness did not instill in him any strain of pessimism or melancholy, both fairly common characteristics of the Irish temper, but strengthened his nerves in times of crisis and imbued him with fatalism. More than most men, he was emotionally prepared for the tragic fate that was his. . . .

Although experts might long dispute about the combination of voters and the strokes of fortune that brought about his narrow victory, John Kennedy in November, 1960, was concerned only with the future. He was determined to be President of all the people. Whether in the exercise of his best abilities he would prove, in Robert Frost's formulation, more Irish or more Harvard was for the future to determine. Yet he was conscious also that he had a special responsibility over and above that of any of his predecessors. The day after his election when a reporter congratulated him on breaking the historic barrier against a Catholic in the White House, Kennedy replied: "No, I have not broken it. I have only been given the opportunity to break it. If I am not a successful President, the barrier will be back higher than ever."

The most significant chapter in the American Irish story was about to begin.

* * *

In the glaring sun of a Dallas afternoon, the nightmare returned. History, which the Irish people on two continents had thought to have mastered for once, asserted its old power with an act of sudden, cruel caprice. John F. Kennedy, their chosen hero, the first Irish Catholic President of the United States, the leader of the free world, a man of intelligence, physical beauty, personal grace, and rare vitality, was dead. Not his sturdy courage nor his coolness in crisis, not his prudent preparations nor his gift for diplomacy had availed him against his enemy. He joined the company of lost leaders—Michael Collins, Terence MacSwiney, Charles Stewart Parnell, Wolfe Tone, Patrick Sarsfield, and all the others reaching back in an unbroken line through the mists of defeat and old pain. He became one with those who "always went forth to battle and . . . always fell." He who wanted so much to cope with real problems and master practical issues became a romantic hero and a tragic martyr; he who had been a leader became a legend. What should have been the Age of Kennedy, "a golden age of poetry and power," became only a brief, shining interlude, measured in days instead of years. The promised land of what was to be now became the forbidden country of what might have been. John Kennedy became one of history's tantalizing if's. He had time only to give a hint of his native power, a glimpse of his developing stature, a preliminary measure of his intended achievement, and then he was gone. Time foreshortened and opportunity foreclosed—this was the essence of John Kennedy's tragedy.

Eugene O'Neill

FROM LONG DAY'S JOURNEY INTO NIGHT

Eugene O'Neill (1888–1953), America's greatest playwright, was the son of the immensely popular Irish-born actor James O'Neill. O'Neill identified strongly with the American

Irish, and was determined to portray the Irish with honesty and without sentiment. In Long Day's Journey Into Night, *he has eloquently laid bare the anguished lives of members of his own family. The play is set in 1912, the year Eugene (Edmund in the play) was diagnosed with tuberculosis, and the year his mother, after a sanitorium cure, relapses into her morphine addiction.*

TYRONE
With guilty resentment.
For God's sake, don't dig up what's long forgotten. If you're that far gone in the past already, when it's only the beginning of the afternoon, what will you be tonight?

MARY
Stares at him defiantly now.
Come to think of it, I do have to drive uptown. There's something I must get at the drugstore.

TYRONE
Bitterly scornful.
Leave it to you to have some of the stuff hidden, and prescriptions for more! I hope you'll lay in a good stock ahead so we'll never have another night like the one when you screamed for it, and ran out of the house in your nightdress half crazy, to try and throw yourself off the dock!

MARY
Tries to ignore this.
I have to get tooth powder and toilet soap and cold cream—
She breaks down pitiably.
James! You mustn't remember! You mustn't humiliate me so!

TYRONE
Ashamed.
I'm sorry. Forgive me, Mary!

MARY
Defensively detached again.
It doesn't matter. Nothing like that ever happened. You must have dreamed it.
He stares at her hopelessly. Her voice seems to drift farther and farther away.
I was so healthy before Edmund was born. You remember, James. There wasn't a nerve in my body. Even traveling with you season after season, with week after week of one-night stands, in trains without Pullmans, in dirty rooms of filthy hotels, eating bad food, bearing children in hotel rooms, I still kept healthy. But bearing Edmund was the last straw. I was so sick afterwards, and that ignorant quack of a cheap hotel doctor—All he knew was I was in pain. It was easy for him to stop the pain.

TYRONE
Mary! For God's sake, forget the past!

MARY
With strange objective calm.
Why? How can I? The past is the present, isn't it? It's the future, too. We all try to lie out of that but life won't let us.
Going on.
I blame only myself. I swore after Eugene died I would never have another baby. I was to blame for his death. If I hadn't left him with my mother to join you on the road, because you wrote telling me you missed me and were so lonely, Jamie would never have been allowed,

when he still had measles, to go in the baby's room.

Her face hardening.

I've always believed Jamie did it on purpose. He was jealous of the baby. He hated him.

As Tyrone starts to protest.

Oh, I know Jamie was only seven, but he was never stupid. He'd been warned it might kill the baby. He knew. I've never been able to forgive him for that.

TYRONE

With bitter sadness.

Are you back with Eugene now? Can't you let our dead baby rest in peace?

MARY

As if she hadn't heard him.

It was my fault. I should have insisted on staying with Eugene and not have let you persuade me to join you, just because I loved you. Above all, I shouldn't have let you insist I have another baby to take Eugene's place, because you thought that would make me forget his death. I knew from experience by then that children should have homes to be born in, if they are to be good children, and women need homes, if they are to be good mothers. I was afraid all the time I carried Edmund. I knew something terrible would happen. I knew I'd proved by the way I'd left Eugene that I wasn't worthy to have another baby, and that God would punish me if I did. I never should have borne Edmund.

TYRONE

With an uneasy glance through the front parlor.

Mary! Be careful with your talk. If he heard you he might think you never wanted him. He's feeling bad enough already without—

MARY

Violently.

It's a lie! I did want him! More than anything in the world! You don't understand! I meant, for his sake. He has never been happy. He never will be. Nor healthy. He was born nervous and too sensitive, and that's my fault. And now, ever since he's been so sick I've kept remembering Eugene and my father and I've been so frightened and guilty—

Then, catching herself, with an instant change to stubborn denial.

Oh, I know it's foolish to imagine dreadful things when there's no reason for it. After all, everyone has colds and gets over them.

Tyrone stares at her and sighs helplessly. He turns away toward the front parlor and sees Edmund coming down the stairs in the hall.

TYRONE

Sharply, in a low voice.

Here's Edmund. For God's sake try and be yourself—at least until he goes! You can do that much for him!

He waits, forcing his face into a pleasantly paternal expression. She waits frightenedly, seized again by a nervous panic, her hands fluttering over the bosom of her dress, up to her throat and hair, with a distracted aimlessness. Then, as Edmund approaches the doorway, she cannot face him. She goes swiftly away to the windows at left and stares out with her back to the front parlor. Edmund enters. He has changed to a ready-made blue serge suit, high stiff collar and tie, black shoes.

With an actor's heartiness.

Well! You look spic and span. I'm on my way up to change, too.

He starts to pass him.

Mary Gordon

FROM THE OTHER SIDE

A Matter of Pride

Mary Gordon, novelist, short story and essay writer, born on Long Island, is a professor of English at Barnard College. In this moving story of Irish immigrant families, self-reliant seventeen-year-old Ellen Costello who has managed her father's grocery store in Ireland for several years, escapes one kind of humiliation at home in Ireland to face another kind on the other side, in America, in service as a lady's maid to a shallow, wealthy Irish-American woman. Ellen's childhood friend Delia meets Ellen's boat at the port of New York, accompanied by her good-natured husband, Jimmy Flaherty.

Delia with her greenhorn's fear, her hiding out among her kind, her terror of the first thing not out of the same bog she came from. "My Jimmy has a cousin has a friend, says there's a place. All ready for you, El, you'd never have a moment's worry." Of course, she took the place, grateful as she was to Delia, and wet behind the ears, not knowing one thing about America, relying on Delia and Jimmy for advice. As good advice as she would have got from their Brendan, who was two when she arrived, or Margaret, who was just six months.

She'd never get over the disgrace of it. Even the words themselves shameful: "in service." And why should she serve? Cleaning the shit of people she was better than? "But, El, you've such a lovely job," Delia would say. "Mrs. Fitzpatrick's lady's maid. I'd give my eye teeth for it. Any girl would, Ellen. All the lovely stuff, the clothes, the hairbrushes. Tell me about those hairbrushes again."

* * *

Claire and James Fitzpatrick. Both of them brought up thinking themselves royalty. The Jesuits, the Madames of the Sacred Heart, the dancing classes for the children of the wealthy Irish so that they might mate. They'd known each other from their cradles, Claire and James Fitzpatrick told Ellen a million times, as if it were a smart remark. It made her sick. "I see you're a good girl, Ellen, and a clever one," Claire Fitzpatrick would say, smiling at Ellen in the mirror while Ellen looked down at the ugly hair, would not meet Mrs. Fitzpatrick's gaze. "Mind that the one does not get in the way of the other." And she'd quote her a poem about the Virgin Mary that was supposed to be clever because the BVM was never mentioned:

And was she clever in her words
Her answers quick and smart?
We know not: we know of the secret love
For her son in her heart.

"I understand from the others you have a quick tongue in your head, and find yourself ready with an answer. But remember, Ellen, a girl in your position can lose everything by forgetting who she is."

"Yes, madame," she would say, refusing in her resoluteness to meet the eye that searched, demanded that she meet it in the glass. I know who I am. And where I've come from. She longed for the relief of the abuse that could come from her own mouth. My father, a gentleman. My education, the Presentation Sisters. And my mother. She would see the mother in these moments, young and running, singing, lifting the towel on the bread dough as she checked its rising. But then it would come to her, the real truth of her mother, silent or gibber-

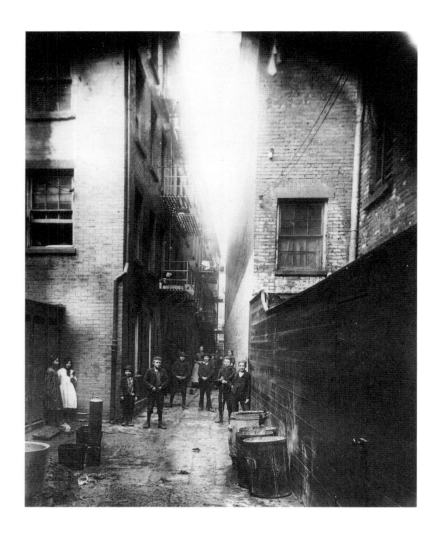

JACOB A. RIIS. *Mullen's Alley,* c. 1890. Photograph. Museum of the City of New York. The Jacob A. Riis Collection, #113.

ing, an animal, no woman now, bearded, with lifeless eyes. Ellen had feared that any slip, any faint hint of her past would reveal the truth of her mother to Claire Fitzpatrick's eye. So she remained above reproach and when Mrs. Fitzpatrick questioned her about her past she made up what she knew the woman wished to hear: the small farm, the countless brothers, cheerful sisters, stoical hardworking father, and her sainted mother, who slaved for the family but was never too busy for a laugh.

"You must think of me as your mother now," Claire Fitzpatrick would say from time to time, in love with herself for her good heart.

"Yes, madame," Ellen would reply. The perfect servant with her eyes kept down because of her emotions: gratitude and missing home. And in her heart: "I'd slap the face of you for that suggestion if there was a way on earth I could. I'd tear out your ugly hair. I'd leave you here, bald and disfigured from the blows of my fist on your face. You'd be unable even to find your underclothes, so little do you know the workings of your own life. Never dare to speak of yourself and my mother in one breath. You are unworthy to kiss the hem of her garments. The strap of her sandals you are unworthy to loose ."

* * *

The work was never hard. It was the nature of the life that killed her. All the lies that stopped her breath.

The room they gave her could so easily have been a pleasant room. Its darkness was no burden to her, nor its size. She brought in small objects for pleasure: a postcard she liked, showing the harbor, and one handpainted one, a scene of Brooklyn Bridge; a tin she'd asked the cook for, Famous Cake Box; a picture of a blonde child and a large black dog. It was the cast-off, the ragendedness that was the room's cruelty to her, and the sense that what was deficient could so easily be fixed. Nails for her clothes instead of hooks. The comforters stained, marked with the waters of who knew what life or what disaster. The mantel and the floor inadequately varnished, ready to splinter, to cause pain. At least the door closed: she

COLORPLATE 87

DEREK HILL. *Tory Island from Tor More*. 20th century. Oil on canvas. Ulster Museum, Belfast.

COLORPLATE 88

PAUL HENRY. *Launching the Currach.* 20th century. Oil on canvas. 16¹/₈ x 23⁵/₈ in. (41 x 60 cm).
National Gallery of Ireland, Dublin.

COLORPLATE 89

PAUL HENRY. *Lakeside Cottages*. 20th century. Oil on canvas. 16⁵/₁₆ x 24 in. (41.5 x 61 cm).
Hugh Lane Municipal Gallery of Modern Art, Dublin.

COLORPLATE 90

LEE WHELAN. *The Kitchen Window*. 20th century. Oil on canvas. 19³/₄ x 18³/₄ in. (50.1 x 47.7 cm).
Crawford Municipal Art Gallery, Cork.

COLORPLATE 91

WILLIAM ORPEN. *The Wash House*. 1905. Oil on canvas. 35¹³/₁₆ x 28³/₄ in. (91 x 73 cm).
National Gallery of Ireland, Dublin.

COLORPLATE 92

PATRICK TUOHY. *A Mayo Peasant Boy*. Early 20th century. Oil on canvas. 36 x 21 1/16 in.
(91.5 x 53.5 cm). Hugh Lane Municipal Gallery of Modern Art, Dublin.

COLORPLATE 93

JOHN B. YEATS. *The Bird Market.* Early 20th century. Oil on canvas. 25 x 18⅞ in. (63.5 x 48 cm).
Hugh Lane Municipal Gallery of Modern Art, Dublin.

COLORPLATE 94

RICHARD T. MOYNAN. *Military Maneuvers*. 1891. Oil on canvas. 58¹/₄ x 94¹/₂ in. (148 x 240 cm).
National Gallery of Ireland, Dublin.

thanked God for that. But it didn't lock. In time, when she thought she had her mistress's favor, she asked: "Could a lock not be put on my door? It would mean something to me." Claire Fitzpatrick didn't hesitate, didn't give it a moment's thought. "Our servants' rooms are never locked." Reminding Ellen of what she hated most, making her hate herself and all of them because she had forgotten or assumed it could be otherwise. She was a servant, what they wanted was that she would not be herself to herself, but lay herself out to them for their own use. The worst of it was living among the others. Coarse, ignorant, filthy girls, thinking themselves so great and fortunate. Matt Corrigan the king among them; the undermaids, fighting for the joy of polishing his boots. The cook a drunk, the housekeeper a pious ninny, always pressing on Ellen holy pictures and novenas, urging her to thank God for her good situation, offering her suggestions about underwear as she offered her mints so strong you'd kill your stomach with them. And all of them—the tradesman, the butcher's boy—thinking they had the right to call her by her first name. The impudence, the theft of it. She'd stopped them talking to her by her coldness, her coldness was her joy.

Delia had begged to visit, wanting to see the inside of the Fitzpatrick house. "Maybe you'd slip me up to the mistress's room itself, one day when she's out, El. I could take a look." But Ellen never would. Her job meant something. She was paid to keep things concealed. The thought of Delia in the mistress's room shocked her. It was Ellen's place to keep back the intruder, the violating eye or foot, the hand that touched and spoiled. She knew her part in the conspiracy: it was her understanding of the nature of the human eye, that thing that leered and gaped and sought to steal the good of everything, that loved defilement and the ruin of a thing, her understanding of all that made her good at her work. She hated the fine lace, the covered buttons, the exact folds, the silk ribbons, veils, false flowers, the embroideries, the small stitches: she knew the blood of slaves went into them. And yet they were her province. She was honorable; she valued, above all, her honor. Why would she let Delia into places that were not hers? Why would she let her into the library, the dining room, let her finger the silver or the coffee set that stood out on the sideboard, the chintz draperies with their pattern of choked carnation hollyhocks, chrysanthemums? Why would she invite her friend? She hated all those objects but they were not hers, and she respected separations. She would not let the trespassers trespass.

So, when the day came that she couldn't stick it, it wasn't the disliking of the job itself that pushed her over, it was the sudden awareness that the Fitzpatricks, in paying her, thought they had bought her life.

Hal Boyle

FROM ASSOCIATED PRESS, MARCH 17
"What Is It To Be Irish?"

This delightful article is full of Irish pride. On the one day of the year when being Irish really matters—St. Patrick's Day, March 17—the Irishman becomes an IRISHMAN who walks the earth as a giant with mythic and mystic powers of understanding, filled with the poetry and music of life, not to mention blarney.

What is it to be Irish? On 364 days of the year, being Irish isn't visibly different from being Scotch, French, Italian, Jewish, Serbian, Dutch, or—yes—even English.

The Irishman pays his bills, complains against taxes, does his work, and listens to his wife,

Ben Bulben Mountain, County Sligo.
Photograph. Irish Tourist Board, Dublin.

like the man of any other race. But on this one day of the year—holy St. Patrick's Day—the Irishman becomes an Irishman. And on this day you have to be Irish to know what it is to be Irish.

The outer signs, of course, can be seen by all. The Irishman overnight grows a foot taller and stalks the earth a giant. All traffic lights turn green before him, and if they don't he sees red. But this air of majesty is only token evidence of interior change. The men of other races who envy the Irishman his bearing on St. Patrick's Day would envy him far more if he could look inside the Irishman's soul.

Beyond Words:

What is it to be Irish?

How can you put the wonder of it into words? If a psychiatrist stretched himself out on his warm couch after his last customer had gone home, and he dreamed of the man he himself would most like to be—well, he might be perfect, but he'd still be only half an Irishman on St. Patrick's Day.

What is it to be Irish?

It is to have an angel in your mouth, turning your prose to poetry. It is to have the gift of tongues, to know the language of all living things. Does an Irishman pause and turn an ear to a tree? It is because on this day he wants to hear what one sleepy bud says to another as it opens its pale hands to the warm sun of spring.

What is it to be Irish?

Oh, on this day it is music. Not just the cornet in the parading high school band, but the deep, deep music of living, the low, sad rhythms of eternity. This Irishman hears the high song of the turning spheres. All the world is in tune, and he is in step with the tune, the tune that only he can hear.

History in a Day:

234

What is it to be Irish?

It is to live the whole history of his race between a dawn and a dawn—the long wrongs, the bird-swift joys, the endless hurt of his ancestors since the morning of time in a forgotten forest, the knock-at-his-heart that is part of his religion.

What is it to be Irish?

It isn't only the realisation that he is descended from kings. It is the realisation that he is a king himself, an empire on two feet striding in power, a strolling continent of awe.

What is it to be Irish?

Why on St. Patrick's Day, to be Irish is to know more glory, adventure, magic, victory, exultation, gratitude, and gladness than any other man can experience in a lifetime.

What is it to be Irish?

It is to walk in complete mystic understanding with God for twenty-four wonderful hours.

THE CELTIC REVIVAL BEGINS

W.B. Yeats

FROM THE CELTIC TWILIGHT

"Kidnappers"

William Butler Yeats (1865–1939), poet, dramatist, and folklorist, was the leader of the Celtic literary revival at the turn of the century. His love of Irish fantasy and folklore is reflected in the charming and mystical tales of The Celtic Twilight *(published in 1893). In this story we are introduced to the "unearthly troop" of fairies who pass to and from the otherworld through the small square white stone high up on Ben Bulben, the mountain over-looking Sligo.*

A little north of the town of Sligo, on the southern side of Ben Bulben, some hundreds of feet above the plain, is a small white square in the limestone. No mortal has ever touched it with his hand; no sheep or goat has ever browsed grass beside it. There is no more inaccessible place upon the earth, and few more encircled by awe to the deep considering. It is the door of faery-land. In the middle of night it swings open, and the unearthly troop rushes out. All night the gay rabble sweep to and fro across the land, invisible to all, unless perhaps where, in some more than commonly 'gentle' place—Drumcliff or Drum-a-hair—the night-capped heads of faery-doctors may be thrust from their doors to see what mischief the 'gentry' are doing. To their trained eyes and ears the fields are covered by red-hatted riders, and the air is full of shrill voices—a sound like whistling, as an ancient Scottish seer has recorded, and wholly different from the talk of the angels, who 'speak much in the throat, like the Irish,' as Lilly, the astrologer, has wisely said. If there be a new-born baby or new-wed bride in the neighbourhood, the night-capped 'doctors' will peer with more than common care, for the unearthly troop do not always return empty-handed. Sometimes a new-wed bride or a new-born baby goes with them into their mountains; the door swings to behind, and the newborn or the new-wed moves henceforth in the bloodless land of Faery; happy enough, but doomed to melt out at the last judgment like bright vapour, for the soul cannot live without sorrow. Through this door of white stone, and the other doors of that land where *geabheadh tu an sonas aer pighin* ('you can buy joy for a penny'), have gone kings, queens, and princes, but so greatly has the power of Faery dwindled, that there are none but peasants in these sad chronicles of mine.

Somewhere about the beginning of last century appeared at the western corner of Market Street, Sligo, where the butcher's shop now is, not a palace, as in Keats's *Lamia*, but an apothecary's shop, ruled over by a certain unaccountable Dr Opendon. Where he came from, none ever knew. There also was in Sligo, in those days, a woman, Ormsby by name, whose husband had fallen mysteriously sick. The doctors could make nothing of him. Nothing seemed wrong with him, yet weaker and weaker he grew. Away went the wife to Dr Opendon. She was shown into the shop parlour. A black cat was sitting straight up before the fire. She had just time to see that the sideboard was covered with fruit, and to say to herself, 'Fruit must be wholesome when the doctor has so much,' before Dr Opendon came in. He was dressed all in black, the same as the cat, and his wife walked behind him dressed in black likewise. She gave him a guinea, and got a little bottle in return. Her husband recovered that time. Meanwhile the black doctor cured many people; but one day a rich patient died, and cat, wife, and doctor all vanished the night after. In a year the man Ormsby fell sick once more. Now he was a good-looking man, and his wife felt sure the 'gentry' were coveting him. She went and called on the 'faery-doctor' at Cairnsfoot. As soon as he had heard her tale, he went behind the back door and began muttering, muttering, muttering—making spells. Her husband got well this time also. But after a while he sickened again, the fatal third time, and away went she once more to Cairnsfoot, and out went the faery-doctor behind his back door and began muttering, but soon he came in and told her it was no use—her husband would die; and sure enough the man died, and ever after when she spoke of him Mrs Ormsby shook her head saying she knew well where he was, and it wasn't in heaven or hell or purgatory either. She probably believed that a log of wood was left behind in his place, but so bewitched that it seemed the dead body of her husband.

She is dead now herself, but many still living remember her. She was, I believe, for a time a servant or else a kind of pensioner of some relations of my own. . . .

Some five miles southward of Sligo is a gloomy and tree-bordered pond, a great gathering-place of water-fowl, called, because of its form, the Heart Lake. It is haunted by stranger things than heron, snipe, or wild duck. Out of this lake, as from the white square stone in Ben Bulben, issues an unearthly troop. Once men began to drain it; suddenly one of them raised a cry that he saw his house in flames. They turned round, and every man there saw his own cottage burning. They hurried home to find it was but faery glamour. To this hour on the border of the lake is shown a half-dug trench—the signet of their impiety. A little way from this lake I heard a beautiful and mournful history of faery kidnapping. I heard it from a little old woman in a white cap, who sings to herself in Gaelic, and moves from one foot to the other as though she remembered the dancing of her youth. . . .

John Kirwan was a great horse-racing man, and once landed in Liverpool with a fine horse, going racing somewhere in middle England. That evening as he walked by the docks, a slip of a boy came up and asked where he was stabling his horse. In such and such a place, he answered. 'Don't put him there,' said the slip of a boy; 'that stable will be burnt to-night.' He took his horse elsewhere, and sure enough the stable was burnt down. Next day the boy came and asked as a reward to ride as his jockey in the coming race, and then was gone. The race-time came round. At the last moment the boy ran forward and mounted, saying, 'If I strike him with the whip in my left hand I will lose, but if in my right hand bet all you are worth.' For, said Paddy Flynn, who told me the tale, 'the left arm is good for nothing. I might go on making the sign of the cross with it and all that, come Christmas, and a Banshee, or such like, would no more mind than if it was that broom.' Well, the slip of a boy struck the horse with his right hand, and John Kirwan cleared the field out. When the race was over, 'What can I do

MAX BEERBOHM. *W. B. Yeats Presenting Mr. George Moore to the Queen of the Fairies.* Early 20th century. Watercolor and ink on paper. 12½ x 7¾ in. (31.8 x 19.7 cm). Hugh Lane Municipal Gallery of Modern Art, Dublin.

for you now?' said he. 'Nothing but this,' said the boy: 'my mother has a cottage on your land—they stole me from the cradle. Be good to her, John Kirwan, and wherever your horses go I will watch that no ill follows them; but you will never see me more.' With that he made himself air, and vanished.

Sometimes animals are carried off—apparently drowned animals more than others. In Claremorris, Galway, Paddy Flynn told me, lived a poor widow with one cow and its calf. The cow fell into the river, and was washed away. There was a man thereabouts who went to a red-haired woman—for such are supposed to be wise in these things—and she told him to take the calf down to the edge of the river, and hide himself and watch. He did as she had told him, and as evening came on the calf began to low, and after a while the cow came along the edge of the river and commenced suckling it. Then, as he had been told, he caught the cow's tail. Away they went at a great pace, across hedges and ditches, till they came to a royalty (a name for the circular ditches, commonly called raths or forts, that Ireland is covered with since Pagan times). Therein he saw walking or sitting all the people who had died out of his village in his time. A woman was sitting on the edge with a child on her knees, and she called out to him to mind what the red-haired woman had told him, and he remembered she had said, Bleed the cow. So he stuck his knife into the cow and drew blood. That broke the spell, and he was able to turn her homeward. 'Do not forget the spancel,' said the woman with the child on her knees; 'take the inside one.' There were three spancels on a bush; he took one, and the cow was driven safely home to the widow.

There is hardly a valley or mountain-side where folk cannot tell you of someone pillaged from amongst them. Two or three miles from the Heart Lake lives an old woman who was stolen away in her youth. After seven years she was brought home again for some reason or other, but she had no toes left. She had danced them off. Many near the white stone door in Ben Bulben have been stolen away.

It is far easier to be sensible in cities than in many country places I could tell you of. When one walks on those grey roads at evening by the scented elder-bushes of the white cottages, watching the faint mountains gathering the clouds upon their heads, one all too readily discovers beyond the thin cobweb veil of the sense, those creatures, the goblins, hurrying from the white square stone door to the north, or from the Heart Lake in the south.

Douglas Hyde
The Piper and the Púca

Douglas Hyde (1860–1949), the first President of Ireland (1937–1945), was a founding member of the Gaelic League (responsible for the revival and cultivation of the Gaelic language) and a collector of folktales in the original Gaelic. In this tale, a marvelous blending of the pagan Celtic and Christian traditions, the Púca, an animal spirit which manifests in many different shapes (a horse, donkey, bull, goat, eagle, etc.) lures the piper to a November night celebration at Croagh Patrick, St. Patrick's holy mountain, still the site of annual pilgrimmages.

In the old times, there was a half fool living in Dunmore, in the county Galway, and although he was excessively fond of music, he was unable to learn more than one tune, and that was the "Black Rogue." He used to get a good deal of money from the gentlemen, for they used to get sport out of him. One night the piper was coming home from a house where there had been a dance, and he half drunk. When he came to a little bridge that was up by his mother's house, he squeezed the pipes on, and began playing the "Black Rogue" (an rógaire dubh). The Púca came behind him, and flung him up on his own back. There were long horns on the Púca, and the piper got a good grip of them, and then he said—

"Destruction on you, you nasty beast, let me home. I have a ten-penny piece in my pocket for my mother, and she wants snuff."

"Never mind your mother," said the Púca, "but keep your hold. If you fall, you will break your neck and your pipes." Then the Púca said to him, "Play up for me the 'Shan Van Vocht' (an t-seann-bhean bhocht)."

"I don't know it," said the piper.

"Never mind whether you do or you don't," said the Púca. "Play up, and I'll make you know."

The piper put wind in his bag, and he played such music as made himself wonder.

"Upon my word, you're a fine music-master," says the piper then; "but tell me where you're for bringing me."

"There's a great feast in the house of the Banshee, on the top of Craogh Patric tonight," says the Púca, "and I'm for bringing you there to play music, and, take my word, you'll get the price of your trouble."

"By my word, you'll save me a journey, then," says the piper, "for Father William put a journey to Craogh Patric on me, because I stole the white gander from him last Martinmas."

JOHN B. YEATS. *Douglas Hyde, Poet and Scholar, First President of Ireland.* 1906. Oil on canvas. 42 1/8 x 33 3/8 in. (107 x 86 cm). National Gallery of Ireland, Dublin.

The Púca rushed him across hills and bogs and rough places, till he brought him to the top of Croagh Patric. Then the Púca struck three blows with his foot, and a great door opened, and they passed in together, into a fine room.

The piper saw a golden table in the middle of the room, and hundreds of old women (cailleacha) sitting round about it. The old woman rose up, and said, "A hundred thousand welcomes to you, you Púca of November (na Samhna). Who is this you have brought with you?"

"The best piper in Ireland," says the Púca.

One of the old women struck a blow on the ground, and a door opened in the side of the wall, and what should the piper see coming out but the white gander which he had stolen from Father William.

"By my conscience, then," says the piper, "myself and my mother ate every taste of that gander, only one wing, and I gave that to Moy-rua (Red Mary), and it's she told the priest I stole his gander."

The gander cleaned the table, and carried it away, and the Púca said, "Play up music for these ladies."

The piper played up, and the old women began dancing, and they were dancing till they were tired. Then the Púca said to pay the piper, and every old woman drew out a gold piece, and gave it to him.

"By the tooth of Patric," said he, "I'm as rich as the son of a lord."

"Come with me," says the Púca, "and I'll bring you home."

They went out then, and just as he was going to ride on the Púca, the gander came up to him, and gave him a new set of pipes. The Púca was not long until he brought him to Dunmore, and he threw the piper off at the little bridge, and then he told him to go home, and says to him, "You have two things now that you never had before—you have sense and music (ciall agus ceól)."

The piper went home, and he knocked at his mother's door, saying, "Let me in, I'm as rich as a lord, and I'm the best piper in Ireland."

"You're drunk," said the mother.

"No, indeed," says the piper, "I haven't drunk a drop."

The mother let him in, and he gave her the gold pieces, and, "Wait now," says he, "till you hear the music, I'll play."

He buckled on the pipes, but instead of music, there came a sound as if all the geese and ganders in Ireland were screeching together. He awakened the neighbours and they all were mocking him, until he put on the old pipes, and then he played melodious music for them; and after that he told them all he had gone through that night.

The next morning, when his mother went to look at the gold pieces, there was nothing there but the leaves of a plant.

The piper went to the priest, and told him his story, but the priest would not believe a word from him, until he put the pipes on him, and then the screeching of the ganders and geese began.

"Leave my sight, you thief," said the priest.

But nothing would do the piper till he would put the old pipes on him to show the priest that his story was true.

He buckled on the old pipes, and he played melodious music, and from that day till the day of his death, there was never a piper in the county Galway was as good as he was.

Lawrence Millman

FROM OUR LIKE WILL NOT BE THERE AGAIN

The Shepherd and the Sunbeam

In 1975 Lawrence Millman traveled through the west of Ireland, the craggy region usually referred to as the last place on earth where conversation is not dead, "the last place God made," to record these stories of people who have lived by the spoken word for generations. The sunbeam motif in this story recalls the legend surrounding St. Brigit.

I used to always go to an old person for to get a few histories. 'Twas an old man that in 1928 told me this: he said that there was a wonderful man living just beyond here, a sheep herder for a Protestant landlord years ago, and this man had no knowledge of anything but his sheep and his lands. He was away up in the mountain beyond minding sheep, and he never seen a chapel, he was miles away from a chapel.

There was a priest crossing one time, and the priest began to talk to this man, and he says, "Do you go to mass?" "What is that?" says he. The priest asked him his age, and he told him, a man well gone in years, a white bawneen he was wearing. "Next Sunday," says the priest, "you'll see the people going to mass, and follow them. Follow them down the mountain." "All right," says he.

Sure enough, the next Sunday he followed them down the mountain and into the chapel. The day was very warm, and after walking, and when he was coming inside, he started to pour sweat. There was a sunbeam coming in from the window, and he thought it was a rope, and he took off his white bawneen and threw it up upon it, and faith, believe it or believe it not, the coat caught up on the sunbeam and the sunbeam kept the coat. Then the priest, seeing the coat

Inishmore House, Aran Islands. Photograph. Irish Tourist Board, Dublin.

hanging there, said to the congregation, "Thanks be to God, there's a Saint at mass today."

After mass, the priest came up to the old man and told him he needn't come anymore. Why? Because he was a true Christian, a living Saint. Because if he continued coming to that chapel, could happen next Sunday, he could fall into sin and the sunbeam wouldn't hold up the coat. He might look at a handsome lassie, that's all the marks you need ever pass, that's a sin for you. So he stayed away for the rest of his life.

You see, the man was an actual Saint. He was in the mountain all his life, out there on his own, and there was more religion in him than there could ever be if he went looking for it, at the chapel. I don't think the sunbeam would have held up that priest's coat.

Lady Augusta Gregory

FROM OUR IRISH THEATRE

The Poet and the Patron Meet

Lady Augusta Gregory (1852–1932) devoted herself to the study of Irish folklore. Her poems, short stories, and plays exhibited her command of the language and her extensive knowledge of folk tales and traditions. Her home at Coole Park was a gathering place for poets, playwrights, and artists, and it was there that she and William Butler Yeats first discussed the possibility of a national Irish theatre, a dream which was eventually realized in The Abbey Theatre.

Mr Edward Martyn came to see me, bringing with him Mr Yeats whom I did not know very well, though I cared for his work very much and had already, through his directions, been gathering folklore. They had lunch with us, but it was a wet day and we could not go out . . . We sat through the wet afternoon, and though I had never been at all interested in theatres, our talk turned on plays. Mr Martyn had written two, *The Heather Field* and *Maeve*. They had been offered to London managers, and now he thought of having them produced in Germany, where there seemed to be more room for new drama than in England. I said it was a pity we had no Irish theatre where such plays could be given. Mr Yeats said that had always been a dream of his, but he had of late thought it an impossible one, for it could not at first pay its way and there was no money to be found for such a thing in Ireland. We went on talking about it, and things seemed to grow possible as we talked, before the end of the afternoon we had made our plan. We said we would collect money, or rather ask to have a certain sum of money guaranteed. We would then take a Dublin theatre and give a performance of Mr Martyn's *Heather Field*, and one of Mr Yeats' own plays, *The Countess Cathleen*.

Andrew E. Malone

FROM THE IRISH THEATRE

The Dream Becomes Reality

This article which places the founding of The Abbey Theatre within an historic context was actually the first of a series of lectures delivered during The Abbey Theatre Festival held in Dublin in August 1938. Andrew Malone, the author, claims that his singular knowledge of The Abbey is not based on his involvement with the production of any of the plays, but derives from his place as "the man in the street," a long-time member of the audience from childhood.

I was a small boy when my first visit was made to the Abbey Theatre; and from the initial glimpse which I had of its stage I was enthralled and enamoured. The audience was very small in those days, and the reputation of Irish plays and players stood higher in other countries and in other cities than it did in Ireland or Dublin. In Dublin a small section of the population was actively hostile to the new theatrical and dramatic development, but the greater part of the city population was magnificently ignorant and indifferent. The early audiences were, in consequence, very small, and the theatre in its formative years was open for only three evenings in each week. Even then, while the sixpenny pit might be thronged—and its uncomfortable bench-seats held a representative assortment of Dublin's youthful enthusiasts—the people in the stalls might be counted easily upon the fingers. . . .

It has to be remembered, of course, that the Irish people at the time had other, and apparently more pressing, things to think about. The echoes of the historic Parnell "split" still reverberated through the land, and the lingering embers of passionate disputation might have been fanned into renewed flame at any moment. In 1898 the mind of the country was occupied in the main by political and social problems, but the celebration of the centenary of the Rebellion of 1798 threw its thoughts back upon events which aroused patriotic passion, yet without giving visible form to anything more enduring than a monument to those who had sacrificed their lives for their country a century earlier.

Beneath the placid surface, however, there was a ferment which was later to break the familiar moulds and re-make the country. The Gaelic League had been founded some fifteen years earlier, and the effort to restore the ancient national language of Ireland brought almost forgotten, or dimly remembered, things to the forefront of the popular mind. The people were

H. OAKLEY. *Yeats, Synge and George Russell (AE),
fishing in Coole Lake.* c. 1910. Ink on paper. Colin
Smythe Ltd.

reminded that history was more than a century; that a community had a past enshrined in special and peculiar forms; that a land rich in heroic legends must know something about them; and that the transient turbulence of party strife and personal rancour make a sorry showing in the pages of recorded history. It was a period of dejection and disillusionment, with only hidden stirrings to mark the maintenance of its vitality.

While Ireland was occupied in the futilities of political party strife, there were developments and stirrings in other countries which came later to exercise a strong influence upon Irish affairs. As early as 1855, while Ireland still was sunk in the slough of the Famine and while the "coffin ships" carried the dispirited people in thousands to the United States, Henrik Ibsen had begun his revolutionary career as a dramatist in Norway. Ibsen . . . focussed attention upon the moral and social problems which clamoured for attention. Without attempting to convert audiences to his views, as his followers did later, Ibsen roused indignation through emotional experience.

The technical innovation consisted mainly in the identification of action with exposition. "What we might have learned from Ibsen," said Bernard Shaw, "was that our fashionable dramatic material was worn out so far as cultivated modern people are concerned: that what really interests such people on the stage is not what we call action . . . but stories of lives, discussions of conduct, unveiling of motives, conflict of characters in talk, laying bare of souls, discovery of pitfalls—in short, *illumination* of life. . . ."

While Free Theatres were being founded in Paris, Berlin, and London, a new ferment of a totally different kind had entered the life of Ireland. Parnell had died and politics had lost its fascination for the younger people, who turned towards the cultural movements. The academic

Society for the Preservation of the Irish Language had given place to the Gaelic League, a more virile body which had for its avowed object the restoration of Irish as the vernacular of the country. The Gaelic League was founded in 1893 by a small band of poets and scholars, in which Douglas Hyde and Eoin MacNeill were prominent; and almost at once it attracted all that was active and vital in the intellectual life of Ireland. Attention was turned towards the Irish language as a literary medium: Edward Martyn thought of writing plays in Irish, and George Moore played with it as a way of escape from cheap and weak English. Douglas Hyde published his *Love Songs of Connacht* and *Religious Songs of Connacht*, from which the dialogue of the earlier plays of the Abbey Theatre derives much of its charm. Irish Literary Societies were founded in Dublin and London, with W. B. Yeats as an initiating force and vigorous member. In these groups the foundations were well and truly laid for the literary renascence and the national theatre in Ireland.

In 1898 W. B. Yeats met Lady Gregory, and that was to be the fateful meeting in the history of the drama and the theatre in Ireland. Lady Gregory has set the authentic details in her diary: "I was in London in 1898, and I find written: 'Yeats and Sir Alfred Lyall to tea. Yeats stayed on. He is very full of play-writing. . . . He, with the aid of Miss Florence Farr, an actress who thinks more of a romantic than of a paying play, is keen about taking a little theatre somewhere in the suburbs to produce romantic drama, his own plays, Edward Martyn's, one of Bridges', and he is trying to stir up Standish O'Grady and Fiona Macleod to write some. He thinks there will be a reaction after the realism of Ibsen, and romance will have its turn. . . .'"

The letter by which this project was commended to the consideration of prospective guarantors asked for no more than £300. "We propose," it said, "to have performed in the spring of every year certain Celtic and Irish plays, which, whatever be their degree of excellence, will be written with a high ambition, and so to build up a Celtic and Irish school of dramatic literature. We hope to find in Ireland an uncorrupted and imaginative audience, trained to listen by its passion for oratory, and believe that our desire to bring upon the stage the deeper thoughts and emotions of Ireland will ensure for us a tolerant welcome, and that freedom of expression which is not found in the theatre of England, and without which no new movement in art or literature can succeed. We will show that Ireland is not the home of buffoonery and of easy sentiment, as it has been represented, but the home of an ancient idealism. We are confident of the support of all Irish people, who are weary of misrepresentation, in carrying out a work that is outside all the political questions that divide us."

J. M. Synge

FROM THE ARAN ISLANDS

John Millington Synge (1871–1909), the great folk-dramatist of the Irish Literary Theatre, grew up comfortably in Dublin and earned a degree in music from Trinity College. In 1906 in Paris, he met Yeats, recently returned from a visit to the Aran Islands—the last outpost of the Irish culture central to his literary movement. Yeats encouraged Synge to "Go to the Aran Islands. Live there as one of the people themselves. Express a life that has never found expression." This is an excerpt from Synge's journal recalling that time and place.

THE GREY HORSE

This evening the old man told me a story he had heard long ago on the mainland:—

There was a young woman, he said, and she had a child. In a little time the woman died and they buried her the day after. That night another woman—a woman of the family—was sitting by the fire with the child on her lap, giving milk to it out of a cup. Then the woman they were after burying opened the door, and came into the house. She went over to the fire, and she took a stool and sat down before the other woman. Then she put out her hand and took the child on her lap, and gave it her breast. After that she put the child in the cradle and went over to the dresser and took milk and potatoes off it, and ate them. Then she went out. The other woman was frightened, and she told the man of the house when he came back, and two young men. They said they would be there the next night, and if she came back they would catch hold of her. She came the next night and gave the child her breast, and when she got up to go to the dresser, the man of the house caught hold of her, but he fell down on the floor. Then the two young men caught hold of her and they held her. She told them she was away with the fairies, and they could not keep her that night, though she was eating no food with the fairies, the way she might be able to come back to her child. Then she told them they would all be leaving that part of the country on the Oidhche Shamhna, and that there would be four or five hundred of them riding on horses, and herself would be on a grey horse, riding behind a young man. And she told them to go down to a bridge they would be crossing that night, and to wait at the head of it, and when she would be coming up she would slow the horse and they would be able to throw something on her and on the young man, and they would fall over on the ground and be saved.

She went away then, and on the Oidhche Shamhna the men went down and got her back. She had four children after that, and in the end she died.

It was not herself they buried at all the first time, but some old thing the fairies put in her place.

JOHN B. YEATS. *John Millington Synge.* Early 20th century. Oil on canvas. 29¹/₂ x 24⁵/₈ in. (75 x 62.5 cm). Hugh Lane Municipal Gallery of Modern Art, Dublin.

THE FUNERAL

The young man has been buried, and his funeral was one of the strangest scenes I have met with. People could be seen going down to his house from early in the day, yet when I went there with the old man about the middle of the afternoon, the coffin was still lying in front of the door, with the men and women of the family standing round beating it, and keening over it, in a great crowd of people. A little later every one knelt down and a last prayer was said. Then the cousins of the dead man got ready two oars and some pieces of rope—the men of his own family seemed too broken with grief to know what they were doing—the coffin was tied up, and the procession began. The old women walked close behind the coffin, and I happened to take a place just after them, among the first of the men. The rough lane to the graveyard slopes away towards the east, and the crowd of women going down before me in their red dresses, cloaked with red petticoats, with the waistband that is held round the head just seen from behind, had a strange effect, to which the white coffin and the unity of colour gave a nearly cloistral quietness.

This time the graveyard was filled with withered grass and bracken instead of the early ferns that were to be seen everywhere at the other funeral I have spoken of, and the grief of the people was of a different kind, as they had come to bury a young man who had died in his first manhood, instead of an old woman of eighty. For this reason the keen lost a part of its formal nature, and was recited as the expression of intense personal grief by the young men and women of the man's own family.

When the coffin had been laid down, near the grave that was to be opened, two long switches were cut out from the brambles among the rocks, and the length and breadth of the coffin were marked on them. Then the men began their work, clearing off stones and thin layers of earth, and breaking up an old coffin that was in the place into which the new one had to be lowered. When a number of blackened boards and pieces of bone had been thrown up with the clay, a skull was lifted out, and placed upon a gravestone. Immediately the old woman, the mother of the dead man, took it up in her hands, and carried it away by herself. Then she sat down and put it in her lap—it was the skull of her own mother—and began keening and shrieking over it with the wildest lamentation.

As the pile of mouldering clay got higher beside the grave a heavy smell began to rise from it, and the men hurried with their work, measuring the hole repeatedly with the two rods of

Tom Lalor. *Yeats Addressing Audience from Stage of Abbey Theatre.* 1907. Ink on paper. National Library of Ireland, Dublin.

bramble. When it was nearly deep enough the old woman got up and came back to the coffin, and began to beat on it, holding the skull in her left hand. This last moment of grief was the most terrible of all. The young women were nearly lying among the stones, worn out with their passion of grief, yet raising themselves every few moments to beat with magnificent gestures on the boards of the coffin. The young men were worn out also, and their voices cracked continually in the wail of the keen.

When everything was ready the sheet was unpinned from the coffin, and it was lowered into its place. Then an old man took a wooden vessel with holy water in it, and a wisp of bracken, and the people crowded round him while he splashed the water over them. They seemed eager to get as much of it as possible, more than one old woman crying out with a humorous voice—

'*Tabhair dham braon eile, a Mhourteen.*' ('Give me another drop, Martin.')

Ulick O'Connor

FROM CELTIC DAWN

Setting the Stage

Ulick O'Connor, biographer, playwright, poet, and a member of the Board of Directors of the Abbey Theatre in Dublin, offers a fascinating "behind the scenes" picture of the realism which Synge considered vital to the production of Riders to the Sea.

For the stage production [of *Riders to the Sea*] which took place the following year, he insisted on realism in the costumes and had Aran flannel sent up, dyed red 'madder' and cut to fit the leading actors. Pampooties were made from a cowhide that had been secured when a customer at a tan yard decided not to have a waistcoat made from it on account of his girlfriend's objections to cowskin, and the tanner sold it cheaply to the prop manager for the Fays. An old peasant woman was discovered living with a married daughter in a city tenement who could teach the actresses the 'caoine' or death chant that the islanders sing round their dead. As if in a trance, beside a crumbling marble fireplace that had once warmed the posteriors of aristocrats, she sang her astonishing lament with thin piping notes while the actresses who were learning from her tried to ignore the noise of passing vehicles outside. She was so successful in training the cast that one of them remembered afterwards how it made 'a scene very terrible and yet beautiful to look on.' A spinning wheel was needed which Lady Gregory provided by buying it from a woman in a cottage who had had it for over a hundred years. It was to remain a prop in the company for many years.

Riders to the Sea, which had its first staged performance in February 1904, has been called the finest one-act play in any language. It lasts barely twenty minutes and has none of the movement of classic tragedy. Its effect is obtained through the stoical acceptance of fate by the main characters. Perhaps in this, his first successful completed play, Synge achieved the ambition of which he spoke to Yeats—to bring three hitherto unrelated emotions together; for in *Riders to the Sea*, besides the stoicism of the central characters, there is the ecstasy of the elements they defy and the asceticism of people's daily lives divorced from material ambition.

The audience becomes gradually aware during the play that a mother has lost three sons by drowning (one dashed from a pony into the sea by a wave); and her last speech, as she finds out that her third son has been taken from her, is drenched in the fatalism that Synge found in the character of his island companions.

J. M. Synge

FROM RIDERS TO THE SEA

Riders to the Sea, *considered one of the finest tragedies ever written, was produced by the Irish National Theatre Society in 1904. The language and the stories of the people of the Aran Islands are incorporated into this haunting, fatalistic one-act drama of one woman's ongoing struggle with the sea. The grey pony in this selection is drawn directly from the story in* The Aran Islands.

NORA: Tell us what it is you seen.

MAURYA: I went down to the spring well, and I stood there saying a prayer to myself. Then Bartley came along, and he riding on the red mare with the gray pony behind him. [*She puts up her hands, as if to hide something from her eyes*] The Son of God spare us, Nora!

CATHLEEN: What is it you seen?

MAURYA: I seen Michael himself.

CATHLEEN: [*Speaking softly*] You did not, mother; it wasn't Michael you seen, for his body is after being found in the Far North, and he's got a clean burial by the grace of God.

MAURYA: [*A little defiantly*] I'm after seeing him this day, and he riding and galloping. Bartley came first on the red mare; and I tried to say, "God speed you," but something choked the words in my throat. He went by quickly; and "the blessing of God on you," says he, and I could say nothing. I looked up then, and I crying, at the gray pony, and there was Michael upon it—with fine clothes on him, and new shoes on his feet.

CATHLEEN: [*Begins to keen*] It's destroyed we are from this day. It's destroyed, surely.

NORA: Didn't the young priest say the Almighty God wouldn't leave her destitute with no son living?

MAURYA: [*In a low voice, but clearly*] It's little the like of him knows of the sea. . . . Bartley will be lost now, and let you call in Eamon and make me a good coffin out of the white boards, for I won't live after them. I've had a husband, and a husband's father, and six sons in this house—six fine men, though it was a hard birth I had with every one of them and they coming to the world—and some of them were found and some of them were not found, but they're gone now the lot of them. . . . There were Stephen, and Shawn, were lost in the great wind, and found after in the Bay of Gregory of the Golden Mouth, and carried up the two of them on the one plank, and in by that door.

[*She pauses for a moment, the girls start as if they heard something through the door that is half open behind them*]

NORA: [*In a whisper*] Did you hear that, Cathleen? Did you hear a noise in the north-east?

CATHLEEN: [*In a whisper*] There's some one after crying out by the seashore.

MAURYA: [*Continues without hearing anything*] There was Sheamus and his father, and his own father again, were lost in a dark night, and not a stick or sign was seen of them when the sun went up. There was Patch after was drowned out of a curagh that turned over. I was sitting here with Bartley, and he a baby, lying on my two knees, and I seen two women, and three women, and four women coming in, and they crossing themselves, and not saying a word. I looked out then, and there were men coming after them, and they holding a thing in the half of a red sail, and water dripping out of it—it was a dry day, Nora—and leaving a track to the door.

[*She pauses again with her hand stretched out toward the door. It opens softly and old women begin to come in, crossing themselves on the threshold, and kneeling down in front of the stage with red petticoats over their heads*]

COLORPLATE 95

HARRY CLARKE. *Eve of St. Agnes*. 1924. Stained-glass window. 60 x 48 in. (152.5 x 122 cm).
Hugh Lane Municipal Gallery of Modern Art, Dublin. Photography: Davison & Associates Ltd., Dublin.

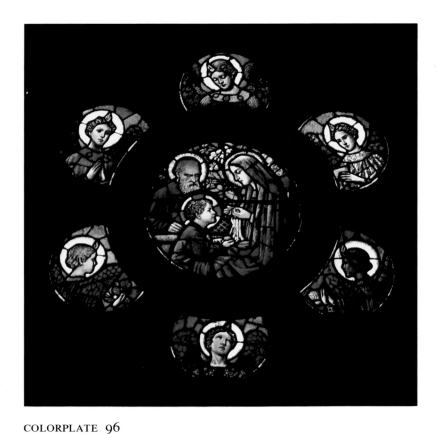

COLORPLATE 96

MICHEAL HEALY. *Rose Window*. 1907. Stained glass.
St. Brendan's Cathedral, Loughrea, County Galway. Photograph.
Cameo Photography, Loughrea.

COLORPLATE 97

MICHEAL HEALY. *Regina Coeli (Queen of Heaven)*. Early
20th century. Stained-glass window. St. Brendan's Cathedral,
Loughrea, County Galway. Photograph. Cameo Photography,
Loughrea. *Celebrated artists of the Celtic Revival provided
decorations and liturgical accessories for this beautiful cathedral
built at the turn of the century, from 1897 to 1903.*

COLORPLATE 98

SARAH PURSER. *The Nativity*. Early 20th century. Stained glass. St. Brendan's Cathedral, Loughrea,
County Galway. Photograph. Cameo Photography, Loughrea.

COLORPLATE 99

EVELYN GLEESON. *Liturgical Vestment.* (Front).
Early 20th century. Silk with embroidered silk
ornament. St. Brendan's Cathedral, Loughrea, County
Galway. Photograph. Cameo Photography, Loughrea.
These vestments were designed by Evelyn Gleeson
and made in her workshop at Dun Emer.

COLORPLATE 100

EVELYN GLEESON. *Liturgical Vestment.* (Back).
St. Brendan's Cathedral, Loughrea, County Galway.
Photograph. Cameo Photography, Loughrea.

COLORPLATE 101

EVELYN GLEESON. *Liturgical Vestment*. (Detail). St. Brendan's Cathedral, Loughrea, County Galway. Photograph. Cameo Photography, Loughrea.

COLORPLATE 102

EVELYN GLEESON. *Liturgical Vestment.* (Back). Early 20th century. Silk with embroidered silk ornament. St. Brendan's Cathedral, Loughrea, County Galway. Photograph. Cameo Photography, Loughrea.

COLORPLATE 103

EVELYN GLEESON. *Liturgical Vestment.* (Detail). Early 20th century. Silk with embroidered silk ornament. St. Brendan's Cathedral, Loughrea, County Galway. Photograph. Cameo Photography, Loughrea. *The striking detail here shows the Chi-Rho symbol for Christ.*

COLORPLATES 104–107.

JACK B. YEATS. *Liturgical Banners.* Early 20th century. St. Brendan's Cathedral, Loughrea, County Galway. Photograph. Cameo Photography, Loughrea. *From the top left: St. Patrick and the snakes of Ireland; St. Brendan; St. Joseph; and St. Jarlath.*

Riders to the Sea. 1906. Production photograph. National Library of Ireland, Dublin. *From left: Maire O'Neill (Molly Allgood), Sara Allgood, Brigit O'Dempsey.*

MAURYA: [*Half in a dream, to* Cathleen] Is it Patch, or Michael, or what is it at all?

CATHLEEN: Michael is after being found in the Far North, and when he is found there how could he be here in this place?

MAURYA: There does be a power of young men floating round in the sea, and what way would they know if it was Michael they had, or another man like him, for when a man is nine days in the sea, and the wind blowing, it's hard set his own mother would be to say what man was it.

CATHLEEN: It's Michael, God spare him, for they're after sending us a bit of his clothes from the Far North.

[*She reaches out and hands* Maurya *the clothes that belonged to* Michael. Maurya *stands up slowly, and takes them in her hands.* Nora *looks out*]

NORA: They're carrying a thing among them and there's water dripping out of it and leaving a track by the big stones.

CATHLEEN: [*In a whisper to the women who have come in*] Is it Bartley it is?

ONE OF THE WOMEN: It is surely, God rest his soul.

[*Two younger women come in and pull out the table. Then men carry in the body of* Bartley, *laid on a plank, with a bit of sail over it, and lay it on the table*]

CATHLEEN: [*To the women, as they are doing so*] What way was he drowned?

ONE OF THE WOMEN: The gray pony knocked him into the sea, and he was washed out where there is a great surf on the white rocks.

[Maurya *has gone over and knelt down at the head of the table. The women are keening softly and swaying themselves with a slow movement.* Cathleen *and* Nora *kneel at the other end of the table. The men kneel near the door*]

MAURYA: [*Raising her head and speaking as if she did not see the people around her*] They're all gone now, and there isn't anything more the sea can do to me. . . . I'll have no call now to be up crying and praying when the wind breaks from the south, and you can hear the surf is in the east, and the surf is in the west, making a great stir with the two noises, and they hitting one on the other. I'll have no call now to be going down and getting Holy Water in the dark nights after Samhain, and I won't care what way the sea is when the other women will be keening. [*To* Nora] Give me the Holy Water, Nora, there's a small sup still on the dresser. [Nora *gives it to her*]

MAURYA:][*Drops* Michael's *clothes across* Bartley's *feet, and sprinkles the Holy Water over him*] It isn't that I haven't prayed for you, Bartley, to the Almighty God. It isn't that I haven't said prayers in the dark night till you wouldn't know what I'd be saying; but it's a great rest I'll have now, and great sleeping in the long nights after Samhain, if it's only a bit of wet flour we do have to eat, and maybe a fish that would be stinking.

[*She kneels down again, crossing herself, and saying prayers under her breath*]

CATHLEEN: [*To an old man*] Maybe yourself and Eamon would make a coffin when the sun rises. We have fine white boards herself bought, God help her, thinking Michael would be found, and I have a new cake you can eat while you'll be working.

THE OLD MAN: [*Looking at the boards*] Are there nails with them?

CATHLEEN: There are not, Colum; we didn't think of the nails.

ANOTHER MAN: It's a great wonder she wouldn't think of the nails and all the coffins she's seen made already.

CATHLEEN: It's getting old she is, and broken.

[Maurya *stands up again very slowly and spreads out the pieces of* Michael's *clothes beside the body, sprinkling them with the last of the Holy Water*]

NORA: [*In a whisper to* Cathleen] She's quiet now and easy; but the day Michael was drowned you could hear her crying out from this to the spring well. It's fonder she was of Michael, and would any one have thought that?

CATHLEEN: [*Slowly and clearly*] An old woman will be soon tired with anything she will do, and isn't it nine days herself is after crying and keening, and making great sorrow in the house?

MAURYA: [*Puts the empty cup mouth downwards on the table, and lays her hands together on* Bartley's *feet*] They're all together this time, and the end is come. May the Almighty God have mercy on Bartley's soul, and on Michael's soul, and on the souls of Sheamus and Patch, and Stephen and Shawn [*bending her head*]; and may He have mercy on my soul, Nora, and on the soul of every one is left living in the world.

[*She pauses, and the keen rises a little more loudly from the women, then sinks away*]

MAURYA: [*Continuing*] Michael has a clean burial in the Far North, by the grace of the Almighty God. Bartley will have a fine coffin out of the white boards, and a deep grave surely. What more can we want than that? No man at all can be living forever, and we must be satisfied.

[*She kneels down again and the curtain falls slowly*]

Sean O'Casey
FROM THE PLOUGH AND THE STARS
A Soldier's Duty and a Wife's Deceit

Sean O'Casey (1880–1964) was born into a poor Protestant family in Dublin, and given a sporadic education. The Plough and the Stars, *his drama of the Easter Rising, produced in 1926 by the Abbey Theatre, caused the audience to riot in protest against both O'Casey's apparent denial of the mythic-heroic stature of the leaders of the 1916 rebellion and the presence of a prostitute on the same stage. In this excerpt, Nora's attempt to keep her husband at home, out of the Citizen's Army, fails.*

NORA: [*A little nervous*] Take no notice of it, Jack; they'll go away in a minute.

[*Another knock, followed by the voice of* Captain Brennan]

THE VOICE OF CAPT. BRENNAN: Commandant Clitheroe, Commandant Clitheroe, are you there? A message from General Jim Connolly.

The Plough and the Stars.
1916. Flag. National
Library of Ireland,
Dublin.

CLITHEROE: [*Taking her arms from round him*] Damn it, it's Captain Brennan.

NORA: [*Anxiously*] Don't mind him, don't mind, Jack. Don't break our happiness. . . . Pretend we're not in. . . . Let us forget everything to-night but our two selves!

CLITHEROE: [*Reassuringly*] Don't be alarmed, darling; I'll just see what he wants, an' send him about his business.

NORA: [*Tremulously—putting her arms around him*] No, no. Please, Jack; don't open it. Please, for your own little Nora's sake!

CLITHEROE: [*Taking her arms away and rising to open the door*] Now don't be silly, Nora. [Clitheroe *opens door, and admits a young man in the full uniform of the Irish Citizen Army—green suit; slouch green hat caught up at one side by a small Red Hand badge; Sam Browne belt, with a revolver in the holster. He carries a letter in his hand. When he comes in he smartly salutes* Clitheroe. *The young man is* Captain Brennan. *He stands in front of the chest of drawers*]

CAPT. BRENNAN: [*Giving the letter to* Clitheroe] A dispatch from General Connolly.

CLITHEROE: [*Reading. While he is doing so,* Brennan's *eyes are fixed on* Nora, *who droops as she sits on the lounge*] "Commandant Clitheroe is to take command of the eighth battalion of the I.C.A. which will assemble to proceed to the meeting at nine o'clock. He is to see that all units are provided with full equipment: two day's rations and fifty rounds of ammunition. At two o'clock A.M. the army will leave Liberty Hall for a reconnaissance attack on Dublin Castle.—Com.-Gen. Connolly."

CLITHEROE: [*In surprise, to* Capt. Brennan] I don't understand this. Why does General Connolly call me Commandant?

CAPT. BRENNAN: Th' Staff appointed you Commandant, and th' General agreed with their selection.

CLITHEROE: When did this happen?

CAPT. BRENNAN: A fortnight ago.

CLITHEROE: How is it word was never sent to me?

CAPT. BRENNAN: Word was sent to you. . . . I meself brought it.

CLITHEROE: Who did you give it to, then?

CAPT. BRENNAN: [*After a pause*] I think I gave it to Mrs. Clitheroe, there.

CLITHEROE: Nora, d'ye hear that? [Nora *makes no answer. Standing* C.—*there is a note of hardness in his voice*] Nora . . . Captain Brennan says he brought a letter to me from General Connolly, and that he gave it to you. . . . Where is it? What did you do with it?

[Capt. Brennan *stands in front of the chest of drawers, and softly whistles "The Soldiers' Song"*]

NORA: [*Running over to him, and pleadingly putting her arms around him*] Jack, please

Jack, don't go out to-night an' I'll tell you; I'll explain everything. . . . Send him away, an' stay with your own little red-lipp'd Nora.

CLITHEROE: [*Removing her arms from around him*] None o' this nonsense, now; I want to know what you did with th' letter? [Nora *goes slowly to the couch and sits down again. Angrily*] Why didn't you give me th' letter? What did you do with it? . . . [*Goes over and shakes her by the shoulder*] What did you do with th' letter?

NORA: [*Flaming up and standing on her feet*] I burned it, I burned it! That's what I did with it! Is General Connolly an' th' Citizen Army goin' to be your only care? Is your home goin' to be only a place to rest in? Am I goin' to be only somethin' to provide merrymakin' at night for you? Your vanity 'll be th' ruin of you an' me yet. . . . That's what's movin' you: because they've made an officer of you, you'll make a glorious cause of what you're doin', while your little red-lipp'd Nora can go on sittin' here, makin' a companion of th' loneliness of th' night!

CLITHEROE: [*Fiercely*] You burned it, did you? [*He grips her arm*] Well, me good lady—

NORA: Let go—you're hurtin' me!

CLITHEROE: You deserve to be hurt. . . . Any letther that comes to me for th' future, take care that I get it. . . . D'ye hear—take care that I get it! [*He lets her go, and she sinks down, crying on the couch. He goes to the chest of drawers and takes out a Sam Browne belt, which he puts on, and then puts a revolver in the holster. He puts on his hat, and looks towards* Nora. *At door* L., *about to go out*] You needn't wait up for me; if I'm in at all, it won't be before six in th' morning.

NORA: [*Bitterly*] I don't care if you never came back!

CLITHEROE: [*To* Capt. Brennan] Come along, Ned.

[*They go out; there is a pause.* Nora *pulls the new hat from her head and with a bitter movement flings it to the other end of the room. There is a gentle knock at door* L., *which opens, and* Mollser *comes into the room. She is about 15, but looks to be only about 10, for the ravages of consumption have shrivelled her up. She is pitifully worn, walks feebly, and frequently coughs. She goes over and sits down* L. *of* Nora]

MOLLSER: [*To* Nora] Mother's gone to th' meetin', an' I was feelin' terrible lonely, so I come down to see if you'd let me sit with you, thinkin' you mightn't be goin' yourself. . . . I do be terrible . . . I'll die sometime when I'm be meself. . . . I often envy you, Mrs. Clitheroe, seein' th' health you have, an' th' lovely place you have here, an' wondherin' if I'll ever be sthrong enough to be keepin' a home together for a man.

[*The faint sound of a band playing is heard in the distance outside in the street*]

MOLLSER: Oh this must be some more of the Dublin Fusiliers flyin' off to the front.

[*The band, passing in the street outside, is now heard loudly playing as they pass the house. It is the music of a brass band playing a regiment to the boat on the way to the front. The tune that is being played is "It's a Long Way to Tipperary"; as the band comes to the chorus, the regiment is swinging into the street by* Nora's *house, and the voices of the soldiers can be heard lustily singing the chorus of the song*]

It's a long way to Tipperary, it's a long way to go;
It's a long way to Tipperary, to th' sweetest girl I know!
Good-bye, Piccadilly, farewell Leicester Square.
It's a long way to Tipperary, but my heart's right there!

[Nora *and* Mollser *remain silently listening. As the chorus ends, and the music is faint in the distance again,* Bessie Burgess *appears at door* L., *which* Mollser *has left open*]

BESSIE: [*Speaking in towards the room*] There's th' men marchin' out into th' dhread dimness o' danger, while th' lice is crawlin' about feedin' on th' fatness o' the land! But yous'll not escape from th' arrow that flieth be night, or th' sickness that wasteth be day. . . . An' ladyship an' all, as some o' them may be, they'll be scatthered abroad, like th' dust in th' darkness! [Bessie *goes away;* Nora *steals over and quietly shuts the door. She comes back to the lounge and wearily throws herself on it beside* Mollser]

MOLLSER: [*After a pause and a cough*] Is there anybody goin', Mrs. Clitheroe, with a tither o' sense?

THE TWENTIETH CENTURY

W. B. Yeats

Poems

THE LAKE ISLE OF INNISFREE

From The Rose *(1893).* *This lyrically rhythmic poem celebrating nature, and especially the island of Innisfree on Sligo's Lough Gill, offers images reminiscent of ascetic monks in their beehive cells. Thoreau's* Walden *is said to have inspired this poem.*

———————

I will arise and go now, and go to Innisfree,
And a small cabin build there, of clay and wattles made:
Nine bean-rows will I have there, a hive for the honey-bee,
And live alone in the bee-loud glade.

And I shall have some peace there, for peace comes dropping slow,
Dropping from the veils of the morning to where the cricket sings;
There midnight's all a glimmer, and noon a purple glow,
And evening full of the linnet's wings.

I will arise and go now, for always night and day
I hear lake water lapping with low sounds by the shore;
While I stand on the roadway, or on the pavements grey,
I hear it in the deep heart's core.

THE WILD SWANS AT COOLE

From The Wild Swans at Coole *(1919).* *Yeats often walked the mile from "Coole House," Lady Gregory's home, to Coole Lake where he observed over the course of nineteen years the swans—beautiful, ageless, and faithful. Here is a poignant, wistful reaction to the "autumn" of life.*

———————

The trees are in their autumn beauty,
The woodland paths are dry,
Under the October twilight the water
Mirrors a still sky;
Upon the brimming water among the stones
Are nine-and-fifty swans.

JACK B. YEATS. *Lough Gill, County Sligo.* 20th century. Watercolor on paper. 10 1/16 x 14 1/2 in. (25.6 x 36.8 cm). National Gallery of Ireland, Dublin.

The nineteenth autumn has come upon me
Since I first made my count;
I saw, before I had well finished,
All suddenly mount
And scatter wheeling in great broken rings
Upon their clamorous wings.

I have looked upon those brilliant creatures,
And now my heart is sore.
All's changed since I, hearing at twilight,
The first time on this shore,
The bell-beat of their wings above my head,
Trod with a lighter tread.

Unwearied still, lover by lover,
They paddle in the cold
Companionable streams or climb the air;
Their hearts have not grown old;
Passion or conquest, wander where they will,
Attend upon them still.

But now they drift on the still water,
Mysterious, beautiful;
Among what rushes will they build,
By what lake's edge or pool
Delight men's eyes when I awake some day
To find they have flown away?

From The Green Helmet and Other Poems *(1910). The image of crowd, riders, and horses all involved in a single process exemplifies Yeats's ideal vision of an Ireland in which the focus is on the activities of country life as opposed to the concerns of mercantilism.*

There where the course is,
Delight makes all of the one mind,
The riders upon the galloping horses,
The crowd that closes in behind:
We, too, had good attendance once,
Hearers and hearteners of the work;
Aye, horsemen for companions,
Before the merchant and the clerk
Breathed on the world with timid breath.
Sing on: somewhere at some new moon,
We'll learn that sleeping is not death.
Hearing the whole earth change its tune,
Its flesh being wild, and it again
Crying aloud as the racecourse is,
And we find hearteners among men
That ride upon horses.

O'Connell's Wager

Daniel O'Connell's friends make bets on his ability to best one of Dublin's most outrageous, irascible characters in a battle of words. The result is a hilarious encounter in which the Kerry barrister pushes the Dublin huckster to her limit.

There was at that time in Dublin, a certain woman, Biddy Moriarty, who had a huckster's stall on one of the quays nearly opposite the Four Courts. She was a virago of the first order, very able with her fist, and still more formidable with her tongue. From one end of Dublin to the other, she was notorious for her powers of abuse, and even in the provinces Mrs. Moriarty's language had passed into currency. The dictionary of Dublin slang had been considerably enlarged by her, and her voluble impudence had almost become proverbial. Some of O'Connell's friends, however, thought that he could beat her at the use of her own weapons. Of this, however, he had some doubts himself, when he listened once or twice to some minor specimens of her Billingsgate. It was mooted once where the young Kerry barrister could encounter her, and some one of the company rather too freely ridiculed the idea of his being able to meet the famous Madame Moriarty. O'Connell never liked the idea of being put down, and he professed his readiness to encounter her, and even backed himself for the match. Bets were offered and taken and it was decided that the matter should come off at once.

The party adjourned to the huckster's stall, and there was the owner herself, superintending the sale of her small wares—a few loungers and ragged idlers were hanging around her stall, for Biddy was a character and in her way was one of the sights of Dublin. O'Connell commenced the attack.

"What's the price of this walking-stick, Mrs. What's-your-name?"

"Moriarty, sir, is my name, and a good one it is; and what have you to say agen it? One-and-sixpence 's the price of the stick. Troth, it's chape as dirt, so it is."

"One-and-sixpence for a walking stick; whew! why, you are not better than an impostor, to ask eighteen pence for what cost you two pence."

"Two pence, your grandmother! Do you mane to say it's chating the people I am? Impostor, indeed!"

"I protest as I am a gentleman . . ."

"Jintleman! Jintleman! The likes of you a jintleman! Wisha, by gor, that bangs Banagher. Why, you potato-faced pippin-sneezer, when did a Madagascar monkey like you pick up enough of common Christian dacency to hide your Kerry brogue?"

"Easy now, easy now," said O'Connell with imperturbable good humour, "don't choke yourself with fine language, you whiskey-drinking parallelogram."

"What's that you call me, you murderin' villain?" roared Mrs. Moriarty.

"I call you," answered O'Connell, "a parallelogram; and a Dublin judge and jury will say it's no libel to call you so."

"Oh, tare-an'-ouns! Oh, Holy Saint Bridget! that an honest woman like me should be called a parrybellygrum to her face. I'm none of your parrybellygrums, you rascally gallows-bird; you cowardly, sneakin', plate-lickin' blaguard!"

"Oh, not you, indeed! Why, I suppose you'll deny that you keep a hypotenuse in your house."

"It's a lie for you. I never had such a thing . . . "

"Why, sure all your neighbours know very well that you keep not only a hypotenuse, but that you have two diameters locked up in your garret, and that you go out to walk with them

JACK B. YEATS. *Robert Gregory on Sarsfield at Gort Horse Show, 1906.* Pen and ink on paper. Colin Smythe Ltd., with permission of Anne Yeats.

264

every Sunday, you heartless old heptagon."

"Oh, hear that, ye saints in glory! Oh, there's bad language from a fellow that wants to pass for a jintleman. May the divil fly away with you, you micher from Munster, and make celery-sauce of your rotten limbs, you mealy-mouthed tub of guts."

"Ah, you can't deny the charge, you miserable sub-multiple of a duplicate ratio."

"Go, rinse your mouth in the Liffey, you nasty tickle-pincher; after all the bad words you speak, it ought to be dirtier than your face, you dirty chicken of Beelzebub."

"Rinse your own mouth, you wicked-minded old polygon—to the deuce I pitch you, you blustering intersection of a superficies!"

"You saucy tinker's apprentice, if you don't cease your jaw, I'll . . . " But here she gasped for breath, unable to hawk up more words.

"While I have a tongue, I'll abuse you, you most inimitable periphery. Look at her, boys! There she stands—a convicted perpendicular in petticoats! There's contamination in her circumference, and she trembles with guilt down to the extremities of her corollaries. Ah, you're found out, you rectilinealantecedent, and equiangular old hag! 'Tis with the devil you will fly away, you porter-swiping similitude of the bisection of a vortex!"

Overwhelmed with this torrent of language, Mrs. Moriarty was silenced. Catching up a saucepan, she was aiming at O'Connell's head, when he made a timely retreat.

"You've won your wager, O'Connell, here's your bet," said the ones who proposed the contest.

Leon Uris

FROM TRINITY

An Irish Rebel Challenges the British Crown

Leon Uris tells the story of Ireland from the famine of the 1840s to the Rising of 1916. In this extract, the fictional, defiant Conor Larkin, on trial for treason in a secret courtroom, evokes the passion and eloquence of Ireland's greatest heroes as he speaks without counsel, disproving the legality of the court and the very presence of the English on Irish soil.

"This court is illegal because your presence on Irish soil is illegal," Conor answered.

"And on what does the prisoner base that assumption?"

"On English common law."

Well, I'll tell you, you could have heard Charles Stewart Parnell and Daniel O'Connell stir in their graves if you listened hard enough.

"Take him away," Scowcroft said with a wave of the hand.

Bobby was on his feet! "The prisoner has the right to speak in his own defense," he said, citing one of the cornerstones of British justice. "Unless, of course, the court is satisfied to have the record bear out that he was silenced."

Sir Lucian Bolt came to the judge's rescue. "The Crown has no objection."

"I am prepared to allow prisoner Larkin to speak," the judge said, "but I advise him in advance that this is a court of law and his arguments will be restricted to issues and issues alone. You may go on, Larkin."

Conor took a few steps toward the bench and looked constantly from Sir Lucian Bolt to Sir Arnold Scowcroft.

"There are thousands of precedents in English common law of cases where a strong neighbor has used force by one means or another to impose his will on a weaker neighbor and such use of force as a method has always been deemed illegal in English courts. Without use of a proper legal library to support my argument, I will, nonetheless, attempt to cite a dozen or so landmark cases with which I am certain you are quite familiar."

Conor then went into the most magnificent extemporaneous dissertation I or anyone else within earshot had ever heard. At first, no one could believe the language coming from a man in rags and chains, then we all became totally swept up. He cited cases known to all lawyers of quarrels where force was declared illegal between neighbors in a close situation in cities, between farmers, between large estate holders, between municipalities, between counties and between British provinces on the mother island, Wales vs. England, Scotland vs. England. He went on to recite another dozen decisions, mostly made by colonial courts in the settlement of disputes between warring tribes and clans or provinces within a colony. His last set of citations dealt with international disputes in which the British had acted as arbitrator and, consistent with English common law, declared the use of force by a stronger neighbor on a weaker neighbor as no legal basis on which to settle a dispute.

"What you are saying through English common law is that you are desirous of existing with your neighbors in a country and a world where force is not permitted in the settlement of disputes because force by itself does not constitute right. As we know, by any definition, Ireland is the neighbor of England."

The place stood in awe. What I think astonished Sir Lucian Bolt, Sir Arnold Scowcroft and the other British who heard Conor's words was that such a profound theory emanated from a man representing a race which they truly believed to be inferior. I had the feeling that the legalists sensed they were hearing no idle rambling doomed to die in this room, but a statement which would be seized upon by every occupied people in the world who longed for their liberation. If English common law was an extension of God's supreme law, they were indeed in trouble in explaining their empire.

"If England had taken the position that we're going to have Ireland because we're stronger and we want it for exploitation, perhaps your presence here would be more understandable. However, the English went to enormous lengths to establish a legal basis for the entry into Ireland. Obviously they wanted to say to future generations, 'This is the reason we have come here.' What was the instrument of English legality for the invasion of Ireland? It was a papal bull issued in the year of 1154 granting you my country. Who gave you Ireland? The document was issued by an English Pope on the request of an English King. . . . for the purpose of amassing kingdoms for his sons. . . .You hold up this document and say in this year of 1908, 'This is our right to Ireland.' Was it legal even then? Did the Pope own Ireland? Didn't an armed invasion negate the legality of the papal bull, according to English common law?"

"Your lordship," Sir Lucian said, rising, "I don't see why the court has to be subjected to what has degenerated into a Fenian tirade."

"I see nothing the prisoner has said to be outside the guidelines laid down by the court," McAloon snapped.

Scowcroft drummed his fingers on the table top. It had gotten to a point where he was afraid he would have to make a ruling on Larkin's thesis and he was a legalist of extreme pride.

"I wish to hear the rest of what Larkin has to say."

Conor drew a breath and took a step toward the judge, pointing his finger.

"On the assumption that England's presence in Ireland was gained on shaky legal grounds, subsequent actions of a quasi-legal nature have no legal foundation in fact. Again, without the facility of a law library I am able to cite some four hundred pieces of legislation enacted against the Irish people to aid, abet and expand British presence in which a deliberate attempt was made to destroy an ancient civilization by laws repugnant to every concept of God and democracy and laws in contradiction to your own public vows to bring civilization to the Irish savage."

He stopped, swallowed a number of times to erase the dryness in his mouth, coughing a bit.

"Laws," Conor cried, "were enacted to destroy the Celtic concept of Catholicism which was the light and the flower of Western civilization at a time when England and the European continent writhed in the dark ages. When your attempt to impose the Reformation failed you

then enacted laws and shamefully bribed the Irish bishops into replacing Celtic Catholicism with Anglo-Catholicism totally alien to the Irish character. Laws were enacted in exactly the same measure to eradicate our language, an advanced system of government by the people, our economy, our customs, our heritage. Your legal basis of justification has come through convincing yourselves that we are an inferior race unfit to share an equitable life, even in our own land, and if we wished to continue to live in it we must become Englishmen. You have attempted to show the world and your own people that we are inferior and this gives you leave to treat us like animals. Nae, animals are fed, only Irishmen are deliberately starved in Ireland. Through the precedent of establishing the Irishman as a savage and the mission to rescue him from himself you have gone on to establish an empire in which you are also saving black, yellow and brown savages from themselves."

Now he paced with his chains clanging but no one was of a mood to stop him.

"These decades, generations and centuries of comic perversion of law and God, these self-serving acts of coercion, these instant laws that flip-flop or are enacted on a moment's notice according to your need of the day, these farcical unions imposed on unwilling people have always been carried out with total contempt for the savage. No Englishman really asks the savage how he would like to be ruled, for that is apparently the God-given right of your fine, advanced, Western culture and your mother of parliaments.

"The men who lead your government this minute are the same men who sat in the back bench of Parliament a few years ago expressing public horror and revulsion over your treatment of the Boers. But now that these fine gentlemen have gained power, their pity and their sense of decency have strangely fled as they always have when it comes to the Irish."

"Must this continue?" Sir Lucian cried out.

"Yes!" McAloon snapped. "Yes, yes, yes."

"I stand here in a world filled with rising and angry voices which will no longer tolerate their lives being manipulated by the perverse whims of greedy men. Before this twentieth century is out it will see you packing your kits and being drummed out of every corner of the world in scorn. You're a bunch of damned hypocrites holding yourselves up to the world as the successors of the ancient democracies while your hands are soaked in blood and your Parliament hosts this mockery. All you're really in it for is the money!"

"Silence! Silence!" Scowcroft burst from crimson cheeks as his mesmerism vanished.

Conor threw his head back and laughed as the guards closed in on him. "But, my lord," he roared, "even the lowest Irishman is allowed his speech from the dock."

"Silence the prisoner!"

"What are you afraid of? No one will hear me. You've made certain of that."

As Conor was seized Major Westcott bowed to the judge. "Does his lordship wish the prisoner gagged?"

"Aye, do that!" Conor shouted. "Let's stop the pretense that I'll get justice from the same lovely people who enacted the penal laws."

Sir Arnold studied himself back into control and waved Major Westcott away. "This court has been overly generous. No further presentation of the prisoner is required."

"Court?" Conor mocked. "I see no court. I see a hidden room buried in the Wicklow Mountains. There are no lawbooks, no journalists, no probing eyes or impartial minds. Are you inferring, sir, that this is a British courtroom?"

The judge was paralyzed with shock.

"Are you telling me you brought me to this place to dispense justice or are you saying that this is the justice you really have in mind for the Irish?"

Conor turned around, rattling his chains, and his eyes reached every man in the room and they backed off from his glare. "Court? This is a star chamber, a day out of the dark ages, a diabolical notion of justice, a reversion to the Inquisition. Are you serious about this?" Conor shuffled to the judge's table and leaned over, looking the man in his eyes, and the man blinked.

"You are a stranger in my land, mister. In the end, your fake legality will be exposed and you'll crawl out of Ireland, reviled."

Silence followed, long, terrible silence.

"The prisoner," the judge said shakily, "is remanded to solitary confinement while the court takes the matter under advisement." As Scowcroft bolted from the room his tipstaff snapped up.

"All rise," he said.

E. Charles Nelson

A Botanist Looks at Shamrock

Here is everything you ever wanted or needed to know about the three-leaved green plant that has become a universal symbol for Ireland. Although St. Patrick never mentioned it in his writings, his association with the near-mystical plant is a fixed part of Irish legend.

But, what *is* Shamrock?

The easiest way to answer that question is to ask country-folk who still have knowledge of the way things used to be. That is what I did a few years ago. I appealed for the true shamrock, as gathered by tradition from fields and byways. Nearly 250 shamrocks, alive and rooted, from almost every Irish county were potted carefully and grown into healthy plants at the National Botanic Gardens, Glasnevin, Dublin.

Everyone in Ireland knows that shamrocks worn on St. Patrick's Day have *no* flowers—the clusters of trefoil leaves are pure green, unsullied by flowers. But a shamrock discarded on St. Patrick's night can be planted and grown until it blossoms. (Every green plant must reproduce, and shamrock is no exception; it must bloom and thereafter set seeds.) By flowering those shamrocks in the Botanic Gardens, I could discover what the true, wild-collected ones really were—to what botanical species, with unfamiliar Latin names, each should be assigned.

One hundred three (46 per cent) of the true shamrocks sent to me in 1988 were plants that

Shamrock. Prelate's Badge. Ulster Museum, Belfast, Northern Ireland.

botanists, anywhere in the world, call *Trifolium dubium* (lesser trefoil, *seamair bhuí* in Irish); it has small clusters of minute yellow pea-flowers. Seventy-eight (35 per cent) were white clover *(Trifolium repens; seamair bhán)* and a very few others proved to be *Trifolium pratense* (red clover, *seamair dhearg*).

This is not startling information! In 1893, Nathaniel Colgan, an amateur Dublin botanist, did exactly the same experiment—he persuaded parish priests to send shamrocks which he grew until they blossomed; his percentages were almost identical with mine.

What conclusions can be drawn from this tale of scientific exactitude? Firstly, there is no agreement among the Irish about one, *and only one,* genuine shamrock—true shamrock has been and continues to be any one of four clovers. Moreover, present-day Irish shamrock-gatherers collect the same plants, in the same proportion, as their predecessors did in the 1890s. But, a majority prefer *Trifolium dubium* (indeed if you buy shamrock in a supermarket, you will wear *Trifolium dubium*).

Secondly, the shamrock is *not unique* to Ireland. Professor Michael Zohari, an Israeli botanist who was the world expert on clovers (*Trifolium* species), and Dr. David Heller reported that *Trifolium dubium* is distributed from Scandinavia to the Caucasus, and is a naturalised alien in North America.

Thirdly, very few self-respecting Irish folk wear wood sorrel *(Oxalis acetosella, seamsóg),* or its garden relatives, although these are the 'shamrocks' often promoted in America. As I say, these revelations are not new. Nathaniel Colgan came to the same conclusions in the 1890s. I have added little to what he wrote, except that the *four* true shamrocks are unchanged in relative popularity.

Whence did shamrock originate, and how did it become the badge of the Irish?

There are several important facts that, again, may startle many devout Irish men and women. Patrick, a British slave who became our patron saint, does not mention shamrock in his surviving writings. There is no historical record to confirm that Patrick preached sermon about the Holy Trinity using a shamrock to illustrate 'Three in One.' There is no account of Patrick's life, written before 1726, in which shamrock is linked with him, though the story is now an inseparable thread in Ireland's unequalled tapestry of myths and legends.

Shamrock is an *English* word; it first appeared in print during the 1500s in plays and poetry but did not then signify a sacred emblem. Shamrock was a vegetable, a famine food that the persecuted, starving Irish were said to eat—shamrock was part of the propaganda of the sixteenth century. The first person to link the word shamrock with a recognisable plant was a famous English herbalist, John Gerard, whose magnificent book, published in London during 1597, is still a delight to read. He wrote that white and red clovers were 'called in Irish *Shamrockes*.' We don't know who told Gerard this, but he was correctly informed. After that, shamrock slowly insinuated itself into the floral emblems of the kingdoms of Britain and Ireland joining English roses, Scottish thistles and Welsh leeks (the daffodil is a modern emblem). Shamrock, for Ireland, was entwined into royal coats-of-arms and heraldic devices.

When was shamrock first worn? In the early eighteenth century it was more usual to wear a cross of ribbons on St. Patrick's Day, but by 1726 shamrock was worn in hats, and then drowned. Towards the close of the same century, shamrocks entered the badges and flags of Irish regiments and Irish patriots. At the beginning of the 1800s, shamrocks made their first appearance carved on churches! Later they were engraved on beautiful glasses and painted on porcelain; they were fashioned from emeralds for elegant ladies to wear and were embroidered on their dresses; they were carved in bog-oak; books overflowed with shamrocks; they were printed on postcards, and sentimental songs were full of them.

Ultimately, the enshrining of shamrock as an Irish badge came to be traced to the poetry of Thomas Moore, and to the activities of King George IV and Queen Victoria. George IV came to Dublin in 1821, and entered the city, standing in a carriage and pointing to a great swathe of shamrock pinned to his hat—he gave his 'blessing' to the Scottish thistle in 1822 in a similar floral display. Queen Victoria's dresses for one of her state visits were embroidered with silver shamrock, and she commanded in 1900 that soldiers in Irish regiments should wear shamrock on St. Patrick's Day to commemorate fellow Irishmen who were killed in the Boer War. Thus the green shamrock is a symbol of remembrance older than the scarlet poppy of Flanders' fields.

Nowadays, it takes no more than a green trefoil to proclaim an Irish connection. But there is a final contradiction. Shamrock is neither the ancient emblem of Ireland nor the modern emblem of state—the harp is the time-honoured, national emblem, used in the Republic on all government publications and on the blue presidential standard. Only in Northern Ireland does the shamrock have official status as an emblem; within the arms of the United Kingdom shamrocks stand proud with roses, thistles and daffodils.

In the end, shamrock is *exactly* what its name means! Shamrock is the English version of the Irish word *seamróg* which can be translated precisely as young clover (from *seamair* = clover, *óg* = little, young). A shamrock is, simply, the winter phase of a clover—nothing less, nothing more.

Conrad Arensberg

FROM THE IRISH COUNTRYMAN

Appeasing the Fairies

Conrad Arensberg was born in 1910 in Pittsburgh, Pennsylvania, graduated from Harvard, and taught at M.I.T., Barnard, and Columbia. In the early 1930s Arensberg conducted field

study in social anthropology in County Clare, Ireland. In this selection from The Irish
Countryman: An Anthropological Study, *he turns his professional eye to "them," the
"pisherogues," visitors from the other world.*

The chief of these powers is usually called the "fairies." The country-people have many other
names for them which they prefer. But, most often, they feel no need of distinguishing them
by particular names. They call them simply "them." In the pronoun they summarize both their
nameless power and their immanence. No greater specification is necessary where such powers crowd so closely in upon one's life. The acts and rituals which spring out of this belief are
similarly broad in scope. They range from minor doings and turns of speech of daily life to the
most hidden practices of rare and deadly black magic. . . .

I have often heard countrymen, steeped in the old lore, say, "They'll leave you alone if you
don't be in their way." One makes a great mistake to think of any holder of popular belief as a
person ridden with superstitious fear, unable to make his way through ordinary life. As one
countryman told another collector, Lady Gregory, in the days before the war: "If we knew how
to be neighbourly with them, they would be neighbourly and friendly with us."

It is a question, then, of giving "them" their due. Where older custom survives, certain
precautions must be taken. You are probably all familiar with many of them. Food and water
must be left for them at night. Dirty water must not be thrown out at night. For the night is a
"lonely time"; "you wouldn't like to be out in it." The fairies are abroad. Were the water
thrown out, there is danger that it might dirty them as they pass along a fairy path or make a

nocturnal visit. Then they will be angry, and disaster will follow. A hen, a pig, a cow, even a child may sicken and die.

But this anger of theirs, you see, results from direct affront. And that affront lies, really, in improper conduct. In the case of dirty water, it lies directly in improper conduct of the household. Throwing out dirty water is slovenly and bad management. The community condemns it as much as do the fairies who might be wetted.

Consequently, one can begin to see the existence of a projection of values into the world of belief. Dangerous as "they" are, they bring good luck and prosperity as well, if they receive their proper due. Their favour follows proper conduct of the household and good household management in daily life. Thus one finds such statements possible as the following, in which an old fellow of North Clare, an authority on such matters, speaks of "their" nocturnal visits:

"They very often put up at a house in the night. They would come to certain houses, and if they liked the house and it was good and clean and everything swept for them, they would come often to the same house, and that house would be prosperous. If it was dirty and they found no comfort in it they would not stop. They'd go to strong houses like the Careys" (he named a comfortable, neat family of small farmers in the neighbourhood). "You often see a little old woman going along the road and stopping in asking for a bite to eat, and you might give it to her, and she looking to see was it a good house for them to stop in it."

Thus many tales of the good people point a moral. In this light such a common tale as that of the herdsman's house is readily understandable. The herdsman, as a landless man, is regarded by the small farmers as being a "cut" below themselves; consequently, his untidiness is a byword among them. One version of the story goes, in synopsis, as follows:

"Many families moved into a herdsman's place, but they were all chased out of it. Finally, one family moved in, cleaned up the house, and a 'paving path' around it. A little old woman visits the wife, borrows a cooking-pot and is similarly well treated. In gratitude she explains that the woman of the house and her husband will always prosper and never be molested, because they alone of all the families had cleaned up the place where 'they' walk."

Patrick Kavanagh

FROM THE GREEN FOOL

"The Wedding"

Patrick Kavanagh (1904–1967), one of Ireland's greatest poets, was the son of a farmer and cobbler, and was raised in County Monaghan in the north of Ireland. He left school early, presumably to become a farmer, but at the age of thirty set out to walk the fifty miles from his home to Dublin. Published in 1938, The Green Fool, *his autobiography, captures the essence of Irish rural life as seen in this account of the business of a country wedding.*

I was going to the fair of Carrick. I was accompanied by a neighbour-man whose daughter was getting married. He was very fidgety on this occasion. He was going to the town to meet his prospective son-in-law and he had in his breast-pocket half the fortune which was to be paid over on that day.

Before we had walked very far together he brought forth the roll of notes.

'Count them, Paddy,' he said, handing me the notes.

I fingered them heedlessly.

'There's a hundred and fifty in that wad,' he said. 'Meself and Judy made all that, and it

COLORPLATE 108

EDMUND DULAC. *W.B. Yeats and the Irish Theatre*. 1915. Ink, pencil, and watercolor on paper.
11 7/16 x 14 in. (29.1 x 35.5 cm). National Gallery of Ireland, Dublin.

COLORPLATE 109 *(above, left)*

JOHN BUTLER YEATS. *Augusta Gregory, Dramatist.* 1903. Oil on canvas. 24³/₈ x 20¹/₂ in. (62 x 52 cm). National Gallery of Ireland, Dublin.

COLORPLATE 110 *(above, right)*

SARAH PURSER. *Dr. Douglas Hyde, Poet, Scholar, and first President of Ireland. (1860–1949).* Early 20th century. Oil on canvas. 30 x 24¹³/₁₆ in. (76 x 63 cm). National Gallery of Ireland, Dublin.

COLORPLATE 111

SARAH PURSER. *Maud Gonne.* Early 20th century. Oil on canvas. 69¹/₂ x 41 in. (176.5 x 106 cm). Hugh Lane Municipal Gallery of Modern Art, Dublin.

COLORPLATE 112

JOHN BUTLER YEATS. *William Butler Yeats, Poet*. 1900. Oil on canvas. 30⁵/₁₆ x 25³/₁₆ in. (77 x 64 cm).
National Gallery of Ireland, Dublin. *Portrait of the poet by his father.*

COLORPLATE 113

SEAN O'SULLIVAN. *Portrait of James Joyce*. 1935. Red chalk and charcoal with white highlights on grey paper. 21⁷/₁₆ x 15 in. (54.5 x 38 cm). National Gallery of Ireland, Dublin.

COLORPLATE 114

MURIEL BRANDT. *Micheal MacLiammoir*. 20th century. Oil on canvas. 23⅝ x 34 in. (60 x 86.3 cm).
National Gallery of Ireland, Dublin. *MacLiammoir founded the Gate Theatre in Dublin.*

COLORPLATE 115

CAROL GRAHAM. *James Galway*. 1980. Oil on canvas. Ulster Museum, Belfast.
Copyright Carol Graham. *Galway, the man with the golden flute, performs all over the world.*

COLORPLATE 116

BARRIE COOK. *John Montague, Portrait.* 1991. Oil on canvas. 38⁵/₁₆ x 40¹/₈ in. (97.3 x 102 cm).
Crawford Municipal Art Gallery, Cork.

COLORPLATE 117

EDWARD MCGUIRE. *Portrait of Seamus Heaney*. 1974. Oil on canvas. 55⁷/₈ x 44¹/₈ in. (142 x 112 cm).
Ulster Museum, Belfast.

Donnybrook Fair in all its Glory, 1830. Color print by Sadler, late 19th century. National Library of Ireland, Dublin.

wasn't by buyin' new hats and fiddle de fols that we made it.'

'Judy was a good woman,' I said.

'Yer own mother was a good savin' woman, and between ourselves I wasn't a bad wee man meself.'

I handed him back the money. 'You were a good man,' I said.

'Yer own father was a good wee man,' he reciprocated, 'no better goin'.'

He looked towards the hills, and his dreams awoke.

'When I came from Scotland thirty years ago,' he said, 'I hadn't what would jingle on a tombstone. As God is me judge it's true, when I came home from Scotland I hadn't as much money as would put earnest in a besom.'

He must have been poor. I knew the ballad.

> *The Castleblaney besoms, the best that ever grew*
> *Were sold for two a penny on the Hill of Mullacrew.*

He invited me to the wedding. There would be a dance.

'Next Wednesday, if all goes well,' he said, 'Mary will be gettin' buckled. She's gettin' the best place in the parish, twenty-five acres of the best of dry land facin' the sun.'

'She's a lucky girl,' I said.

'No luckier than she deserves,' he said, 'there's not the batin' of Mary in Ireland.'

I knew by his talk that he had some slight misgivings. Strong, fifty-year-old twenty-five-acre farmers are not caught in the net of romance. They often wriggle out at the last moment. I knew a man who walked out of the church on the morning of his wedding. He left a fine young girl behind him for the sake of ten pounds. Marrying off a family of daughters was an expensive item for a poor farmer. A hundred pounds was the smallest fortune—fifty pounds down before the marriage and the other half by the instalment system.

You could easily know a farmer who owed his son-in-law part of the fortune. The son-in-law would come and take away a load of potatoes or turnips, or in the red-summer a load of mangolds for the pigs. Or he would be sure to run short of seed corn in spring and be forced to call on his wife's father for a few barrels.

The man with whom I travelled to Carrick met his future son-in-law on arrival in the town. They entered a pub and sat in one of the snugs. They were joined by a couple of amateur lawyers.

The pub in which they sat was opposite the sucker-pig-market. I was in the pig-market. We wanted a few young pigs. My mother arrived by train.

The marriage-bargainers came out of the pub. My travelling companion looked a trifle

Irish Tent, Blind Piper, the Moreen Jig. Drawing used for engraving in Mr. and Mrs. S.C. Hall's *Ireland (1841–43)*. National Library of Ireland, Dublin.

pale. My mother ran up to him.

'Is it all settled?' she asked.

'It's all settled,' he sighed.

'Well, thank God,' mother said.

The wedding was a success. There were three motor-cars. After the breakfast they drove off on a tour. Generally those wedding-tours went no farther than Dundalk. A pub at the Lower End was the rendezvous of wedding-parties.

The dance was held in a corn-loft over the pigsty. I got there about seven o'clock. The farmer himself was fixing candles to jutting stones around the loft walls. There was a half-barrel of porter standing in a corner.

'We didn't "tap" that porter yet,' the man said. 'We'll wait till the weddeners come home.'

In the dwelling-house was a great stir. Young girls were rushing around—slicing bread, setting the tables, singing and laughing all at once. Around the fire sat a few old women talking in low, peaceful tones.

'Run out and see if ye can hear the weddeners comin',' I was asked.

I went out to the yard and listened.

'No sign of them yet,' I said.

'I hope nothin' happened to them,' one of the old women said.

The invited guests were now pouring in, and some uninvited guests, too, such as servant boys and the professional philanderers of the parish. The fiddler arrived with his fiddle stuck under his coat.

'Is she "tapped" yet?' was the first thing he said. He was referring to the half-barrel.

'Very soon now, Pat, very soon,' the farmer said.

The tables were set. There were several kinds of currant cakes, plum pudding, rice pudding, ham and jam sandwiches. My lips watered. I knew that we could not touch the groaning table until the wedding-party had got the first run. We would get the leavings.

The fiddler played a few melancholy airs. It was easy to see that he was thirsty. The woman of the house called him to the room. I heard the pop of a cork and the woman's voice: 'This is a special drop I kept on the quiet.' The fiddler coughed.

'As good a drop of whisky as I ever tasted. Where did ye get it?'

'Backhouse's,' she said, 'it's Punchenstown.'

The fiddler coughed again. 'No, no,' he said, 'it's too dacent ye are.'

'Arrah drink it off, Pat,' she said.

'Ah, well, here's luck to the newly-weds.'

'The same to you, Pat.'

'Mary's gettin' a good man,' the fiddler said. 'A good man surely, no better.'

'She's gettin' a good place, Pat,' the woman said, 'thirty-five acres of the best of dry land.'

'He has forty acres, woman dear,' the fiddler said. I heard the clink of glasses again.

'Here now, ye'll have another wee tint.'

'Yer a wonderful woman, Judy.'

Over the rarefied atmosphere of February there came to our ears the sound of wild cheering. We rushed out to the yard.

'The weddeners are comin', the weddeners are comin'.'

The three cars drove up the short laneway to the house of the bride's people. The wedding party were drunk. As they left the cars and approached us they were cracking very private jokes.

'That was a great yarn Micky toul to Molloy.'

'Aw sure ye may be talkin'.'

And they laughed loudly. Two of the men went behind the door of the horse-stable: they were using this place as a urinal.

The bride and bridegroom entered the house. They were welcomed. All of us shook hands with them and wished them a 'gradle of joy.' The best man was explaining how they had fared during the day.

'We went as far as Dundalk. Nothin' would do Micky but we'd have to go into the pub at the Lower End. Aw, we had a great day. We had a dance in the taproom of the pub. Went all round the country after that—to Annagassan and back by Ardee. Aw, we had a great day.'

Among the wedding-party there had been a melodeon but no melodeon-player. However, one of the boys pulled the music-box in and out and nobody minded the absence of harmony. They cheered above the noise of the melodeon on the outward journey, and, coming home, the tormentor of music was too drunk to be able to do any harm to a sensitive ear.

We went to the loft while the wedding-party was eating. The fiddler came too.

'Take yer partners for a set,' the fiddler said.

We were about twenty boys and there was only one girl. She was well danced. A feeling of poignancy undertoned our merriment.

'This would make a very good wake,' a philanderer said.

'Only the corpse is missin',' another said.

And the bride and bridegroom and all the relations and satellites came out. The bride and bridegroom sat together on a sack of corn which had been laid along the wall. The bridegroom was sixty years old if he was a day, the bride was around twenty-one.

'A great match she made,' all the bridegroom's friends said.

'A young wife is the ruination of an oul' man,' a fellow beside me remarked. That stirred my curiosity. 'Why?' I asked.

'She'll run the life outa him. Why, man, he won't be worth a second-hand chew of tobacco when he's after sleepin' a week with that one.'

The dance. We took our partners for an Irish dance. We tapped around the floor. Even the sixty-year-old bridegroom was trying to walk on the music.

After the dance we sat on our hunkers around the walls while the porter was handed round. The man of the house and his son distributed the frothy liquor in pint mugs. I didn't want to drink, porter is cold stuff.

'Come on, drink up,' they forced me, 'there's others waitin' for that mug.'

I drank.

'He wanted to be forced,' somebody said; 'shy, but willin', like a bride in bed,' he added.

We were invited to supper in relays. Within the kitchen everyone was talking beyond himself. Even the old women let themselves go and said the wildest and most ridiculous things. Romance was in the air.

Cuchulainn. 20th century. Bronze sculpture in General Post Office, Dublin, erected as a memorial to the executed leaders of the Easter Rising. Irish Tourist Board, Dublin. *Cuchulainn, the mythic hero of* The Cattle Raid of Cooley *wanted to die standing up facing his enemy. After receiving a lethal wound, his warriors helped to bind him to a rock by the river where he could be seen by the enemy. It was only when a crow landed on his shoulder that the warriors knew he was dead.*

'Who'll give meself a squeeze?' an old crone by the hob sang: 'I seen the day when the boys would give their eye for a hoult with Bessy.'

'What kind of a night are yez havin' out there?' the bride's mother inquired.

'A holy livin' terror,' we told her, 'never saw the batin' of it for a dance.'

She was pleased. 'I must go out there meself when we get the tables cleared off,' she said.

By far the best part of the dance was the supper. The porter-sharks said the best part was the half-barrel.

Some time after midnight the bride started to cry, and a few of the girls joined her.

'You are as well to sing sorrow as to cry it,' I used to hear people say. The maxim, or whatever it is, worked both ways, for here were people crying joy. The girl was really lonely. In normal times in a normal country her husband wouldn't get a young girl like her even if he had fifty acres of land. But in South Monaghan marriages were becoming a rare event. The girls were losing their smiling self-confidence and alluring *hauteur*.

The horse was put in the cart. It was four o'clock. The bride's furniture and clothes were put on the cart. This load was called the 'flitting.' An old woman, a relation of the bride, got up on the load, as was the custom.

'Who's goin' with the flittin'?' strangers inquired.

'Maggy Malone,' was the answer.

The dancers dispersed. There was weeping and wailing as the 'flitting' rattled off. Only Maggy Malone, perched on top amid tables and wardrobes, kept her equilibrium both physically and emotionally. One would imagine it was a funeral was starting off. The bride's mother and sisters cried and laughed by turns. The father watched the cart out of sight.

'There goes a hundred and fifty pounds,' was probably what he was thinking. And a further hundred and fifty to be raised and paid by the end of the year. He was beggared, and he knew it. All his hard savings gone to purchase a husband.

'Oh, God, what did I do on you at all,' I once heard a man say after God had sent him the third consecutive daughter. No wonder he was displeased with Providence: daughters were a fragile and expensive commodity.

James Connolly

FROM THE IRISH FLAG, 1916

James Connolly (1868–1916) was born in Edinburgh and emigrated to Ireland in 1896. He founded the Irish Socialist Republican Party, eventually became a leader in the labor movement, and, with Patrick Pearse, led the violent 1916 Easter Rising, which culminated in his execution on May 9 at Kilmainham Jail. This article appeared in his newspaper, The Workers' Republic, *two weeks before the Rising. The green flag was hoisted over Liberty Hall on April 16, one week later.*

We are out for Ireland for the Irish. But who are the Irish? Not the rack-renting, slum-owning landlord; not the sweating, profit-grinding capitalist; not the sleek and oily lawyer; not the prostitute pressman—the hired lairs of the enemy. Not these are the Irish upon whom the future depends. Not these, but the Irish working class, the only secure foundation upon which a free nation can be reared.

The cause of labour is the cause of Ireland, the cause of Ireland is the cause of labour. They cannot be dissevered. Ireland seeks freedom. Labour seeks that an Ireland free should be the sole mistress of her own destiny, supreme owner of all material things within and upon her soil. Labour seeks to make the free Irish nation the guardian of the interests of the people of Ireland, and to secure that end would vest in that free Irish nation all property rights as against the claims of the individual, with the end in view that the individual may be enriched by the nation, and not by the spoiling of his fellows.

Having in view such a high and holy function for the nation to perform, is it not well and fitting that we of the working class should fight for the freedom of the nation from foreign rule, as the first requisite for the free development of the national powers needed for our class? It is so fitting. Therefore on Sunday, April 16th, 1916, the green flag of Ireland will be solemnly hoisted over Liberty Hall as the symbol of our faith in freedom, and as a token to all the world that the working class of Dublin stands for the cause of Ireland, and the cause of Ireland is the cause of a separate and distinct nationality.

In these days of doubt, despair, and resurgent hope we fling our banner to the breeze, the flag of our fathers, the symbol of our national redemption, the sunburst shining over an Ireland re-born.

PROCLAMATION OF THE IRISH REPUBLIC, 1916

The Easter Rising erupted violently on April 24, 1916, when the Irish Citizen's Army and the Irish Volunteers under Patrick Pearse and James Connolly seized the general post office and several other buildings in central Dublin. Pearse read this Proclamation of the Provisional Government from the front steps of the post office, calling on all Irish men and women to fight for their freedom from British rule. When it was over six days later, 64 rebels, 132 policemen and soldiers, and over 300 civilians were dead.

———————

The Provisional Government of the Irish Republic to the People of Ireland

Irishmen and Irishwomen: In the name of God and of the dead generations from which she receives her old tradition of nationhood, Ireland, through us, summons her children to her flag and strikes for her freedom.

Having organized and trained her manhood through her secret revolutionary organizations, the Irish Republican Brotherhood, and through her open military organizations, the Irish Volunteers, and the Irish Citizen Army, having patiently perfected her discipline, having resolutely waited for the right moment to reveal itself, she now seizes that moment, and, supported by her exiled children in America and by gallant allies in Europe, but relying in the first on her own strength, she strikes in full confidence of victory.

We declare the right of the people of Ireland to the ownership of Ireland, and to the unfettered control of Irish destinites, to be sovereign and indefeasible. The long usurpation of that right by a foreign people and government has not extinguished the right, nor can it ever be extinguished except by the destruction of the Irish people. In every generation the Irish people have asserted their right to national freedom and sovereignty; six times during the past three hundred years they have asserted it in arms. Standing on that fundamental right and again asserting it in arms in the face of the world, we hereby proclaim the Irish republic as a sovereign independent state, and we pledge our lives and the lives of our comrades-in-arms to the cause of its freedom, of its welfare, and of its exaltation among the nations.

The Irish republic is entitled to, and hereby claims, the allegiance of every Irishman and Irishwoman. The republic guarantees religious and civil liberty, equal rights and equal opportunities to all its citizens, and declares its resolve to pursue the happiness and prosperity of the whole nation and of all its parts, cherishing all the children of the nation equally, and oblivious of the differences carefully fostered by an alien government, which have divided a minority from the majority in the past.

Until our arms have brought the opportune moment for the establishment of a permanent national government, representative of the whole people of Ireland, and elected by the suffrages of all her men and women, the Provisional Government, hereby constituted, will administer the civil and military affairs of the republic in trust for the people. We place the cause of the Irish republic under the protection of the Most High God, whose blessing we invoke upon our arms, and we pray that no one who serves that cause will dishonour it by cowardice, inhumanity, or rapine. In this supreme hour the Irish nation must, by its valour and discipline, and by the readiness of its children to sacrifice themselves for the common good, prove itself worthy of the august destiny to which it is called.

Signed on behalf of the provisional government,

THOMAS J. CLARKE, SEAN MacDIARMADA, THOMAS MacDONAGH, P. H. PEARSE, EAMONN CEANNT, JAMES CONNOLLY, JOSEPH PLUNKETT

Aftermath of the 1916 Easter Rising in Dublin. 1916. Photograph. The Metropole Hotel, Post Office and Nelson Column along O'Connell Street. Colin Smythe Ltd.

Patrick Pearse

FROM THE MURDER MACHINE

"Back to the Sagas"

Patrick Pearse (1879–1916), born in Dublin of an English father and Irish mother, was educated at the Christian Brothers School, University College, and King's Law. A much-loved educator, Pearse founded St. Enda's school in Rathfarnham, where he was able to institute his progressive educational ideas, not the least of which was the concept that education should be fun. This selection, from a pamphlet comprised of Pearse's articles on Irish education, expresses his conviction that schools need to look to the heroic spirit for inspiration.

That freedom may be availed of to the noble ends of education there must be, within the school system and within the school, an adequate inspiration. The school must make such an appeal to the pupil as shall resound throughout his after life, urging him always to be his best self, never his second-best self. Such an inspiration will come most adequately of all from religion. I do not think that there can be any education of which spiritual religion does not form an integral part; as it is the most important part of life, so it should be the most important part of education, which some have defined as a preparation for complete life. And inspiration will come also from the hero-stories of the world, and especially of our own people; from science and art if taught by people who are really scientists and artists, and not merely persons with certificates from Mr. T. W. Russell; from literature enjoyed as literature and not studied as 'texts'; from the associations of the school place; finally and chiefly from the humanity and great-heartedness of the teacher.

A heroic tale is more essentially a factor in education than a proposition in Euclid. The story of Joan of Arc or the story of the young Napoleon means more for boys and girls than all the algebra in all the books. What the modern world wants more than anything else, what Ireland wants beyond all other modern countries, is a new birth of the heroic spirit. If our

JACK B. YEATS.
*Communicating with
the Prisoners.* 1922.
Oil on board.
Sligo County Library.

schools would set themselves that task, the task of fostering once again knightly courage and strength and truth—that type of efficiency demanded by the English Civil Service—we should have at least the beginning of an educational system. And what an appeal an Irish school system might have! What a rallying cry an Irish Minister of Education might give to young Ireland! When we were starting St. Enda's I said to my boys: 'We must re-create and perpetuate in Ireland the knightly tradition of Cuchulainn, "better is short life with honour than long life with dishonour"; "I care not though I were to live but one day and one night, if only my fame and my deeds live after me"; the noble tradition of the Fianna, "we, the Fianna, never told a lie, falsehood was never imputed to us"; "strength in our hands, truth on our lips, and cleanness in our hearts"; the Christ-like tradition of Colmcille, "if I die it shall be from the excess of the love I bear the Gael."' And to that antique evangel should be added the evangels of later days: the stories of Red Hugh and Wolfe Tone and Robert Emmet and John Mitchel and O'Donovan Rossa and Eoghan O'Growney. I have seen Irish boys and girls moved inexpressibly by the story of Emmet or the story of Anne Devlin, and I have always felt it to be legitimate to make use for educational purposes of an exaltation so produced.

The value of the national factor in education would appear to rest chiefly in this, that it addresses itself to the most generous side of the child's nature, urging him to live up to his finest self. If the true work of the teacher be, as I have said, to help the child to realise himself at his best and worthiest, the factor of nationality is of prime importance, apart from any ulterior propagandist views the teacher may cherish. The school system which neglects it commits, even from the purely pedagogic point of view, a primary blunder. It neglects one of the most powerful of educational resources.

It is because the English education system in Ireland has deliberately eliminated the national factor that it has so terrifically succeeded. For it has succeeded—succeeded in making slaves of us. And it has succeeded so well that we no longer realise that we are slaves. Some of us even think our chains ornamental, and are a little doubtful as to whether we shall be quite as comfortable and quite as respectable when they are hacked off.

It remains the crowning achievement of the 'National' and Intermediate systems that they have wrought such a change in this people that once loved freedom so passionately. Three-quarters of a century ago there still remained in Ireland a stubborn Irish thing which Cromwell had not trampled out, which the Penal Laws had not crushed, which the horrors of '98 had not daunted, which Pitt had not purchased: a national consciousness enshrined mainly in a national language. After three-quarters of a century's education that thing is nearly lost.

A new education system in Ireland has to do more than restore a national culture. It has to restore manhood to a race that has been deprived of it. Along with its inspiration it must, therefore, bring a certain hardening. It must lead Ireland back to her sagas.

Finally, I say, inspiration must come from the teacher. If we can no longer send the children to the heroes and seers and scholars to be fostered, we can at least bring some of the heroes and seers and scholars to the schools. We can rise up against the system which tolerates as teachers the rejected of all other professions rather than demanding for so priest-like an office the highest souls and noblest intellects of the race. . . .

The fact is that, with rare exceptions, the men and women who are willing to work under the conditions as to personal dignity, freedom, tenure, and emolument which obtain in Irish schools are not the sort of men and women likely to make good educators. This part of the subject has been so much discussed in public that one need not dwell upon it. We are all alive to the truth that a teacher ought to be paid better than a policeman, and to the scandal of the fact that many an able and cultured man is working in Irish secondary schools at a salary less than that of the Viceroy's chauffeur.

Patrick Pearse

Poems

I am Ireland

Patrick Pearse wrote stories, plays, and poetry in both Gaelic and English. In this poem, written in the last year of his life, Pearse identifies with the familiar Gaelic folk figure and suffers the disappointment of unfulfilled promises.

I am Ireland:
I am older than the Old Woman of Beare.

Great my glory:
I that bore Cuchulainn the valiant.

Great my shame:
My own children that sold their mother.

I am Ireland:
I am lonelier than the Old Woman of Beare.

LAST LINES, 1916

On the eve of his execution as one of the leaders of the 1916 Easter Rising, Pearse remembered the beauty of his beloved world. At his trial, the president of the court remarked, "I have had to condemn to death one of the finest characters I have ever come across."

———————

The beauty of the world hath made me sad,
This beauty that will pass;
Sometimes my heart hath shaken with great joy
To see a leaping squirrel in a tree,
Or a red ladybird upon a stalk,
Or little rabbits in a field at evening,
Lit by a slanting sun,
Or some green hill where shadows drifted by,
Some quiet hill where mountainy man hath sown
And soon shall reap near to the gate of Heaven;
Or children with bare feet upon the sands
Of some ebbed sea, or playing on the streets
Of little towns in Connacht,
Things young and happy.
And then my heart has told me:
These will pass,
Will pass and change, will die and be no more,
Things bright and green, things young and happy;
And I have gone upon my way
Sorrowful.

I have no treasure trove
The wealth of fame is gone
Even the very joys of love
Have vanished and left me alone.

Gold I haven't piled
Nothing of this I leave behind
My wish to be remembered by a child
By something said which pleased his mind.

Níor cruinníodh liomsa ór—
I have not garnered gold.

George Bernard Shaw

A Letter of Condolence on the Death of Michael Collins

Michael Collins (1890–1922), one of Ireland's great revolutionary heroes, was largely responsible for negotiating the 1921 treaty which established the boundaries between

JOHN LAVERY. *Michael Collins, Rebel Leader.* 20th century. Oil on canvas. 17 1/2 x 25 9/16 in. (44.5 x 65 cm). Hugh Lane Municipal Gallery of Modern Art, Dublin.

Northern Ireland and the Republic. On August 22, 1922, just ten days after taking over the leadership of the Irish Free State, Collins was ambushed and killed by extremists who thought he had betrayed the Republic to the English. In this letter of condolence to Collins's sister Johanna, George Bernard Shaw fondly recounts his only meeting with Collins at a dinner at Horace Plunkett's home just a few days earlier.

DEAR MISS COLLINS,

Don't let them make you miserable about it: how could a born soldier die better than at the victorious end of a good fight, falling to the shot of another Irishman—a damned fool, but all the same an Irishman who thought he was fighting for Ireland—"a Roman to a Roman"?

I met Michael for the first and last time on Saturday last, and am very glad I did. I rejoice in his memory, and will not be so disloyal to it as to snivel over his valiant death.

So tear up your mourning and hang up your brightest colors in his honor; and let us all praise God that he had not to die in a snuffy bed of a trumpery cough, weakened by age, and saddened by the disappointments that would have attended his work had he lived.

Sincerely,

BERNARD SHAW

Denis Devlin

"The Tomb of Michael Collins"

Denis Devlin (1908–1959) was born in Scotland, educated in Dublin, Munich, and Paris, and served in the diplomatic service in Rome, New York, Washington, London, and Tokyo. He wrote this elegy for the slain hero Michael Collins.

———————

I
Much I remember of the death of men,
But his I most remember, most of all,
More than the familiar and forgetful
Ghosts who leave our memory too soon—
Oh, what voracious fathers bore him down!

It was all sky and heather, wet and rock,
No one was there but larks and stiff-legged hares
And flowers bloodstained. Then, Oh, our shame so massive
Only a God embraced it and the angel
Whose hurt and misty rifle shot him down.

One by one the enemy dies off;
As the sun grows old, the dead increase,
We love the more the further from we're born!
The bullet found him where the bullet ceased,
And Gael and Gall went inconspicuous down.

II
There are the Four Green Fields we loved in boyhood,
There are some reasons it's no loss to die for:
Even it's no loss to die for having lived;
It is inside our life the angel happens
Life, the gift that God accepts or not,
Which Michael took with hand, with harsh, grey eyes,
He was loved by women and by men,
He fought a week of Sundays and by night
He asked what happened and he knew what was—
O Lord! how right that them you love die young!
He's what I was when by the chiming river
Two loyal children long ago embraced—
But what I was is one thing, what remember
Another thing, how memory becomes knowledge—
Most I remember him, how man is courage.

And sad, Oh sad, that glen with one thin stream
He met his death in; and a farmer told me
There was but one small bird to shoot: it sang
'Better Beast and know your end, and die
Than Man with murderous angels in his head.'

III

I tell these tales—I was twelve-year-old that time.
Those of the past were heroes in my mind:
Edward the Bruce whose brother Robert made him
Of Ireland, King; Wolfe Tone and Silken Thomas
And Prince Red Hugh O'Donnell most of all.

The newsboys knew and the apple and orange women
Where was his shifty lodging Tuesday night;
No one betrayed him to the foreigner,
No Protestant or Catholic broke and ran
But murmured in their heart: here was a man!

Then came that mortal day he lost and laughed at,
He knew it as he left the armoured car;
The sky held in its rain and kept its breath;
Over the Liffey and the Lee, the gulls,
They told his fortune which he knew, his death.

Walking to Vespers in my Jesuit school,
The sky was come and gone; 'O Captain, my Captain!'
Walt Whitman was the lesson that afternoon—
How sometimes death magnifies him who dies,
And some, though mortal, have achieved their race.

James Joyce

FROM A PORTRAIT OF THE ARTIST AS A YOUNG MAN

Christmas Dinner

James Joyce (1882–1941) was born in Dublin and educated by the Jesuits and the Christian Brothers, eventually attending University College, Dublin. Joyce left Ireland in 1904 under a self-imposed exile, and spent the rest of his life in Europe, with only infrequent visits to Ireland. Although now considered by many to be the most influential writer of the 20th century, he died in Zurich disappointed that his major works had not brought more success. In this selection the Dedalus' Christmas dinner disintegrates into squabbling about the dead-king Parnell.

———————

—Tell me, did I tell you that story about a very famous spit?
—You did not, John, said Mr Dedalus.
—Why then, said Mr Casey, it is a most instructive story. It happened not long ago in the county Wicklow where we are now.
He broke off and, turning towards Dante, said with quiet indignation:
—And I may tell you, ma'am, that I, if you mean me, am no renegade catholic. I am a catholic as my father was and his father before him and his father before him again when we

Georgian Houses, Dublin.
Photograph.
Irish Tourist Board.

gave up our lives rather than sell our faith.

—The more shame to you now, Dante said, to speak as you do.

—The story, John, said Mr Dedalus smiling. Let us have the story anyhow.

—Catholic indeed! repeated Dante ironically. The blackest protestant in the land would not speak the language I have heard this evening.

Mr Dedalus began to sway his head to and fro, crooning like a country singer.

—I am no protestant, I tell you again, said Mr Casey flushing.

Mr Dedalus, still crooning and swaying his head, began to sing in a grunting nasal tone:

> *O, come all you Roman catholics*
> *That never went to mass.*

He took up his knife and fork again in good humour and set to eating, saying to Mr Casey:

—Let us have the story, John. It will help us to digest.

Stephen looked with affection at Mr Casey's face which stared across the table over his joined hands. He liked to sit near him at the fire, looking up at his dark fierce face. But his dark eyes were never fierce and his slow voice was good to listen to. But why was he then against the priests? Because Dante must be right then. But he had heard his father say that she was a spoiled nun and that she had come out of the convent in the Alleghanies when her brother had got the money from the savages for the trinkets and the chainies. Perhaps that made her severe against Parnell. And she did not like him to play with Eileen because Eileen was a protestant and when she was young she knew children that used to play with protestants and the protestants used to make fun of the litany of the Blessed Virgin. *Tower of Ivory*, they used to say, *House of Gold!* How could a woman be a tower of ivory or a house of gold? Who was right then? And he remembered the evening in the infirmary in Clongowes, the dark waters, the light at the pierhead and the moan of sorrow from the people when they had heard.

Eileen had long white hands. One evening when playing tig she had put her hands over his eyes: long and white and thin and cold and soft. That was ivory: a cold white thing. That was the meaning of *Tower of Ivory*.

—The story is very short and sweet, Mr Casey said. It was one day down in Arklow, a cold bitter day, not long before the chief died. May God have mercy on him!

He closed his eyes wearily and paused. Mr Dedalus took a bone from his plate and tore some meat from it with his teeth, saying:

—Before he was killed, you mean.

Mr Casey opened his eyes, sighed and went on:

—It was down in Arklow one day. We were down there at a meeting and after the meeting was over we had to make our way to the railway station through the crowd. Such booing and baaing, man, you never heard. They called us all the names in the world. Well there was one old lady, and a drunken old harridan she was surely, that paid all her attention to me. She kept dancing along beside me in the mud bawling and screaming into my face: *Priesthunter! The Paris Funds! Mr Fox! Kitty O'Shea!*

—And what did you do, John? asked Mr Dedalus.

—I let her bawl away, said Mr Casey. It was a cold day and to keep up my heart I had (saving your presence, ma'am) a quid of Tullamore in my mouth and sure I couldn't say a word in any case because my mouth was full of tobacco juice.

—Well, John?

—Well. I let her bawl away, to her heart's content, *Kitty O'Shea* and the rest of it till at last she called that lady a name that I won't sully this Christmas board nor your ears, ma'am, nor my own lips by repeating.

He paused. Mr Dedalus, lifting his head from the bone, asked:

—And what did you do, John?

—Do! said Mr Casey. She stuck her ugly old face up at me when she said it and I had my mouth full of tobacco juice. I bent down to her and *Phth!* says I to her like that.

He turned aside and made the act of spitting.

—*Phth!* says I to her like that, right into her eye.

He clapped a hand to his eye and gave a hoarse scream of pain.

—*O Jesus, Mary and Joseph!* says she. *I'm blinded! I'm blinded and drownded!*

He stopped in a fit of coughing and laughter, repeating:

—*I'm blinded entirely.*

Mr Dedalus laughed loudly and lay back in his chair while uncle Charles swayed his head to and fro.

Dante looked terribly angry and repeated while they laughed:

—Very nice! Ha! Very nice!

It was not nice about the spit in the woman's eye. But what was the name the woman had called Kitty O'Shea that Mr Casey would not repeat? He thought of Mr Casey walking through the crowds of people and making speeches from a wagonette. That was what he had been in prison for and he remembered that one night Sergeant O'Neill had come to the house and had stood in the hall, talking in a low voice with his father and chewing nervously at the chinstrap of his cap. And that night Mr Casey had not gone to Dublin by train but a car had come to the door and he had heard his father say something about the Cabinteely road.

He was for Ireland and Parnell and so was his father: and so was Dante too for one night at the band on the esplanade she had hit a gentleman on the head with her umbrella because he had taken off his hat when the band played *God save the Queen* at the end.

Mr Dedalus gave a snort of contempt.

—Ah, John, he said. It is true for them. We are an unfortunate priestridden race and always were and always will be till the end of the chapter.

Uncle Charles shook his head, saying:

—A bad business! A bad business!

Mr Dedalus repeated:

—A priestridden Godforsaken race!

He pointed to the portrait of his grandfather on the wall to his right.

—Do you see that old chap up there, John? he said. He was a good Irishman when there was no money in the job. He was condemned to death as a whiteboy. But he had a saying about our clerical friends, that he would never let one of them put his two feet under his mahogany.

Dante broke in angrily:

—If we are a priestridden race we ought to be proud of it! They are the apple of God's eye. *Touch them not*, says Christ, *for they are the apple of My eye.*

—And can we not love our country then? asked Mr Casey. Are we not to follow the man that was born to lead us?

—A traitor to his country! replied Dante. A traitor, an adulterer! The priests were right to abandon him. The priests were always the true friends of Ireland.

—Were they, faith? said Mr Casey.

He threw his fist on the table, and frowning angrily, protruded one finger after another.

—Didn't the bishops of Ireland betray us in the time of the union when bishop Lanigan presented an address of loyalty to the Marquess Cornwallis? Didn't the bishops and priests sell the aspirations of their country in 1829 in return for catholic emancipation? Didn't they denounce the fenian movement from the pulpit and in the confessionbox? And didn't they dishonour the ashes of Terrence Bellew MacManus?

His face was glowing with anger and Stephen felt the glow rise to his own cheek as the spoken words thrilled him. Mr Dedalus uttered a guffaw of coarse scorn.

—O, by God, he cried, I forgot little old Paul Cullen! Another apple of God's eye!

Dante bent across the table and cried to Mr Casey:

—Right! Right! They were always right! God and morality and religion came first.

Mrs Dedalus, seeing her excitement, said to her:

—Mrs Riordan, don't excite yourself answering them.

—God and religion before everything! Dante cried. God and religion before the world!

Mr Casey raised his clenched fist and brought it down on the table with a crash.

—Very well, then, he shouted hoarsely, if it comes to that, no God for Ireland!

—John! John! cried Mr Dedalus, seizing his guest by the coatsleeve.

Dante stared across the table, her cheeks shaking. Mr Casey struggled up from his chair and bent across the table towards her, scraping the air from before his eyes with one hand as though he were tearing aside a cobweb.

—No God for Ireland! he cried. We have had too much God in Ireland. Away with God!

—Blasphemer! Devil! screamed Dante, starting to her feet and almost spitting in his face.

ROSE BARTON. *St. Patrick's Cathedral, Marsh's Library, Dublin.* c. 1897. Watercolor on paper. 7 1/16 x 10 13/16 in. (18 x 27.5 cm). Courtesy Crawford Municipal Art Gallery, Cork, Ireland. Private collection.

COLORPLATE 118

Silver Rococo Coffee Pot. Sterling silver. Ulster Museum, Belfast.

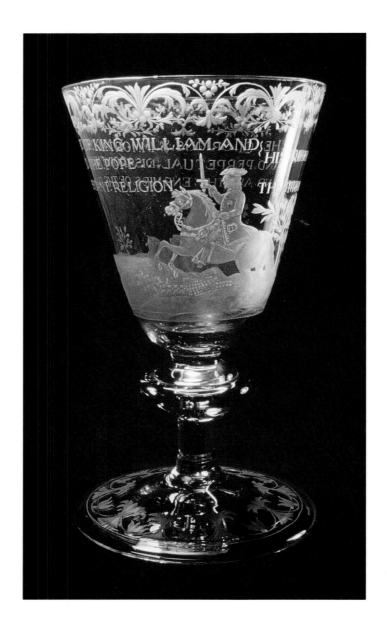

COLORPLATE 119

Williamite Goblet. Etched glass. Ulster Museum, Belfast.

COLORPLATE 120

Sugar bowl and stand. c. 1820–1830.
Waterford, cut glass. 4³/₄ x 8 in.
(12 x 20 cm). National Museum of
Ireland, Dublin.

COLORPLATE 121

Waterford Crystal Goblet. "Ballylee." Contemporary cut glass. Waterford Crystal, Inc.

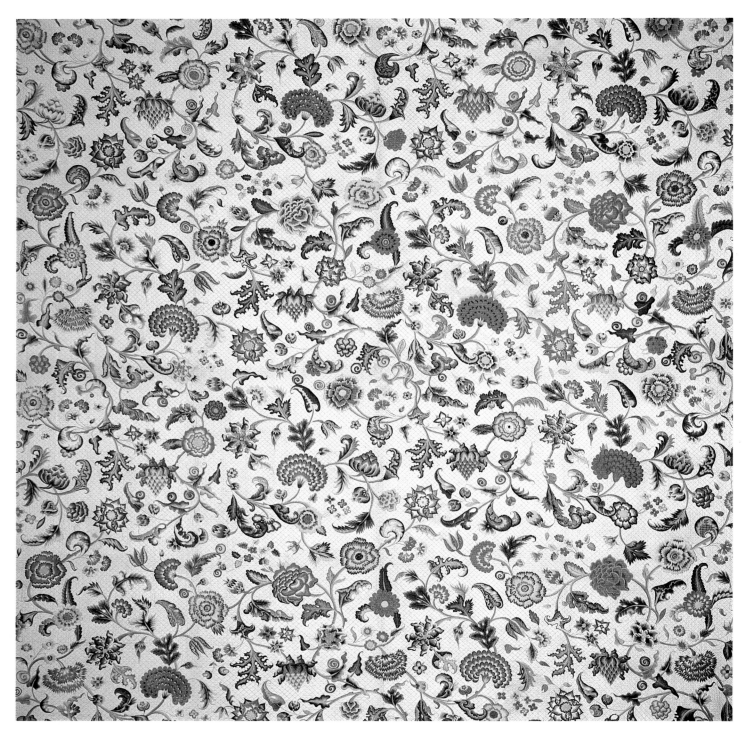

COLORPLATE 122

Lennox Quilt. 19th century. Ulster Museum, Belfast.

COLORPLATE 123

HARRY CLARKE. *Textile Design for Sefton Fabrics, Belfast.* 1919. Watercolor over ink on paper.
9⁵/₁₆ x 7 ¹/₁₆ in. (23.6 x 18 cm). National Gallery of Ireland, Dublin. *Sefton Fabrics commissioned
Clarke to design a set of eight silk handkerchiefs. This pattern of butterflies and sea urchins is one
of the unused designs.*

COLORPLATE 124

ANNE MORROW. *Donegal tweed scarves.* Village Donegal. Photograph. Irish Tourist Board, Dublin.

COLORPLATE 125

Clones Lace. County Monaghan. Contemporary lace-making. Photograph. Irish Tourist Board, Dublin.

COLORPLATE 126

HARRY KERNOFF. *Costumes for an officer, his daughter and a workman.* 1928. Watercolor over ink and pencil on paper. 7 x 8⁷/₈ in. (17.8 x 22.5 cm). National Gallery of Ireland, Dublin.

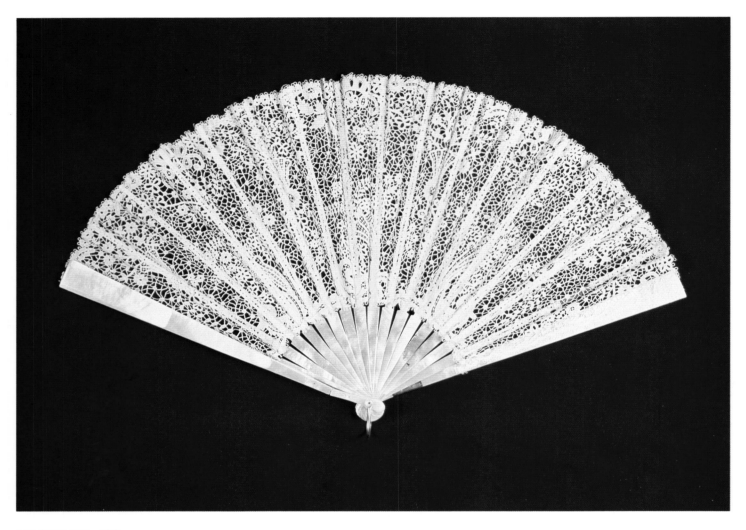

COLORPLATE 127

Lace Fan. c. 1890. Made in Carrickmacross, County Monaghan. 23¹/₂ x 8¹/₂ in. (59.7 x 21.6 cm).
National Museum of Ireland, Dublin.

Uncle Charles and Mr Dedalus pulled Mr Casey back into his chair again, talking to him from both sides reasonably. He stared before him out of his dark flaming eyes, repeating:

—Away with God, I say!

Dante shoved her chair violently aside and left the table, upsetting her napkinring which rolled slowly along the carpet and came to rest against the foot of an easychair. Mrs Dedalus rose quickly and followed her towards the door. At the door Dante turned round violently and shouted down the room, her cheeks flushed and quivering with rage:

—Devil out of hell! We won! We crushed him to death! Fiend!

The door slammed behind her.

Mr Casey, freeing his arms from his holders, suddenly bowed his head on his hands with a sob of pain.

—Poor Parnell! he cried loudly. My dead king!

He sobbed loudly and bitterly.

Stephen, raising his terrorstricken face, saw that his father's eyes were full of tears.

Elizabeth Bowen

FROM SEVEN WINTERS: MEMORIES OF A DUBLIN CHILDHOOD

"Sundays"

Elizabeth Bowen (1899–1973), celebrated short-story writer, novelist, and essayist, was born in Dublin, but spent most of her life in England. After inheriting the family home, Bowen's Court, in County Cork, she lived there part of each year. This memoir of her comfortable childhood winters in Dublin presents a matter-of-fact picture of the Protestant Anglo-Irish daily life.

On Sundays we went to St. Stephen's, our parish church, a few minutes' walk along the canal. St. Stephen's Georgian facade, with its pillars and steps, crowns the Upper Mount Street perspective, and looks down it into the airy distance of Merrion Square. To the ascending sound of bells we went up the steps—my mother with a fine-meshed veil drawn over her features, my father already removing his top-hat, I in my white coat. The Sunday had opened with mysterious movements about the staircase of Herbert Place—my mother's and father's departure to 'early church.'

About this Matins *I* went to there was no mystery. I could be aware that this was only an outer court. None the less, I must not talk or look behind me or fidget, and I must attempt to think about God. The church, heart of and key to this Protestant quarter, was now, at mid-morning, packed: crosswise above the pews allotted to each worshipping family ran galleries, with, I suppose more people up there. The round-topped windows let in on us wintry, varying but always unmistakably Sunday light, and gas burned where day did not penetrate far enough. The interior, with its clear sombreness, sane proportions, polished woodwork and brasswork and aisles upon which confident feet rang, had authority—here one could feel a Presence, were it only the presence of an idea. It emphasized what was at once august and rational in man's relations with God. Nowhere was there any intensity of darkness, nowhere the point of a small flame. There was an honourable frankness in the tone in which we rolled out the General

PATRICK HENNESSY. *Portrait of Elizabeth Bowen at Bowenscourt.* 20th century. Oil on canvas. 35 7/8 x 28 in. (91 x 71 cm). Crawford Municipal Art Gallery, Cork, Ireland.

Confession—indeed, sin was most felt by me, in St. Stephen's, as any divagation from the social idea. There was an ample confidence in the singing, borne up by the organ's controlled swell.

Bookless (because I could not read) I mouthed my way through the verses of hymns I knew. Standing packed among the towering bodies, I enjoyed the feeling that something was going on. During prayers I kneeled balanced on two hassocks, and secretly bit, like a puppy, sharpening its teeth, into the waxed prayer-book ledge of our pew. Though my inner ear was already quick and suspicious, I detected, in the course of that morning service, no hypocritical or untrue note. If I did nothing more, I conformed. I only did not care for the Psalms, which struck me as savage, discordant, complaining—or, sometimes, boastful. They outraged all the manners I had been taught, and I did not care for this chanted airing of troubles.

My mother attended St. Stephen's out of respect for my father's feeling that one should not depart from one's parish church. He mistrusted, in religion as in other matters, behaviour that was at all erratic or moody; he had a philosophic feeling for observance and form. But she liked St. Bartholomew's better because it was 'higher,' and once or twice in the course of every winter she would escape and take me there. Archbishop Trench and his daughters were her cousins; the happiest days of her girlhood had been spent at the Palace, and for the rest of her days she remained High Church. She spoke of 'Prods' (or, extreme, unctuous Protestants) with a flighty detachment that might have offended many. I was taught to say 'Church of Ireland,' not 'Protestant,' and 'Roman Catholic,' not simply 'Catholic.'

It was not until after the end of those seven winters that I understood that we Protestants were a minority, and that the unquestioned rules of our being came, in fact, from the closeness of a minority world. Roman Catholics were spoken of by my father and mother with a courteous detachment that gave them, even, no myth. I took the existence of Roman Catholics for granted but met few and was not interested in them. They were, simply 'the others,' whose world lay alongside ours but never touched. As to the difference between the two religions, I was too discreet to ask questions—if I wanted to know. This appeared to share a delicate, awkward aura with those two other differences—of sex, of class. So quickly, in a child's mind, does prudery seed itself and make growth that I remember, even, an almost sexual shyness on the subject of Roman Catholics. I walked with hurried step and averted cheek past porticos of churches that were 'not ours,' uncomfortably registering in my nostrils the pungent, unlikely smell that came round curtains, through swinging doors. On Sundays, the sounds of the bells of all kinds of churches rolled in a sort of unison round the Dublin sky, and the currents of people quitting their homes to worship seemed to be made alike by one human habit, such as of going to dinner. But on weekdays the 'other' bells, with their (to my ear) alien, searching insistence had the sky and the Dublin echoes all to themselves. This predisposition to frequent prayer bespoke, to me, some incontinence of the soul. . . .

James Stephens

Preparing for a Dinner Party

James Stephens (1882–1950), short-story writer, lyricist, and journalist, grew up in Dublin's slums, and worked as a clerk until George Russell (AE) discovered his poems and included him in Dublin's fashionable literary circle. He became Registrar of the National Gallery of Ireland and a popular radio broadcaster for the BBC. The following account of his first meeting with George Moore reveals a self-involved Mr. Moore offering advice on the art of dinner-party conversation to the naive Stephens.

I was Registrar of the Dublin National Gallery at one time. My man came in and said: "Mr. George Moore to see you, sir." "Ah," said I to myself, "the famous novelist that everybody talks about and nobody reads, and of whom I've never read a word either!" . . . "Show him in," said I.

In ten more seconds George Moore stepped into my lovely office. There were three or four pictures on each of my walls, and a beautiful fire in the grate. Moore looked very carefully at all my pictures before he looked at me, and said: "Ah, copies, I presume."

"I think not," I replied, "but you are more of an expert than I am." Moore sat down. "You are an expert, *ex officio*," said he. "Oh, no," I answered. "I am merely a very superior official: my Director is Quattro-centro and my Board is Byzantine. They are our experts."

An odd thing happens when two writers meet. Without a word being uttered on the subject, each knows in thirty seconds whether the other has ever read a line of his work or not. Neither of us had, and we were both instantly aware that life is not perfect, but, while I was full of patience and hope, Moore was scandalised.

Still, literature was his subject, and this was so in a deeper sense than in any other writer I have ever met. In the way of being dedicated to the craft of writing, Moore was that. He lived for the prose way of thinking—wine, women and murder—and I am sure that when he was asleep he dreamed that he was writing a bigger and better book than any he had yet managed to produce. He loved the art of prose; for poetry he had the traditional reverence that we all have; but I fancy that he had small liking for it.

Poetry presents a problem to the prose men, for it can exist very energetically without character, without humour, it can even get along without action, where prose must have all of these. The novelist may often think of poetry as almost a complete destitution, or as the stock-in-trade of a beggarman: "Poetry is nothing written by no one."

"What are you working at now, Stephens?" said Moore.

"This morning," I replied, "I translated the *County of Mayo*."

"That is my own county," said he, "and so I am interested. But, my dear Stephens, that poem has been translated so many times already, that you are wasting your, ah, talent, yes, perhaps talent, on a job that every literate person in Ireland has done before you."

"Why, Moore?" said I.

Here he broke in, "Don't you think, Stephens, that I have come to the years in which younger men should address me as Mr. Moore?"

"Certainly, Mr. Moore," said I—and he smiled a grave, fattish and reprobating smile at me.

"You were going to say," he prompted, turning on me his pale fattish face and his sloping, thinnish shoulders, and his air of listening to me almost as through a keyhole.

"Only, sir, that a translation is never completed until it has become a piece of original verse in the new tongue."

"That is an excellent and beautifully impossible definition," said Moore. "Perhaps,' he went on, "you would like to say the verses to me. How many are there?" he added hastily.

"Only four," I answered, "and as it is about your own county, sir, you should be the first one to hear them."

"Thank you, Stephens," said he, unnecessarily, for I intended to say that poem to someone. So I said the little poem, and he praised it highly, mainly I think because I had called him "sir."

"I must leave you very soon," said he, "for I have a lunch engagement, but if you ever need literary advice, I hope you will write to me. In fact, I beg that you will do so, for I have a proposition to make to you."

"I am in need of advice right now, Mr. Moore," said I, "and although some might think the matter not literary I consider that everything that has to do with a speech problem has to do with literature."

Moore agreed. "Psychological problems," said he, "are women and religion and English grammar. All other problems are literary. Tell me the matter that is confusing you, Stephens."

"Well, sir," said I, "I have been invited to the first formal dinner party of my life."

"Your first dinner party?" he queried.

"I have eaten," I explained, "with every kind of person and at every kind of table, but I have never dined with anybody."

"At a dinner," said he, "formal or informal, you just eat your dinner."

"Oh, no, Mr. Moore," said I, "the problem has nothing to do with mastication and is quite a troublesome one. I shall be sitting at a strange table and on my right hand there will be a lady whom I have never seen before and may never see again."

"Quite," said he.

"On my left hand," I continued, "there will be another lady whom I've never seen before. In the name of heaven, Mr. Moore, what shall I say to these ladies?"

"Why," said Moore thoughtfully, "this is a problem that never struck me before. It is a very real one," said he, sitting up at me and at it. "If you were an Englishman," he went on, "you could talk a little about the weather, vaguely, you know, a number of Dirty Days and How are You's, and then you could say a few well-chosen words about the soup, and the meat, and subsequently about the pudding—pudding, Stephens."

"Dammit," said I.

"An Irishman," Moore said, "can always find something to say about the cattle, and the crops, the manure, and the . . . No, no," he continued energetically, "no manure—ladies think it is very strange stuff: they prefer to talk about the theaters, actors, I mean, and hats. I'll tell you, talk to the first woman about how pretty her dress is; say that you have never seen so lovely a dress in your life. Then turn to the other hussy, and say that she is the most beautiful person in the room. Admire her rings: don't ask her where she got them: never ask a woman where or how she got anything whatever; questions like that often lead to divorce proceedings. In short, Stephens, talk to them about themselves, and you are pretty safe."

He enlarged on this matter: "You may talk to them about their hair and their eyes and their noses, but," he interrupted hastily, "don't say anything whatever about their knees."

"I will not, Mr. Moore," said I fervently.

"In especial, Stephens, do not touch their knees under any circumstances."

"I will not, Mr. Moore."

"Restraint at a formal dinner party, Stephens, is absolutely necessary."

"I quite understand, sir."

"Moreover, Stephens, women are strangely gifted creatures in some respects, all women have a sense akin to absolute divination about their knees."

"Ah, sir?" I queried.

"When a woman's knee is touched, Stephens, however delicately, the lady knows infallibly whether the gentleman is really caressing her or whether he is only wiping his greasy fingers on her stocking. But formal dinner parties are disgusting entertainments anyhow. Goodbye, Stephens."

"Goodbye, Mr. Moore," said I fervently, "and thank you very much for your help. I shall never forget those ladies' knees."

Moore smiled at me happily, almost lovingly. "Write to me about this dinner party, Stephens."

"I shall certainly do so, Mr. Moore."

And that was our first meeting.

John Montague
"Tyrone: the Rough Field"

John Montague, poet and teacher, was born in 1929 in Brooklyn, New York, but grew up on a farm in County Tyrone. He was educated at St. Patrick's College, Armagh and University College, Dublin. After living for a time in France, he returned to the United States to teach

The Turf Cutter.
Photograph. National Library of Ireland, Dublin. Valentine Photographic Collection.

at Berkeley, among other universities. He lectures at University College, Cork, returning from time to time to teach in the United States. In this simple remembrance of the ordinary life of "the heart land of Ulster" the passage of time is obliterated, as the past merges with the present through vivid images of the farm life of forty years ago.

The parish in which I was brought up lies in Tyrone, what a Belfast poet (John Hewitt) once called 'the heart land of Ulster.' A seventeenth century survey, on the other hand, describes it as 'cold mountainous land' which may explain why it escaped resettling at the time of the Plantation. Across the road from our house were the crumbling remains of stables, a halt on the old Dublin-Derry coach road. And with its largely Catholic population (MacRory, MacGirr, Farrel, Tague) Errigal Kieran could still be taken for a parish in Southern Ireland, artificially marooned. Most of the place names were pure Gaelic: Garvaghey (The Rough Field), Glencull (The Glen of the Hazels), Clogher (The Golden Stone). On a clear day, working at turf on the top mountain, one could see straight down to North Monaghan.

But there were defiant differences. The post-van which came down the road was royal-red, with a gold crown on either side. And the postman himself was an ex-Serviceman who remembered Ypres and the Somme, rather than 1916 or the Eighteenth day of November. In school we learnt the chief industries of Manchester, but very little about Cuchulainn or Connemara. And none of the farmers had enough Gaelic to translate the names of the town-lands. A dark-faced fanatical priest tried to teach us some after school hours. I thought him a fearsome bore until I greeted the last Gaelic speaker in the area after mass one Sunday, and saw the light flood across her face.

The ordinary life of the people, however, took little stock of racial or religious differences; they were submerged in a pre-industrial farming pattern, where the chief criterion was 'neighbourliness.' True, there were social differences which betrayed the historical cleavage. The depressed class of farm labourers were largely Catholic, just as the majority of the stronger farmers were Protestant. There were also the sexual fantasies which emerge when, as in the American South, two cultures rub uneasily together. Pedigree bulls were mainly owned by Protestants: indeed, there was a curious legend that Catholic bulls were rarely as potent. And when I went to fetch the local gelder for our young bulls, it seemed oddly appropriate that he should take down his cloth-covered weapon from beside a stack of black family bibles.

But in the seasonal tasks that pushed the wheel of the year the important thing was skill, based on traditional practice. Turf-cutting, which began in late spring, revealed all the instinctive layers of a craft. First there was the stripping of the bank, the rough sods being saved for the back of the fire. Then the three-man team moved in, one to cut (using the traditional slane or flanged spade), one to fill (grasping the wet turves in rows) and one to wheel (emptying the barrow sideways, so that the turf fell uncrushed, but open to the sun). At mealtime, they sat around the basket in a circle, their hobnailed boots shining with wet, and talked of great teams of the past.

But turf-cutting was not as delicate a task as building a stack. To begin, a circle of stones and whins was laid, 'to let the air in under her.' Upon this the stack rose, the builder riding with it, to catch and place the sheaves forked to him, until he slithered down to round the conical roof of thatch. One of our hands, slovenly enough in other ways, was held to be a master builder. In winter, when the thresher came, his stacks unpeeled in smooth slices, like an orange.

Such tasks determined the character of the people, hard-working, frugal, completely escaping the traditional view of the Celt. Kitchens were usually well lit, with a dresser of delph along one wall, a curtained settle bed in another, a shotgun or fiddle resting on a third. But the centre was the great blackened tent of the hearth, where the crook swung, supporting a hierarchy of pots and pans. From this fire to the dairy, with its meal bins and churns, the farmer's wife bustled, until the men came tramping in for their evening meal.

The hearth was also the focus of the strongest custom in Ulster farming communities, the habit of dropping in, for a visit or *ceilidh,* after milking time. One rarely knocked, your approach being heralded by the dog's bark, the shadow crossing the window. Sometimes a worn pack of cards was produced, for a game of 'twenty-five.' Sometimes a song was called for, but the district was not rich in balladry, except for a version of the north-country 'Barbary Allen' and one or two patriotic songs, like 'The Mountains of Pomeroy.'

It was at such times that one came closest to the secret life of the countryside. Starting from practical details, the chat drew a thick web of speculation over local affairs: who was 'failing fast,' who was threatening 'the law' on some neighbour, who was going to give birth (inside or outside the blanket, a third of the children in the local school being illegitimate). Fact soon drowned in fancy: how so-and-so had broken his leg after ploughing down a fairy fort, how a B-Special's hair had turned white because he arrested a priest on his way to a dying man, how Father Mackey had put a poltergeist in a bottle.

For behind the flat surface of daily life beat memories of a more resonant past, now half-regretted, half-feared. When I was five I was brought to my first wake and remember the neat row of clay pipes beside the snuff and porter. But by the time I was going to secondary school my aunt had given up planting the rushy St Brigid's Crosses which used to hang over the lintel in kitchen and byre. Even barn dances had become a thing of the past, although I made the last one in the Fintona area famous when, climbing to get a swig of poteen from the local fiddler, I fell straight through the loft into a nest of squealing pigs.

For a long time Carleton's Tyrone survived in the remote areas, under the shadow of the mountains, but since the war, the rate of change has become relentless. The replacing of the hearth fire by a stove dealt a blow not merely to turf-cutting and breadmaking (most farmers' wives now buy shop bread) but also to the practice of ceilidhing. The battery wireless was an endearing faulty messenger from outside, but with the arrival of electric light and television the Rough Field has become a part of the twentieth century. The old coach-road is now a magnificent highway, running straight as a die through the built-up valley. The public-house, surrounded by cars, looks like a roadhouse; the shop sells ice-cream to children from the pre-fabricated village where the road workers and lorry drivers (formerly farm labourers) live.

But one must avoid seeing all this through a haze of nostalgia. The last time I was back I was talking to a strong farmer in his byre. Behind us the milking-machine hummed, the pans and cylinders swaying under the cow's udder. He was lamenting the decline of neighbourliness, how farming had become mechanized, how the young had no time for anything but cars and dancehalls. Then a smile crossed his face, and he described how the oldest crone in the district had come down to see his television set. 'She had a stick in either hand, and her bent over like a hoop. She came into the kitchen—we had to pull back the dogs off her—and she said she be to see the picture box. She sat in front of it for an hour and then rose to go, saying that 'a wee man you could turn on like that would be a great comfort on a cold winter's night.'

Patrick Kavanagh

Poems

SHANCODUFF

His native black hills in North Monaghan are the poetic inspiration for this celebration of the natural life as Kavanagh expresses his love for the living landscape.

My black hills have never seen the sun rising,
Eternally they look north towards Armagh.

HUMBERT J. CRAIG.
Going to Mass. 20th
century. Oil on board.
14³/₈ x 19³/₈ in. (37.7 x
50.5 cm). Crawford
Municipal Art Gallery,
Cork, Ireland.

Lot's wife would not be salt if she had been
Incurious as my black hills that are happy
When dawn whitens Glassdrummond chapel.

My hills hoard the bright shillings of March
While the sun searches in every pocket.
They are my Alps and I have climbed the Matterhorn
With a sheaf of hay for three perishing calves
In the field under the Big Forth of Rocksavage.

The sleety winds fondle the rushy beards of Shancoduff
While the cattle-drovers sheltering in the Featherna Bush
Look up and say: 'Who owns them hungry hills
That the water-hen and snipe must have forsaken?
A poet? Then by heavens he must be poor.'
I hear and is my heart not badly shaken?

INNISKEEN ROAD: JULY EVENING

The isolation of the poet, the outsider who can observe as the bicycles or the cars ride up to,
but not into, *the dance, may enhance the vision of his work but can leave him feeling distant
and remote.*

The bicycles go by in twos and threes—
There's a dance in Billy Brennan's barn to-night,
And there's the half-talk code of mysteries

And the wink-and-elbow language of delight,
Half-past eight and there is not a spot
Upon a mile of road, no shadow thrown
That might turn out a man or woman, not
A footfall tapping secrecies of stone.

I have what every poet hates in spite
Of all the solemn talk of contemplation.
Oh, Alexander Selkirk knew the plight
Of being king and government and nation.
A road, a mile of kingdom, I am king
Of banks and stones and every blooming thing.

A CHRISTMAS CHILDHOOD

The religious nature of Christmas takes on new reality as the child becomes part of the mystery of the Nativity and the images of the Nativity become part of the child's landscape.

I
One side of the potato-pits was white with frost—
How wonderful that was, how wonderful!
And when we put our ears to the paling-post
The music that came out was magical.

The light between the ricks of hay and straw
Was a hole in Heaven's gable. An apple tree
With its December-glinting fruit we saw—
O you, Eve, were the world that tempted me

To eat the knowledge that grew in clay
And death the germ within it! Now and then
I can remember something of the gay
Garden that was childhood's. Again

The tracks of cattle to a drinking-place,
A green stone lying sideways in a ditch
Or any common sight the transfigured face
Of a beauty that the world did not touch.

II
My father played the melodeon
Outside at our gate;
There were stars in the morning east
And they danced to his music.

Across the wild bogs his melodeon called
To Lennons and Callans.
As I pulled on my trousers in a hurry
I knew some strange thing had happened.

Outside the cow-house my mother
Made the music of milking;
The light of her stable-lamp was a star
And the frost of Bethlehem made it twinkle.

A water-hen screeched in the bog,
Mass-going feet
Crunched the wafer-ice on the pot-holes,
Somebody wistfully twisted the bellows wheel.

My child poet picked out the letters
On the grey stone,
In silver the wonder of a Christmas townland,
The winking glitter of a frosty dawn.

Cassiopeia was over
Cassidy's hanging hill,
I looked and three whin bushes rode across
The horizon—the Three Wise Kings.

An old man passing said:
'Can't he make it talk'—
The melodeon. I hid in the doorway
And tightened the belt of my box-pleated coat.

I nicked six nicks on the door-post
With my penknife's big blade—
There was a little one for cutting tobacco.
And I was six Christmases of age.

My father played the melodeon,
My mother milked the cows,
And I had a prayer like a white rose pinned
On the Virgin Mary's blouse.

Blarney Bridge in County Cork. Engraving. National Library of Ireland, Dublin.

James Plunkett

FROM THE GEMS SHE WORE

On Reaching Blarney Castle

James Plunkett, born in 1920 and educated in Dublin, is a critic, musician, short-story writer, novelist, and a former program head of Telefís Eirann. Here he traces the derivation of the word "blarney" and explains why so many people feel compelled to bend over backwards to kiss the Blarney Stone.

———————————

A few miles to the north-west of Cork city lies Blarney and its famous Castle, where you kiss the Blarney Stone and are ever afterwards endowed with eloquence. Blarney (like Captain Boycott) has the distinction of having given a word to the English language through Queen Elizabeth's impatience with McCarthy, Baron of Blarney, who had an inexhaustible supply of answers and excuses for going his own sweet way instead of submitting to her Majesty's much reiterated commands.

'All Blarney,' pronounced the Queen, when she received yet another polite enquiry after her health, accompanied by yet another reasonable explanation as to why McCarthy had not yet done what he kept on and on promising to do. A man with the gift of the Blarney is fair of word and soft of speech and, as they say, can swear a hole through an iron bucket.

The stone is set in the battlements, one hundred and twenty winding steps up from the ground. One legend says it was given to the McCarthys by Robert Bruce after the battle of Bannockburn; another that it was given to a Cormac McCarthy by a woman whom he rescued from drowning and who turned out to be a witch. The countryside around is well wooded and peaceful and much traversed by gaily coloured horse drawn caravans, with their complement of holiday makers who fancy a few weeks of Romany life.

Father Prout

"Blarney Castle"

Father Prout (Francis Sylvester Mahony, 1804–1866), a native of Cork, was a Jesuit priest known for his witty verses. He eventually left the Church and worked as a journalist and translator in Europe. Surely he kissed the Blarney Stone before writing these verses.

———————————

There is a boat on the lake to float on.
And lots of beauties which I can't entwine;
But were I a preacher, or a classic teacher,
In every feature I'd make 'em shine!

There is a stone there, that whoever kisses,
O! he never misses to grow eloquent;

Blarney Castle, Cork.
Late 18th century.
Engraving. National
Library of Ireland,
Dublin.

'Tis he may clamber to a lady's chamber,
Or become a member of parliament:

A clever spouter he'll soon turn out, or
An out-and-outer, "to be let alone."
Don't hope to hinder him, or to bewilder him.
Sure he's a pilgrim from the Blarney stone!

Sean O'Faolain

FROM AN IRISH JOURNEY

Advice to the Traveller

Sean O'Faolain was born in 1900 in Cork and educated both there and at Harvard (MA 1929). He was an early volunteer in the Irish Republican movement. In this colorful guide to his home county he describes Cork as a town with a sting, and its citizens as shrewd masters of the irreverent — in both intonation and gesture. His portrait of Kinsale conveys how the town's history continues to pervade every aspect of its landscape.

CORK

I have described Cork city, or parts of it, several times in stories and novels: but I have always seen it there through the eyes and heart of some character for whom it was the world. It is not my world now, though I was born here, and lived here for twenty-six years. So, I am not a stranger; and yet I am not part of it because I have left it for so long. This town is coloured by my idea of it in boyhood and youth and first manhood, and it is coloured again by that which our memories do to the early part of our lives after we have married experience. I cannot be objective about Cork.

There is only one tune for Cork. It is one of those towns you love and hate. Some wag said that in Cork you do not commit sin; you achieve it. You do not, likewise, enjoy life in Cork; you experience it. For it is a town with a sting, inhabited by the Irish Gascons, the most acidulous race we breed, the most alive, the keenest, sharpest, and toughest, typified at their best and worst by a man like Tim Healy, or a man like Anthony Carroll, or a man like Jasper Wolfe. To a stranger entering Cork I would say: "Be on the defensive. These smothering, Blarneying folk have the mountains of Cork and Tipperary to the North of them, the sea to the South of them, the wilds of West Cork and Kerry at their backs, and as for the valley to the East down to Youghal, it seems to be asleep, and I always found it asleep, but since it is part of Cork it is safer not to believe for a moment that it is asleep."

To be born, to grow, and to live here in this apparently languorous south is to live tautly all the time. It is that; sleep; or drink.

One lives every experience, every growing-pain with the greatest possible poignancy here. One is persistently made aware of what one should experience without awareness. For as these people are full of brains and full of ideas, they are also full of alertness, shrewdness, cynicism, and bitter humour, which communicates itself. Put a flower into their hands and they will admire it with a delicate perception and a fine phrase (every Corkman has the gift of words), and then . . . you will see the eyebrows flicker, and an impish look come into the eyes, and out will come some word that crushes it in the fist.

I have never forgotten, and when somebody asks me about the Cork people, I always recall a tiny incident that illustrates this side of their nature, the smiling, eyelash-peering murder. There was a young fellow at the university, who was to grow to be a sensitive poet, admired and claimed by the city because he wrote of it with that excess of affection known only to the exile. The new president, Sir Bertram Windle, was due to arrive in the city, and this lad thought it would be a nice thing if the students could meet him and welcome him. The students agreed; he composed an address of welcome which his fellows approved; they met the president; the poet read the address and all went off well. The day after, still elated, the poet chanced to meet a student in the street, and this conversation followed. Every Corkman will hear the intonation, the faint rise of tone, the gentle flick of the lash in the last phrase. I do not

Cork. Hand-colored drawing used for engraving in Mr. and Mrs. S. C. Hall's *Ireland* (1841–43). National Library of Ireland, Dublin.

know if the stranger can appreciate it.

"Hello, Dan!"

"What cheer!" from the poet.

"Er . . . I see ye presented an address to the president, aw?"

"That's right."

"I see . . . er . . . I see you wrote it yourself, aw?"

"Ay!"

"Er . . . I see you read it out to him yourself, aw?"

"I did."

Pause. The accoster's eyebrows flicker. His eyelashes come together. He smiles gently.

"I . . . er . . . I suppose 'twas the way you couldn't get anyone else to do it?"

To this day the poet, now a man of years, curls up as he remembers the sting of that casual question, with all its ungenerous implications. Then he laughs, and seeing the little scene I laugh, and no Corkman for whom I have ever acted it but laughs, and then grinds his teeth and then laughs again. Connoisseurs in sadism.

KINSALE

Kinsale is, as we say sometimes in the south, "crawling" with history. It must go back to Norman times at least. There is high up on the hills to the west, over the old town, a field, and in that field a protuberance which is the remains of a far earlier religious settlement. But for every Irishman the word means only one phrase—1601—the Spanish landing under Don Juan del Aquila—the hosting of O'Neill and O'Donnell from the north of Ireland—the all-but-last stand of the old medieval Gaelic Ireland against the new power of the Renaissance—the ten weeks siege of Mountjoy and Carew—the fatal and fateful battle on Christmas morning, and then the "flight of the earls"—that phrase which rings in the mind of Ireland the knell of its ancient order.

There is hardly a field about this old town which does not, for that siege and battle, still the mind with memories. Here in this dyke, overrun by brambles, the Irish dead were piled. There a farm carries the word of "slaughter" in its Gaelic name: *Cnocanair.* If you go for a walk here with a local inhabitant, he will, as casually as inevitably interrupt the conversation, as you pass from vantage point to vantage point over the rolling hills, to indicate where O'Donnell approached the town, where the English trenches lay, where Carew encamped. One picks (even still) musket bullets out of the ground. The impress of that siege and battle is as fresh in Kinsale as if it were only yesterday that the Irish burst on the English camp at dawn and found to their dismay the troops ready and waiting. I spent a whole day walking the hills with a friend who has served in several campaigns; a soldier to his marrowbones. His expert elucidation made me feel the thing come to life in field after field: especially so when he said, "But it is in winter one should walk here. The battle was fought in winter. Then the trees would be bare and we would see the terrain just as they saw it, when the morning broke."

It all reminded me of Egdon Heath in its suffusion of association with times past. This is rare in Ireland. Our history has seemed to fade from the land like old writing from parchment. Traditional memory is broken. Our monuments are finest when oldest, but then so old that their echoes have died away. The *pietas* which is so cherished and nourished in other countries, has here an inadequate number of actual moulds to hold it. National emotion is a wild sea-spray that evaporates like a religion without a ritual. We are moved by ghosts. Something powerful and precious hangs in the air that holds us like a succubus; but what it is we can hardly define because we have so few concrete things that express it. Only in the most rare and most precious places throughout the entire land is there this urn-burial of Kinsale, where the ashes may still be revered in the very vessel which still holds them before our eyes. Aughrim is another such place. The fields of Wexford. Some corners of Limerick city. Derry, Killala, Ballina, Sligo. None of these has the monumental significance of Kinsale, the sense of the die cast, the doom of the decisive hour. Kinsale was one of the decisive battles of these islands.

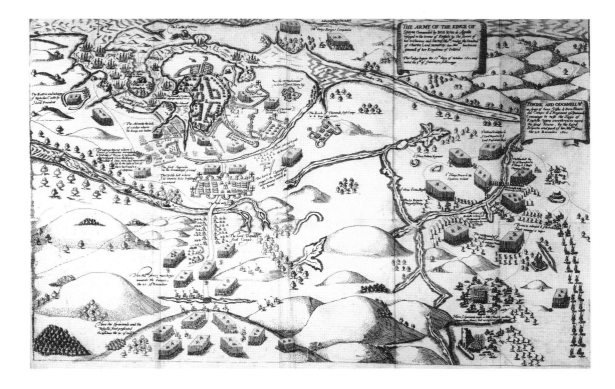

To this day it carries the import which fell on it that bitter winter morning over three hundred years ago.

The first impression the town makes on the traveller is the dignity of age, the sorrow of decline, and the final, hopeless topsy-turveydom of everything. Hood cloaks on the women, slated fronts, ruins, winding lanes—these are the motifs. There are few streets in Kinsale. The vagaries of time have thrown down passages that call themselves streets, but in fact are antique pathways. The footsteps of the generations have beaten the town into shapelessness. At every corner one is lost.

Alice Taylor

FROM TO SCHOOL THROUGH THE FIELDS

Some Colorful Characters

Alice Taylor has written a warm remembrance of a 1940s childhood in the Irish countryside of County Cork. The simple world of family loyalty and togetherness is embodied in the formidable grandmother and the on-again off-again farm worker who knew the true meaning of traveling light, and is touchingly expressed through the ritual of the family rosary.

A TOUCH OF OLIVER

My grandmother was a formidable old lady. She was six feet tall and, dressed in flowing black with a crochet shawl around her shoulders, she carried herself with grace and dignity. In later years she used a walking stick, but she walked with regal bearing until the day she died at ninety-eight years of age. It could be that she needed the stick to maintain law and order when she was unable to move as fast as she wanted, for while grandmothers are supposed to be loving and soft-bosomed, mine certainly did not fit into that picture: she was strong willed and domineering and ruled the house with a rod of iron. Her husband was dead with years so she ran the large farm herself and thrived on it. She was a forerunner of the struggle for equality and she was confident that most women could run a business as well if not better than men. She did just that, but in her time she was no ordinary woman. She killed her own pig and seldom sent for a vet as she could dose cattle and repair fractures like an expert. Some of her mother's people were doctors so she maintained that medicine was in her blood and, indeed, when one of her workmen was gored by a bull her fast, skilful action saved his life.

Though in some ways she was ahead of her time, in others she belonged to the era of the French Revolution. When our revolution came and the Black and Tans rampaged around the country my grandmother, a staunch Republican, was in the thick of it. Anyone on the run knew that they could get safe harbouring in her house. The Black and Tans knew this as well and many nights when the family were fast asleep the lorries drove into the yard, loud banging started on the door and the house was searched.

One night a young man called Larry, who was on the run, was asleep upstairs in the same room as her young son. Her two daughters were in another room. Suddenly the loud knocking started and she woke up. Realizing that they had not heard the warning noise of the lorries, she got out of bed slowly, hoping to give Larry time to get away, but she did not know that the house was surrounded. She still delayed in answering and the knocking turned to banging, demanding that she: "Open in the name of the King!" Eventually she opened the door and the soldiers trooped in past her. They searched the house thoroughly, even turning the bedclothes out on the floor, but finding nothing they became very annoyed because they seemed certain that there should have been somebody there.

My grandmother was a tough woman who did not know the meaning of fear: she asked them to leave now that they had searched her house. She refused to get drawn into an argument with them but stayed tight-lipped—which could not have been easy for her as silence was not one of her virtues.

The officer in charge, who had called many times, looked at my grandmother and remarked, "You remind me of my mother."

"Well, indeed," she snapped back, "your mother must not be up to much to raise a blackguard like you."

At last they left, warning her that they'd be calling again and that she'd be caught eventually. She went to the door and listened to hear the lorries starting up down the lane; then she put her children back to bed and sat by the fire for a long time. Opening the front door she checked in the half light of the dawn to make sure there was nobody about. It had happened before that the Tans had doubled back, hoping to catch them unprepared. Eventually, when she was convinced that they were safe, she stood in the middle of the kitchen and called aloud: "In the name of God where are you?"

Beside the fire in the kitchen was an old settle bed which appeared to be a timber seat when it was closed up. The Tans had checked it but when the cover did not rise they had assumed that it was just a seat. Out of this, with his face white as a sheet, rolled Larry. It had been a narrow escape. She was convinced that the Tans had known that somebody was there that night so they must have been tipped off; she suspected a family further back in the valley and she never forgave them. If ever their name came up in conversation her face would darken and she would say, "Bad blood there."

GIVE ME MY SHIRT

He was not blessed with a sunny disposition but possessed a razor-sharp brain and a biting wit. His role in life could best be described as a part-time travelling farmworker. How much he travelled and for how long he worked was entirely of Dan's own choosing; he was a free spirit

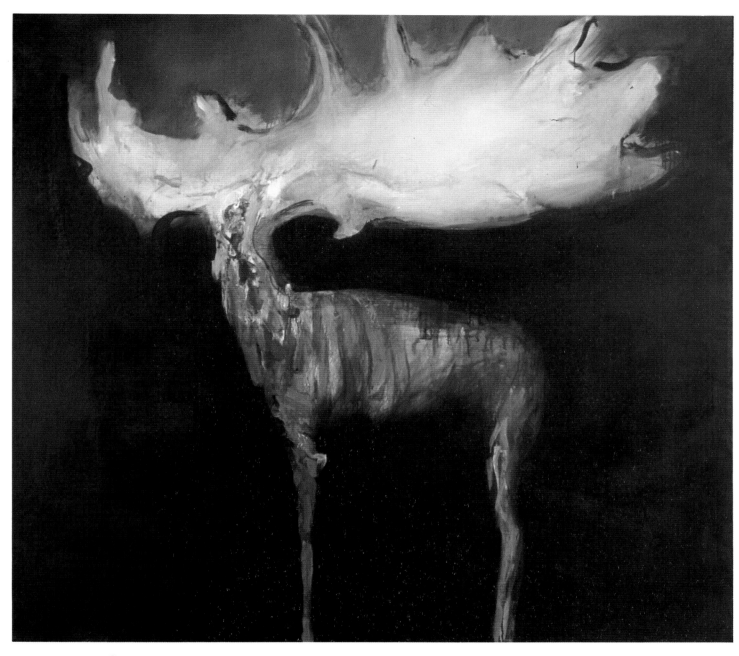

COLORPLATE 128

BARRIE COOK. *Megaceros Hibernicus*. 1983. Oil on canvas. 66⁵/₁₆ x 72 in. (168.4 x 182.9 cm).
Irish Museum of Modern Art, Dublin. The Gordon Lambert Collection.

COLORPLATE 129

JACK B. YEATS. *A Cleric*. 1913. Oil on board. 14⁵/₁₆ x 9³/₁₆ in. (36.3 x 23.3 cm).
National Gallery of Ireland, Dublin.

COLORPLATE 130

JACK B. YEATS. *No Flowers*. 20th century. Oil on canvas. 24 x 36¹/₄ in. (61 x 92 cm).
National Gallery of Ireland, Dublin.

COLORPLATE 131

JACK B. YEATS. *"Before the Start" Galway Point to Point*. 20th century. Oil on canvas.
18¹/₈ x 24 in. (46 x 61 cm). National Gallery of Ireland, Dublin.

COLORPLATE 132

JOAN JAMIESON. *Ardmore Church*. c. 1950. Oil on canvas. 24¹/₂ x 29¹/₂ in. (62.2 x 74.9 cm).
Crawford Municipal Art Gallery, Cork.

COLORPLATE 133

MAINE JELLETT. *The Virgin of Eire*. 20th century. Oil on canvas. 25³/₁₆ x 36¹/₄ in.
(64 x 92 cm). National Gallery of Ireland, Dublin.

COLORPLATES 134, 135 *(opposite)*

The Great Book of Ireland/ Leabhar Mor na h Eireann. 20th century. Vellum. Courtesy Theo Dorgan, Poetry Ireland, Dublin. *A contemporary Book of Kells, the work of 120 poets and 140 artists. Artists: Eamon O'Doherty (above), Charles Cullen, Daniel-Day Lewis, Brian Bourke, Charles Harper, Louis Le Brocquy, Barrie Cook, Rita Duffy, Yehuda Bacon. Poets: Micheal Longley (above), Derek Mahon, Tony Barry, Cathal O'Searcaigh, Gerry Murphy, Samuel Beckett, Seamus Heaney, Ciaran Carson, Mhaire Mhoc an tSoi.*

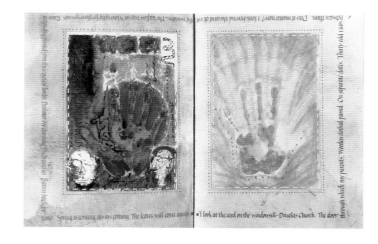

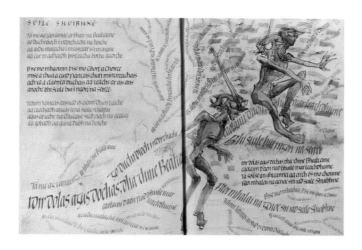

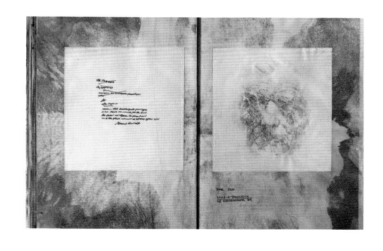

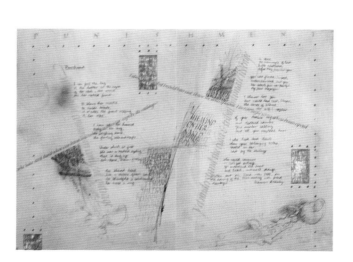

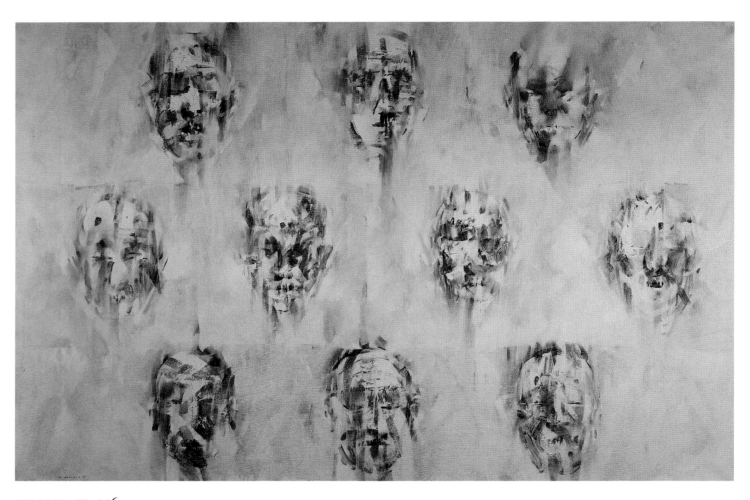

COLORPLATE 136

LOUIS LEBROCQUY. *Homage to Clonfert.* 20th century. Oil on canvas. 38 x 57¹/₂ in. (96.5 x 146 cm). Hugh Lane Municipal Gallery of Modern Art, Dublin.

and marched to the sound of his own drum. Trade unions would have been completely unnecessary to Dan because if conditions did not suit him he just moved on. He was master of his own destiny, but he never wronged anybody and he was completely honest.

Dan came to our house a couple of times a year and the length of his stay depended on many factors. His wardrobe consisted of a brown paper bag containing his spare shirt which he entrusted to my mother on arrival and demanded back when he made his sometimes hasty exit. Some people believe in making an entrance, but Dan was one for making an exit and his parting shot was always: "Give me my shirt—I'm going."

He usually arrived at Christmas time, because then he had the farmyard more or less to himself. At that time farmworkers went home on Christmas Eve and did not return until the 1st of February, which was the beginning of the working year, and Dan would survive longer if he had only my father to contend with, though even he was too much at times. At the end of our house was a large room where my brother slept, with a bay window opening onto the garden. There was always a spare bed in the room and some mornings Dan would be in the bed, having arrived during the night without disturbing anyone. More mornings the bed would have been slept in but Dan missing as he would have gone to bring in the cows for the early milking. He was a light sleeper and an early riser, and when he had the cows brought in he'd rattle around the kitchen and make such an infernal racket that he would wake the whole household. If anyone complained the only satisfaction Dan gave them was to remark: "Don't be sleeping your life away."

Among the other farm houses that he favoured with his presence was a widow woman who lived across the river from us. She was very mean where food was concerned and Dan enjoyed dragging the last bite from her. One day for dinner she gave him a huge plate of cabbage, which was plentiful on the farm, and a tiny bit of beef. Dan demanded more beef and got a little, with still more cabbage, and when he demanded more beef again she said:

"Dan, that heifer will be bellowing inside in you if you eat more beef."

"Jakus me, ma'am," Dan snorted, "If she will it won't be because she's looking for cabbage."

Eventually he got fed up with the widow woman and one morning, bright and early, demanded his shirt and was gone. She met him a couple of months later in town, and complained bitterly about how wrong it had been of him to desert her when she had needed him so badly.

Dan drew himself up to his full five foot two and, glaring at her from under his bushy eyebrows, he snapped: "Madam, I deserted the King of England, so where does that leave you?"

The Last Litany

Despite the fact that my mother was tolerant and flexible in most situations, she did have streaks of uncompromising rigidity. The family rosary was one of these: sick, maimed or crippled, we were all on our knees for the rosary, and helpers, visitors, or anyone who happened to call at the wrong time were apt to be included.

During the summer months I knelt inside the kitchen window looking down over the fields where the cows were grazing after milking. When my turn came to give out the decade I used the cows in the field to count my ten Hail Marys. I mentally sectioned off ten in a corner, but as my mind floated back and forth across the valley the cows naturally moved around so my ten could decrease to five or six. If I said the Glory before schedule my mother gently intervened in the background—"Two more." Or if my herd increased and my Hail Marys swelled beyond the ten she interrupted with "Glory, now, Glory." She also fought gallantly to keep us all supplied with rosary beads but they were continually getting lost or broken. She never tried to convert my father to beads, so he cracked his knuckles as he went along to keep count.

Her rosary was one thing, but her additions to it were something else. First came the litany starting "Holy Mary," and we would all chant, "Pray for us" in response. After Holy Mary came a long list and somewhere down along the list came "Ark of the Covenant" and "Gate of

Heaven." After "Gate of Heaven" one night my mother lost her concentration and she floundered and repeated it a few times, failing to remember what came next. Finally a little voice in the background piped up helpfully: "Try Nelson's Pillar!" Everybody fell around the floor laughing, and my father took advantage of the opportunity to call a halt to the litany for the night.

But the litany was only one of the many additions. There were three Hail Marys for this neighbour and a second lot for another one, until my father would start complaining, "For God's sake, we'll be here till morning." We prayed diligently for years for one neighbour who was studying to be a teacher and of whom my father voiced the opinion that "if a bumble bee had his brains he'd fly backwards," but despite this pronouncement on the neighbour's grey matter he still qualified. It was my mother's conviction that prayer could move mountains and indeed hers often did; at least they moved mountains of ignorance. During exam time she always lit a candle in the centre of the parlour table. I would come home during exams and peep into the parlour to check if she had remembered. It was always lighting. It was a symbol of caring and in later years her children wrote as adults to her from many corners of the world asking her to light her candle and pray for their special problems.

Cormac MacConnell
"Help for the Hay"

Cormac MacConnell has many avid followers as a columnist for the Irish Press *in Dublin. In this column, he encounters a Mayo character, a farmer with a real plan of action.*

It was the lone and lonesome look of the old man alone in the middle of the five-acre meadow which made me stop last Wednesday in Mayo and jump the ditch and go across the felled sways of crackling hay to him. I'd give him a half-hour, I thought and maybe get some story or other out of him, or the skeleton of a story and at the worst of times, a mug of tea out of the bottle.

Nothing tastes as good as meadow tea, ten minutes away from the kitchen, one minute from Heaven. I felt like a very good Samaritan approaching an old haymaker in such obvious need of assistance.

"You could do with a hand," says I, heading towards a pile of pitchforks and rakes lying beside him. "Are you by yourself?" says he. "Who in the name of God are you?"

I told him.

"Then," says he, "for the love of God hide over there behind the ditch or you'll ruin me altogether."

"That's no way to treat a good Samaritan," says I hiding nevertheless under a sally bush and raising the voice so that he could still hear me. "I often worked in a meadow and any help is better than none."

"No offence, and I'm thankful to you for stopping," says he. "But you'd have blistered hands and you'd be gone out of here in an hour at most, one crooked cock of hay only, and the sight of anyone with me in the meadow will chase away the men I'm after."

"Oh fair enough," says I, still a bit offended.

"You're too wise a man to be annoyed," says he. "Do you think I'm standing here by accident, just in this spot in the red shirt. Did you see me the minute you came over the hill?"

"Yes."

"That's my plan," says he feebly shaking out a fork of hay so that it wisped around his

NATHANIEL HONE
THE YOUNGER.
Haymaking by the Sea.
Late 19th century. Oil on
board. 11 3/8 x 17 11/16 in.
(29 x 45 cm). National
Gallery of Ireland,
Dublin.

legs. "You have to use the head these days."

"Yes?"

"If you saw me, the postman Masterson will see me coming over the hill finishing his rounds and he'll half brake the bicycle and he'll say to himself 'poor Martin is by himself, I can't pass him.' And he'll stop the bike and come in the gate and pick up a handful of hay and he'll say 'it's in great form for going up Martin' and he'll pick up a fork and get stuck in.

"As good as three men and he won't leave until the field is finished. He's due in five minutes, ten if he takes two pints, but he won't because it's only Wednesday."

"Where did you park the car?"

"Round the bend."

"All right, he won't see it. Stay well-hidden now."

"Is he the only one you'll catch?"

"Not at all."

"About 4 o'clock young Master Toole will be coming home and since I'll have Masterson down in the corner, he won't see him until it's too late and he'll stop the Volkswagen and say to himself, 'poor Martin, no help' and come in the gate intending to stay an hour only and then I'll get him talking about the big win last Sunday and he'll be, here to finish in time as well—two bad blisters tomorrow, for him, but he's not a bad lad."

"Will that be enough?"

"It would be in a pinch. But about half six the two Lallys will get off the bus at the cross, coming out from town—they work in the factory, you know—and by that time we'll be having the tea sitting up beside where you are now, maybe eight or nine cocks made, and one will say to the other 'we'll hear a couple of ould Martin's yarns, there's great sport in him,' and I'll have them too and the best of workers they are, hardy young lads, until I need them no more, and every cock of hay is up clean and decent as you like."

"You are a smart man," I said.

"You have to be these days," says he. "Stay well hid now, well hid, for the postman is due."

He worked the fork feebly again, the red shirt sleeve making a pathetic enough show in the middle of all the whitening swathes of labour and, together, we watched the top of the hill.

The postman Masterson had only the one pint, for he was dead on time. I saw him braking the bike on the top of the hill. He disappeared into the dip and then after a half-minute or so, the bike clanged against the gate and this fine, strong-looking man walked into the field.

I saw him take up a handful of hay and he came up the field and he said: "It's in good form for making up Martin."

I slipped the back way over the ditch and they never saw me go.

Ita Daly

FROM THE LADY WITH THE RED SHOES

Ita Daly was born in 1944 in County Leitrim and educated at University College, Dublin. She is a novelist and short-story writer who won The Irish Times *short story competition in 1975. In this hauntingly beautiful story a privileged narrator/guest at a longtime favorite North Mayo resort discovers the secret of another guest, one who courts such privilege.*

The West of Ireland, as every schoolboy knows, is that part of the country to which Cromwell banished the heretical natives after he had successfully brought the nation to heel. Today, it is as impoverished and barren as ever it was, bleak and lonesome and cowering from the savagery of the Atlantic which batters its coastline with all the fury that it has gathered in over three thousand miles. But the West of Ireland can also be heartbreakingly beautiful; and on a fine April morning with the smell of gorse and clover filling the air and the bees showing the only evidence of industry in a landscape that is peopleless as far as the eye can see—on such a morning in the West of Ireland you can get a whiff of Paradise.

It is an irony which pleases me mightily that we as a family have such a strong attachment to the West. Our ancestors, you see, came over with Cromwell, foot soldiers who fought bravely and were rewarded generously and have never looked back since. And every Easter we leave Dublin and set out westwards where we spend a fortnight in McAndrews Hotel in North Mayo. It is a family tradition, started by my grandfather, and by now it has achieved a certain sacredness. Nothing is allowed to interfere with the ritual, and so when I married Judith one April day, some twenty-five years ago, it seemed quite natural that we should spend our honeymoon there. We have gone there every Easter since and if Judith has found it somewhat dull on occasion, she accepts gracefully a period of boredom in the knowledge that it gives me so much pleasure, while I in turn have been known to accompany her to Juan-les-Pins. An experience which, however, I have not been foolish enough to repeat.

McAndrews is one of the puzzles of the world. Built on the outskirts of Kilgory, looking down on the hamlet and on the sea, it dates back to the late nineteenth century. A large, square house, red-bricked and turreted, it is a reminder of the worst excesses of the Gothic revival, and every time I see its monstrous outline, lonely on the hill, my heart bounds and my pulse quickens. Nobody knows whether it was there before Kilgory and the village grew up around it or whether Kilgory was there first. But certainly it seems an odd place to have built a hotel, miles from a town, or a church, or even a beach. It is situated on a headland overlooking the Atlantic, but the cliffs are so steep and the sea so treacherous here that there is neither boating nor swimming available. Strange to build a hotel in such a place, stranger still that there have been enough eccentrics around to keep it in business for almost a century. My father, as a boy, used to arrive by train. The main line ran from Dublin to Westport and from there a branch line went to the hotel—not to Kilgory mark you, but to the actual hotel grounds. 'Any guests for McAndrews?' the porters used to shout as one disembarked at Westport and was ushered onto a toy train with its three or four first-class carriages, to be shunted along the fifteen miles and deposited a stone's throw from the grand front door of McAndrews with its noble stone balustrade. . . .

This year, Judith was ill and did not accompany me. To say that she was ill is something of

an exaggeration, for if she had been, I would certainly not have left her. But she was some-what under the weather, and as her sister was in Dublin from London, she decided to stay there with her while I went to Mayo alone. In truth, I was somewhat relieved, for I am only too aware of how difficult it must be for Judith, gay and outgoing, to be married to a dry stick like myself all these years. I am glad when she gets an opportunity to enjoy herself and I had no doubt that Eleanor and she would be much happier without my inhibiting presence. Still, I was going to miss her, for like many solitary people I am very dependent on the company of those few whom I love.

But the magic of McAndrews began to re-assert itself as soon as I got down to breakfast the first morning and found Murphy, with his accustomed air of calm and dignity, presiding over the dining-room. Murphy has been head waiter here for over thirty years now, although I always see him more as a butler, a loyal family retainer, rather than as a smart *maître d'hôtel*. His concern for each guest is personal and his old face is suffused with genuine pleasure when he sees you again each year. . . .

I quickly re-established my routine, falling into it with the ease and gratitude one feels on putting on again an old and much-worn jacket. Breakfasts were latish but hearty, then a walk as far as the village and back. Afterwards an hour or two spent in the library in the delightful company of Boswell, a man to be enjoyed only in leisured circumstances—I never read him in Dublin. Lunch and an afternoon in a deck-chair in the gardens, looking out to sea, dozing, dreaming, idling. After dinner another walk, this time more strenuous, perhaps two miles along the coast road and then back to McAndrews for a final glass of port followed by early bed with a good detective novel. The bliss of those days is hard to convey, particularly the afternoons, when it never seemed to rain. I would take my deck-chair and place it in a shel-tered spot and sit, hour upon hour, and watch the Atlantic at its ceaseless labours. I'd watch as the light changed—from blue to green and from green to grey—until an occasional sea-gull would cut across my line of vision and I would raise my eyes and follow its soaring flight to the great vault of heaven. A couple of afternoons like that and things were back in perspective. The consciousness of one's encroaching age, the knowledge that one is regarded as a has-been, became less painful, and there, on the edge of the Atlantic, a peace began to make itself felt. . . .

By dinner-time the light had changed outside and a soft blue opacity was flooding in from the Atlantic through the great windows of the dining-room. This is the Irish twilight, most beautiful of times and that part of the day I missed most during those few years I spent in West Africa as a young man. It is a time that induces a half-wilful melancholia—helped no doubt by the glass in one's hand—and in McAndrews they respect this mood, for the curtains are never drawn nor the lights switched on until darkness finally descends. As I moved through the flickering pools of yellow light—for there were many diners already present and many candles lit—I was struck again by the solemnity of the room. Years and years of ritual have given it a churchlike quiet, a hint of the ceremony and seriousness with which eating is invested by both guests and staff. I took my usual seat against the wall, facing out towards sea, and as Murphy murmured, priest-like, over the wine, we were both startled by a raised and discordant voice. 'Waiter, come here please.'

Together we turned towards the voice, both acutely conscious of the solecism that had been committed in referring to Murphy as 'Waiter.' The offender was sitting about six feet away at a small table in the middle of the room. It was an unpopular table, unprotected, marooned under the main chandelier, seldom occupied except when the hotel was very busy. I guessed now that some underling, flustered by the novelty of the situation, had forgotten himself to such an extent as to usher this person to it without first consulting Murphy. And the arrival of this new diner *was* a novelty. She was not a resident, which was odd in itself, for McAndrews has never been the sort of place to seek out a casual trade; then she was alone, unescorted, a sight which was not only odd, but simply not done: ladies, one feels, do not dine alone in public. But the most striking thing of all about our newcomer was her appearance. She was in her fifties, maybe sixty, with hair and dress matching, both of an indeterminate pink. She wore spectacles which were decorated with some kind of stones along the wings. These shone and sparkled as she moved her head, but no more brightly than her teeth, which were of an amazing and American brightness. She flashed them up at Murphy now, and as he shied away from their brilliance, I could see that for once he was discomposed. But Murphy is a gentleman and within seconds he had himself again in hand. Stiffening his back, he bowed slightly in the direction of the teeth. 'Madam?' he enquired, with dignity.

'Could I have a double Scotch on the rocks, and I'd like a look at the menu.' Her voice had that familiarity which so many aspects of American life have for Europeans who have never even crossed the Atlantic. I don't think I have ever met an American, but I have a great fondness for their television thrillers, and I immediately identified the voice as a New York voice, tough New York, like so many of my favourite villains. Proud of my detective work, I sat back to listen.

The whiskey had appeared with that speed to which we McAndrews guests are accustomed, and if Murphy disapproved of this solitary diner, his training was too perfect to even suggest it. . . .

Murphy coughed encouragingly behind a genteel hand and began, 'Perhaps Madam, I could recommend tonight the—.' But she gathered her shoulders together and threw back her head. 'No, you could not, waiter. I know exactly what I want.' Her voice had taken on an added stridency. 'I want a filet mignon with a green salad. Surely a place like this can produce that—huh?'

'It is not on the menu, Madam, but certainly if that is what you require, we can arrange it.' I thought I noticed a hint of disapproval in Murphy's silky tones.

'Yeah, that's what I want. Nothing to start and I want the steak medium-rare, and I mean medium-rare. All you Irish overcook meat .' . . .

As I watched my fellow-diner I wondered how on earth she had ever found her way to McAndrews. It was not a fashionable spot, not the sort of place that attracted tourists. There was a hideous motel only ten miles away, much smarter than McAndrews, flashing neon lights, full of Americans, supplying what they called an ensemble for the gratification of their guests. Surely this woman would have been much more at home in such a place? But as I studied her, I began to realize that this strange creature was actually impressed by McAndrews. I was sure now that she hadn't accidentally happened upon it as I had at first surmised, but that for some unknown reason she had chosen it deliberately. And I saw too that her apparent rudeness was no more than awkwardness, an effort to hide her awe and inexperience in such surroundings . . . As the waiter placed the steak in front of her, Murphy approached, disapproval in every line of his stately person. 'Medium rare, as you required,' he said, and even I, sitting some distance away, drew back from the sting of his contempt. . . .

The Burren, County Clare. Photograph. Irish Tourist Board, Dublin.

Decency demanded that I leave her some privacy to eat so reluctantly I looked away. Soon, I was glad to see, the other guests lost interest in her, and when after a safe interval I glanced back at her table, she had finished her meal and was wiping her mouth with an air of well-being and relaxation. It must have been a satisfactory filet mignon. When Murphy brought the menu again, she actually smiled at him. 'No, no,' she said waving it away, 'nothing more for me. We women have to watch our figures—eh?' And as she glanced at him archly, I thought for an awful moment that she was going to dig him in the ribs. Murphy looked at her coldly, making no effort to return her smile. 'Very well, Madam.' The words hung between them and as she sensed his unfriendliness, indeed hostility, the smile, still awkward upon her lips, became transfixed in an ugly grimace. 'I guess you'd better bring me another Scotch.' Defeat was now beginning to edge out defiance in her voice. She grasped her drink when it arrived, and gulped it, as a drowning man gulps air. This seemed to steady her somewhat and taking another, slower sip, she drew out a cigarette from her bag and lit it. It was then that she discovered, just as Murphy was passing on his way towards my table, that there was no ashtray. 'Excuse me,' she sounded embarrassed, 'could you bring me an ashtray please?' Murphy turned slowly in his tracks. He looked at her in silence for fully five seconds. 'I am sorry, Madam,'—and it seemed to me now that the whole dining-room was listening to his even, slightly heightened tones—'I am sorry, but our guests do not smoke in the dining-room.' In essence this is true, it being accepted among the guests that tobacco is not used in here—a measure of their consideration for each other as smoke fumes might lessen someone's enjoyment of an excellent meal. I thoroughly approve of this unwritten rule—it seems to me to be eminently civilized—but I know well that on occasion, people, newcomers for example, have smoked in McAndrews dining-room, and Murphy, though perhaps disapproving, has never demurred. I looked at him now in amazement and maybe he caught my expression of surprise, for he added, 'Coffee is served in the blue sitting-room, Madam, there are ashtrays there. However, if you'd prefer it, I can—' The woman stood up abruptly, almost colliding with Murphy. Her face and neck were flooded with an ugly red colour and she seemed to be trying to push him away. 'No, not at all, I'll have the coffee,' and she blundered blindly towards the door. It seemed a long, long journey.

I finished my cheese and followed her thoughtfully into the sitting-room. All evening something had been niggling me, something about that voice. I have a very sensitive ear I believe—I am rather proud of it—and although, as I had noticed, this woman spoke with an American accent, there was some underlying non-American quality about it. Something familiar but different about those vowels and th's. Now as I sat and lit my cigar, I realized what it was—it was so obvious that I had missed it until now. Her voice, of course, was a local voice, a North Mayo voice with that thick and doughy consistency that I was hearing around me since I had come down. It had become Americanized, almost completely so, but to my ear its origins were clear. I could swear that that woman had been born within ten miles of this very hotel.

We both sipped our coffee, the tinkle of coffee-spoons falling between us. I watched her as she sat alone, isolated and tiny in the deep recess of the bay window, looking out at the darkening gardens. Beyond, there were still some streaks of light coming from the sea, and I knew that down below on the rocks the village children would be gathering their final bundles of seaweed before heading off home to bed. The seaweed is sold to the local factory where it is turned into fertilizer of some kind and the people here collect it assiduously, sometimes whole families working together, bare-footed, for the salt water rots shoe-leather. Even the little ones often have hard and calloused feet, sometimes with ugly cuts. Life is still hard in the West of Ireland. I looked across at my lady—*her* feet were encased in red high-heeled shoes with large platform soles. Her face, as she gazed out unseeing, was sad now, sad and crumpled-looking. I recalled again her voice, and as we sat there, drinking our coffee, I suddenly knew without any shadow of doubt what she was doing there. I knew *her* intimately—her life was spread out in front of me. I could see her as a little girl, living nearby in some miserable cottage. Maybe, when I was out walking as a child with my Mama, I had even passed her, not noticing the tattered little girl who stood in wonder, staring at us. McAndrews must have been a symbol to her, a world of wealth and comfort, right there on the doorstep of her own poverty-stricken existence. Perhaps she had even worked in the hotel as a maid, waiting to save her fare to America, land of opportunity. And in America, had she been lonely, frightened by that alien place, so different from her own Mayo? Had she wept herself to sleep many nights, sick for a breath of home? But she had got on, sent money back, and always, all those years, she had kept her dream intact: one day she would return home to Kilgory, a rich American lady, and she would go into McAndrews Hotel, not as a maid this time but as a guest. She would order a fine dinner and impress everyone with her clothes and her accent and her wealth.

She sat now, a rejected doll in her pink dress and red shoes, for tonight she had seen that dream disintegrate like candy-floss. I wanted to go to her, to tell her, explain to her that it didn't matter any more—the world itself was disintegrating. She should realize that places like McAndrews weren't important any longer, people only laughed at them now. She had no need to be saddened, for she, and all those other little Irish girls who had spent their days wash-

JACK B. YEATS. *The Liffey Swim.* 20th century. Oil on canvas. 24 x 35 13/16 in. (61 x 91 cm). National Gallery of Ireland, Dublin.

ing other people's floors and cooking other people's meals, they would inherit the earth. The wheel had come round full circle.

Of course I didn't approach her. I finished my coffee and went straight to bed thinking how the world is changing, my world, her world. Soon McAndrews itself will be gone. But for me, this landscape has been caught forever—caught and defined by its heroine, the lady with the red shoes. Of course, you, on reading this, are going to see me as a sentimental old codger, making up romantic stories about strangers, because I am lonely and have nothing better to do. But I know what I know.

Sean O'Faolain

Persecution Mania

Although Sean O'Faolain is a writer of short stories, novels, plays, criticism, essays, and travel books, he is most acclaimed as a short-story writer. It is said that most Irishmen tolerate criticism well; if it is witty, the subject will accept and even enjoy the comment, repeating it to others with a smile. Meet Ike Dignam.

There are two types of Irishman I can't stand. The first is always trying to behave the way he thinks the English behave. The second is always trying to behave the way he thinks the Irish behave. That sort is a roaring bore. Ike Dignam is like that. He believes that the Irish are witty, so he is for ever making laborious jokes. He has a notion that the Irish have a gift for fantasy, so he is constantly talking fey. He also has a notion that the Irish have a magnificent gift for malice, mixed up with another idea of the Irish as great realists, so he loves to abuse everybody for not having more common sense. But as he also believes that the Irish are the most kind and charitable people in the world he ends up every tirade with an "Ah, sure, God help us, maybe the poor fellow is good at heart." The result is that you do not know, from one moment to the next, whom you are talking to—Ike the fey, or Ike the realist, Ike the malicious, or Ike the kind.

I am sure he has no clear idea of himself. He is a political journalist. I have seen him tear the vitals out of a man, and then, over a pint, say, with a shocked guffaw,

"I'm after doin' a terrible thing. Do you know what I said in my column this morning about Harry Lombard? I said, 'There is no subject under the sun on which the eloquence does not pour from his lips with all the thin fluidity of asses' milk.' Honest to God, we're a terrible race. Of course, the man will never talk to me again."

All as if Right Hand had no responsibility for Left Hand. But the exasperating thing is that his victims do talk to him again, and in the most friendly way, though why they do it I do not know considering some of the things he says and writes about them. He is the man who said of a certain woman who is in the habit of writing letters to the press in defence of the Department of Roads and Railways: "Ah, sure, she wrote that with the Minister's tongue in her cheek." Yet the Minister for Roads and Railways is one of his best friends, and he says, "Ike Dignam? Ah, sure! He's all right. The poor divil is good at heart." And the cursed thing is that Ike *is* good at heart. I have long since given up trying to understand what this means. Something vaguely connected with hope and consolation and the endless mercy of God?

Ike naturally has as many enemies as friends, and this is something that *he* cannot understand. Somebody may say,

"But you're forgetting, Ike, what you said about him last year. You said every time he sings 'Galway Bay' he turns it into a street puddle."

Ike will laugh delightedly.

"That was only a bit o' fun. Who'd mind that?"

"How would you like to have things like that said about yourself?"

He will reply, valiantly,

"I wouldn't mind one bit. Not one bit in the world. I'd know 'twas all part of the game. I'd know the poor fellow was really good at heart."

A few weeks ago he got a taste of his own medicine. He committed the folly of granting to his rivals the ancient wish of all rivals, "That mine enemy would write a book." The subject of his book—it was a pamphlet rather than a book—was *The Irish Horse in Irish History*, and it was savagely disembowelled in an anonymous review in one of the popular weeklies. The sentence that wounded him, as it was intended to do, said: "Mr. Dignam's knowledge of hunters is weak, of hacks most profound."

That very afternoon I met him in Mooney's on the quay. He was staring into the boghole deeps of a pint of porter. Seeing me he turned such a morose eye on me that I could tell he had been badly hit.

"You saw what the *Sun* said about my book?" he asked, and when I nodded: "That's a low paper. A low rag. A vicious-minded rag. That's what it is. Full of venom and hate and lust for power. And," he added, slapping the counter, "destruction!"

"Somebody getting his own back, I suppose?"

"What did I ever do to anybody? Only a bit of give and take. What's done every day of the week in journalism. Surely to Gawd nobody takes me as seriously as all that!"

"Well, that's more or less all your reviewer did with your book."

Again the indignant palm slapped the mahogany.

"That's exactly what I dislike about that review. The mean implication. The dirty innuendo. Why couldn't he come out and say it in the open like a man? It's the anonymity of the thing that's so despicable." Here he fixed me with a cunning eye. "Who do ye think wrote it?"

I spread my hands.

"I think," he said sourly, "that it was Mulvaney wrote it. I made a hare of him one time in my column. But I'm not sure. That's the curse of it. He hasn't enough brains to write it." He gazed at me for a moment through his eyelashes. "You didn't write it yourself, by any chance?"

I laughed and told him I hadn't read his book. I'd bought it, of course (which I had not), and had every intention of reading it (which was also untrue).

"Or could it be that drunk Cassidy," he said. "That fellow has it in for me ever since I said that he spoke in the Dail with the greatest sobriety." He laughed feebly. "Everyone knew what I meant. Do you think it might be Cassidy?"

"Ikey, it might be a dozen people."

"It could be anybody," he snarled. "Anybody! Damn it all if I ever say a thing I say it straight out from the shoulder. Why can't they come into the open?" He leaned nearer and dropped to a whisper. "I was thinking it might be that redheaded bastard from the All Souls Club. That fellow thinks I'm anti-clerical. And," he guffawed, "I'm not! That's the joke of it, I'm not!"

"What in the name of all that's holy," I asked crossly, "has anti-clericalism got to do with horses?"

He scratched his head fiercely and moaned and shook it.

"Ye never know. The people in this country have as much sense when it comes to religion. . . . Tell me, did ye ever hear of a thing called Discovery of Documents?"

It was only then I fully realized how badly he had been hit.

"You're not being such an idiot as to be thinking of taking this thing to law?"

"Look't! I don't give one tinker's curse about what anybody says against me, but the one thing I *must* know is who wrote it! If I don't find out who wrote it I'll be suspecting my best friends for the rest of my born days."

"Well," I said, finishing my drink and leaving him, "happy hunting to you."

A couple of days later I saw him cruising towards me along O'Connell Street glowing like a sunrise.

"I'm on the track of that," he shouted at me from fifteen yards off. "I'm off on the right scent," he babbled, and I had time to remember what he was talking about while he explained how he had worked up a friendship with a girl in the office of the *Sun*. 'Tis none of the people I suspected at all. Do you know who I think wrote it now?"

"God knows, maybe you wrote it yourself."

He shook with laughter.

"'Twould be great publicity if I could say I did." Then he glowered. "They're entirely capable of saying I did. If they thought anybody would believe 'em. No!" he gripped my arm. "'Twas a woman did it. I should have guessed it from the word Go."

"Who is she?"

"I don't know," he said, sadly.

"Then why did you say . . . ?"

"I had a dream about it. Didn't I see the long, lean, bony hand holding the pen, coming out like a snake from behind a red curtain! Didn't I see the gold bangle on the wrist and all?"

"Did you pull the curtain to see who it was?"

"I pulled and I pulled," Ike assured me enthusiastically. "Dear Gawd, I was all the night pullin'!"

"And," I suggested bitterly, "I suppose the curtain was made of iron? You know, Ikey, you'll go crackers if you go on like this."

With his two hands he dragged his hat down on his head as if he wanted to extinguish himself.

"I will," he cried, so loudly that passers-by turned to look at the pair of us. "I'll go stark, staring, roaring mad if I don't find out who wrote that dirty thing about me."

"Look," I pleaded, "what does it all matter? The whole thing is gone completely out of everybody's head but your own. It's all over and done with. And even supposing you did find out who wrote it, what could you do then?"

He folded his arms and gazed down O'Connell Street like Napoleon looking over the Atlantic from Saint Helena.

"I'd write a Limerick on him. I'd *shrivel* him. I wouldn't leave a peck on his bones. As a matter of fact," cocking an eye on me, "I've done it already. I wrote ten Limericks the other night on ten different people who might have written that review. I'm thinking of publishing the whole lot of 'em, and if the cap fits they can share it and wear it."

And before I could stop him he recited to the sky four blistering quatrains on *Irish Bards and Botch Reviewers*. I took his arm:—

"Ikey, that'll be ten enemies you'll make instead of one! Come in here, Ikey, and let me talk to you like a father."

We went across to Mooney's and I talked for half an hour. I told him we had all been through this sort of thing. I told him that no man who cannot grow an epidermis against malice should try to live in small countries like ours. I said that all that matters is a man's work. I assured him, Heaven forgive me, that he had written a masterly record of *The Irish Horse in Irish History* and that that was the main thing. I developed this soundly into the theory that everything is grist to the mill, and that instead of worrying about this silly review he should go home and write a comic piece about it for *Dublin Opinion*, which, indeed, he could do very well. I built him up as Dignam *solus contra mundum*. He agreed to every word of it. We parted cordially. He was in the happiest temper.

Three days later he came striding towards me, beaming. From afar he hailed my passing ship, roaring like a bosun:—

"I found out that bastard! Mulvaney! A friend of mine charged him with it and he didn't deny it."

"Good. You're satisfied now."

"I am. I don't give a damn about it now. Sure that fellow's brains are all in his behind. Who'd mind anything he'd say?"

"The whole thing is of no importance."

"None what-so-ever."

"Splendid. It's all over now."

"Finished. And done with."

"Grand."

"I sent him a hell of a postcard."

"No!"

"I did," he chortled, "I did. All I wrote on it was what I said to yourself:—'Your Second Front is your Behind.' An open postcard. It was a terrible thing to do," he beamed. "Oh, shocking!" His laughter gusted.

"And you put your name to that?"

"I did not. What a fool I'd be! That'll keep him guessing for a while. 'Twill do him no harm in the world. He's not a bad poor gom. Ah! Sure! The poor divil is good at heart."

Off he went, striding along, as happy as a child. I went into Mooney's. There at the counter was Mulvaney, sucking his empty pipe, staring in front of him, his bushy eyebrows as black as night. I wheeled quickly but he caught the movement and called me. His hand strayed to his breast pocket.

"I'm after receiving a very myst-e-e-rious communication," he said sombrely.

I did not hear what else he said. I realized that you could do nothing with these people. I realized that the only sensible thing to do was to write a satire on the whole lot of them. I began to wonder could I get any editor anywhere to publish it anonymously.

Myles na Gopaleen

FROM KEATS AND CHAPMAN

"Keatsiana"

Brian Nolan (1911–1966), had a responsible job in Irish government, and wrote short stories, poems, plays, and a well-loved column in The Irish Times *under a variety of pseudonyms, including Flann O'Brien (novelist) and Myles na Gopaleen (newspaper columnist of 25 years). Over the years he received hundreds of attempted puns suggested by the readers, most of them very bad. These, Keats and Chapman's own, are irresistible. As Flann O'Brien himself said about the Keats and Chapman material, "This thing is a genuine disease."*

Keats was once presented with an Irish terrier, which he humorously named Byrne. One day the beast strayed from the house and failed to return at night. Everybody was distressed, save Keats himself. He reached reflectively for his violin, a fairly passable timber of the Stradivarius feciture, and was soon at work with chin and jaw.

Chapman, looking in for an after-supper pipe, was astonished at the poet's composure, and did not hesitate to say so. Keats smiled (in a way that was rather lovely).

'And why should I not fiddle,' he asked, 'while Byrne roams?'

* * *

Keats, when living in the country purchased an expensive chestnut gelding. This animal was very high-spirited and largely untrained and gave the novice owner a lot of trouble. First it was one thing, then another but finally he was discovered one morning to have disappeared from his stable. Foul play was not suspected nor did the poet at this stage adopt the foolish expedient of locking the stable door. On the contrary he behaved very sensibly. He examined the stable to ascertain how the escape had been effected and then travelled all over the yard on his hands and knees looking for traces of the animal's hooves. He was like a dog looking for a trail, except that he found a trail where many a good dog would have found nothing. Immediately the poet was off cross-country following the trail. It happened that Chapman was on a solitary walking-tour in the vicinity and he was agreeably surprised to encounter the poet in a remote mountainy place. Keats was walking with his eyes on the ground and looked very preoccupied. He had evidently no intention of stopping to converse with Chapman. The latter, not understanding his friend's odd behaviour, halted and cried:

'What are you doing, old man?'

'Dogging a fled horse,' Keats said as he passed by.

* * *

Keats and Chapman once called to see a titled friend and after the host had hospitably produced a bottle of whiskey, the two visitors were called into consultation regarding the son of the house, who had been exhibiting a disquieting redness of face and boisterousness of manner at the age of twelve. The father was worried, suspecting some dread disease. The youngster was produced but the two visitors, glass in hand, declined to make any diagnosis. When leaving the big house, Chapman rubbed his hands briskly and remarked on the cold.

'I think it must be freezing and I'm glad of that drink,' he said. 'By the way, did you think what I thought about that youngster?'

'There's a nip in the heir,' Keats said.

Seamus Heaney

FROM THE SENSE OF PLACE

Nourishment for the Imagination

Seamus Heaney, poet, essayist, teacher, was born in 1939 in County Derry and educated at St. Columb's and Queen's College, Belfast. He has taught in the United States at Berkeley and Harvard and has been the recipient of most of the major literary prizes. This selection, from a lecture given in the Ulster Museum in January 1977, is a wondrous exploration of the conscious and unconscious sense of place central to the Irish poets.

Although it has long been fashionable to smile indulgently at the Celtic Twilight, it has to be remembered that the movement was the beginning of a discovery of confidence in our own ground, in our place, in our speech, English and Irish. And it seems to me undeniable that Yeats's sense of the otherness of his Sligo places led him to seek for a language and an imagery other than the ones which were available to him in the aesthetic modes of literary London.

He had, of course, a double purpose. One, to restore a body of old legends and folk beliefs that would bind the people of the Irish place to the body of their world, in much the way that I have suggested the name Ardee meshes the old saga with the Ardee man's sense of who he is and where he is. Yeats in this way would have commended the remarks made by Carson McCullers, that to know who you are, you have to have a place to come from. But his other purpose was to supplement this restored sense of historical place with a new set of associations that would accrue when a modern Irish literature, rooted in its own region and using its own speech, would enter the imaginations of his countrymen. And the classic moment in this endeavour was his meeting with Synge, in a hotel in Paris, the young Synge in search of *la vie de bohème*, struggling with the idioms of decadence, whom Yeats sent west to express the life of Aran, in the language of the tribe. At that moment a new country of the

HENRY BROCAS. *Carlingford Castle, County Louth.* Early 19th century. Watercolor on paper. 11 5/8 x 16 1/2 in. (29.5 x 42 cm). National Gallery of Ireland, Dublin.

mind was conceived in English, the west that the poets imagined, full of tragic fishermen and poetic peasants.

Synge, in his preface to *The Tinker's Wedding*, used a phrase which is apposite to my concerns in this discussion. 'The drama is made serious,' he wrote, 'not by the degree in which it is taken up with problems that are serious in themselves, but by the degree in which it gives the nourishment, not very easy to define, on which our imaginations live.' That nourishment, it seems to me, became available more abundantly to us as a result of the achievements of the Irish Literary Revival, and much of its imaginative protein was extracted from the sense of place. There is, for example, this short but very revealing moment in a review which Yeats wrote in 1874, when he was twenty-nine. 'The final test of the value of any work of art to our particular needs, is when we place it in the hierarchy of those recollections which are our standards and our beacons. At the head of mine are a certain night scene long ago, when I heard the wind blowing in a bed of reeds by the border of a little lake, a Japanese picture of cranes flying through a blue sky, and a line or two out of Homer.' Yeats is here talking about what Matthew Arnold called 'touchstones,' high points of imaginative experience, 'those recollections which are our standards and our beacons.' Arnold's touchstones were literary, drawn from the whole field of European poetry, but it is typical and significant, I think, that first in the hierarchy of Yeats's recollections is an experience that was obviously local and deeply involved with his apprehension of the spirit of a place. The wind among those night reeds stayed with him and was so pervasive in his mental weather that it formed the title of a collection of poems that he published four years later, a book that brought the moods of the Irish weather into English poetry and changed the atmosphere of that poetry.

However, we have to understand also that this nourishment which springs from knowing and belonging to a certain place and a certain mode of life is not just an Irish obsession, nor is the relationship between a literature and a locale with its common language a particularly Irish phenomenon. It is true, indeed, that we have talked much more about it in this country because of the peculiar fractures in our history, north and south, and because of the way that possession of the land and possession of different languages have rendered the question particularly urgent. But I like to remember that Dante was very much a man of a particular place, that his great poem is full of intimate placings and place-names, and that as he moves round the murky circles of hell, often heard rather than seen by his damned friends and enemies, he is recognized by his local speech or so recognizes them. And we could also talk about the sense of place in English poetry and find it rewarding with talents as diverse as Tennyson and Auden, Arnold and John Clare, Edward Thomas and Geoffrey Hill.

But I want to turn the plough back into the home ground again and see what can be turned up in Co. Monaghan. Patrick Kavanagh's place was to a large extent his subject. As I have said before, his quarrel with himself was the quarrel between himself and it, between the illiterate self that was tied to the little hills and earthed in the stony grey soil, and the literate self that pined for 'the city of Kings/Where art, music and letters were the real things.' His sonnet 'Epic' is his comprehension of this about himself and his affirmation of the profound importance of the parochial. Where Yeats had a conscious cultural and, in the largest sense, political purpose in his hallowing of Irish regions, Kavanagh had no such intent. Yeats would have probably called him local rather than national, as he had called William Allingham; and Kavanagh would have called himself parochial. He abjured any national purpose, any belief in Ireland as 'a spiritual entity.' And yet, ironically, Kavanagh's work probably touches the majority of Irish people more immediately and more intimately than most things in Yeats. I am not going to say that this makes Kavanagh a more important writer, but what I do say is that Kavanagh's fidelity to the unpromising, unspectacular countryside of Monaghan and his rendering of the authentic speech of those parts gave the majority of Irish people, for whom the experience of life on the land was perhaps the most formative, an image of themselves that nourished their sense of themselves in that serious way which Synge talked about in his preface. Kavanagh's grip on our imaginations stems from our having attended the intimate hedge-school that he attended. For thirty years and more he lived the life of a small farmer's son in the parish of Inniskeen, the life of fairs and football matches, of mass-going and dance-going. He shared his neighbours' fundamental piety, their flyness, their brusque manners and their vigorous speech. He gambled and rambled among them. He bought and sold land and cattle and corn. Yet all the time, as he stitched himself into the outer patterns of his place, there was a sensitivity and a yearning that distinguished him. For this poet whom we recognize as being the voice of a communal life had a fiercely individual sense of himself. 'A poet is never one of the people,' he declared in his *Self Portrait*. 'He is detached, remote, and the life of small-tune dances and talk about football would not be for him. He might take part but he could not belong.' And that statement could stand as a gloss on the first important poem that Kavanagh wrote, a poem which is about his distance from what is closest to him, a poem too where the life of small-time dances which he affects to disdain is lovingly particularized.

Eavan Boland

"The Emigrant Irish"

Eavan Boland (b. 1944), poet, lecturer, and reviewer, is a native of Dublin, and was educated there and in London and New York before graduating from Trinity College, Dublin. She played a central role in the development of Arlen House, a feminist publishing house in that city. In this elegantly spare poem, the emigrants from the famine are remembered for their strength and ability to survive.

Like oil lamps we put them out the back,

of our houses, of our minds. We had lights
better than, newer than and then

a time came, this time and now
we need them. Their dread, makeshift example.

They would have thrived on our necessities.
What they survived we could not even live.
By their lights now it is time to
imagine how they stood there, what they stood with,
that their possessions may become our power.

Cardboard. Iron. Their hardships parcelled in them.
Patience. Fortitude. Long-suffering
in the bruise-coloured dusk of the New World.

And all the old songs. And nothing to lose.

John Montague

FROM THE ROUGH FIELD

"A Lost Tradition"

In this poem, Montague remembers the landscape of his past, of his childhood, as a manuscript which we have lost the skill to read. The ancient Gaelic language and culture are represented only by "the shards of a lost tradition."

All around, shards of a lost tradition:
From the Rough Field I went to school
In the Glen of the Hazels. Close by
Was the bishopric of the Golden Stone;
The cairn of Carleton's homesick poem.

Scattered over the hills, tribal
And placenames, uncultivated pearls.
No rock or ruin, dun or dolmen
But showed memory defying cruelty
Through an image-encrusted name.

The heathery gap where the Rapparee,
Shane Barnagh, saw his brother die—
On a summer's day the dying sun
Stained its colours to crimson:
So breaks the heart, Brish-mo-Cree.

The whole landscape a manuscript
We had lost the skill to read,
A part of our past disinherited;
But fumbled, like a blind man,
Along the fingertips of instinct.

SEAN KEATING.
Economic Pressure.
20th century. Oil on
board. 48 x 48 in. (122 x
122 cm). Crawford
Municipal Art Gallery,
Cork, Ireland.

The last Gaelic speaker in the parish
When I stammered my school Irish
One Sunday after mass, crinkled
A rusty litany of praise:
Tá an Ghaeilge againn arís . . .

Tír Eoghain: Land of Owen,
Province of the O'Niall;
The ghostly tread of O'Hagan's
Barefoot gallowglasses marching
To merge forces in Dun Geanainn

Push southward to Kinsale!
Loudly the war-cry is swallowed
In swirls of black rain and fog
As Ulster's pride, Elizabeth's foemen,
Founder in a Munster bog.

Seamus Heaney

Poems

REQUIEM FOR THE CROPPIES

From Door into the Dark *(1969).* *The Croppies were the rebel farmers, identified by their close-cropped hair, who rose against the British in the United Irish rising of 1798. The final image of this poem is haunting: the rebels, killed on the fields of Vinegar Hill in June, were buried quickly with dirt, and by August the barley they had carried in their coat pockets had sprouted out of the grave. Nature's cycles are eternal.*

———————————

The pockets of our great coats full of barley—
No kitchens on the run, no striking camp—
We moved quick and sudden in our own country.
The priest lay behind ditches with the tramp.
A people, hardly marching—on the hike—
We found new tactics happening each day:
We'd cut through reins and rider with the pike
And stampede cattle into infantry,
Then retreat through hedges where cavalry must be thrown.
Until, on Vinegar Hill, the fatal conclave.
Terraced thousands died, shaking scythes at cannon.
The hillside blushed, soaked in our broken wave.
They buried us without shroud or coffin
And in August the barley grew up out of the grave

THE MASTER

From Station Island. *The schoolmaster is isolated, disengaged from the action of the present. Those who seek to learn must do so consciously and cautiously.*

———————————

He dwelt in himself
like a rook in an unroofed tower.

To get close I had to maintain
a climb up deserted ramparts
and not flinch, not raise an eye
to search for an eye on the watch
from his coign of seclusion.

Deliberately he would unclasp
his book of withholding
a page at a time and it was nothing
arcane, just the old rules

we all had inscribed on our slates.
Each character blocked on the parchment secure
in its volume and measure.
Each maxim given its space.

Like quarrymen's hammers and wedges proofed
by intransigent service.
Like coping stones where you rest
in the balm of the wellspring.

How flimsy I felt climbing down
the unrailed stairs on the wall,
hearing the purpose and venture
in a wingflap above me.

John Hewitt

"Ireland"

John Hewitt (1907–1987), poet, critic, museum official, was born in Belfast and educated at Methodist College and Queen's University. He retired in 1972 from directing the Herbert Art Gallery and Museum in Coventry, England. In this poem, Hewitt explores his relationship with his harsh, lonely home.

———————————

We Irish pride ourselves as patriots
and tell the beadroll of the valiant ones
since Clontarf's sunset saw the Norsemen broken . . .
Aye, and before that too we had our heroes:
but they were mighty fighters and victorious.
The later men got nothing save defeat,
hard transatlantic sidewalks or the scaffold . . .

We Irish, vainer than tense Lucifer,
are yet content with half-a-dozen turf,
and cry our adoration for a bog,
rejoicing in the rain that never ceases,
and happy to stride over the sterile acres,
or stony hills that scarcely feed a sheep.
But we are fools, I say, are ignorant fools
to waste the spirit's warmth in this cold air,
to spend our wit and love and poetry
on half-a-dozen peat and a black bog.

We are not native here or anywhere.
We were the keltic wave that broke over Europe,
and ran up this bleak beach among these stones:
but when the tide ebbed, were left stranded here
in crevices, and ledge-protected pools

that have grown saltier with the drying up
of the great common flow that kept us sweet
with fresh cold draughts from deep down in the ocean.

So we are bitter, and are dying out
in terrible harshness in this lonely place,
and what we think is love for usual rock,
or old affection for our customary ledge,
is but forgotten longing for the sea
that cries far out and calls us to partake
in his great tidal movements round the earth.

Niall Sheridan

FROM RACING

Hippomania

Niall Sheridan (b. 1912), writer, physician, literary and television personality, was educated at University College, Dublin. In this article on the sport of kings, Sheridan considers the racecourse a microcosm of life.

In Ireland, what used to be called the sport of kings is the bond which cements a vast, colourful and heterogeneous democracy—the vivid world of owners, trainers, jockeys, punters, tipsters and the racing public. The breeding, training and racing of horses is an important industry, an endless topic of conversation, almost a national obsession. Among a race of fervent individualists, hippomania is a great unifying force cutting clean across all social, cultural and economic barriers. It may be significant that while thousands of punters regularly put a half-crown on a horse, Ireland is the only country in the world which, in designing its official currency, has put a horse on a half-crown.

I was reared in the great horse-breeding area of County Meath and the exploits of famous local horses were part of the folklore of my childhood. Steeplechasing was the main topic of the endless discussions which centered around pedigrees and bloodlines, riding tactics, training methods and recollections of memorable races, often relived stride by stride and fence by fence. Interest in the sport was, of course, practical as well as academic, and I well remember how I first experienced the impact of the racing world on our own household in a curious little domestic drama.

Three days before the Grand National of 1928, my mother and two lady visitors, over tea and seed-cake, took the notion of having a collective flutter and went into close consultation over their selection. Unencumbered by any expert knowledge of the subject, their minds were open to other helpful influences from outer space.

We had at that time, among our canine menage, a scruffy mongrel terrier, given to us by a Tipperary cousin. He had been christened 'Tim'—a studied insult to Tim Healy because of his betrayal of Parnell. This pointed firmly to Tipperary Tim as the probable winner. My aunt, a strong supporter of the temperance movement, approved of the initials 'TT.' And the matter was clinched when one of the visitors noted that the horse was to be ridden by a man called Dutton—this being the maiden name of her maternal grandmother.

In these circumstances, the selection of Tipperary Tim was logical—indeed, inevitable.

The total investment of the syndicate (or consortium, as it might nowadays be called) was fifteen shillings, and it was decided that the placing of the commission should be entrusted to Bartley, the gardener and general handyman, a recognized expert on Turf matters.

He, in his turn, acted with a more rational logic. As a keen student of racing form, he could scarcely approve of a bunch of crazy women throwing money away on a rank outsider that seemed to have about as much of a chance as a snowball in hell. So he decided to hold the bet himself and let the matter drop.

There was great jubilation among the ladies when Tipperary Tim—the only horse left standing out of forty-two starters—won at 100 to 1, but everything turned to gloom when it was found that Bartley had disappeared. It was rumoured that he had found it necessary to make an urgent visit to a distant cousin and that he had taken to his bed with an unspecified ailment. At any rate, like a guilty bureaucrat pursued by the Press, he remained unavailable for comment. But all was forgiven in the end, though the name of Tipperary Tim had for long afterwards the power to inject a chilly pause into the liveliest discussion.

In that lush Meath countryside, which has bred so many famous jumpers, the Grand National was an inexhaustible topic. As the days grew shorter, friends and neighbours would drop in, and around the fire in the parlour there would be the tinkle of glasses and the gurgle of pouring whiskey. As the early dusk thickened over the sleeping fields outside, the talk would go back and back to the great Irish heroes of Aintree, men and horses.

How the Beasleys won it three times in the 'eighties, and how Jack Gourlay steered Drogheda to victory through a blinding snowstorm in '91 (or was it '92?), with the horse's hooves stuffed full of butter to prevent the snow from packing in them during the race. How the immortal Manifesto, trained only a few miles away, won it for the second time in '99 with twelve-stone-seven on his back, bringing off a great betting coup for his owner and enriching every punter in the county.

And what about the mighty Troytown, who once made such a leap at Becher's Brook that he put four feet of daylight between himself and that formidable fence? There were other magic names as the years rolled on—Easter Hero and Golden Miller, Reynoldstown, Workman, Royal Danieli. Would we ever see their like again?

Those fireside talkers, like their equine heroes, are dead and gone now, but if they could return they would find other names to conjure with—Ballymoss, Cottage Rake, Hatton's Grace and the incomparable Arkle, the greatest 'chaser in the whole history of racing. They would marvel at a trainer like Vincent O'Brien who could win three Cheltenham Gold Cups, three Cheltenham Hurdles and three Grand Nationals in successive years—apart from winning the Epsom Derby with Larkspur and the St Leger with Ballymoss. They would revel in the feats of Paddy Prendergast, Tom Dreaper and Pat Taaffe, who have become legends in their own lifetimes.

For Irish-bred and Irish-trained horses have, during the past twenty-five years, made a tremendous impact on the international racing scene. Indeed, the Irish racing and breeding industry has never been in a more flourishing state, because of several favourable factors. The administration of the sport is highly efficient, and funds available from the tote are wisely used to improve amenities and increase the value of stakes. The leading trainers can rely on the support of wealthy patrons (many of them American) who can afford to buy the best breeding and wait for results. An important landmark was the inauguration in 1962 of the sponsored Irish Sweeps Derby (with total prize-money of approximately £70,000), which has already established itself as one of the great classic races of Europe. And finally, there has been the emergence, during the post-War period, of two Irish trainers unsurpassed in skill and virtuosity— Vincent O'Brien in County Tipperary and Paddy ('Darkie') Prendergast at the Curragh in County Kildare. It is an astonishing fact that these two trainers, based in Ireland, have topped the table of winning trainers in Britain for the past four years—Prendergast taking the laurels in three successive years, with O'Brien repeating the feat in 1966.

The figures alone tell an impressive story. During 1965 (later statistics are not available) Irish-bred horses, racing in seventeen countries, won stakes valued more than £2,000,000. In the same year Irish exports of bloodstock were worth £3,723,000. In 1966 Irish-bred horses won four of the five classic races run in Britain; the winner of the remaining classic (the Oaks) was bred in France but trained in Ireland.

The figures indicate what an important part the breeding and racing industry plays in the Irish economy, but statistics cannot reflect the perpetual drama, excitement and expertise which lies in the background. The late-night study of the form book and the pre-dawn gallops, as a trainer brings his horse to peak fitness for a big coup. The slow-talking, long-sighted countrymen, who can pick out the jockeys' colours a mile away and store in a computer-like memory every vital move in a race.

The racecourse is a microcosm of life, a focus for triumph and disaster, glory or defeat, a setting for the endless duel with fate or chance or destiny, call it what you will. As starting-time approaches, there are swift dramatic changes in the betting-market when the 'inspired' money moves in. There is that tense hush just before the start, and the rising fervour of the crowd as the horses rise together to the final fences or the two-year-olds—a wavering spectrum of colour—come thundering down the five-furlong stretch.

Ray Bradbury

FROM GREEN SHADOWS, WHITE WHALE

Finding Grist for the Writer's Mill

Ray Bradbury (b. 1920), American screenwriter, novelist, and science fiction writer, spent seven months in Ireland in 1953 at the invitation of movie director John Huston, writing the screenplay for the movie Moby Dick. *That trip inspired many of Bradbury's stories, as well as* Green Shadows, White Whale. *In this excerpt he recalls some memorable Irish charac-*

ters, from the taxi driver who charges less for the long way around to the old bicyclist who proudly introduces the screenwriter to his "family."

———————

On and off the boat train and along the rainy streets by taxi, I finally signed in at the Royal Hibernian Hotel and telephoned Kilcock to see how I might find the Devil Himself, as the reception clerk put it while handing my luggage to the bellboy, who shuddered me by elevator up to my room to plant my luggage where it wouldn't take root, as he said, and backed off from me as if he had searched a mirror and found no image.

"Sir," he said. "Well, are you some sort of famous author?"

"Sort of," I said.

"Well." The bellboy scratched his head. "I been asking around the pub and the lobby and the kitchen, and no one ever *heard* of you."

At the door, he turned.

"But don't worry," he said. "Your secret's safe with *me*."

The door shut quietly.

I was suddenly mad for Ireland or the Whale. Not knowing which, I grabbed a cab that veered through streets filled with tens of thousands of bicycles. We headed west along the Liffey.

"Is it the long or short you'd want?" asked my driver. "The long way around or the short arrival?"

"Short—"

"*That's* expensive," interrupted my driver. "Long is cheaper. Conversation! Do you *talk*? By trip's end, I am so relaxed I forget the tip. Besides, it's a map, chart, and atlas of Liffey and beyond that I am. Well?"

"The *long* way around."

"Long it *is!*" He kicked the gas as if it needed awakening, skinned a dozen bicyclists, and sailed out to snake the Liffey and mind the air. Only to hear the motor cough and roll over dead, just short of Kilcock.

We peered in at an engine long gone in mystery and leaning toward the tomb. My driver hefted a large hammer, decided against giving the engine a coup de grace, slung the hammer aside, and walked to the rear of the taxi to detach a bike and hand it over. I let it fall.

"Now, now." He reinstalled the vehicle in my hands. "Your destination's but a short drive down this road." He shook the bike. "Climb on."

"It's been a few years . . . "

"Your hands will remember and your ass will learn. Hop."

I hopped to straddle and stare at the dead car and the easy man. "You don't seem upset . . ."

"Cars are like women, once you learn their starters. Off with you. Downhill. Careful. There's few brakes on the vehicle."

"Thanks," I yelled as the vehicle rolled me away.

* * *

Ten minutes later, I stopped at the top of a rise, listening.

Someone was whistling and singing "Molly Malone." Up the hill, wobbling badly, pedaled an old man on a bike no better than mine. At the top he fell off and let it lie at his feet.

"Old man, you're not what you once was!" he cried, and kicked the tires. "Ah, lay there, beast that you are!"

Ignoring me, he took out a bottle. He downed it philosophically, then held it up to let the last drop fall on his tongue.

I spoke at last. "We both seem to be having trouble. Is anything wrong?"

The old man blinked. "Is that an American voice I hear?"

"Yes. May I be of assistance . . . ?"

The old man showed his empty bottle.

"Well, there's assistance *and* assistance. It came over me as I pumped up the hill, me and the damned vehicle"—here he kicked the bike gently—"is both seventy years old."

"Congratulations."

"For what? Breathing? That's a habit, not virtue. Why, may I ask, are you staring at me like that?"

I pulled back. "Well . . . do you have a relative in customs down at the docks?"

"Which of us hasn't?" Gasping, he reached for his bike. "Ah, well, a moment's rest, and me and the brute will be on our way. We don't know where we're going, Sally and me—that's the damn bike's name, ya see—but we pick a road each day and give it a try."

I tried a small joke.

"Does your mother know you're out?"

The old man seemed stunned.

"Strange you say that! She *does!* Ninety-five she is, back there in the cot! Mother, I said, I'll be gone the day; leave the whiskey alone. I never married, you know."

"I'm sorry."

"First you congratulate me for being old, and now you're sorry I've no wife. It's sure you don't know Ireland. Being old and having no wives is one of our principal industries! You see, a man can't marry without property. You bide your time till your mother and father are called Beyond. Then, when their property's yours, you look for a wife. It's a waiting game. I'll marry yet."

"At *seventy*!?"

The old man stiffened.

"I'd get twenty good years of marriage out of a fine woman even this late—do you *doubt* it?!" He glared.

"I do not."

The old man relaxed.

"Well, then. What are you up to in Ireland?"

I was suddenly all flame and fire.

"I've been advised at customs to look sharp at this poverty-stricken, priest-ridden, rain-filled, sleet-worn country, this—"

"Good God," the old man interjected. "You're a writer!"

"How did you guess?"

The old man snorted, gesturing.

"The country's overrun. There's writers turning over rocks in Cork and writers trudging through bogs at Killashandra. The day will come, mark me, when there will be five writers for every human being in the world!"

"Well, writer I am. I've been here only a few hours now and it feels like a thousand years of no sun, only rain, cold, and getting lost on roads. My director will be waiting for me somewhere if I can find the place, but my legs are dead."

The old man leaned at me.

"Have you begun to dislike your visit? Look *down* on?"

"Well . . . "

The old man patted the air.

"Why not? Every man needs to look down on someone. You look down on the Irish, the Irish look down on the English, and the English look down on everyone else in the world. It all comes right in the end. Do you think I'm bothered by the look on your face, you've come to weigh our breath and find it sour, measure our shadows and find us short? *No!* In fact, I'll help you solve this dreadful place. Come along where you can witness an awful event. A dread scene. A meeting of Fates, *that's* it. The true birthplace of the Irish . . . Ah, God, how you'll *hate* it! And yet . . . "

"Yet?"

"Before you leave us, you'll love us all. We're irresistible. And we know it. More's the pity. For knowing it makes us all the more deplorable, which means we must work harder to become irresistible again. So we chase our own behinds about the country, never winning and never quite losing. There! Do you see that parade of unemployed men marching on the road in holes and tatters?"

"Yes!"

"That's the First Ring of Hell! Do you see them young fellows on bikes with flat tires and no spokes, pumping barefoot in the rain?"

"Yes!"

"That's the Second Ring of Hell!"

The old man stopped. "And here . . . can you read? The Third Ring!"

I read the sign. "'Heeber Finn's' . . . why, it's a *pub*."

The old man pretended surprise. "By God, now, I think you're right. Come meet my . . . family!"

"Family? You said you weren't *married*!"

"I'm not. But—in we go!"

The old man gave a great knock on the backside of the door. And there was the bar, all bright spigots and alarmed faces as the dozen or so customers whirled.

"It's *me*, boys!" the old man cried.

"Mike! Ya gave us a start!" said one.

"We thought it was—a crisis!" said another.

"Well, maybe it is . . . for *him* anyway." He jabbed my elbow. "What'll ya have, lad?"

I scanned the lot, tried to say wine, but quit.

"A whiskey, please," I said.

"Make mine a Guinness," said Mike. "Now, introductions all around. That there is Heeber Finn, who owns the pub."

Finn handed over the whiskey. "The third and fourth mortgage, that is."

Mike moved on, pointing.

"This is O'Gavin, who has the finest bogs in all Kilcock and cuts peat turf out of it to stoke the hearths of Ireland. Also a fine hunter and fisher, in or out of season!"

O'Gavin nodded. "I poach game and steal fish."

"You're an honest man, Mr. O'Gavin," I said.

"No. As soon as I find a job," said O'Gavin, "I'll deny the whole thing."

Mike led me along. "This next is Casey, who will fix the hoof of your horse."

"Blacksmith," said Casey.

"The spokes of your bike."

"Velocipede repair," said Casey.

"Or the spark plugs on any damn car."

"Auto-moe-beel renovation," said Casey.

Mike moved again. "Now, this is Kelly, our turf accountant!"

"Mr. Kelly," I said, "do you count the turf that Mr. O'Gavin cuts out of his bog?"

As everyone laughed, Kelly said: "That is a common tourist's error. I am an expert on the races. I breed a few horses—"

"He sells Irish Sweepstakes tickets," said someone.

"A bookie," said Finn.

"But 'turf accountant' has a gentler air, does it not?" said Kelly.

"It does!" I said.

"And here's Timulty, our art connoisseur."

I shook hands with Timulty. "Art connoisseur?"

"It's from looking at the *stamps* I have the eye for paintings," Timulty explained. "If it goes at all, I run the post office."

"And this is Carmichael, who took over the village telephone exchange last year."

Carmichael, who knitted as he spoke, replied: "My wife got the uneasies and she ain't come right since, God help her. I'm on duty next door."

"But now tell us, lad," said Finn, "what's your crisis?"

"A whale. And . . . " I paused. "Ireland!"

"Ireland?!" everyone cried.

Mike explained. "He's a writer who's trapped in Ireland and misunderstands the Irish."

After a beat of silence someone said: "Don't we *all*!"

To much laughter, Mr. O'Gavin leaned forward. "What do you misunderstand, specific like?"

Mike intervened to prevent chaos. "Underestimates is more the word. Confused might be the sum! So I'm taking him on a Grand Tour of the Worst Sights and the Most Dreadful Truths." He stopped and turned. "Well, that's the lot, lad."

"Mike, there's one you missed." I nodded to a partition at the far end of the bar. "You didn't introduce me to . . . *him*."

Mike peered and said, "O'Gavin, Timulty, Kelly, do you *see* someone there?"

Kelly glanced down the line. "We do not."

I pointed. "Why, it's plain as my nose! A man—"

Timulty cut in. "Now, Yank, don't go upsetting the order of the universe. Do you see that partition? It is an irrevocable law that any man seeking a bit of peace and quiet is automatically gone, invisible, null and void when he steps into that cubby."

"Is that a fact?"

"Or as close as you'll ever get to one in Ireland. That area, no more than two feet wide by one deep, is more private than the confessional. It's where a man can duck, in need of feeding his soul without converse or commotion. So for all intents and purposes, that space, until he breaks the spell of silence himself, is uninhabited and *no one's there*!"

Everyone nodded, proud of Timulty.

"Fine, Timulty, and now—drink your drink, lad, stand alert, be ready, watch!" said Mike.

I looked at the mist curling through the door. "Alert for what?"

"Why, there's always Great Events preparing themselves out in that fog." Mike became mysterious. "As a student of Ireland, let nothing pass unquestioned." He peered out at the night. "*Anything* can happen . . . and always *does*." He inhaled the fog, then froze. "Sssst! Did you *hear*?"

Beyond, there was a blind stagger of feet, heavy panting coming near, near, near!

"What . . . ?" I said.

Mike shut his eyes. "Sssst! Listen! . . . *Yes!*"

Heinrich Böll

FROM IRISH JOURNAL

Heinrich Böll (b. 1917), German novelist, won the Nobel Prize for Literature in 1972. This journal of a trip through Ireland with his wife and children is a charming, tender testament to Ireland and the Irish. Translated by Leila Vennewitz.

IRISH ROADS

It had seemed blasphemous when someone once said to me in Germany: The road belongs to the automobile. In Ireland I was often tempted to say: The road belongs to the cow. Indeed, cows are sent as freely to pasture as children to school: they fill the road with their herds, turn round haughtily when you blow your horn, and the driver has a chance here to show a sense of humor, behave calmly, and test his skill. He drives carefully right up to the herd, timidly forces his way into the condescendingly formed passage and, the minute he has reached the leading cow and overtaken it, he can step on the gas and count himself lucky to have escaped a danger—and what is more exciting, what better stimulus is there for human gratitude, than danger averted? So the Irish driver remains a creature to whom gratitude is not foreign; he must constantly fight for his life, his rights, and his speed: against schoolchildren and cows. He would

WILLIAM MAGRATH. *Landscape.* 20th century.
Watercolor on paper. 29³/₄ x 21⁷/₈ in. (75.5 x 55.5 cm).
Crawford Municipal Art Gallery, Cork, Ireland.

never be able to coin a snobbish slogan such as: The road belongs to the automobile. Ireland is a long way from deciding who the road belongs to. And how beautiful these roads are: walls, walls, trees, walls and hedges; the stones of Irish walls would be enough to build the tower of Babel, but Irish ruins are proof that it would be useless to begin such a building. In any event, these beautiful roads do not belong to the automobile; they belong to whoever happens to occupy them and whoever allows those desiring passage to prove their skill. Some roads belong to the donkey: donkeys playing truant from school, there are plenty of those in Ireland; they nibble away at the hedges, mournfully contemplate the countryside—turning their rumps toward the passing car. Whatever else, the road does not belong to the automobile.

IN A MANNER OF SPEAKING

When something happens to you in Germany, when you miss a train, break a leg, go bankrupt, we say: It couldn't have been any worse; whatever happens is always the worst. With the Irish it is almost the opposite: if you break a leg, miss a train, go bankrupt, they say: It could be worse; instead of a leg you might have broken your neck, instead of a train you might have missed Heaven, and instead of going bankrupt you might have lost your peace of mind, and going bankrupt is no reason at all for that. What happens is never the worst; on the contrary, what's worse never happens: if your revered and beloved grandmother dies, your revered and beloved grandfather might have died too; if the farm burns down but the chickens are saved, the chickens might have been burned up too, and if they do burn up—well, what's worse is that you might have died yourself, and that didn't happen. And if you should die, well, you are rid of all your troubles, for to every penitent sinner the way is open to Heaven, the goal of our laborious earthly pilgrimage—after breaking legs, missing trains, surviving all manner of bankruptcies. With us—it seems to me—when something happens our sense of humor and imagination desert us; in Ireland that is just when they come into play. To persuade someone who has broken his leg, is lying in pain or hobbling around in a plaster cast, that it might have been worse is not only comforting, it is an occupation requiring poetic talents, not to mention a touch of sadism: to paint a picture of the agonies of a fractured vertebra, to demonstrate what a dislocated shoulder would be like, or a crushed skull—the man with the broken leg hobbles off much comforted, counting himself lucky to have suffered such a minor misfortune.

Thus fate has unlimited credit, and the interest is paid willingly and submissively; if the children are in bed, racked and miserable with whooping cough, in need of devoted care, you must count yourself fortunate to be on your feet and able to look after the children. Here the imagination knows no bounds. "It could be worse" is one of the most common turns of speech, probably because only too often things are pretty bad and what's worse offers the consolation of being relative.

J. P. Donleavy

FROM IRELAND IN ALL OF HER SINS AND SOME OF HER GRACES

Behan Visits

J. P. Donleavy, was born in 1926 in Brooklyn, New York, to Irish-born parents. He went to Ireland in 1946 to study at Trinity College, and stayed. Here is his tribute to the land of his fathers which he adores, and which he chose as his home. In this excerpt, Brendan Behan, wild and unpredictable, pays Donleavy a most unusual visit.

With my then wife Valerie away, I preceded on my own that day at Kilcoole to clean up the shambles of used pots and strewn furnishings. Then later that afternoon covered in dust and sweat I heard whistling coming down my long entry lane. And I went out to my front gate to see Behan in his shambling duck walk approaching me. Sockless as usual, and sporting an unlaced up pair of my shoes. I asked him where were the remaining pairs.

'Ah, Mike, now I hate the countryside. I hate cunning country ways. I hate country people. And I nearly hate getting my feet wet just as much. Sure I knew you were already out somewhere in a pair of your own shoes yourself. So I took a bag full of the rest of them you weren't needing and wore a pair till they got wet on the way to the pub. And a bloody soaking wet walk it was too. As I went along, I had to fling the wet pair into the field and put on a dry pair. You'll find them with no bother. Start there just over the fence is your first pair. And the rest every fifty yards or so up to the pub.'

* * *

Behan disappeared off to my studio to collect up his manuscript of *Borstal Boy*. In which many songs and verse appeared. Behan maintaining the advantage of such was the space you could leave before and after each, thus with fewer words necessary to write to fill out the page. Behan always, as he did, would heft a manuscript in his hand, estimating its weight and then would proceed to calculate the number of words, choosing a page and with his little stub of a pencil, counting down the lines and then the words across and then his fingers flicking over the pages to the last one upon which he would scribble down his figures and then frowning in his act of multiplication would with satisfaction announce the result just as a farmer might, assessing the number of bales of hay stacked safely in the barn. An analogy, alas, which was as near as ever describing Behan's associations with country life. On this late afternoon standing at the corner outside my studio, and as Behan would in such profound moments of written words tabulated, he out of the blue became serious on another serious subject.

'Mike I regret as others might not that I have been sentenced to death in my absence by the I.R.A.'

'I'm sorry to hear that Brendan.'

'Well it's not as bad as it would be if I were sentenced to death and it were carried out in my presence. I have this little bit of the present geography situating me here to be thankful for that I'm not in my coffin. And now I'll tell you another thing. To your credit and not mine. I was behind your back complaining to McInerney that there you were bringing him bags from this place of old dirty potatoes and cabbages for him to use to feed his kids and that you wouldn't be that fast or generous when it came to buying a thirsty man a drink in a pub. And McInerney turned on me and nearly tore my head off, saying it was more than the fucking likes of me or anybody else had done.'

But such was Behan's concern for my present safety that it was only as he was leaving after four days, and singing me a small bit of commendation if not praise, that he made his announcement about the I.R.A. and that they were presently in search of him in every nook, cranny and pub of Dublin and might have already drawn their own conclusions that he was out peacefully sojourning in the countryside. And so informed, would acquaint with the friends he knew there and might now at this very moment be advancing belly down from every direction across the fields with Thompson sub-machine guns and gelignite ready to spray bullets and blast me, Behan, the whole place and both our manuscripts to kingdom come.

Paul Durcan

"Bewley's Oriental Cafe, Westmoreland Street"

Paul Durcan was born in 1944 in Dublin and was educated at University College, Cork. With a definite attitude, the poet seems to enjoy keeping an eye on things in Bewley's Oriental Cafe (a tea room), although it may not be politically correct.

When she asked me to keep an eye on her things
I told her I'd be glad to keep an eye on her things.
While she breakdanced off to the ladies' loo
I concentrated on keeping an eye on her things.
What are you doing?—a Security Guard growled,
His moustache gnawing at the beak of his peaked cap.
When I told him that a young woman whom I did not know
Had asked me to keep an eye on her things, he barked:
Instead of keeping an eye on the things
Of a young woman whom you do not know,
Keep an eye on your own things.
I put my two hands on his hips and squeezed him:

Shooting Reaction,
Belfast. 1974.
Photograph. AP/Wide
World Photos.

Look—for me the equivalent of the Easter Rising
Is to be accosted by a woman whom I do not know
And asked by her to keep an eye on her things;
On her medieval backpack and on her spaceage Walkman;
Calm down and cast aside your peaked cap
And take down your trousers and take off your shoes
And I will keep an eye on your things also.
Do we not cherish all the children of the nation equally?
That woman does not know the joy she has given me
By asking me if I would keep an eye on her things.
I feel as if I am on a Dart to Bray,
Keeping an eye on her things;
More radical than being on the pig's back,
Keeping an eye on nothing.
The Security Guard made a heap on the floor
Of his pants and shoes,
Sailing his peaked cap across the café like a frisbee.
His moustache sipped at a glass of milk.
It is as chivalrous as it is transcendental
To be sitting in Bewley's Oriental Café
With a naked Security Guard,
Keeping an eye on his things

Derek Mahon

"Derry Morning"

From The Hunt by Night *(1982). Derek Mahon, poet, television writer, teacher, and lecturer, was born in 1941 in Belfast and was educated at Trinity College in Dublin. In this poem the mist clears to offer an emerging picture of urban ruin.*

———————

The mist clears and the cavities
Glow black in the rubbled city's
Broken mouth. An early crone,
Muse of a fitful revolution
Wasted by the fray, she sees
Her *aisling* falter in the breeze,
Her oak-grove vision hesitate
By empty wharf and city gate.

Here it began, and here at least
It fades into the finite past
Or seems to: clattering shadows whop
Mechanically over pub and shop.
A strangely pastoral silence rules
The shining roofs and murmuring schools;
For this is how the centuries work—
Two steps forward, one step back.

Hard to believe this tranquil place,
Its desolation almost peace,
Was recently a boom-town wild
With expectation, each unscheduled
Incident a measurable
Tremor on the Richter Scale
Of world events, each vibrant scene
Translated to the drizzling screen.

What of the change envisioned here,
The quantum leap from fear to fire?
Smoke from a thousand chimneys strains
One way beneath the returning rains
That shroud the bomb-sites, while the fog
Of time receives the ideologue.
A Russian freighter bound for home
Mourns to the city in its gloom.

Charles Lucey

FROM THE NORTH IN AGONY

Charles Lucey, Irish-American newspaperman, researched this book of personal observations and impressions of Ireland over many years spent wandering through the country. In this selection on Northern Ireland, Lucey juxtaposes the pastoral scene of the surrounding countryside with the ravaged city of Derry.

––––––––––

It is, in the airy rhetoric of the tourist guidebook, "a country where you relax and go as you please along open roads to unspoilt beaches, shimmering lakes and rivers that beckon anglers and boatmen . . . peace and beauty of mountain, glen and forest . . . the friendliest of people extend an openhanded welcome."

The travel brochure hyperbole seemed within allowable limits and I thought, rolling easily through fertile Armagh and Tyrone in Northern Ireland, that here indeed could be haven from a world's discord and jackassery. The day had a late summer indolence about it; tractors crawled like great beetles across fields coming golden with harvest from the fast-running Blackwater to the old fortress-town of the O'Neills at Dungannon. The beauty of "mountain, glen and forest" is alive and real enough. It is more pastoral, less spectacular than the beauty of Donegal or Kerry on this same island but, the ubiquitous British Union Jack notwithstanding, it is unmistakably part of Ireland.

The miles slip away quickly through Omagh and Newtownstewart and Strabane and then one drops down into the green valley of the River Foyle and after that the fan-out into Lough Foyle and an endless northern sea.

Here above the Foyle, behind the finest old city wall in Ireland and one of the finest in all Europe, is the ancient city of Derry, arrogantly called Londonderry by the English, its high hills climbed by winding streets of cobbles long bloodied by hate and history.

But I find no peace in Derry, as I find none in Belfast. I find British troops in full battle dress and with automatic rifles, with bayonets at the ready, patrolling streets barricaded with barbed wire, timbering, and overturned trucks and buses. In both cities I see gaping holes in business and residential blocks that bring a flash-back to the devastation I saw in London and in Germany and Italy at the end of World War II. Here and now it is vengeance by incendiary gasoline bomb. No midnight is safe from the tension that bursts into violence. Physical fear is as strong as a hand in the face and families intimidated by bigots flee from their homes.

In Derry I walk block after block where plate-glass windows are smashed jaggedly open to a melancholy drizzle. Sidewalks are littered with broken glass. A car, burned and overturned to block off an area of Derry's Catholic Bogside ghetto, lies derelict. A bulldozer pushes away the brick and mortar of a burned-out building.

Small shopkeepers go about the task of boarding up shop fronts. Some wonder whether it is worth while to try to go on. Pitifully, after windows are boarded, a "Business as Usual" legend is lettered crudely across the boards. It is not business as usual, of course, but business under terrible strain. No one knows where it ends or what new rioting night may bring. . . .

It will take time to rebuild the bombed, burned-out blocks of old Belfast. It will take longer, no matter with what earnestness the North approaches civil reforms, to try to rebuild a real measure of trust into human and community relations in this province.

Yet all is not mayhem and madness and there has to be hope that the peace promised by the tourist brochures will one day be restored. On one of my last visits to the Six Counties I drove the beautiful coast road that runs from the Mountains of Mourne, skirts Belfast, and then climbs the Northeast coast to and beyond the Glens of Antrim. Here again, as often earlier, I

WILLIAM CONOR. *The Jaunting Car.* c. 1933. Oil on canvas. $27^{15}/_{16}$ x $35^{3}/_{4}$ in. (70.9 x 90.9 cm). Ulster Museum, Belfast. © Mrs. Edna Vitty.

had that deep feeling of how unmistakably, the Union Jack and other British paraphernalia notwithstanding, this indeed is Ireland.

I was sure of it one night when I went with an Irish newspaper editor to a pub in a lovely little seacoast town in County Down. The company was good and talk went late. I remarked to one of the natives that I was astonished at the lack of concern about pub-closing time. In reply he told me of the local policeman who, hearing a great raillery long after lights should have been out and patrons dispatched homeward, thumped loudly on the pub door with his baton. The barman opened the door cautiously.

"For God's sake, man," said the policeman quietly, "you have thirty bicycles in one heap here by the door. Get someone out here to scatter them about so you're not getting me told off by my sergeant."

This is Ireland, authentically, and not England.

The next day my newspaper friend talked of an ancient time before the O'Neills were high kings of Ulster. There is a legend that when they first came to Ireland it was agreed that he would be king who first touched Irish soil.

Their boats were stranded on the reefs. Sailors struggled to free their vessels to be first ashore.

As they strove a chieftain, The O'Neill, with a courage that has marked many of that name, drew his sword, severed his own hand at the wrist, and hurled it far and away to the strand with his remaining hand.

The O'Neill claimed and won the kingship.

The Red Hand became the family coat of arms and to this day it is there, the *Lamh dhearg* in the crest and shield of Ulster.

"Dire as this recent time has been," my friend mused, "who can say there may not still be men of courage in Ulster who will one day find a better way?"

361

Seamus Heaney

FROM PREOCCUPATIONS

"Belfast: Christmas, 1971"

Living in Belfast under siege at Christmas involves surviving explosions and funerals, remembering to carry your packages close to you so they won't be suspected of detonating.

People keep asking what it's like to be living in Belfast and I've found myself saying that things aren't too bad in our part of the town: a throwaway consolation meaning that we don't expect to be caught in crossfire if we step into the street. It's a shorthand that evades unravelling the weary twisted emotions that are rolled like a ball of hooks and sinkers in the heart. I am fatigued by a continuous adjudication between agony and injustice, swung at one moment by the long tail of race and resentment, at another by the more acceptable feelings of pity and terror. We live in the sickly light of TV screens, with a pane of selfishness between ourselves and the suffering. We survive explosions and funerals and live on among the families of the victims, those blown apart and those in cells apart.

And we have to live with the Army. This morning I was stopped on the Falls Road and marched to the nearest police barracks, with my three-year-old son, because my car tax was out of date. My protests grew limp when the officer in charge said: 'Look, either you go to the police up the road or we take you now to Holywood'—their own ground. It hasn't been named martial law but that's what it feels like. Everywhere soldiers with cocked guns are watching you—that's what they're here for—on the streets, at the corners of streets, from doorways, over the puddles on demolished sites. At night, jeeps and armoured cars groan past without lights; or road-blocks are thrown up, and once again it's delays measured in hours, searches and signings among the guns and torches. As you drive away, you bump over ramps that are specially designed to wreck you at speed and maybe get a glimpse of a couple of youths with hands on their heads being frisked on the far side of the road. Just routine. Meanwhile up in the troubled estates street-lights are gone, accommodating all the better the night-sights of sniper and marksman.

If it is not army blocks, it is vigilantes. They are very efficiently organized, with barricades of new wood and watchmen's huts and tea rotas, protecting the territories. If I go round the corner at ten o'clock to the cigarette machine or the chip shop, there are the gentlemen with flashlights, of mature years and determined mien, who will want to know my business. How far they are in agreement with the sentiments blazoned on the wall at the far end of the street I have not yet enquired. But 'Keep Ulster Protestant' and 'Keep Blacks and Fenians out of Ulster' are there to remind me that there are attitudes around here other than defensive ones. All those sentry boxes where tea and consultation are taken through the small hours add up to yet another slogan: 'Six into Twenty-Six won't go.' I walk back—'Good-night now, sir'— past a bank that was blown up a couple of months ago and a car showroom that went three weeks ago. Nobody was killed. Most of the windows between the sites are boarded up still. Things aren't too bad in our part.

There are few enough people on the roads at night. Fear has begun to tingle through the place. Who's to know the next target on the Provisional list? Who's to know the reprisals won't strike where you are? The bars are quieter. If you're carrying a parcel you make sure it's close to you in case it's suspected of being about to detonate. In the Queen's University staff common-room, recently, a bomb-disposal squad had defused a bundle of books before the owner had quite finished his drink in the room next door. Yet when you think of the corpses in the rubble of McGurk's Bar such caution is far from risible.

Then there are the perils of the department stores. Last Saturday a bomb scare just pipped me before I had my socks and pyjamas paid for in Marks and Spencer, although there were four people on the Shankill Road who got no warning. A security man cornered my wife in Robinson and Cleaver—not surprisingly, when she thought of it afterwards. She had a timing device, even though it was just an old clock from an auction, lying in the bottom of her shopping bag. A few days previously someone else's timing device had given her a scare when an office block in University Road exploded just as she got out of range.

There are hardly any fairy lights, or Christmas trees, and in many cases there will be no Christmas cards. This latter is the result of a request by the organizers of the civil disobedience campaign, in order that revenue to the Post Office may be cut as much as possible over the joyous season. If people must send cards, then they are asked to get the anti-internment cards which are being produced by the People's Democracy and the Ardoyne Relief Committee to support, among others, the dependents of the internees in Long Kesh camp. Which must, incidentally, be literally the brightest spot in Ulster. When you pass it on the motorway after dark, it is squared off in neon, bright as an airport. An inflammation on the black countryside. Another of our military decorations.

The seasonal appeals will be made again to all men of goodwill, but goodwill for its proper exercise depends upon an achieved self-respect. For some people in this community, the exercise of goodwill towards the dominant caste has been hampered by the psychological hoops they have been made to jump and by the actual circumstances of their lives within the state, British and all as it may have been. A little goodwill in the Establishment here towards the notion of being Irish would take some of the twists out of the minority. Even at this time it is difficult to extend full sympathy to the predicament of that million among us who would ask the other half-million to exalt themselves by being humbled. You see, I have heard a completely unbigoted and humane friend searching for words to cope with his abhorrence of the Provisionals and hitting on the *mot juste* quite unconsciously: 'These . . . these . . . Irish.'

Instead of the Christmas tree, which will be deliberately absent from many homes, people will put the traditional candle in the window. I am reminded of Louis MacNeice, 'born to the Anglican order, banned for ever from the candles of the Irish poor'; and of W. R. Rodgers, whose *Collected Poems* have appeared in time for Christmas; and of John Hewitt, that Ulsterman of Planter stock whose poetry over the years has been an exploration of the Ulster Protestant consciousness. All three men were born to a sense of 'two nations' and part of their imaginative effort was a solving of their feelings towards Ireland, a new answer to the question that Macmorris asked Fluellen in the Globe Theatre almost four hundred years ago: 'What is my nation?' As Northern Protestants, they each in different ways explored their relationship to the old sow that eats her farrow. They did not hold apart and claim kin with a different litter. Although, in fact, I have never seen farrow eaten by a sow in my life: what usually happens is that the young pigs eat one another's ears.

Last Sunday, at an interdenominational carol service in the university, I had to read from Martin Luther King's famous 'I have a dream' speech. 'I have a dream that one day this nation will rise up and live out the full meaning of its creed'—and on that day all men would be able to realize fully the implications of the old spiritual, 'Free at last, free at last, Great God Almighty, we are free at last.' But, as against the natural hopeful rhythms of that vision, I remembered a dream that I'd had last year in California. I was shaving at the mirror of the bathroom when I glimpsed in the mirror a wounded man falling towards me with his bloodied hands lifted to tear at me or to implore.

It used to be that you could predict the aftermath of Christmas: 'How did your Christmas go?' 'Oh quiet, very quiet.' There isn't much predictable now, except that the sirens will blare out the old and blare in nothing very new. In some parts of the country they will have killed the wren on St. Stephen's Day. In some houses they will still be hoping for a first-footer to bring a change of luck.

Brendan Kennelly

"The Essence of Being Irish"

Brendan Kennelly, poet, born in 1936 in County Kerry, was educated at St. Ita's College and Trinity College, Dublin, where he is currently professor of modern literature. In this article written for Bord Failte in Dublin, Kennelly asserts that the essence of being Irish derives from the notion that in Ireland "you are, on the whole, cherished for your uniqueness."

I work in Trinity College, Dublin, a very active yet relatively easygoing university. Around the College spreads the ancient, chatty city of Dublin, the streets of which always have people ready to stop and talk in an immediately interesting way. What we may call The Great Book of Dublin, James Joyce's *Ulysses*, was once described by a sharp American critic as being "a novel about talking and walking." I have yet to meet a better description of the book and of the city. I would say that Dublin is the most articulate city I've been in throughout the decades. Perhaps it's for that very reason that sometimes I leave it for another Ireland, the uncrowded West and South. Ireland literally gets in under your skin, steals into your dreaming mind, taking possession of it like a memory of love or a spontaneous kindness from stranger or friend.

If you asked me to name one factor that makes Ireland the quietly irresistible land it is, I would reply that time has failed to establish its customary tyranny over the lives of many of the people and so they are free to develop their personalities, indulge their natural inclination toward talk and animated story-telling while always giving the impression that you, the second party in the leisurely dialogue, are a much more interesting and articulate person than you ever dreamed yourself to be. This is not flattery, this is acute recognition of your human value. Ireland is a place where character and personality are cherished far ahead of theory and abstraction. This generates a special warmth in the social atmosphere which nurtures the heart and stimulates the mind. It also means that the Irish take time to find the right words, the most apt and evocative images, the most precise phrases in which to state their views on every topic under the sun.

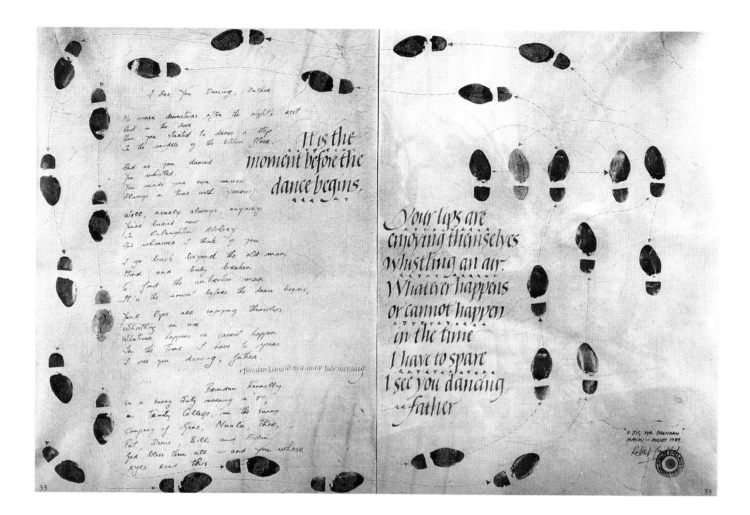

ROBERT BALLAGH, artist;
BRENDAN KENNELLY,
poet. *The Moment Before
the Dance.* 1990.
Contemporary illuminated
manuscript. Vellum.
The Great Book of
Ireland, Dublin.

Recently an old friend of mine died in Cork. He was one of the most inspiring talkers and story-tellers I've known; and as I traveled over the Kerry and Cork mountains to pay my last respects to him, the people with whom I was traveling spoke nonstop about his stories and wit, his escapades and adventures, his passion for sport and his love of people, his fiery interest in politics, his love of staying up all night and welcoming in the dawn light with stories of old friends and enemies. As I listened, I knew in my heart that one of the greatest Irish qualities is the passionate refusal to commit a dead friend to oblivion; instead, there is this eloquent loving insistence on talking about the strands of his personality, the events of his life, his favorite phrases, the quality of his humor, his outbursts of temper, his loves, prejudices, weaknesses, virtues, vices, stories. Stories, always stories. Fair enough, when you take time to think of it. What's a man or a woman in the end, and after the end, but the loving, lively, incisive ways in which we remember and tell our stories about him or her? That's an individual's history. History, his story. It is also the most acute expression of the Irish love of a person's uniqueness. This is a true and reassuring value in a world where individuals are increasingly treated as cogs in a machine. In Ireland you are, on the whole, cherished for your uniqueness. After all, that's what you deserve because that's what you are. Unique. There's nobody quite like you; no story quite like your story.

Everywhere you go in Ireland you meet beautiful children. I fondly cherish the thought that they too will grow to be people-lovers, nature-lovers and story-lovers like so many of those it has been my privilege to meet, travelling in this old land that has preserved a startling youthfulness through all its trials and tribulations. Ireland, still resisting the dull tyranny of time, the mechanical dominance of clock, watch and calendar, retains this wonderful blend of a child's sparkling enthusiasm with an old survivor's gritty wisdom as it offers, calmly and almost shyly, its many heart-warming charms to a needy world. The more you get to know this little country, the more fascinating it becomes. It is, in the deepest sense, one of the richest corners of the earth.

INDEX

Page numbers in italic denote illustrations. Colorplate numbers are given in parentheses.

PHOTO CREDITS